The UNHCR and the Afghan Crisis

Humanitarianism and Security

General Editor:
Antonio De Lauri, Chr. Michelsen Institute

Amid the growing convergence between the politics of aid and policing, emergency and military governance, securitization and the production of collective fear, this series examines humanitarianism and security as both ideology and practice. To this end, it offers ethnographic and theoretical analyses that contribute to the development of critical approaches at the intersection of anthropology, sociology, geography, international relations, and other disciplines.

THE UNHCR AND THE AFGHAN CRISIS

The Making of the International Refugee Regime

Giulia Scalettaris

berghahn
NEW YORK · OXFORD
www.berghahnbooks.com

First published in 2024 by
Berghahn Books
www.berghahnbooks.com
© 2024 Giulia Scalettaris

Library of Congress Cataloging-in-Publication Data
Names: Scalettaris, Giulia, author.
Title: The UNHCR and the Afghan crisis : the making of the international
refugee regime / Giulia Scalettaris.
Other titles: HCR et la crise afghane. English
Description: New York : Berghahn Books, 2024. | Series: Humanitarianism and
security ; volume 3 | Translation of: Le HCR et la crise afghane : une
bureaucratie internationale à l'épreuve. | Includes bibliographical
references and index.
Identifiers: LCCN 2023021772 (print) | LCCN 2023021773 (ebook) | ISBN
9781805391685 (hardback) | ISBN 9781805390817 (ebook)
Subjects: LCSH: Refugees--Services for--Afghanistan. | Office of the United
Nations High Commissioner for Refugees. | Refugees--International
cooperation. | Afghan War, 2001-2021--Refugees.
Classification: LCC HV640.5.A28 S4313 2024 (print) | LCC HV640.5.A28
(ebook) | DDC 362.8709581--dc23/eng/20230830
LC record available at https://lccn.loc.gov/2023021772
LC ebook record available at https://lccn.loc.gov/2023021773

British Library Cataloguing in Publication Data
A catalogue record for this book is available from the British Library

ISBN 978-1-80539-168-5 hardback
ISBN 978-1-80539-169-2 epub
ISBN 978-1-80539-081-7 web pdf

https://doi.org/10.3167/9781805391685

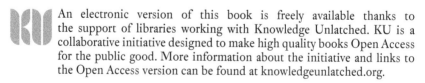

CONTENTS

☻☻☻☻☻

Figures and Tables

Figures

Table

Acknowledgements

First and foremost, I would like to thank the individuals I have called Saverio and Eric. These two UNHCR officials accepted my application for an internship and supervised my work in Kabul with wisdom and generosity. Without the trust they placed in me, this book would not exist. I wish to express my respect and gratitude to them.

I am also extremely grateful to all the researchers who, through their skill, generosity and friendship, helped to advance my thinking. First Michel Agier, who always placed the greatest trust in me to conduct my research. Then Alessandro Monsutti, whose valuable advice guided me throughout this work, and Marion Fresia for her attentive and generous reading. Among all the others, I am particularly grateful to Sabine Dini and Azita Bathaïe, whose willingness to comment on some chapters enriched this work.

This research was conducted within the framework of two projects funded by the Agence Nationale de Recherche (French National Research Agency), 'Asiles' ('Asylum') and 'Transguerres' ('Trans-war'). Conferences of the Association euro-africaine pour l'anthropologie du changement social et du développement (APAD) were highly enriching occasions. In Kabul the Afghanistan Research and Evaluation Unit kindly made its resources available to me. A Swiss Confederation Excellence Scholarship at the Graduate Institute of International and Development Studies made it possible for me to finalise my manuscript.

Finally, I am grateful to Rachel Gomme, who carefully translated the manuscript from French, and to the five institutions that funded the translation: the Centre for Administrative, Political and Social Studies and Research (CERAPS, UMR 8026) at the University of Lille, the University of Lille itself, the ANR-18-CE41-0013 PACE project supported by the French National Research Agency, the French Collaborative Institute on Migration (coordinated by the CNRS under the reference ANR-17-CONV-0001) and the European

Centre for the Humanities and Social Sciences (MESHS) sponsored by the Hauts de France region in Northern France.

Abbreviations

ACSU: Afghanistan Comprehensive Solutions Unit

ANDS: Afghanistan National Development Strategy

AREU: Afghanistan Research and Evaluation Unit

BAFIA: Bureau for Aliens and Foreign Immigrants (Iran)

BPRM: Bureau of Population, Refugees and Migration (United States)

CAR: Commissionerate for Afghan Refugees (Pakistan)

CIA: Central Intelligence Agency (United States)

CSSR: Collective for Social Science Research

ECHO: European Commission Humanitarian Aid Office

ECOWAS: Economic Community of West African States

EU: European Union

FATA: Federally Administered Tribal Areas (Pakistan)

GCIM: Global Commission for International Migration

HRW: Human Rights Watch

ILO: International Labour Organization

IOM: International Organization for Migration

ISAF: International Security Assistance Force

ISI: Inter-Service Intelligence

MoRR: Ministry of Refugees and Repatriation (Afghanistan)

MSF: Médecins Sans Frontières

NATO: North Atlantic Treaty Organization

NGO: nongovernmental organisation

NRC: Norwegian Refugee Council

NWFP: North-West Frontier Province (Pakistan)

OCHA: United Nations Office for the Coordination of Humanitarian Affairs

PDES: Policy Development and Evaluation Service (UNHCR)

POR: Proof of Registration

SAFRON: Ministry of States and Frontier Regions (Pakistan)

UN: United Nations

UNAMA: United Nations Assistance Mission in Afghanistan

UNHCR: United Nations High Commissioner for Refugee

UNDP: United Nations Development Project

UNICEF: United Nations Children's Fund

UNRWA: United Nations Relief and Works Agency for Palestinian Refugees in the Near East

USSR: Union of Soviet Socialist Republics

WFP: World Food Programme

Introduction

A United Nations (UN) agency set up after the Second World War to over-see the application of the 1951 Refugee Convention, the office of the United Nations High Commissioner for Refugees (UNHCR) has the mission to find 'international protection' for migrants[1] who have lost the protection of the state to which they belong. Whilst the UNHCR's initial mandate was re-stricted to refugees in Europe, it now operates worldwide. Although the or-ganisation used to be primarily active in the legal and diplomatic spheres, its large-scale expansion during the 1990s was accompanied by an increase in its humanitarian activities. Today, the UNHCR is a huge bureaucracy operating in 135 countries and responsible for some 90 million people whom the agency terms 'displaced'. It is also the core component of a larger mechanism for the government of refugees, which has also become highly institutionalised and extends throughout the world. It now involves a multiplicity of actors in diverse capacities – states, nongovernmental organisations (NGOs), think tanks, local advocacy organisations and others whose work is framed by the 1951 Convention.

This volume presents a political anthropology of the UNHCR. Its aim is to understand this UN agency and its activity. How does the UNHCR operate? In what ways does it exercise its power? What is the impact of its activity? These questions arose for me following my degree in international relations. On the one hand, sympathetic to UN and humanitarian values, I saw the UNHCR as a potential career path. On the other hand, I was troubled by the vehement criticism to which the organisation had been subject since the 1990s. My research project emerged from the desire to understand the impact of the UNHCR's activity on the basis of my own experience as an apprentice officer by studying the organisation's internal functioning.

In answer to these questions, this study focuses on the UNHCR's inter-vention in the Afghan crisis during the 2000s. This was (and remains) a key crisis for the UNHCR. For over thirty years, Afghans have constituted the largest refugee population in the world, only surpassed in recent years by Syrians.[2] Even before Afghanistan was ravaged by four decades of conflict, it was already one of the world's poorest countries, and migration was a widespread subsistence strategy. The UNHCR intervened in the region in the early 1980s, following the Soviet invasion of the country, and it based itself mainly in Pakistan. By the end of the 1980s, the organisation had reported some six million refugees, mainly resident in Iran and Pakistan. Following the overthrow of the Taliban regime, immediately after the 9/11 attacks, a UN-sponsored reconstruction project aimed at re-establishing political stability in Afghanistan was initiated. It was in this context that the UNHCR established the biggest repatriation and reintegration programmes in its history. But in 2008 the organisation was still reporting some three million refugees (one-seventh of the Afghan population according to current estimates, and one-tenth of the persons under the UNHCR's mandate), while Afghanistan was once again plunged into conflict.

In order to understand how the UNHCR's policies are developed and organised, between 2006 and 2008 I conducted an ethnographic study in the organisation's offices in Geneva and Kabul, cities that in the mid-2000s represented the nerve centres of multilateralism and international aid. The study began with an internship at the UNHCR Headquarters in Geneva, at the Afghanistan Desk (March–July 2006). Under the United Nations Volunteers programme, I was then taken on in the Kabul Branch Office, where as Donor Reporting Officer I was responsible for relations with funders and writing memos for external circulation (April 2007–March 2008). During this period I was able to observe the work of the UNHCR *in process*, to grasp the dispersed nature of its bureaucratic apparatus and to dissect its internal functioning, the technocratic procedures through which the UNHCR wields its authority and the relations it maintains with its many interlocutors.

The linking theme of this study is an innovative project, devised in 2003, that aimed to promote 'comprehensive solutions to Afghan displacement'. The project was original in its recognition of mobility as indispensable for Afghans' subsistence, and as an irreversible phenomenon. While the 'traditional solutions' implemented by the UNHCR ('integration', 'resettlement' or 'repatriation') always entail the sedentarisation of people fleeing conflict, this strategy proposed that mobility should be incorporated into the solutions. I was able to shadow the two authors of this project when they were posted in Geneva and when they were assigned to the Kabul office, where they directed the Afghan Operation between 2007 and 2009. I was thus able to follow this innovative strategy from its conception to its implementation, and the obstacles that it encountered that ultimately prevented it from shifting the organisation's nation- and state-centred vision of the world.

Retracing the trajectory of this project offers a way to grasp the UNHCR in its material nature as a network of offices and agents linked together by bundles of practices and a bureaucratic habitus. Rather than being a monolithic entity acting in accordance with a single line of thinking, as it is often presented and as it presents itself, the UNHCR thus emerges as a polymorphous, multi-positioned bureaucratic apparatus, shaped from within by its multiple contexts of intervention and by the topography of broader power relations.

Moreover, tracking this project highlighted the limitations of a mission that leads the UNHCR to reproduce the (nation-based) order at the root of the 'problem' that it was set up to resolve. While this groundbreaking project testifies to the organisation's capacity to innovate and reflect on its activity, the obstacles it encountered also reveal a paradox: the UNHCR seeks to assist migrants, but sets its work in the same state-centred, sedentary order that restricts movement and gives meaning to and legitimises the organisation's existence and mission. In other words, the interstate nature of the organisation justifies the existence of the UNHCR and its universalist moral claims, but by the same token, it limits the UNHCR's repertoire of action and its range of options, making the problem it is designed to solve insoluble. The attempt to incorporate Afghan migrants into a state jurisdiction thus contributes to a mechanism aimed at their emplacement in Afghanistan, and the containment and illegalisation of Afghan mobility.

Liisa Malkki (1992) has shown how the international refugee regime is rooted in the UN system, which propagates a sedentary and territorialised view of identities and constructs mobility as a problem. My study shows that the nation-based order substantially restricts the UNHCR's activities, but also shapes the way in which the organisation changes the world. Structured by a sedentary, state-centred rationale, the effect of the UNHCR's activity is to implant the national order and consolidate the allegedly 'superior' liberal-democratic model of the state. By acting on states, migrants and collective imaginaries, the UNHCR's interventions in fact imprint the nation-based order on the material and/or symbolic levels.

The UNHCR and the international refugee regime continued to evolve during the 2010s. The use of big data, the requirement for 'evidence-based policy', the New Public Management turn and attention to environmental issues, for example, were reinforced; since 2015, the so-called 'refugee crisis' in Europe and, more recently, the Ukrainian crisis have forced the organisation to devote more attention and resources to the continent; the organisation's interventions are more strongly influenced by the 'cluster' system; and the aims of the 2019 Global Compact on Refugees now shape its language. In Afghanistan, the takeover by the Taliban put a definitive end to the two-decade international intervention and was followed by an unprecedented economic and food crisis. But these developments in no way change the conclusions of my study, either concerning the UNHCR's functioning or concerning the structural limitations of the international refugee regime. The configuration is the same: a country in crisis, major migration flows, few possibilities of residence elsewhere, an organisation trapped in global power relations and its nation-based view of the world that prevents it from accepting the fundamental characteristic of those who are its concern – their mobility.

Although less studied than the major international economic and development organisations, the UNHCR has been the subject of a number of studies in international relations (Barnett 2001; Betts 2009a, 2009b; Garnier 2014; Gilbert 1998; Hall 2013; Hammerstad 2014; Lavenex 2016; Loescher 1993, 2001a, 2001b; Loescher et al. 2008; McKittrick 2008; Roberts 1998). These studies highlight its endeavour to remain autonomous of states, that are seen as factors determining constraint and opportunity, and they emphasise the influence of interstate relations on the UNHCR's policies. But they tend to reify the organisation, presenting it as a disembodied, monolithic actor, and to overlook the actors and arenas that do not belong to the interstate sphere.

More recently, social science studies have documented the UNHCR's functioning and the consequences of its activities. Some of these studies (which are often critical) shed light on the organisation's work of containing mobility and screening migrants that they see as major forms of domination during the post-Cold War era (Agier 2003, 2011; Barnett 2001; Duffield 2008; Harrell-Bond 1986; Scheel and Ratfisch 2014). Focusing mainly on refugee populations and contexts of intervention, they pay little attention to the organisation's internal workings. Nor are the effects of the UNHCR's activities outside the management of migration taken into consideration. Other studies, by contrast, explore the organisation's functioning on the basis of internal empirical studies or detailed analyses of certain procedures (Cole 2018; Crisp 2017; Fresia 2010, 2012; Glasman 2017; Hyndman 2000; Jacobsen and Sandvik 2011; Morris 2017; Sandvik 2011; Valluy 2009). These studies 'unveil' the UNHCR, taking us from preparatory meetings for the Executive Committee to asylum application hearings in France and to the evaluation of resettlement applications in Kampala; they decipher the classification operations, the mechanisms of accountability or the creation of a professional identity among expatriate staff. They thus reveal the plurality and diversity of the contexts, procedures and agents that underpin the organisation's functioning, and they furnish a more fine-grained understanding of a number of specific facets of its activity. But the larger structural effects of this complex institutional activity often remain unexplored.

Based on embedded ethnography and analytical tools derived from anthropology and political sociology, the approach taken in this study is both empirical and encompassing. Its aim is to grasp the impact of the UNHCR's global activity during the 2000s on the basis of a study of its internal functioning.

Going to the core of the UNHCR's transglobal apparatus, following a key situation from within it, and then undertaking a process of distancing, deconstruction and contextualisation enabled me to bring several levels of analysis together: the micropolitics of practices, the institution as well as the multiscalar power relations that shape its environment and its organisation (relations that encompass, but are not limited to, the interstate system).

After a chapter that presents the theoretical and methodological context, this book is divided into two main parts. The first part (Chapters 2–6) explores the internal functioning of the UNHCR: the organisation's epistemic framework, its deployment across the globe, the main bureaucratic procedures underpinning it, and its agents (expatriate and so-called 'local' staff). The second part (Chapters 7–11) examines the UNHCR's work with Afghan refugees: the procedures used to identify 'refugees', the repatriation programme, the programme for reintegration in Afghanistan, the production of consistent narratives on Afghan mobility, and the administrative surveillance mechanisms the organisation put in place. Each of these chapters seeks both to understand an important aspect of how the UNHCR operates and/or wields its authority, and to grasp the complex and ambivalent, tense and entangled relationship that the organisation maintains with the interstate system.

Notes

1. In this study, I use the term 'migrant' in the sociological sense of a person who migrates. I therefore use it to denote all Afghans who migrate, including those who are the focus of the UNHCR's activity. When I use the term 'migrant' as a label in the context of immigration policy, I place it in inverted commas. For more on the institutional labelling of individuals who migrate, see Chapter 7.
2. This evaluation does not take Palestinian refugees into account, because they are the focus of a dedicated UN agency: the United Nations Relief and Works Agency for Palestine Refugees in the Near East (UNRWA).

CHAPTER 1

An Embedded Bureaugraphy

This chapter presents the theoretical and methodological foundations of my research.[1] I describe how I developed an approach to the UNHCR that allowed me to grasp the significance of the organisation's activity worldwide during the 2000s, through a study of its internal functioning. I propose the term 'bureaugraphy' to describe my research process. This term articulates the way in which I conceptualised the UNHCR as a bureaucratic structure operating on a planetary scale, constructed this international organisation as an object of analysis, studied it ethnographically and located it in a political configuration broader than the system of interstate relations.

My approach was informed by the reflections of Michael Barnett and Martha Finnemore (Barnett and Finnemore 2004). However, while these authors argue that the activity of international organisations can be understood by thinking of them as bureaucracies, I consider the bureaucracy of the UNHCR from a more empirical point of view, as concrete material that can form a basis for ethnographic analysis. Unlike states, whose machinery is not comprised solely of bureaucratic bodies and that govern large territories, international organisations are materialised primarily through their offices and their staff. Apart from its Executive Committee, which meets once a year in the Palace of Nations in Geneva in the presence of representatives of member states, at the time of my study the UNHCR consisted concretely of a body of around 7,000 employees and some 300 offices spread over 110 countries. The offices, in effect, constitute the UNHCR's 'territory', being the only spaces the organisation is free to shape at its discretion.

While it underscores the centrality of bureaucracy in my approach, the term 'bureaugraphy' also states a position: a UN bureaucracy can be the subject of ethnographic study just as much as a community or a tribe. The term thus highlights a specific theoretical approach in political anthropology: treating different forms of organisation and exercise of power in the same way and on an equal footing, whether they are centred on relationships between individuals or organised around offices dominated by computers and stacks of files. While several authors have already demonstrated the pertinence of an ethnographic approach to bureaucratic institutions (Abélès 1992; Latour 2010; Weller 2018), the use of the term *bureau*graphy rather than *ethno*graphy articulates the theoretical regeneration of anthropology, as it reorients a method initially developed to study remote ethnic groups towards familiar institutions.

Following an introductory discussion of the renewal of international organisation studies, I present my own research process in four stages.[2] I first explain how I 'uninstituted' the UNHCR and constituted its dispersed bureaucratic structure as a field. I then show how I defined the limits of my field and describe the process whereby I moved from localised observation to reflect on the organisation as a whole. Finally, I describe the essential process of epistemological distancing that enabled me to produce anthropological, rather than expert knowledge on the UNHCR.

The Regeneration and the Challenges of International Organisation Studies

International organisation studies has been revitalised in recent years, at the level of both methods and themes. While international relations studies is certainly a rich field, from the point of view of a social scientist, it tends to be overly positivist and state-centred.[3] There is now a growing body of literature documenting the internal operation and forms of authority of international organisations, based on empirical research, discourse analysis and archive studies. Four issues of the journal *Critique Internationale*[4] testify to this trend, which arises in the context of a broader theoretical shift in the social sciences, with the development of tools to grasp international and large-scale objects of study (Burawoy 2000; Siméant-Germanos 2012).

These studies have helped to open the 'black box' of international organisations by situating them in a context more complex than the system of states. They reveal the actors who interact within them (officers, diplomats, experts, etc.), their careers (Ambrosetti and Buchet de Neuilly 2009; Pouliot 2006), and the practices and routines underpinning their operation (Abélès 2011; Bendix 2012). While historians shed light on the processes of institutionalisation (Karatani 2005; Kott 2011), sociologists reveal an open and porous institutional space, situated at the crossroads between national and international arenas, traversed by transnational circulations of ideas, norms and knowledges, a site of negotiation between diverse understandings and interests (Abélès

1995; Cling et al. 2011; Decorzant 2011; Kott 2011). International organisations are true bureaucratic entrepreneurs, and also modify their repertoires so as to establish their authority in response to changes in their environment (Fouilleux 2009; Nay 2012; Nay and Petiteville 2011). Focusing on the activity of these institutions, a number of studies emphasise the work of constructing public problems and large-scale dissemination of paradigms and codes of conduct (Andrijasevic and Walters 2010; Barnett and Finnemore 2004; Fresia 2010; Lavenex 2016; Merlingen 2003; Revet 2009), and also consider how these norms are articulated in local contexts (Merry 2006; Murray Li 2007). Many studies emphasise the production of expert knowledge, as a source of legitimacy and intellectual influence (Boome and Seabrooke 2012; Littoz-Monnet 2017; Nay 2014) and of mechanisms of depoliticisation (Ferguson 1994; Müller 2013; Pécoud 2015).

These studies open up numerous avenues of research, but present three challenges to an empirical understanding of the activity of an international organisation. The first difficulty is to develop an understanding of the institution as both a singular, integrated entity and an arena, a complex space traversed by social, political and professional relations. Most studies are forced to choose between these two approaches – the institution-actor or the institution-arena. The second challenge is to define the field: how to design a study capable of examining bodies that operate on a planetary scale, whose activities have impact at many different levels? Is it possible to go beyond the choice between case study and comparison? A few ethnographic studies manage to achieve an encompassing vision of the organisation or its activity, working from strategic sites of power or circulating within the organisation (Atlani-Duhault 2005; Fresia 2018; Mosse 2005). A third challenge is to avoid falling under the intellectual sway of the organisation. International organisations produce particularly influential discourses and norms, and the researcher's proximity often goes hand in hand with a desire to influence the organisation's activity, and therefore to formulate more or less explicit recommendations or criticisms.

The UNHCR as an Object of Study: Uninstituting the Organisation

Many studies of the UNHCR and refugee policy are conducted from within a state-centred and normative perspective. The two myths of state sovereignty (the absolute and final power that states are deemed to have within their jurisdiction) and of national and international law (as both a lens of understanding and a regulator of reality) ultimately structure their analytical frameworks. These studies naturalise, essentialise and reify the interstate system and international institutions, creating an implicit hypothesis from the existing order.

The UNHCR is thus seen as a homogeneous and monolithic actor, with defined outlines, and possessing its own rationality and coherence. The organisation 'does', 'says', 'decides', etc., as if it were reduced to its status as a moral person. Relatively disembodied, abstracted from any context, it seems to act like a *deus ex machina* from above, somewhere 'up there', over the top of states. The interstate character of the UNHCR forms the foundation for analysis of the way in which it works, and the 1951 Refugee Convention with its principle of nonrefoulement appears sufficient for explaining its activity. Internal operation is governed by the organisation's statutes, administrative regulations, and hierarchical and operational relations between officers and offices.

Guglielmo Verdirame and Barbara Harrell-Bond's assessment that 'the rights of refugees have been violated by the UNHCR' (2005: 332) is typical of this approach. It incorporates the assumption of the UNHCR as monolithic in its action (violating a person's rights), which also essentialises 'refugees' as discernible persons who exist outside of the UNHCR's activity and the application of law, and conceives of the law as a higher norm to which behaviours and phenomena should conform. As another example, a number of authors who have analysed the repatriation programmes managed by the UNHCR ask whether people's return was *really voluntary* (see, for example, Barnett 2004). Here too, the 'voluntary nature of return' emerges as a sacred, universally valid principle to which programmes should conform, and a criterion on which to judge the substance of the UNHCR's action.

From the outset of my field study, I found it difficult to reconcile this normative and positivist approach with what I was observing within the institution. As an organisation, the UNHCR only existed in the form of multiple offices and officers, among whom tensions regularly arose. These often derived from different understandings of the organisation's priorities, and of how the principles of international law were to be interpreted and realised. How, then, was the institution UNHCR to be constructed as an empirically 'studiable' object?

It was in Michel Foucault's theory of power that I found the tools to 'blow apart' the institution and work on the basis of what remained: the operation of its bureaucratic infrastructure. Foucault exhorts us to dejuridicise and deinstitutionalise our approach to politics (Foucault 1979; Abélès 2008):

> It is this image that we must break free of, that is, of the theoretical privilege of law and sovereignty, if we wish to analyze power within the concrete historical framework of its operation. (Foucault 1979: 90)

The viewpoint is thus reversed: it is the state and its laws that are to be explained in terms of relations of power, not the other way around. The state and its laws are a 'terminal form' (Foucault 1979: 94) in which relations of power are crystallised. In this sense, compared with normative and state-centred approaches, the Foucauldian approach inverts the relationship between norms and practices: it is not the norm that determines or explains practices, but practices that make, unmake and modify the norm. Foucault contrasts the juridical view of politics with a conception of power as a 'mode of action upon actions', and with an analysis of positive mechanisms as they are played out and produced in the relations that run through societies and institutions. He invites us to grasp 'the most immediate, most local power relations that are at work' (1979: 97) by way of an 'ascending' process, starting from detailed analysis of the most infinitesimal mechanisms of power.

If power traverses institutions rather than being embodied in them, then the ethnographer is in a position to offer valuable insight, since they have the tools to go beyond official documents, and hence beyond the image of order and coherence that the organisation presents. Overturning the myths of state and law paves the way for uninstituting and disassembling the organisation. It then becomes possible to approach it in its actual form, that is, as a translocal bureaucracy that operates through offices, officers and procedures linked by clusters of practices and relations that can be observed locally. Indeed the UNHCR's activity takes shape and acquires meaning in the density of relations (meetings, discussions, professional relationships, friendships and rivalries) and in the materiality of offices (meeting rooms, workspaces and corridors), texts (writing occupies much of employees' time, whatever their role) and institutional procedures (for example, circulation of staff). The growing number of recent social science works that base their study of state institutions on observation of bureaucratic procedures, such as the production of documents (Dubois 2012; Hull 2012; Mosse 2005; Sharma and Gupta 2006; Shore and Wright 1997; Weller 2018), encouraged me to take this approach.

Fieldwork within a Dispersed Bureaucracy

Once the UNHCR is constructed as an object open to ethnographic analysis, the question arises as to what kind of fieldwork can be contemplated within this dispersed bureaucracy. Challenges to the assumption of territory/culture isomorphism that long held sway in anthropology have shaken up the binary oppositions that underpinned the perception of the field (here/there, self/other). The question facing ethnographers today is the relevance and the heuristic potential of ethnographic research – a method based on prolonged immersion that calls for close-up observation – when the research context is not territorially circumscribed, and the increasingly interconnected world often constitutes the background of the phenomenon being studied (cf. Gupta and Ferguson 1997b). How, then, are large-scale phenomena, or processes and institutions with a scant territorial base, to be studied?

In response to these questions, George Marcus (1995) suggests multiplying sites of investigation in order to follow flows, objects and histories; others have shown that a well-organised localised study can be used to approach and examine large-scale phenomena. Michael Burawoy (2000, 2001), for example, proposes that globalisation can be grasped ethnographically by finding ways to observe, at the local level, connections (or disconnections) between global-level actors and processes. This enables him to portray globalisation as a phenomenon that is more contingent and less inexorable than is commonly imagined, emerging out of conflictual processes negotiated within a 'global chain' and between its 'nodes'.

My methodology draws from these two approaches and involves three phases.[5] The first was the entry into an institutional space, defined by features such as a professional habitus, specific frames of understanding of the world and an esprit de corps. Becoming integrated into this space required a phase of apprenticeship. I had, for example, to rapidly learn the meaning of acronyms: widely used, they form a language closed to anyone not integrated into the space of shared professional knowledge. The second phase was that of circulating within the institution. My main shift was the transfer from headquarters in Geneva to the Kabul office. As I spent the longest time there and was able to participate more fully in the institution's activities, this experience forms the core of my research. An internship in the Rome office prior to beginning my research, visits to Sub-Offices in Bamyan and Jalalabad and UNHCR project sites in Afghanistan, participating in meetings with other bodies, and more broadly my stay in Kabul as well as my periods of leave, when I lived and travelled as an 'expat', all form part of my fieldwork. This ended when I left the UNHCR, which constitutes the third and last phase.

My research took place in a situation of intense personal involvement that can be described as embedded ethnography. Following a degree in international relations, the UNHCR seemed a potential career prospect, since I saw UN and humanitarian values as close to my own. On the other hand, I also found the virulent criticism the organisation had been subject to since the 1990s troubling. My research project emerged out of a desire to understand the reach of the UNHCR's activity, on the basis of my own experience as an apprentice officer. Thus, during my fieldwork, the roles of apprentice UN officer and ethnologist merged, as the two projects (professional work experience and research study) developed in parallel, with true interest in each of them.

My status as an embedded observer enabled me to conduct a long ethnography within the institution without having constantly to negotiate access. The period of one year, traditionally recommended in anthropology handbooks, proved particularly apposite for studying the UNHCR, as its internal rhythm is determined by the financial year, and its programmes in Afghanistan are strongly influenced by changes of season. My superiors were very open to the world of research and, as I was myself fully dedicated to my work, this dual status posed no problem for my colleagues. At the same time, it enabled me to produce a remarkable wealth of data: in addition to my field journals, where I recorded each evening what had happened during the day, I accumulated a number of work notebooks that enabled me to retrace my activities with precision, as well as all the documents I had worked on (applications for funding, reports, newsletters and pamphlets), most of them public documents whose history I knew in precise detail. Institutional activity in general leaves enormous numbers of written traces: emails, reports, statistics, certificates, etc. While I was unable to use some of these for reasons of confidentiality, they nevertheless enabled me to reconstruct key sequences, to retrace the positions of the various people involved, and always to retain a sense of the heterogeneity of the simultaneous activities that constitute the existence of the institution.

The counterpoint to this wealth of data was the limited control I had over the trajectory of my fieldwork. Given that I had had no choice in my posting to Kabul and that my working hours were taken up by the work, it was my role in the institution that determined the situations I was able to observe. I thus had to 'give myself over' to the institution and let go of planning my field study, formulating hypotheses in advance, regularly reviewing the data I had gathered and so on. This was manifested in a 'loose' observation that required subsequent lengthy and substantial cutting and weeding of the data. It was only once my fieldwork was over that I was able to define the precise boundaries of my research by selecting my data in such a way as to maximise their heuristic power. I did not conduct any formal, in-depth interviews. However, my presentation of myself as a young colleague planning doctoral research on the Afghan refugee regime regularly sparked discussions and debate with one or more colleagues in off-duty moments such as dinner or tea breaks. I would ask Afghan colleagues, for example, about their views on their work, on expatriates and on the UN, or expatriates what they thought about the UNHCR strategy in Afghanistan, the limits of the UNHCR activities, or the pleasures and challenges of being a UNHCR officer. In addition, occasional discussions with the senior managers of the Afghan Operation allowed me to keep track of the progress of the innovative strategy.

There were two aspects of my study that enabled me to make best use of the data gathered in Geneva and Kabul, and to link them together. First, the Desk in Geneva and the Kabul office were both pivotal to the work of the UNHCR at the time of my study, in the strategic planning and implementation of a flagship programme. In the mid-2000s, Afghans were still the largest group of refugees in the world, as they had been since the late 1970s.[6] Following the NATO intervention in Afghanistan in 2001, the 'Afghan operation' had become the largest in terms of both staff and budget, owing to its strategic importance. The Desk in Geneva linked offices in the field with all departments at headquarters, and thus offered me an overview of all the internal actors involved in managing the project, from operations managers in the field to the Protection, Operations and Administrative Officers and the office of the High Commissioner. The Kabul office was the nerve centre of the intervention for the whole region, the crossover point in a high-volume circulation of personnel. I thus met a large number of officers posted to Sub-Offices, to neighbouring countries or at Headquarters, some of whom stayed in the building where I was living. As well as this access to the organisation, working in these two offices gave me an insider's view of the organisation's strategic thinking, thanks to my proximity with senior staff. I was thus able to follow internal debates in the two offices closely, as well as their relationships with the external actors with whom they were in contact.

Second, my transfer from Geneva to Kabul coincided with that of two staff members who had developed an innovative project. I was thus able to follow them from their posting in Geneva, where they created the strategy in 2003, to their appointment at the Kabul office, where they directed the 'Afghan operation' from 2007 to 2009. I decided to take this project as the central focus of my work. The project's originality lay in its recognition of mobility as an indispensable element of Afghans' subsistence, and an irreversible phenomenon. At a time when the UNHCR's 'traditional solutions' invariably involved sedentarisation, this strategy proposed integrating mobility into such solutions (UNHCR 2003a). To return to Marcus' suggestions, my study therefore follows at the same time persons (the two who created the strategy), an idea (the project itself) and a history (the trajectory of an innovative idea within the institution).

Tracking the design and implementation of this project enabled me first to organise my observations in such a way as to describe and analyse the UNHCR's bureaucracy at work: the powerful standardisation procedures (against which this tailor-made project had to forge its path), for example, or the perennial negotiation between the different perspectives that coexist within the organisation (which explain, among other things, the support and the resistance that the strategy encountered). Second, the project enabled me to consider the paradigms underlying the institution. Indeed, the obstacles that ultimately prevented this project from shifting the UNHCR's state-centred and nation-based view of the world helped me to reflect on how the organisation is integrated into the interstate system, preventing it from thinking, and thinking of itself, outside of this system.

From Localised Observation to an Encompassing Reflection

Many studies of the UNHCR and refugee policy focus on a particular site (a camp, a reception counter, a border, a multilateral forum), on a national context and/or on a binary relationship (UNHCR/state(s), UNHCR/refugees, state(s)/refugees). While this approach often produces detailed and insightful studies, the risk is that it overlooks the view of the whole and passes over the ways in which these sites, relationships and structures are articulated.

Some recent studies have endeavoured to develop a broader perspective, in order to give an account of the interactions between the multiple actors and political intentions that shape refugee policy. Some authors take a historical approach, revealing how particular UNHCR procedures have evolved over time and in space (Chimni 2004; Glasman 2017). Alexander Betts (2010b) reflects on the complexity of the international refugee regime through an analysis of how it overlaps with other international regimes, while a number of monographs written from within the context of a UNHCR intervention reveal the articulations between the UNHCR and other nonstate legal systems (Centlivres and Centlivres-Demont 1999; Fresia 2009a; Turner 2010). Other studies, based on multisite analysis of the UNHCR's interventions in different locations throughout the world, have revealed domination on a massive scale, particularly in terms of confining people in camps and containment (Agier 2011; Duffield 2008; Scheel and Ratfisch 2014; Valluy 2009). Marion Fresia (2018) also draws on her series of studies of the UNHCR to build up an efficient portrait of the organisation.

Getting a view of the whole was a central concern for me during both the gathering and the analysis of my data. I saw my fieldwork as a lens through which I might grasp a phenomenon that operates on a planetary scale (the bureaucratic structure of the UNHCR and how it functions) and examine its effects (effects that include, but are not limited to, those on displaced populations). The studies cited above strengthened my determination to consider the links between procedures implemented in different spaces, and to take into account the UNHCR's interactions with nonstate actors.

Michel Foucault's theory of power once again proved pertinent. The strength of this theory lies in its invitation to grasp power relations on the basis of the smallest details, while at the same time bearing in mind the need to develop a global perspective by setting local power relations in the context of broader strategic configurations. The aim is to trace the distribution of discrete elements in order to detect their 'economy', the 'order' in which they arise. Thus Foucault invites us to examine relations of power 'on the two levels of their tactical productivity ... and their strategical integration' (Foucault 1979: 102). The point is to consider the 'series of sequences' through which a 'local centre' of power is set within an 'over-all strategy' that generates 'comprehensive effects' (1979: 98–99). The concept of the apparatus is one of Foucault's significant contributions. To offer a somewhat schematic definition, the apparatus is a historical formation arising out of a heterogeneous set of elements (discourses, institutions, laws, knowledges, etc.) that play into and around one another in such a way as to generate comprehensive effects (Foucault 1994: 299–300). This conceptualisation is very apt for the bureaucracy of the UNHCR.

Understanding the UNHCR as a complex assemblage of heterogeneous elements drove me to locate the relations and practices I observed within the UNHCR apparatus, and, indeed, to use these relations and practices as a basis for examining the interplay between the heterogeneous elements of which it is composed. This interplay is not just a matter of hierarchical relations; it also takes place through the circulation of agents and knowledges, for example, and reveals major differences between offices and members of staff. In practical terms, I built this overview through a continuous process of placing my data in perspective (by cross-referencing them with one another and with those of other studies of the UNHCR) and comparing them (picking out, for example, the diversity of relations the UNHCR may have with a given interlocutor depending on the context, or how an officer's view changes in relation to their postings).

In this way, by comparing the Kabul, Tehran, Islamabad and Rome offices, which all have the same administrative status but very different structures, activities and views of the organisation's priorities, I came to understand that the UNHCR is shaped internally by the multiple contexts in which it operates: each office is immersed in a particular arena, within which it must establish the organisation's legitimacy and reputation, and ensure its activity is relevant and viable. It was by bringing to light the regional scale, and hence the selective application, of the new strategy – recognising the importance of mobility for Afghans, but only in Iran, Afghanistan and Pakistan – that I was able to show to what extent this strategy was in fact consistent with the containment of asylum seekers that European countries – the UNHCR's main donors – were aiming for. Similarly, while many studies place the emphasis on refugee camps, I was able to recognise placement in camps as one among the wide range of procedures (including the award of refugee status and administrative surveillance of migrants) implemented by refugee policies.

While the concept of the apparatus enabled me to construct an encompassing understanding and analysis of the UNHCR's bureaucratic machinery, I drew on recent writings in political anthropology to also set the UNHCR apparatus in a context more complex than the system of relations between states. Rather than a quantitative conception of power, in which power is measured as if it were something homogeneous and quantifiable held by one or other actor, in a zero-sum game, these studies argue that the plurality of political authorities and modes of exercising power should be seen as a continuum (Bayart 2004; Fresia 2009b; Ferguson and Gupta 2002; Hansen and Stepputat 2005; Hibou 1998; Randeria 2007; Sharma and Gupta 2006). Hansen and Stepputat define the set of heterogeneous forms of political organisation and holders of power that coexist in the world as 'overlapping sovereignties' (Hansen and Stepputat 2005). In doing so, they consider 'sovereign' power as a prerogative of all political authorities. Marc Abélès' detailed comparison (1995) of an Ethiopian ethnic group, a French *département*[7] and the European Commission enables him to develop an anthropology of institutions that places the phenomenon of the state in perspective. The political space thus emerges as a composite, fragmented landscape, shaped by a constellation of actors involved in governing populations and territories; the point is then to reconstruct its topography. Taking this encompassing approach to power, the issue is not to understand who wields power (or who governs), but rather to grasp the modalities by which power is exercised within diverse configurations. These studies strive to grasp the articulations between projects and political authorities, in order to identify 'configurations of political authority' (Abélès 1995: 3) or 'processes of governance' (Sending and Neumann 2006).

I therefore strove systematically to situate the UNHCR in a broader political landscape. My aim was to identify the organisation's position within this landscape, to distinguish its particular mode of exerting its authority, and to understand the scope of its activity and how it is diffused, while at the same time making sense of its proper proportions. More specifically, I sought to think all the political authorities, governance projects and legal systems involved in the governance of Afghan migration together as a whole (states, of course, but also smugglers, NGOs, the Taliban, etc.). I wanted to analyse the particular way in which the UNHCR participates in this governance, and how its project articulates (or does not articulate) with those of the other actors involved. Do these actors further, facilitate, sidestep or resist the work of the UNHCR? This approach is far from self-evident, for the *shura* (Afghan local councils) and international organisations, the Taliban and NGOs are often studied by different disciplines, or in isolation, as if they belonged to different worlds.

In order to reconstruct this topography, I drew on all the interactions I was able to observe between UNHCR officers and external interlocutors; I also examined UNHCR documents and the discourse of UNHCR staff, paying attention to the understandings of actors who have a significant role in the governance of Afghan mobility. Through a range of experiences, some fortuitous and some sought-out, I was offered a number of viewpoints from outside the organisation, which helped me to frame it and the effects of its activity, and locate them within this complex context.[8]

Incorporating nonbureaucratic forms of power into the analysis confirms the major role that bureaucracy plays in the UNHCR's exercise of its power. But, more than this, it enables an understanding of the regime of which the UNHCR is the hub, and makes it possible to see how it is integrated into the interstate system. UNHCR officers see states as primary interlocutors, and state sovereignty as the absolute power with which the organisation's actions must comply. In addition to states, there are also nonstate actors involved in the international refugee regime: NGOs and experts, for example, who recognise the UNHCR's authority (as either donor and/or expert) and help to further its activities (by implementing aid programmes or producing knowledge). By contrast, other nonstate actors remain external to the regime. Afghan local councils and tribal authorities, for example, are not treated as political interlocutors in their own right by the UNHCR staff, despite the fact that they play a major role in the subsistence and mobility of Afghans, and influence the effects of UNHCR programmes on the populations concerned, as key channels in the delivery of these programmes. Smuggling networks do not interact with the UNHCR bureaucracy and are rarely mentioned within the organisation. When they are, it is through the lens of national legal systems, as criminals who exploit displaced populations – despite the fact that during the 2000s, it was mainly these networks, rather than states, that enabled Afghans to be mobile.

The Embedded Ethnographer and the Institutional Episteme

My status as a UNHCR employee resulted in intense social and intellectual immersion, leading to deep absorption of the institution's episteme. As a Reporting Officer, I was required to produce texts for external publication. I therefore had to learn to speak, write and think like a UNHCR official and in the name of the organisation. In addition, the UNHCR exerts a powerful intellectual hold over its staff, which goes hand in hand with socialisation and socioprofessional identity. This is particularly evident in 'hardship duty stations' such as the postings in Afghanistan, where the UNHCR expatriate staff remained enclosed in their own space throughout their time there. In this context, the organisation becomes the main social and affective referent. The UNHCR's conceptions and categories, their rationale and their terminology, thus acted on me like a magnet, paralysing analysis of the institution for a time.

How does the researcher detach themself from a discursive space that is itself their subject? For example, I needed descriptive terms to help me analyse how the UNHCR understood the phenomenon of migration, and developed and applied labels such as 'refugee' and 'migrant'. But when I myself was referring to migratory flows, it was difficult, terminologically, to avoid these same labels. Putting the strategic reflection that takes place within the institution in perspective was also difficult. Initially, I was inclined to praise the innovative strategy I was studying, thus expressing a value judgement on this policy.[9]

While my profound absorption of the UNHCR worldview was partly due to my limited connection with academic contexts at the time of my fieldwork, detached assessment of the institutional episteme is an essential and often uncomfortable step in the process for any researcher embedded in an international organisation. Michael Barnett and David Mosse's reflections on their ethnographic studies (within the US mission at the UN and the British International

Development Agency respectively) show that for the insider-researcher, the production of sociological knowledge proceeds through recognition of the socially situated nature of their own ideas and professional practices – what Pierre Bourdieu called 'participant objectivation' (Bourdieu 2003). Barnett (1997) offers a retrospective description of the process that made him into a bureaucrat, and ultimately led him to take the reputation of the institution as the fundamental criterion for judging the UN's interventions. Mosse (2006) recounts the social cost of the break with the epistemic community of which he was part, when the epistemological shift he made was seen as a threat by those who defended the institution's thinking.

More generally, it is essential for any researcher studying international organisations or similar subjects to avoid intellectual co-optation, given the influence of the power-knowledge fields over which these organisations hold sway. This influence is due partly to the scale of the organisations' intervention, and the fact that their cognitive frameworks are often embedded in hegemonic ones.[10] Studies of refugees and asylum policies demonstrate that such distancing is neither comfortable nor automatic.

As the lively debates between researchers about their relations with asylum organisations show (see, for example, van Hear 2012), relations between the academic world and the UNHCR are close, complex and at times ambiguous. Since its expansion in the 1980s, the UNHCR has stepped up its collaboration with researchers. The emergence of the discipline of refugee studies, accompanied by the establishment of research centres (such as the Refugee Studies Centre in Oxford) and journals (such as the *Journal of Refugee Studies*, the *International Journal of Refugee Law* and the *Forced Migration Review*), which the UNHCR helps to fund, is indicative in this regard. This field of study has enshrined the figure of the 'refugee', established by international law and refugee policy, as an academic discipline in its own right.

Collaborating with researchers enables institutional actors to produce a knowledge that informs, and even legitimises, their policies, can sometimes neutralise and absorb criticism, and may also build external alliances in favour of reformative goals (Fresia 2018). Researchers themselves often undertake to produce studies that are more or less explicitly addressed to the organisation. This may derive from an ethical commitment, the desire to produce useful knowledge, to introduce new questions into public debate, to propose reforms, to destabilise dominant representations or indeed to gain access to institutional contexts that would otherwise be inaccessible.

While it has to be recognised that the influence is mutual, and the literature places more emphasis on the risk of subordination and co-optation of researchers (Black 2001; Chimni 1998) than on the institutional reforms they have helped to drive (Fresia 2018), these studies nevertheless testify to the influence of conceptualisations propagated by the UNHCR in the contemporary world. The growth of a body of knowledge (consultancy reports, programme evaluations, strategic papers, academic articles, etc.), situated to varying degrees in the same cognitive framework as the international government of refugees, naturalises the UNHCR's view of the world and gives it more power. This work demonstrates that anthropology can give us the tools (reflexivity, theory) to put the UNHCR's 'regime of truth' into perspective, to avoid intellectual co-optation and to produce a knowledge incommensurable with that of the institution, which can thus open up a new frame of analysis.

Notes

1. An earlier version of this chapter was published in the French journal *Critique internationale* in 2020: 'Bureaugraphier le HCR : approche empirique et englobante d'une organisation internationale', 88(3), 153–72, https://www.cairn.info/revue-critique-internationale-2020-3-page-153.htm (retrieved 12 April 2022).
2. These four stages are presented in logical rather than chronological order in order to give a clear account of the tools I used to conduct an empirically grounded analysis of the UNHCR. The research process was not so linear.
3. For a critical review of international relations literature, see Ambrosetti and Buchet de Neuilly (2009) and Nay and Petiteville (2011). Wanda Vrasti (2008) also notes how international relations studies has become more open to social science methods.
4. 'L'anthropologie des organisations internationales' (no. 54), 'Le changement dans les organisations internationales' (no. 53), 'Une autre approche de la mondialisation : socio-histoire des organisations internationales' (no. 52) and 'La (dé)politisation des organisations internationales' (no. 76).
5. In some of the literature, the global political space is conceptualised in terms of a vertical spatiality (see, for example, Nader 1972). According to this approach, a field study in the UNHCR would involve 'going up'. I did not adopt this approach, in order to avoid naturalising the spatiality of the system of relations between nation-states.
6. At the time of my fieldwork, Afghan refugees represented one-tenth of the persons under the UNHCR's responsibility.
7. *Département* – the administrative regions into which mainland France and its overseas territories are divided (translation).
8. These consisted of two years volunteering with Cimade (a migrant and refugee support NGO) in France, several sessions observing hearings at the French National Court for Asylum Rights, a visit to an Afghan refugee camp near the port of Patras in Greece and a conference of the International Association for the Study of Forced Migration in Cyprus.
9. For a more detailed account of the process of distancing that accompanied my socio-professional transition, see Scalettaris (2019).
10. Liisa Malkki (1992) in particular has shown how the international refugee regime is rooted in the nation-state system, which propagates a sedentary, territorialised view of identities and constructs mobility as a problem.

CHAPTER 2

The 'Refugee Problem' and the Reality of Afghan Mobility

Geneva, spring 2006. I arrive at the UNHCR Headquarters to begin a four-month internship in the section housing the Afghanistan, Iran and Pakistan Desks, located on the third floor of the huge building, within the Operations Department, of the Asia Bureau. This section acts as the interface between Headquarters and the offices in Iran, Afghanistan and Pakistan that together run the 'Afghan Operation', one of the UNHCR's biggest programmes in terms of both funding and staffing. In 2006 the predicament of Afghan refugees was still one of the UNHCR's main concerns. In late 2001, regime change following the NATO intervention in Afghanistan had helped to unblock a situation that had become untenable for the UNHCR. Several million Afghans then returned to the country under the largest repatriation programme the organisation had ever mounted. Nevertheless, the three million or so Afghans living in Iran and Pakistan still represented one-tenth of the total of those falling under the UNHCR's responsibility. Pakistan and Iran remained the countries hosting the largest and third-largest number of refugees worldwide.

Since 2003, the section I was assigned to had also housed the Afghanistan Comprehensive Solutions Unit (ACSU), a small unit tasked with developing long-term strategy for Afghan refugees. The two members of this unit accepted my request for an internship. From my first meeting with Eric and Saverio,[1] and reading the programme documents, I realised that the strategy designed by the Afghanistan Comprehensive Solutions Unit diverged from the organisation's usual approach, particularly in terms of the way in which it understood Afghans' migration and the 'solutions' it envisaged. I was also surprised to learn that, under the auspices of the Afghanistan Research and Evaluation Unit, the anthropologist Alessandro Monsutti, a specialist in Afghan migration, a leading light in transnational migration studies and the author of a monograph on the Hazaras, had been involved in this project; it was in fact through Saverio that I met him for the first time. I also observed that, original though it was, this strategy had gone largely unnoticed at headquarters. My surprise was met with enigmatic smiles by Eric and Saverio. I had the sense that they were keen to initiate an unorthodox venture, which must remain discreet in order to be carried through successfully.

The strategy developed for Afghan refugees post-2001 did indeed incorporate original and unconventional elements that could shake the foundations of the 'refugee problem' the UNHCR is responsible for addressing. In this chapter I describe the conceptualisations of mobility and politics underlying the paradigm of the 'refugee problem', before analysing the unorthodox elements constituting the innovative strategy designed by the ACSU project, and tracing the circumstances that led to its development. In particular, I show that in its view of mobility as an irreversible phenomenon and a potential resource, and in its holistic approach to migration, this project exposes the limits of the 'refugee problem' paradigm and of the three 'durable solutions' meant to address it. It revealed the gap between the conceptual, normative and institutional apparatus established by states, anchored in the premise of the nation-state, and the reality of Afghan migration.

Refugees: Dis-Placed Persons within the National Order

Introduced between the First and Second World Wars, the international refugee regime expanded significantly and became substantially more institutionalised during the second half of the twentieth century. By the early 2000s, it included the activity of not only the UNHCR but also a huge range of bodies operating throughout the world – agencies of various states, NGOs, human rights organisations, law practices, training and research centres. These bodies shared a set of norms, knowledges and procedures rooted in the paradigm of the 'refugee problem', as articulated in the 1951 Convention Relating to the Status of Refugees. These had emerged progressively over sixty years: they included the three 'durable solutions' ('voluntary repatriation', 'local integration' and 'resettlement'); a plethora of legal instruments and procedures (including, for example, the procedures for granting refugee status); techniques for managing populations (construction and management of camps, compilation of statistics, etc.); and a specialist terminology. At the centre of this apparatus sat the figure of the 'refugee' and the organisation of the UNHCR. Loss of the 'protection' of their state of belonging makes the refugee a priority recipient of legal assistance and humanitarian aid, as stipulated in the 1951 Convention. The UNHCR's mission is to seek 'solutions' for this population. I will examine the cognitive foundations of the international refugee regime, for while the regime has developed over time, the paradigm of the 'refugee problem' has remained substantially unchanged. And it is this set of ideas about politics and human mobility that determines the conceptual repertoire and reasoning of actors involved in the international refugee regime, first and foremost officers of the UNHCR.

The first fundamental feature is that the 'refugee problem' as formulated in international law is based on a nation-based understanding of society, politics and mobility. Consequently, the reasoning of those who act to resolve this 'problem' is also rooted in the *national order*. Following Ulrich Beck, it could thus be said that UNHCR staff adopt a *national outlook*.[2] I borrow the concept of *the national order of things* from Liisa Malkki (1992, 1995a) to refer to a set of representations of the world marked out in terms of the nation-state, that is, a model of the state based on the specific experience of the states that were established in Western Europe from the eighteenth century onwards.[3] The national order posits, and thereby naturalises, a world composed of a finite number of territorially sovereign and mutually exclusive states, and isomorphism between the members of national communities and the territory of the state to which they belong. The nation-state forms the basic political unit, a sort of modular 'political shell' (Scott 2009) through which global government of people and things operates. Simply looking at what is commonly known as a 'political map' of the contemporary world is enough to get a sense of this order: each state jurisdiction is demarcated by clear boundaries and distinguished from others by a different colour. In this order, the 'natural' place of each individual is the territory of their state, among their co-nationals. This territorialised jurisdiction forms the 'natural' space of their existence, and their social and political life. Leaving the territory of the state where one belongs thus constitutes deviance, and requires that other states determine whether the entry of non-nationals into their territory is legitimate or not. This is, then, a sedentary order, which by positing mutually exclusive sets of populations, territories and states establishes a powerful criterion for the sociopolitical and spatial distribution of the whole of humanity based on national belonging.

The assumption of nation that underpins both the 1951 Convention and the UNHCR's mandate is primarily a matter of history. The countries that worked to create the interstate regime of protection for refugees were nation-states. This regime emerged in Europe, during the period when the model of the nation-state was spreading throughout the continent, as the treaties that ended the First World War had dissolved empires and redrawn the map of Europe on the basis of the nation principle. This was also the period when the earliest forms of national border control were being put in place: it was precisely the introduction of passports that made the intervention of a High Commissioner for Refugees necessary, to negotiate refugees' entry into national territories

(Noiriel 1997). As Kelly and Kaplan note, with Wilson's Fourteen Points and the creation of the League of Nations, the nation-state became, like the principle of state sovereignty,[4] one of the sources of legitimacy of multilateralism. As the term 'inter-national' and the very name of the League of Nations, later to become the United Nations Organisation, suggest, multilateralism presupposes a world where states and nations are congruent and where those who govern therefore represent the will of their nations (Kelly and Kaplan 2001). This hypothesis is clearly evident in the founding Charter of the United Nations: its preamble states that the 'peoples of the United Nations', through the intermediary of representatives of their governments, have created the organisation. The assumption of nation has only grown stronger subsequently, hand in hand with the global spread of the state. The repertoire of nation was taken up by the liberation struggles that ended colonialism, and it was as nation-states that the new states of Africa and Asia entered the interstate arena (Kelly and Kaplan 2001). From the point of view of the UN agents of multilateralism, the planet is now solidly bolted down in nation-states. Moreover, the legitimacy of the restrictive immigration policies adopted by Western countries from the 1970s onwards was based on the logic of the nation-state. Thus, in the early 2000s, the nation-state was the hegemonic norm of global political life and the dominant mode of representation of the global (Malkki 1998), both within and well beyond intergovernmental multilateralism.

With this understanding of the assumption of nation, I now turn to the thinking that underlies the 'refugee problem'. A refugee, as defined by international law in the mid-twentieth century, is an individual who has lost the 'protection' of their state. It is the failure of the political bond between state and citizen, formulated in terms of absence of 'protection', that prompts them to leave the territory of the state in question and results in absolute distress. Thus, the spatial distancing from the state's jurisdiction marks a fundamental rupture that is political before it is territorial, the equivalent of 'uprooting' (and, indeed, within the UNHCR, refugees are often described as 'uprooted'). What distinguishes refugees from other persons who have left the territory of their state of nationality is that the latter can return there or claim the 'protection' of their state of nationality wherever they are in the world. Refugees, on the other hand, deprived of the context where they could exercise rights, are totally politically destitute. This situation of distress results in a 'protection need' – a key UNHCR phrase identifying those persons for which the organisation is responsible. Thus, the figure of the refugee as defined in international law is a person out of place, and without place in the national order – a place that corresponds to a political context in which their livelihood, political and social life should be made possible. The term 'displacement', often used by the UNHCR to describe this phenomenon, powerfully conveys this idea of being out of place, of painful separation from a situation assumed to be the original and natural order. In the eyes of all other states, the refugee is then simply a *non-national*: there is no place on earth where they can automatically exercise rights.

The condition of political destitution resulting from loss of the protection of one's state of nationality was highlighted by Hannah Arendt, who witnessed in person the political upheavals and migration of populations during and after the Second World War, the context in which the international refugee regime emerged. In a situation where belonging to a state remains the fundamental and essential condition for access to rights, those who no longer enjoy the protection of their own government have lost all political status and all protection. This equates to being deprived of the 'right to have rights':

> the moment human beings lacked their own government and had to fall back upon their minimum rights, no authority was left to protect them and no institution was willing to guarantee them. (Arendt 2017: 381)

In the absence of a sovereign world government and a political community that includes the entirety of the human race, rights can only be protected and upheld as national rights (Arendt 2017). Therefore, when a human being loses the protection of their state of belonging, they are effectively, to use another of Arendt's famous phrases, expelled from humanity altogether. In the wake of Arendt's seminal reflections, a number of researchers have highlighted the functional link between the figure of the refugee, as instituted by international law, and the interstate system, conceived as a closed system of nation-states from which the refugee has been ejected (Agier 2008, 2011; Haddad 2008; Malkki 1992, 1995a; Noiriel 1997, 2001; Nyers 2006). Agier (2008, 2011), for example, understands refugees collectively as a residual humanity of stateless people 'incarcerated outside'. Malkki (1992, 1995a) has emphasised the liminal nature of this figure who finds himself by definition external to the national order – 'between, rather than within sovereign states', as Haddad (2008: 7) notes. Nyers (2006) points out that the refugee shows us the 'inverted mirror image of the citizen', for they are located in a nonplace and is also out of step with what are seen as normal identities and spaces.

The UNHCR's activity can thus be construed as an attempt to create a *place-in-the-world* for refugees. International refugee law and the UNHCR were in fact created in order to establish a new place for these persons, and to *emplace* them in this location. Indeed, the UNHCR often makes reference to the 'asylum space' it has a duty to preserve. In addition, it asks host countries to maintain their 'capacity to host'. Thus, the UNHCR seeks 'durable solutions' in order to provide refugees with 'protection'. There are three of these solutions: 'integration' in the first safe country they reach, 'resettlement' in a further country and 'repatriation' to the country of origin. In each case, the aim is to restore a situation where the individual is integrated as of right in a nation-state. This may be either their country of origin, provided the necessary conditions have been restored, or through the hosting of other countries that guarantee full and lasting inclusion of these vulnerable non-nationals. In a world now entirely made up of nation-states, there is no space outside of them or any substitute for sovereign nation-states. The place to be accorded to refugees must therefore necessarily be created within one of these state jurisdictions. The issue is therefore the access of non-nationals to a state jurisdiction, and the status granted them within it. Since, within the interstate arena, only sovereign states may authorise the entry and stay of non-nationals in their territory, the UNHCR's only way of restoring alignment between the law of sovereign nation-states and the distribution of populations through the world is to strive to influence states' policies on non-nationals.

During the early years of the Cold War, resettlement in industrialised countries was the 'durable solution' most commonly used. The need for labour to support economic revival in Europe combined with the strategic and ideological objectives of the Western bloc nations. This convergence of interests resulted in admission policies that were generous towards refugees from communist countries. Resettlement became a symbol in the ideological war and was widely used to assert the failure of communism and the benevolence of the West. Subsequently, as the rich industrialised countries became increasingly less inclined to welcome non-nationals from war-torn African and Asian countries, or to provide long-term funding for humanitarian interventions in host countries, the hierarchy of 'solutions' shifted. During the 1990s, after a number of conflicts had been resolved with the end of the Cold War, repatriation became established as 'the preferred solution' (Chimni 2004). A number of researchers identify the 1990s as a crucial turning point in the international refugee regime, which henceforth had to come to terms with Western countries' desire to contain flows (see, for example, Crisp 2003). Refugees, who were previously represented as heroes, were now seen as burdens – as suggested by the expression 'burden sharing', sometimes euphemistically rephrased as 'sharing responsibility'. According to this principle, which was increasingly promoted by the UNHCR, 'protection' of refugees should be shared among states in accordance with their capacities. A new rhetoric, still more strongly centred on the national outlook, emerged in the language of the UNHCR (Black and Koser 1999; Chimni 1998; Crisp 2004). This discourse idealised the bond with the country of origin and stressed isomorphism between a person and their jurisdiction of nationality as the ideal and normal situation: the country of nationality was considered the 'home', and the aspiration to 'go back home' – that is, to one's country of origin – was held to be universal.

With regard to Afghan refugees, the UNHCR was thus striving to solve what is often described in UNHCR documents as 'the complex equation for the resolution of Afghan displacement' (UNHCR 2004a: 2). This telling expression reveals the 'mathematical' approach (Warner 1994) underpinning the paradigm of the 'refugee problem', a sort of 'international mathematics'. Solving this 'equation' involves creating a both material and legal space within the Iranian, Pakistani and Afghan state jurisdictions, in order to arrive at an appropriate distribution of Afghan refugees, one capable of ensuring the conditions for subsistence and safety for this population.

The 'Refugee Problem' and Afghan Mobility

When applied to Afghan migration, the conception of the 'refugee problem' itself becomes a problem. Some of the most convincing critiques of this paradigm have been formulated by anthropologists observing the disconnection between the UNHCR's conceptual apparatus and the reality of Afghan migration (see Table 2.1). They join a range of researchers, in both transnational migration studies and refugee studies, who have highlighted the limits of the 'refugee problem' paradigm, as defined in international law, as a way of understanding the social and political situation of populations fleeing conflict.

In *War and Migration*, his monograph on the migrations of the Hazaras, Alessandro Monsutti (2005) shows how this people from central Afghanistan, faced with endemic insecurity and poverty, established extensive socioeconomic and commercial networks throughout the region, extending from Iran to Pakistan and Afghanistan. These networks are based on geographical dispersal of kin groups and diversification of their members' means of subsistence. Monsutti's study encapsulates the gap between the 'refugee problem' paradigm and the concrete reality of migration and politics.

Table 2.1. Differences between the 'refugee problem' paradigm and the sociological approach in the early 2000s

'Refugee problem' paradigm	Migration studies
Migration is an exception	Migration is normal
Migration is problematic	Migration is a resource or solution
The refugee is a victim	The refugee has agency
Selective approach to migration focused on individual cases	Holistic approach to migration
Return to the country of origin is the preferred solution	Return does not represent the end of the migration cycle, nor the restoration of a pre-existing order
Nation-states	There are sociopolitical systems other than states (e.g. ethnic or tribal solidarity)

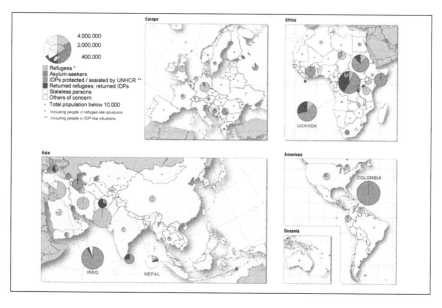

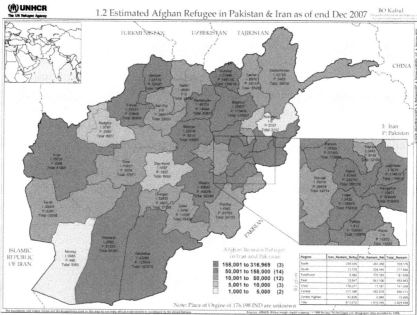

Figure 2.1. Representations of migration. Maps produced by the UNHCR show the population 'under its mandate at the end of 2006' (above) and Afghans in Iran and Pakistan at the end of 2007 (below) (UNHCR 2008a: 24; 2007d: 11). © UNHCR

Set alongside one another, Monsutti's book and the UNHCR reports produced during the same years appear to discuss two different realities. While in the UNHCR reports migration is treated as a problematic exception, Monsutti's study shows that for the Hazaras, it is an everyday reality that has become integrated into their way of life. Historians and anthropologists have shown that migration is a normal and structural element of human societies (Lucassen and Lucassen 1999). All studies of Afghan migration show that for the populations of Afghanistan migration, in its diverse forms, has a long history in the region, dating back to a time well before the beginning of the conflict and the current geopolitical organisation. Even in the 1970s, Afghanistan, a landlocked, mountainous country with only 12% agricultural land, had one of the lowest levels of development in the world and a high birth rate. Migration has therefore historically been a basic socioeconomic strategy that enables people to cope with both droughts and political instability. Furthermore, the Iranian and Pakistani economies have long presented attractive labour markets. Movement is also facilitated by cultural, tribal and linguistic links that span state borders.[5] Thus, the conflict has simply amplified a pre-existing phenomenon.

These contradictory conceptions of mobility, as a deviation on the one hand versus an everyday phenomenon on the other, are underscored by the different understandings of the relationship between people and space in Monsutti's study and the UNHCR documents. The latter perceive migratory flows in terms of a spatiality rigorously anchored in the geopolitics of the nation-state system. This contrasts with the space of multidirectional circulation and recurrent cross-border movements described by Monsutti. These differences are particularly evident in the graphic representations offered by the UNHCR (see Figure 2.1) compared with those in Monsutti's studies (see Figure 2.2). The UNHCR often shows migrations as static population 'reserves' within states, using circles rather than arrows. In addition, it classifies migration flows by country or province of origin. The second map, designed to facilitate management of programmes for the reintegration of returnees, shows very clearly how the migrant population is viewed through the lens of its link with a specific physical place in Afghan territory. By contrast, Monsutti's studies emphasise routes and movements, indicated by arrows. In the first map in particular, it is worth noting that routes have the same 'graphic status' as international borders. Centlivres and Edwards, who studied Pashtun Afghans in Pakistan, observe that the category 'refugee' as defined by international law is incommensurate with the social, cultural, tribal and religious context in which Pashtun movements take place within Pashtunistan, a region that straddles the Afghanistan-Pakistan border (Centlivres 1988; Centlivres and Centlivres-Demont 1999; Edwards 1986).

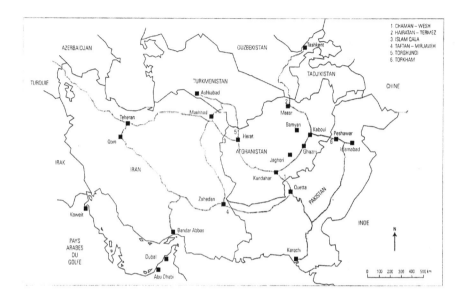

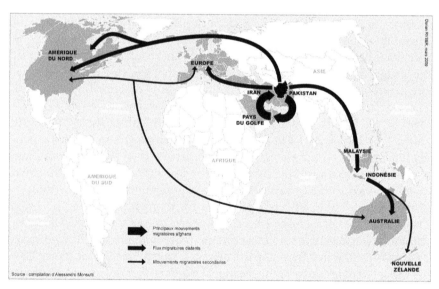

Figure 2.2. Representations of Afghan migration. Maps produced by Alessandro Monsutti show the main migration routes in the Iran-Afghanistan-Pakistan region (above) and Afghan migration throughout the world (below) (Monsutti 2004: 21; 2009: 104). © Alessandro Monsutti

While the UNHCR documents present refugee mobility as a traumatic experience and an expression of distress, Monsutti argues that in the case of the Hazaras, mobility should be seen as a resource instead of a problem. Rather than leading to the breakdown of structures, geographical dispersal allows groups to reproduce social links despite war and dispersal. Transnational networks and relations of solidarity generate a substantial flow of funds to Hazarajat, in amounts much higher than the international aid channelled by NGOs and UN agencies. Monsutti contrasts the victim image frequently presented by humanitarian organisations with the agency of migrants, who are seen as social actors capable of taking charge of their lives. Many studies have recognised the importance of mobility and transnational networks for the survival and subsistence of displaced populations (Bakewell 2000a; Horst 2006; Huttunen 2010; Stepputat 2004; van Hear 2002), and a number of authors have reflected on UNHCR officials' tendency to see refugees as victims, denying them all agency (Malkki 1996; Nyers 2006; Pupavac 2006).

The gap between the 'refugee problem' paradigm and the approach of researchers is also evident in the classification underlying the UNHCR's population of concern: the difference between forced and voluntary migration. This distinction is the foundation of the UNHCR's activity, for the concept of the refugee defines its sphere of competence. In each case, then, the organisation strives to understand whether it is dealing with persons who have been forced by persecution to leave their country or with people leaving of their own free will in order to better their living conditions. Monsutti, however, argues trenchantly that a conceptual framework based on causes is unable to take into account the complexity of the migration strategies developed by the Hazaras, and is therefore both descriptively and analytically inadequate. He views war and poverty as factors that combine with and mutually reinforce one another, driving hundreds of thousands of young Hazaras to move across borders. This argument chimes with those of a growing number of researchers who have also questioned the analytical usefulness of the distinction between 'refugees' and 'voluntary migrants', pointing out that it is impossible to apply it and to distinguish discrete categories of migrants, both empirically (Bakewell 2000a; Fresia 2006) and theoretically (Richmond 1988: 20; Turton 2003: 7). Historians and anthropologists studying migration prefer a global approach that addresses contemporary mobility as part of a continuity. They aim to analyse migratory configurations from a historical and socioeconomic standpoint, and examine how the categories defined by migration policies influence the identities and strategies of migrants (Adelkhah and Bayart 2007; Bakewell 2000a; Black 2001; Malkki 1995b; Lucassen and Lucassen 1999; Turton 2003).

A further disparity emerges with the concept of return. While repatriation has been presented by the UNHCR as the 'preferred solution' since the 1990s, researchers question the idea that return constitutes the 'end of the migration cycle', or a move backwards, and argue that repatriation cannot be conceived as simply restoring a prior order (Al-Ali and Koser 2002; Black and Koser 1999; Cassarino 2004; Hammond 2004; Ray 2000; van Aken 2003; Warner 1994). These researchers in fact show that migration trajectories are rarely linear and that return is often just one stage in a broader trajectory of migration (as in the case of visits to the country, for example). They demonstrate how both migrants and living conditions in the country alter to the extent that return can come to resemble a new departure, and show that migrants' multiple belongings call into question the idea of the country of origin as the definitive 'home'.

Lastly, the gap between the UNHCR's conceptual framework and the reality of Afghan migration is also apparent in the political arena. Because UNHCR officials favour the national outlook, the organisation fails to recognise any sociopolitical order and any kind of solidarity other than those based on nation. However, in Monsutti's work, the state is not seen as the sole and principal context for people's livelihood and the circulation of resources; from this point of view, ethnic solidarity can often be more efficient than the protection of a state. Anthropologists Centlivres and Edwards have shown that in Pashtunistan, displaced people could easily find refuge with neighbouring tribes, in accordance with the tradition of Pashtunwali[6] and Islamic precepts (Centlivres 1988; Centlivres and Centlivres-Demont 1999; Edwards 1986; Shahrani 1995). Many studies also show that ethnic solidarity can have a greater impact than state policies on the living conditions of people fleeing conflict (Fresia 2009a). The exercise of power in the contemporary world cannot be reduced purely to the logic of the state. As Malkki points out, in response to an article by Habermas where he analyses the formation and limits of the nation-state while at the same time representing this form of political organisation as the universal and exhaustive key to reading the state of world politics, although the 'family of nations' has become the dominant mode of representation of the 'global', it cannot represent all of the complex, emergent and only partially articulated forms of association and political solidarity at work in the contemporary world (Malkki 1998: 435).

'Toward Comprehensive Solutions'

The strategy developed by the Afghan Comprehensive Solutions Unit[7] departed from the traditional understanding of the 'refugee problem' and incorporated a number of elements drawn from research conclusions. It started from the basis that the repatriation of all Afghans from Iran and Pakistan should be excluded from consideration:

even an extension of existing arrangements for repatriation *sine die* may resolve neither the immediate tensions between the rate of return and absorption capacity inside
Afghanistan, nor provide a definitive solution. (UNHCR 2004a: 2)

Despite the large-scale repatriation that had taken place, definitive and full
return was not possible owing to the irreversibility of the social and economic
processes arising from the prolonged conflict in Afghanistan. The strategy
based this conclusion on three main considerations.

First, the 2001 change in regime could not transform Afghanistan into a
welcoming country overnight. The process of political transition was in its in-
fancy, and much of the country lacked sufficient means of subsistence, education and employment opportunities. Thus, even with an optimistic prediction
for political stabilisation and gradual economic growth, the reconstruction
supported by the international community would take time.

Second, a proportion of the Afghan population that left the country more
than twenty years earlier was now durably settled in Iran and Pakistan. A
whole generation had been born outside of Afghanistan and had grown
up without ever having known the country. Despite precarious conditions,
this population had become used to higher standards of living than in
Afghanistan, for example, in terms of access to education and healthcare. It
was therefore highly unlikely that this section of the population would wish
to leave these countries.

Finally, the Afghan presence in Iran and Pakistan was a product of major migration flows. Cross-border migration had seen an unprecedented rise
during the decades of conflict, and remained high, particularly since it was
now supported by solid transnational networks. A considerable proportion of
these movements was not necessarily due to persecution or conflict, but rather
stimulated by what appear to be persistent economic and social factors. There
remained a marked economic differential between Afghanistan, where demographic growth continued to outstrip economic growth, and its two neighbours. Moreover, migration was the source of substantial transfers of funds.
These funds were both a crucial contribution to the subsistence of Afghan families and a factor in the country's economic recovery.

It was thus clear that full return was impossible, and the way in which states
and the international bodies concerned managed Afghan populations outside of Afghanistan needed to be rethought. The new strategy subdivided the
Afghan population living in neighbouring countries into four categories, for
each of which appropriate solutions needed to be created:

(1) 'Prospective returnees'. For those Afghans in Iran and Pakistan who
    intended to return to Afghanistan, repatriation and reintegration pro-
    grammes represented a genuine solution. The UNHCR planned to main-
    tain its repatriation and reintegration programmes in partnership with

the Afghan authorities, so that in future the Afghan government had the capacity to integrate and protect the repatriated population.

(2) 'Persons in need of continuing protection'. While for some Afghans the persecution that had led to migrations in the past was decreasing, the fall of the Taliban regime did not automatically eliminate the 'need for international protection' against all forms of human rights violation and persecution. It was therefore essential to establish national asylum regimes in Iran and Pakistan that met international standards, incorporating procedures for granting refugee status and robust official forms of protection.

(3) 'Longstaying Afghans'. Some Afghans who were stably settled in Iran and Pakistan probably did not wish to return to Afghanistan. But although they were not strictly in 'need of international protection', they should enjoy less precarious conditions of residence, based on a long-term right of residence. Development programmes in regions with a large Afghan population, established in collaboration with the World Food Programme (WFP), could facilitate this process.

(4) 'Migrant workers'. A system for managing migration flows could give the many migrant workers regular channels for travelling and working in neighbouring countries, enhancing the benefits of this socioeconomic strategy. This would require the International Labour Organization (ILO) and the International Organization for Migration (IOM) to participate in setting up a migration regime, which would make it possible to establish agreements on migration flows and support capacity building within the government bodies concerned.

To sum up, the strategy recommended reconfiguring the way in which states, in collaboration with international organisations such as the UNHCR, the IOM, the ILO and the WFP, address and manage the presence of Afghans in Iran and Pakistan, and migration flows in the region. It proposed introducing a set of four provisions that were adjustable depending on the type of migration. These were: the repatriation and reintegration programme; an asylum regime aligned with international standards; more stable conditions of residence for Afghans long settled in Iran and Pakistan; and a bilateral agreement governing the status of migrant workers. Once the transition had been achieved, the role of the UNHCR would be much reduced, in terms of both staffing and funding. Its role would be confined to monitoring procedures for granting asylum and the standard of treatment of persons recognised as refugees. In order to encourage this transition, the two members of the Afghanistan Comprehensive Solutions Unit began by commissioning research into population movements in the region, setting up collaborations with the IOM and the ILO, and engaging in a process of 'strategic consultations' with the governments concerned.

An Innovative Project

In its approach to the phenomenon of Afghan migration, and its perception of the UNHCR's mandate in this context, the strategy developed by the Afghanistan Comprehensive Solutions Unit stepped back from the UNHCR's habitual framing of the 'refugee problem'. The implementation of the strategy would involve shifting from a refugee-centred perspective to a mobility-centred one. The problem was redefined not as one facing states that had to manage often unwanted non-nationals, but as a problem of the *relationship* between populations, territories and states. In this the strategy recognised that the national order has intrinsic limits, and attempted to find a way out of the zero-sum game that would result from the pursuit of repatriation for all. By taking into consideration the historical and socioeconomic reality of migration, it proposed that mobility should be seen as natural and positive, while adopting a holistic approach to migration flows.

Under the conventional view of the 'refugee problem', the fact that individuals move across state borders is problematic. It poses a problem to the other states, which must decide how to treat non-nationals often perceived as undesirable within their jurisdiction. All the 'traditional solutions' involve settlement, either in the country of origin, where citizens may be able to return following changes that ensure their safety and livelihood are provided for, or in another country if it agrees to grant them legitimate residence. Limiting migration is therefore always considered desirable, or at least as evidence of the success of the solutions implemented.

However, in the strategy developed for Afghanistan Afghan mobility was considered normal. The strategy recognised the historicity and irreversibility of Afghan migrations: 'it is understood that the Afghan population is an inherently mobile one' (internal document).

This migration constituted a concrete fact that must be taken into account in any consideration of the situation, an unavoidable and irreversible reality that cannot be ignored in policy-making: 'border crossings between Afghanistan and Pakistan are a reality' (internal document).

Moreover, Afghan mobility was seen as an asset, an important economic and social resource for the livelihood of families and also for the viability of the state, thanks to the transfer of money it generated. It should therefore be valued. This means recognising the agency of migrants, the importance of transnational networks and their fundamental role in supporting the livelihood of the Afghan population. As Saverio put it at a conference in Kabul in 2007, the 'comprehensive solutions' project aimed to put the 'human element' at the centre of the equation.

This view meant asserting unequivocally that in the case of Afghanistan – a country with limited natural resources that has suffered decades of political instability – isomorphism between population and territory was not a viable solution. The strategy also took into account the economic disparities between Afghanistan and the neighbouring countries, particularly with regard to their capacity to provide people with a livelihood. From this point of view, migration is necessary and fundamental to the livelihood of Afghan populations and the viability of the Afghan state. Rather than seeking to reduce it, what was needed was to legitimise the presence and movement of Afghans outside their country of origin. Mobility therefore featured among the solutions proposed. In the strategy, the permanent presence of substantial numbers of Afghans in Iran and Pakistan, and cross-border mobility itself, were not completely eliminated, even in the scenario where Afghanistan returned to a state of stability. The strategy recommended a direct approach to the Iranian and Pakistani author-ities, using continuous and persistent pressure to encourage the states in the region to accept first that migration will continue and second that a proportion of the Afghan population will remain permanently in their countries.

Furthermore, the strategy adopted a holistic approach to Afghan migra-tion within the region: rather than distinguishing refugees from other kinds of migrants, it proposed solutions adapted to several categories of migrants. It thus asserted a continuity between forms of migration and how these should be addressed in state policy – hence the expression *'comprehensive solutions'*. In this case, the UNHCR should not prioritise its mandate and the population strictly within its area of competence (persons 'in need of pro-tection'), but should adopt a broader perspective, situating this population within the larger category of migrants as a whole. For example, the strategy repeatedly spoke of 'population movements', which is not an official policy term, using it to describe the overall phenomenon of migration. Provisions relating to persons who fall within the organisation's competence were con-sidered within the 'broader policy framework for displacement' (UNHCR 2007a: 1). 'Migrant workers' were therefore also taken into consideration and it was recommended that a legal framework be put in place to regulate the conditions of both their residence in Iran and Pakistan and their cross-bor-der movements.

Thus, the strategy was distinctive in the way in which it stepped back from the categories and mandates of international organisations. The documents re-peatedly highlighted the fact that the situation extended beyond the UNHCR's mandate and competence. It required a more multifaceted programme of ac-tion than the organisation was able to offer 'additional solutions that lie outside UNHCR's mandate need to be found ... [This] type of challenge can only be addressed by innovative arrangements that go beyond UNHCR's mandate and competence' (UNHCR 2003a: 2–6).

The UNHCR needed to become active in sectors where it has no author-ity – development, the fight against poverty, migrant workers – by setting up collaborations with other organisations. During my placement, I observed Saverio and Eric planning studies on the impact of Afghan migration on the labour markets in Iran and Pakistan. They also discussed the details of projects for training Afghan consular officials in Tehran and Islamabad with officers from the IOM, and development projects planned for areas with a high Afghan presence in Pakistan with officers from the United Nations Development Project (UNDP).

The proposed strategy thus did not take its line from the compartmentalised areas of competence of international organisations or existing policy categories (primary among them those of 'refugee' and 'durable solutions'), imposing them on reality from above. On the contrary, the aim was to take the complex and fluid reality as the starting point. This meant adopting an analysis that set Afghan migration in a historical and socioeconomic perspective, in order to create policies better fitted to this reality by shifting existing areas of competence – even if this meant challenging pre-established categories and domains. Planning documents repeatedly emphasised the need to move away from a 'humanitarian'- or 'refugee'-focused position that could not encompass the phenomenon facing the organisation, which had evolved 'beyond the parameters of a refugee paradigm into a more complex, multi-faceted challenge that will require additional solutions' (UNHCR 2003a: 6). Solutions should be adapted to contextual reality rather than the other way round.

The Emergence of the Strategy

A number of factors converged to create an institutional context favourable to the origin of this innovative strategy: First, the scale and complexity of the Afghan situation, which represented a major test for the UNHCR in the early 2000s, and the need for it to reformulate its role during a delicate transition phase called for in-depth analysis and strategic reflection; second, the meeting between two individuals with complementary personalities and shared affinities, who found a way to assert their point of view; third, a supportive environment at Headquarters, where senior managers were seeking to encourage research into comprehensive and innovative approaches. Seen from the point of view of sociology of institutions (Bezes and Le Lidec 2010; Nay and Petiteville 2011), the situation thus combined exogenous change (the new context in Afghanistan at the end of 2001), two norm entrepreneurs (Saverio and Eric) and a political window (UNHCR Headquarters becoming open to the development of innovative solutions). I will now consider these three factors in more detail.

In the early 2000s, Afghanistan was a key issue for the UNHCR, which needed to demonstrate its capacity to meet the challenge. For two decades,

Afghans had represented the largest population under its remit. In the new geopolitical context (see next section below), this became the largest intervention, in terms of both funding and staffing, that the organisation had ever managed. When Afghanistan moved to the centre of the international stage, the UNHCR had to redefine its activity in a new, postconflict context that was highly sensitive thanks to the intermeshed defence and national security interests of a number of states, including the 'fight against terrorism' being conducted by the United States and its allies.[8]

Ruud Lubbers, the High Commissioner at the time of the 9/11 attacks, had only been in post since the beginning of that year. According to an employee who was involved in the redeployment of the UNHCR in the region between 2001 and 2002, Lubbers felt that Afghanistan would be 'his operation' – the great mission that would go down in history as the key issue under his leadership. Aware of the repercussions the attacks would have in Afghanistan, he entrusted a team based in Pakistan with the task of monitoring how the situation developed during the military campaign. He was therefore receiving daily detailed telephone reports of the team's activities.

Once the military campaign was over, Lubbers handed over the reins of the operation to Mr Gortani, whom he considered one of the brightest and most trustworthy of the senior officials. Gortani in his turn took care to appoint equally trustworthy colleagues in Kabul, thus forming an efficient and close-knit team. Over the course of 2002, this team organised the redeployment of the UNHCR in Afghanistan, established the massive repatriation programme[9] and designed a strategy for reintegrating returnees. Yet while all the organisation's resources and public focus were turned towards the repatriation programme, these officials realised that major challenges would come once the flow of returnees had dwindled. A new impasse loomed on the horizon, owing to the peremptory expectations of the Iranian and Pakistani governments, which continued to encourage total repatriation. Even in late 2001 the Iranian and Pakistani statements and arguments were unequivocal: after two decades, it was time to put an end to the problems posed by the Afghan presence in their territories. They continued to insist that the crisis situation in which Afghans had found themselves was now resolved. These declarations also pointed to donor involvement in Afghanistan and the transition donors were putting in place, which was supposed to guarantee stabilisation of the country and facilitate the reintegration of repatriated Afghans. But in the view of Gortani and his close colleagues, given the situation in Afghanistan and the scale of Afghan migration, definitive return of millions of Afghans was unthinkable. Resolving this difficulty therefore required clear-sightedness and the development of a strategy that went beyond the single question of repatriation.

Afghan Refugees 1979–2001

The 1979 Soviet invasion marked the beginning of a long period of conflict and political instability in Afghanistan. Clashes between Mujahideen and Russian-backed forces were followed by a state of civil war between various factions within the country, which continued until the Taliban came to power. Migration soared, primarily to neighbouring Iran and Pakistan. It is estimated that by the end of the 1980s, the conflict had resulted in at least one million deaths and the internal migration of three million more people. In addition, six million Afghans – approximately one-fifth of the population – had left the country, mainly for Iran and Pakistan. By the end of the 1990s, the number of Afghans in these two countries was estimated at four million.

While the Iranian and Pakistani governments initially welcomed these Afghans, their attitude changed radically during the 1990s, as they began to hold Afghans responsible for social and economic destabilisation in their countries.[10] They also accused them of criminality and drug trafficking. During this period, the two governments' statements led to a sharp deterioration in the living conditions of Afghans settled in their countries. Their access to social services was cut, and they regularly suffered harassment. They were also often expelled, despite the fact that the civil war, the establishment of the Taliban regime and the food crisis had worsened conditions for subsistence and safety in Afghanistan. Donor countries had been reducing their funding since the strategic issue had disappeared with the end of the Cold War.

The 9/11 attacks, the US military intervention in Afghanistan, the fall of the Taliban regime and the start of the international reconstruction project led to a massive geopolitical upheaval, which had a major impact on UNHCR programmes in the region. Afghanistan became the focus of an international political transition and economic reconstruction project, in which the UN was fully involved. The Security Council sponsored an inter-Afghan agreement for a political transition leading to the re-establishment of government institutions. It also set up a UN Assistance Mission in Afghanistan (UNAMA) and commissioned a NATO-led international force to train the Afghan security forces and ensure maintenance of security of the country. The great powers' unprecedented political and financial investment in reconstruction of the country and regime change raised hopes of lasting peace and stability in Afghanistan. This regime change encouraged the return of tens of thousands of Afghans as soon as military operations ended in November 2001.

This realisation prompted intense high-level discussion in the Geneva, Kabul, Islamabad and Tehran offices. In July 2003 these debates resulted in an initial discussion paper entitled 'Towards a Comprehensive Solution for Displacement from Afghanistan' (UNHCR 2003a). The approach recommended in this persuasive and well-argued document was presented by the authors as the only hope for achieving a durable solution. Three months later, the Afghanistan Comprehensive Solutions Unit was set up at UNHCR Headquarters, its purpose being to develop a long-term strategy for the region. The unit at that point comprised two individuals who had been centrally involved in writing the discussion paper. Saverio had served as Regional Liaison Officer since 2002, acting as the link between the Tehran, Kabul and Islamabad offices. Eric had been Policy Advisor at the Geneva Headquarters for the Afghanistan Operation for about a year. As Saverio's posting was coming to an end, the idea of setting up a policy unit to support 'operations' came into being.

Such an ad hoc unit is unusual for the UNHCR. Decisions on strategy are generally taken by senior officers themselves within each operation; in addition, there is a department attached to the High Commissioner's office, the Policy Development and Evaluation Service, that was concerned with analysis and evaluation of the organisation's policy. The strategic importance and exceptional nature of the Afghan situation, and the risk of an impasse that had been highlighted by those promoting the new strategy, help to explain why this ad hoc unit was set up and how the strategic objectives were defined. As Dulong (2010: 262) notes, in situations of institutional crisis, the costs of subversion are reduced amid uncertainty and the loosening of containing structures. The immediate, concrete priority was to manage the situation on the ground in the best way possible, and to redefine the UNHCR's mission in the new, postconflict context, rather than to preserve the refugee paradigm.

Leadership of the Afghanistan Comprehensive Solutions Unit was entrusted to Saverio and Eric, despite the fact that they did not hold senior management-level positions in the UNHCR. They had nevertheless established themselves as authorities on Afghan refugees. Saverio and Eric did not know one another personally before they began working together, but they formed a dynamic, efficient partnership. Their complementary experience and approaches surely contributed to the successful launch of the 'comprehensive solutions': Saverio had followed a career that was both international and internal to the UNHCR, and Eric an Afghan-centred career outside the UNHCR, Saverio's more focused on action, Eric's on analysis. Saverio could be seen as the charismatic insider and Eric as the intellectual outsider. Between them, they combined a wide range of resources that helped to back up their vision: in-depth knowledge of the Afghan context and of the UNHCR, a solid network both within and outside the organisation, strategic acumen, and excellent persuasion and negotiation skills.

Saverio began a promising career with the UNHCR at a young age, with numerous postings in Congo, Djibouti, Cambodia, Lebanon, New York and the Balkans where he was able to demonstrate his capacities. Skilled, confident and ambitious, over the course of his career he had also developed detailed knowledge of the internal mechanisms of the UNHCR, and a critical clear-sightedness about the dysfunctional aspects of the organisation. Over the course of his missions, he had established close relationships within the UNHCR, and his relationship of trust with Mr Gortani, who had invited Saverio to join his team in Kabul, was crucial to the launch of the initiative. Over a lunch where he told me about the origins of the project, Saverio recounted how, as they admired the Afghan mountain landscape over which they were flying, the two had enthusiastically developed the plan to set up this unit, which among other things would allow them to continue working together. Mr Gortani's privileged relationship with the High Commissioner probably helped him gain a level of legitimacy with the organisation's reputedly somewhat conservative senior officers that was otherwise difficult to achieve (Fresia 2010).

Eric had only been at the UNHCR since 2002, having previously worked for a long time with other organisations in Afghanistan. His experience of working in the field in Afghanistan was thus much longer than Saverio's eighteen months. Afghanistan was the country in which he specialised. With a doctorate in economics, his thinking did not start from the premise of the 'refugee problem'. He sifted and evaluated the pertinence of the terms he used, even if it meant shaking up pre-established ideas. He followed the news, and current research in the region, closely; he had established close relationships with a number of researchers, experts and officers of organisations such as the UNDP, the WFP, the IOM and the European Commission who were working on or in Afghanistan. His office housed an extensive library that brought together academic publications, research reports and grey literature, organised in large cardboard file boxes. This explains how he already knew the work of Alessandro Monsutti, which was still little known at the time, as the original French version of his book *War and Migrations* was not published until 2004. Eric's way of thinking, as an English-speaking expert on Afghanistan rather than on refugees, meant that the content, terminology and style of the unit's strategy documents stood out from the organisation's standardised format and set vocabulary. The writing style is fluid, and the structure original and persuasive. Detailed analysis of the context takes priority, preceding recommendations.

The supportive environment at Headquarters further helps to explain how the 'comprehensive solutions' project came into being. The UNHCR generally promotes strategic reflection as a characteristic of a robust, authoritative and flexible organisation. The strategy proposed by Saverio and Eric also fitted well with the new drive towards 'finding solutions' instilled by Ruud Lubbers when he took over as High Commissioner. This impetus generated a climate of discussion and reflection around 'durable solutions' and resulted, among other things, in the 'Convention Plus' launched by the High Commissioner in 2001. This initiative, in a spirit of research and openness to innovative solutions, specifically aimed to promote 'comprehensive' approaches to crises that had hitherto remained intractable (UNHCR 2004b, 2006a: 121–26). Saverio and Eric's strategy fitted perfectly into this initiative, finding a place and an institutional justification as one of the cases that adopted the 'Convention Plus approach', despite the fact that in practice, as noted above, the strategic drive came from elsewhere. Two other Comprehensive Plans of Action were developed under the 'Convention Plus' initiative, for the contexts of Somalia (UNHCR 2005c) and Colombia.[11]

During my posting at the UNHCR Headquarters, I also noted that the theme of mobility also interested the 'higher echelons' on the eighth floor, particularly the Policy Development and Evaluation Service. The director of this service had influence with international decision-makers on matters of asylum and migration. Himself the holder of a doctorate, his long experience of international institutions combined with close links with the world of academic research. He demonstrated a lucid awareness of the challenges that the UNHCR, and UN institutions responsible for managing migration more generally, faced in the new global context at the turn of the twenty-first century (Crisp 1999a, 2003; Crisp and Dessalegne 2002). During the early 2000s, he had temporarily left the UNHCR to sit on the Global Commission on International Migration, set up by the UN Secretary-General to make recommendations for strengthening the 'international governance of migration'.[12] Its final report, which calls for new approaches, is the first international document to address international migration as a unitary, global issue, while highlighting protection of migrants' rights (Global Commission on International Migration 2005). When I met him in his office in 2006, he had just resumed the directorship of the Policy Development and Evaluation Service. On a scrap of paper that I kept, he sketched a drawing with arrows, representing the mobility of Afghan refugees. He explained that the UNHCR was then beginning to see 'migration as a fourth solution'. He was following the developing strategy of the Afghanistan Comprehensive Solutions Unit from a distance, but with interest.

In the situation opened up by the NATO intervention in Afghanistan, would this original, well-thought-out strategy enable the UNHCR to create conditions of livelihood and security for the Afghan populations concerned? And on another level, would it give the organisation the opportunity to re-think the paradigm of the 'refugee problem', given how this paradigm failed to encompass the phenomenon of migration and the political space of the contemporary world? A failure that was becoming increasingly difficult to ignore within the UNHCR, whether it emerged in the concrete limits facing the organisation in the pursuit of its mission or in the rising criticism from researchers studying its work. At that point, the 'comprehensive solutions' strategy represented an exceptional response to an exceptional situation – this was one of the conditions that had enabled it to be established. As I have noted, this strategy had been developed for the very concrete purpose of managing a crucial, thorny issue in the best way possible rather than with the aim of attacking or reforming the institution. Its unconventional aspects remained, for the time being, without fanfare. But, as I have also noted, this strategy carried a potentially destabilising message: if you really want to find a viable solution, you need to change the terms of the equation. Given allies within the organisation and in the academic world, the new direction in the Afghan case could thus usher in a change of mindset that would completely recast the international refugee regime. The remainder of this book follows the institutional journey of the 'comprehensive solutions', opening a window onto the bureaucratic apparatus of the UNHCR in action.

Notes

1. These and all other names that appear in this text are pseudonyms in order to protect the identity of my interlocutors both within and outside the UNHCR.
2. Beck introduces the distinction between *methodological nationalism*, the attitude of those sociologists who locate their reflections within the framework of the national order, and the *national outlook*, the same attitude as adopted by social actors (Beck 2006).
3. From the Enlightenment onwards, liberal democracies, and the principle of self-determination of the people, began to become established in Western Europe. The sovereignty of the state was redefined as national sovereignty. The nation, understood as a limited, culturally homogeneous community of equal citizens, emerged as the basic polity, and as such underpinned the legitimacy of the state as sole guarantor of the rights and wellbeing of citizens. The state's laws and the means of coercion it possesses are legitimate, in that they emanate from the will of the members of the nation who have elected those who govern them. The boundaries of the nation determine the members who enjoy civic and political rights, are entitled to the services provided by the state, and have duties in return (payment of taxes, conscription) (Anderson 2006; Habermas 1998; Hobsbawm 1992; Noiriel 1997).
4. Since the seventeenth century, the interstate system has been legally and politically organised on the principle of state sovereignty, under which the state has supreme and absolute authority in its jurisdiction. The principle of non-interference in the internal affairs of other states was recognised for the first time by the 1648 Peace of Westphalia.

5. For a historical and anthropological perspective on Afghan migration, see Adelkhah (2007), Dupree (1975), Green (2008), Hanifi (2008), Monsutti (2005), Nichols (2008) and Roy (1988).
6. The customary code of the Pashtun people.
7. The outline that follows draws from the UNHCR (2003a) and (2004a) papers.
8. For an overview of the post-2001 geopolitical context, see Rashid (2008), Roy (2004, 2007) and Majidyar and Alfoneh (2010).
9. This programme had been launched in the late 1980s following the 1988 Geneva Accords providing for the withdrawal of Soviet forces. It was suspended several times during the 1990s.
10. For more details on the evolution of reception policies in Iran and Pakistan in the 1980s and 1990s, see Adelkhah and Olszewska (2006), Kronenfeld (2008), Marsden (1992), Rajee (2000), Rizvi (1990), Schöch (2008), and Turton and Marsden (2002).
11. See UNHCR (2005c) and the *Mexico Declaration and Plan of Action to Strengthen the International Protection of Refugees in Latin America*, Mexico City, 16 November 2004. However, in these cases the 'toolbox' remained unchanged. These plans aimed instead to reinforce each of the three 'durable solutions' by finding new ways of implementing them. In this case, the term 'comprehensive' indicates the focus on how the three 'solutions' can complement one another, rather than a holistic approach to migration flows. The only initiative comparable to the strategy developed for the Afghan context after 2001 was the approach adopted by the UNHCR during the mid-2000s in West Africa, when it called for the application of the Economic Community of West African States (ECOWAS) treaty on freedom of movement in the region (Adepoju et al. 2007).
12. In the early 2000s the UN Secretary-General attempted to put the issue of 'migration' back on the agenda. In a famous report, Kofi Annan asserted that 'it [was] time to take a more comprehensive look at the various dimensions of the migration issue' (United Nations 2002: 10).

CHAPTER 3

Cartography of a Diffused Presence

When I arrived at the Kabul office, I immediately printed out the map of Afghanistan produced by the Data Section (see Figure 3.5) in order to locate the UNHCR bases in this unfamiliar context. This same map was to be found at every workstation in the office. Pinned to the wall or kept close to hand, maps are omnipresent in UNHCR offices and are an indispensable work tool, the principal material UNHCR officers use to familiarise themselves with the organisation's presence and intervention sites across the world. The ubiquity of these maps also reveals the anxiety of employees of an organisation that is not rooted in any specific location: how to get to grips with vast territories where access is often difficult. While they provide information on the location of UNHCR offices, these maps also offer evidence of how the institution understands the space in which it intervenes, and the perspective from which it attempts to change it (Anderson 2006: 163). I will consider these documents as a basis for mapping the UNHCR's deployment during the 2000s.

The day after the UNHCR was founded, its staff team was small enough to gather around a piano to celebrate Christmas (Loescher et al. 2008: 79). In the years that followed, as its geographical area of intervention expanded, its infrastructure and staffing also grew and diversified. In 2006 the organisation had some 300 offices distributed through about 110 countries, and employed around 7,000 people.[1] Though a 'lightweight' by the standard of state administrations, the UNHCR operates over a much larger area, but has a more limited physical presence. The UNHCR's mandate is not defined by a relationship to a specific territorialised space; it is determined by a sector of the global population, its 'people of concern' (who numbered around 33 million in 2006), who live in different parts of the world, or are on the move. The UNHCR's infrastructure is continually reconfigured, as it launches new programmes and withdraws others. Offices also take very different forms, from the headquarters in Geneva, where a thousand employees work at desks and in meeting rooms, to the small Bamyan office in central Afghanistan, which also serves as the living quarters for the only expatriate on site.

James Ferguson and Akhil Gupta (2002) identify two principles underlying the spatiality of the state: verticality (the state is above society) and encompassment (the state encompasses its localities). They argue that these two dimensions correspond to the way in which the state sees itself and the way in which it perceives its relations with other authorities. Supported by bureaucratic practices, verticality and encompassment produce spatial and scalar hierarchies that help the state to legitimise and naturalise its authority. Drawing on this approach, in this chapter I analyse the UNHCR's spatial deployment on the basis of four cartographic representations produced by it. These maps reveal how the UNHCR's physical presence is shaped both by the paradigm of the 'refugee problem' and by interactions with a multiplicity of interlocutors. Analysing how the UNHCR situates itself in relation to other actors then makes it possible to situate the organisation and its worldview in the global political space.

To begin with, I discuss the tension underlying the relationship between the UNHCR and states. The UNHCR's deployment is based on the spatiality of the interstate system and subject to the approval of state authorities. But while it relies on the legitimacy conferred upon it by states, the organisation materialises a suprastate political space based both on verticality and on the encompassment of states – a space that putatively encompasses the entire planet. I then consider the nonstate actors with whom the organisation has to interact in order to reach its recipient populations within Afghan territory, such as the village councils and the Taliban. Even though the UNHCR does not consider them political actors in their own right, it must establish legitimacy with them, despite the fact that they do not recognise its claim to encompass the world. Taking into account both the geographical dispersal of the UNHCR's network of offices and the organisation's need to reach many heterogeneous interlocutors, I identify a third principle of *diffusion* that, together with verticality and encompassment, underlies the spatialisation of the UNHCR.

A State-Centred Operation

On the map the UNHCR produces to show its presence in the world (see Figure 3.1), the land masses, represented physically, are divided by state borders. The map also gives the names of all the states officially recognised by the UN, from the vast extent of the United States to the small islands of the Pacific.

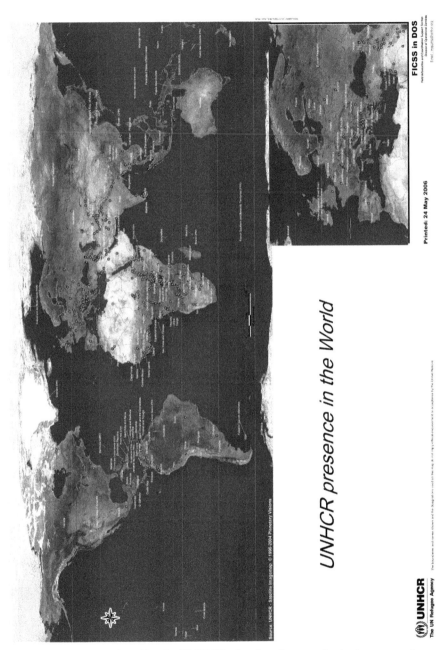

Figure 3.1. Map produced by the UNHCR, showing the organisation's presence in the world in 2006. © UNHCR

Mary Douglas (1986) showed that naturalisation works by establishing an analogy with the natural world (or another domain that is not considered to be socially determined). Here the naturalisation of the interstate system is clearly apparent, since the division of the world into territorialised state jurisdictions is assimilated into a physical representation of the planet. This map shows the extent to which the system of states rooted in nature marks the confines of the UNHCR's view of the world.

James Scott (1998) has highlighted the logic of standardisation and homogenisation of space that characterises the way in which the developmentalist and socialist state views and intervenes in reality. The UNHCR adopts a similar mechanism of homogenisation and standardisation of the global space, using the state as the central criterion of legibility. The state forms the geographical unit and scale of reference, making it possible to grasp the world and compare its parts. In this way, the UNHCR can maintain a synoptic overview that embraces all the territories and populations of the planet. This appears clearly in the division of labour and internal operation. Programmes at the scale of a country, headed by a Representative, known as the Head of Mission, form the 'unit of measurement' of the UNHCR's activity, and programmes to be conducted and aims to be achieved are developed on the basis of a Country Operation. The Country Operation Plan is the main standardised tool through which programmes are developed and annual funding is distributed. With the 'refugee problem' as the basic paradigm, states are classified as 'country of origin' or 'country of asylum' ('host country'), depending on the nationality of the populations concerned.

The state is also the pivot around which the UNHCR's presence in the world is structured. In the interstate sphere from which it arose, every section of the planet is governed by a state jurisdiction. State authorities are the UNHCR's priority interlocutors. As the creators, funders and members of the organisation, states constitute its primary source of legitimacy and resources, and create the policies the UNHCR is tasked with overseeing. It should also be noted that the distribution of UNHCR offices strictly follows the hierarchy of state administrations. Where they are present, these offices sit alongside those of the national administration. In each country where the organisation has an office, it must be present in the capital; this is sometimes the only office it has. The regions of competence of each office are determined by states' administrative boundaries, even down to the district level. The hierarchy of the organisational structure thus reasserts the verticality and encompassment of the state highlighted by Gupta and Ferguson.

In Iran, Afghanistan and Pakistan (see Figure 3.2), the central offices where the senior officers are based and programmes are coordinated are located in the capital, and have the highest status. The UNHCR's Operation is then structured as a pyramid, through the Branch Office, followed by bases established in the remainder of the country. The main cities are often the location of Sub-Offices, while the smaller Field Offices are located on the border or outside of the main cities. Thus, the Herat and Mashhad offices, located on either side of the Afghan-Iranian border, are geographically very close, but belong to two different Country Operations, within which they each occupy a peripheral position. With the rise in expulsions from Iran in the summer of 2007, these zones became the nerve centre for information gathering and the emergency intervention. Several attempts were made to improve direct communication between the two offices, but these met with little success.

Figure 3.1 shows that while the UNHCR operates throughout the world, its presence varies widely in different continents and countries. Its vast geographical range stems from the gradual expansion that led it to intervene outside Europe as new crises arose. To begin with, interventions were concentrated in 'host countries'. Later, with the expansion of repatriation programmes during the 1990s, interventions extended to 'countries of origin'. When a crisis is over, the UNHCR often maintains a presence, at least in the capital, as a base for monitoring asylum policies. Looking at the varied distribution of offices, a much higher density is immediately apparent around what were the epicentres of crisis in 2006, where UNHCR programmes were concentrated: Colombia, Liberia and Sierra Leone, the Democratic Republic of the Congo, the Great Lakes region, Sudan, Iraq, Afghanistan, Sri Lanka and the Balkans. But on closer inspection (see Figure 3.2), it becomes clear that the number of offices does not always correspond to the size of the recipient populations concerned. Iran and Pakistan, which at the time when the map was made were among the countries hosting the world's largest refugee populations, had only four and three offices respectively!

The size and distribution of the UNHCR's presence in a country, like its freedom for action and the kinds of programme it manages, primarily reflect the compatibility between its objectives and the interests of the state authorities responsible for authorising the presence of a body that is mandated, among other things, to monitor their asylum polices. By virtue of its interstate nature, the organisation is inclined to recognise territorialised state jurisdictions as the effective authorities. In order to set up an office and undertake any activity, the UNHCR must therefore obtain the authorisation of the state in question, which is then, significantly, described as a 'host country'.[2] The relationship between the UNHCR and each 'host country' is governed by an agreement. The model proposed by the UNHCR, which forms the basis for negotiation, stipulates among other things that the government of the 'host country' must allow the UNHCR access to the population, must not impose charges on it, must guarantee the safety of its employees and must facilitate their residence. State authorities are also required to approve the organisation's representatives.[3] If the government of a country does not appreciate the UNHCR's activity, it may

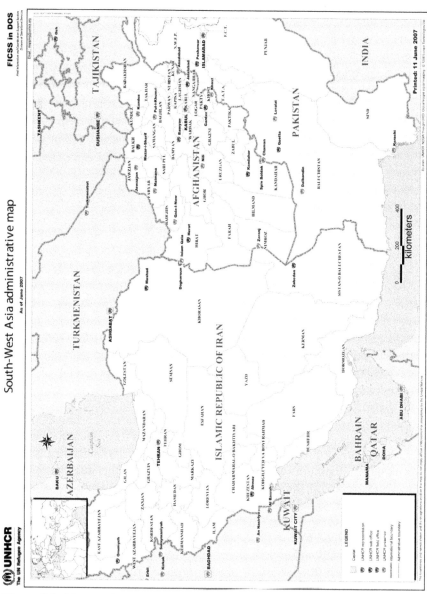

Figure 3.2. Map produced by the UNHCR, showing Iran, Afghanistan and Pakistan, and the organisation's presence in these countries in 2007. © UNHCR

create obstacles to its work. Typically, when the organisation sets up a base swiftly in emergency situations, its presence is welcomed for its material and logistical support. But states may suddenly withdraw their authorisation as soon as the agency's activity becomes too troublesome for them.[4] Thus, a separate negotiation is required for each state. In some cases state jurisdictions are porous, and it is easy for the UNHCR to set up there; in others, the state raises an impenetrable shield.

The UNHCR's presence in Central Asia dates back to the start of the conflict in 1979, following the Soviet invasion of Afghanistan. The evolution of the organisation's programmes in the region shows that while donor funding is essential for financing its infrastructure and programmes, the position of the central authorities in the states concerned is the determining factor shaping its presence and programmes in their countries.

In 2006 the UNHCR's presence in Iran was limited to four offices: Tehran (the capital), Mashhad, Zahedan and Ahwaz. Owing to tensions with the West, the Iranian authorities had restricted the presence of international organisations since the Islamic Revolution, mainly by limiting the number of visas granted. Despite the resources that the UNHCR could have offered, Iranian governments had never been in favour of its establishment in the country. They preferred to manage programmes for Afghans independently through the Bureau for Aliens and Foreign Immigrants Affairs (BAFIA), the body within the Ministry of the Interior that dealt with policy relating to foreigners. Iran did not ask the UNHCR for help in 1979, only doing so at the end of 1980 when the war with Iraq had begun to weigh on state finances. A first agreement for the establishment of a UNHCR office in Tehran was concluded in 1984. The Mashhad and Zahedan offices were not set up until 1992 when the repatriation programme was launched. The Zahedan office was subsequently closed and transferred to Kerman in 2008, following the Iranian government's decision to forbid foreigners access to the province of Sistan-Baluchistan. Thus, the UNHCR's effective access to the territory and to Afghans is very limited: contact with the Afghan population is possible only at the UNHCR offices or in repatriation centres. Any other access must be negotiated on a case-by-case basis and requires the prior agreement of the BAFIA.

The UNHCR presence in Pakistan was more quickly established: in 1979 the Pakistani authorities asked the UNHCR for help in dealing with the influx of Afghans, who had gathered in camps in the border areas. The Islamabad office was opened that year, and those in Peshawar and Quetta the following year. In this case, both donor countries and the host country were favourable to a UNHCR intervention. The United States, which had just adopted a more proactive strategy of containing its Soviet adversary, was fomenting the resistance of the Mujahideen movements based in the camps in order to destabilise the communist regime. The Pakistani government aligned with the United

States so as to break out of its international isolation and increase its influence in Afghanistan, as part of its anti-India strategy. The presence of camps to be managed also allowed the central government to establish a presence in the tribal regions of the North-West Frontier Province, which had retained semi-autonomous status since the colonial era. In this way, it was able to allay the fears of an independent Pashtunistan.[5] Nevertheless, the Pakistani authorities also took care to limit the UNHCR's freedom of action and its access to territory and population. The first agreement authorised the agency to intervene in Pakistani territory on condition that it worked alongside the national authorities. Administration of the camps and of UN aid was entrusted to the Commission for Afghan Refugees (CAR), which was set up in 1979 for this purpose. The UNHCR therefore did not set up field offices in or near the camps. Subsequently, the drastic reduction in funding once the strategic objective had been achieved led to the suspension of a number of programmes during the 1990s. Missions in the camps and the activity of the three UNHCR offices were cut back. In late 2001 they increased again thanks to the repatriation programme, which was wholeheartedly welcomed by the Pakistani government and required major logistical support from the UNHCR.

The situation in Iran and Pakistan contrasts with that in other 'countries of asylum' that saw large inflows of people fleeing conflict, such as Kenya and Tanzania. In these countries, which have received more attention from researchers (Agier 2008, 2011; Hyndman 2000; Turner 2005), the state authorities took a different approach: they did not raise obstacles to the UNHCR's work provided that the organisation offered material support in isolated, specifically demarcated zones. The state authorities willingly left management of aid to the UNHCR, especially if their country was poor, as was often the case. The result was 'humanitarian enclaves': the UNHCR effectively had free rein to establish its bases there, and in these contexts has been described as a 'state surrogate' (Slaughter and Crisp 2008). However, this often went hand in hand with the confinement of migrants in camps, with international organisations installed in the zone around the camps.

As the maps show, in 2006 the Afghan state was particularly permeable, with many offices scattered over its territory. This had been the situation since late 2001. The UNHCR had then been present in the territory for nearly twenty years, but with much reduced staffing owing to the conflict.[6] A first repatriation programme had been launched following the Soviet withdrawal in 1989. Subsequently, the Branch Office was transferred to Islamabad during the 1990s, owing to safety concerns and the restrictions imposed by the Taliban (Centlivres and Centlivres-Demont 1999: 962). At the end of 2001, with the fall of the Taliban and the launch of the reconstruction project, the UNHCR's presence in Afghanistan was reconfigured within the space of a few months. The Branch Office in Kabul was reopened in new, more spacious premises. In total, twenty-two offices have been opened since 2002 to manage returns and the implementation of projects at the local level. By the end of 2002, there were 880 UNHCR employees in the country (including almost one hundred expatriates). In the new geopolitical context, programmes ran unhindered. The Afghan state, which was highly dependent on international funding, raised no resistance to the presence of international organisations in its territory. Moreover, since Afghanistan was the country of origin of the returnees, the UNHCR was intervening in order to help the state take charge of them rather than to claim a status for non-nationals as it did in Iran and Pakistan. Thus, the UNHCR was able to operate as it wished: offices were located in the regions that received the highest number of returnees and where the UNHCR programmes were concentrated.

In Europe, North America, Australia and Japan, the UNHCR's presence is more localised, often limited to a single office in the capital. There are exceptions: the dual office in Brussels, which maintains relations with both the Belgian authorities and the European Commission, and the offices in Italy and Greece that deal with the massive influxes of asylum seekers arriving by sea. Although, as landing points for asylum seekers, these are 'countries of asylum', their main relationship with the UNHCR is as 'donor countries', major funders that enable the organisation to finance its infrastructure and its programmes.

For the last few decades, the UNHCR's only activities in most European countries have consisted of monitoring asylum policies, advocacy and fundraising.[7] The organisation's scope for intervention is relatively small in Europe. While criticism from the UNHCR could damage European countries' status as champions of human rights and democracy, in these contexts it does not have the leverage of its aid programmes, since they are deemed sufficiently wealthy and capable of managing the protection of refugees in their territories themselves. During my posting in Rome in 2005, for example, the Italian maritime police's actions in pushing migrants back to sea elicited the disapproval of the UNHCR office. But while the organisation was unsparing in its criticism, it had nevertheless to tread carefully. Strong public condemnation would have been very embarrassing for the Italian government, which was one of the organisation's principal funders. It was therefore important to maintain positive relations and a basic level of agreement.

Supranational Verticality, Global Encompassment

The UNHCR is enmeshed in the system of states in a complex interlocking, an inextricable entanglement of affirmation and bypassing. As discussed earlier, its interventions are structured on the basis of the interstate order, which is underpinned by the principle of state sovereignty. In accordance with this principle, state authorities always have the power to shape the organisation's presence in their country, for example by hindering officers' travel. From this point of view, the UNHCR's interventions reassert states' supreme authority, and their claims to verticality and encompassment. At the same time, the offices the organisation sets up and the activities it is authorised to undertake circumvent and undermine the absolute authority states are supposed to exercise. Once the UNHCR has established itself in a territory, it pierces state jurisdiction and subverts their spatiality as 'sealed envelopes', setting up another scale of government at the UN and supranational levels. Although supported by states, this scale of government rises 'above' them and encompasses them.

The fact that the UNHCR was created and mandated by states might indicate that it should be seen as subordinate to them. So how is it that representations of verticality and encompassment prevail within the organisation? The UNHCR's claim to occupy a higher moral dimension and embody a political community that encompasses those of states is supported by a number of factors. First, as a UN agency, the UNHCR is deemed to be *super partes* ('above parties') in relation to states – in other words, to be in a relation of neutrality, impartiality and therefore equidistant to them. Second, the UNHCR is the custodian of UN values such as peace, interstate cooperation, equality between states and between persons, and human rights. These principles are considered supreme to the extent that they are the subject of broad consensus among states. UN agencies are tasked with ensuring that these principles are applied throughout the world, a role that no state on its own could assume. Thus, where protection of refugees is concerned, the UNHCR articulates standards (models that are therefore by definition 'superior' to actual situations) and oversees states' asylum policies to ensure conformity with these norms. As the term (*over*see) suggests, this can only be done from above. In order to fulfil its mission, the UNHCR must therefore hold states, their policies, their territories and the refugee populations located there in one all-encompassing gaze.

The UNHCR's claim to global encompassment derives from the UN, the body that represents the entire interstate system. While only about two-thirds of the world's states are members of the UNHCR, almost all are members of the UN. Through its existence and activity, the UN brings into being a political space rooted in the interstate system, where there is nothing outside the set of states of the world. The planet, conceived as the ensemble of all territorial states, is seen as a single, unified space. Thus, the UNHCR's sphere of activity extends over the whole world. Any crisis therefore involves the organisation, wherever it occurs and whatever the populations and territories concerned. The reference space is no longer seen as an inside and an outside in relation to a territory of competence (in the manner of state jurisdictions), but as one single interior that extends across the entire world. It is this global range that forms the basis for the UN and its agencies' claim to universalism, which is apparent for example in the normative tone of their documents.

At the material level, the number, frequency and scale of material and immaterial flows (personnel, documents and humanitarian aid) necessary to the organisation's operation and to its very existence help to support representations of verticality and encompassment. These flows constantly cross or circumvent state borders.

This positioning as encompassing, impartial and morally superior is clearly evident in the UN's emblem. It shows an azimuthal equidistant projection of the planet centred on the North Pole, on which all land masses are visible. Around this is an olive wreath, the symbol of peace. State borders are not shown. It is neither a country nor a capital that has been chosen as the centre of the map, as is often the case in state representations, but a physical location that is deemed neutral. This image evokes a single shared global habitat. The fact that all of the world's land masses appear emphasises the UN's global remit (an aspiration when the logo was created, and a real one today). The principle of equality of states in relation to the UN is also evident in the alphabetical order in which they are always listed by the UN. Their flags are always ordered in the same way, whether at the entrance to the UN headquarters in New York or at the Palace of Nations in Geneva. As well as asserting the organisation's source of legitimacy, this flattening of relations between states evokes the sovereign equality between them and thus symbolises the *super partes* position claimed by the UN.

It is clear, then, why and in what sense UNHCR and UN officers, and many observers, see these organisations as 'global'. The term emphasises the vast scale of their field of intervention, but the concept remains analytically and descriptively weak, for this representation conveys their claims to encompassment and universality.

The UN's claims to verticality, encompassment and universalism are both supported and rejected by states. Its political positioning is constructed and reconstructed in the perennial process of negotiations between UN officials and state representatives. This tension is also reflected in two distinct kinds of institutional space: multilateral forums and UN bureaucracies.

Multilateral forums are held at the UN's two centres in New York and Geneva. The UN headquarters and the Palace of Nations house large conference and meeting halls (primary among them the General Assembly Hall and the Security Council Chamber). States are present here as singular entities represented by their delegations, as members, funders and agents of the UN and its agencies. However, states are not directly present in the UNHCR infrastructure. Its administration is therefore a decision-making body in its own right and is relatively autonomous. This could be seen as a more advanced 'stage' in the UN's development: it is no longer simply the sum of states, but a body generated by their coming together that has freed itself from the umbilical cord linking it to its creators, embodying multilateralism in a single new institution.

Of course, the UNHCR remains institutionally linked to states: they make up its Executive Committee, which meets once a year in one of the Palace of Nations conference halls, and the UN General Assembly appoints the High Commissioner and receives its annual report. The UNHCR is also firmly 'plugged in' to the UN's centres of multilateralism in New York and Geneva, where staff regularly travel and where the UNHCR convenes and leads multilateral conferences. But the UNHCR offices have no venue for interstate conferences. Its infrastructure consists primarily of workspaces for UN officers and meeting rooms. Similarly, it is not the flags of the world's countries (symbolising a gathering of all states) that are displayed at the UNHCR, but a single logo, where the olive wreath makes reference to the UN flag and thus indicates its affiliation.

An Archipelago of Offices

The UNHCR is dotted over the globe in small spaces within state jurisdictions, creating an archipelago of offices. These spaces, often contained within a single building or even an apartment, act as bases from which the UNHCR engages in the global political space. Unlike embassies, UNHCR offices are not organised around a 'continental territory' to which they are legally and morally attached, but rather around an island of reference. The UNHCR Headquarters is the most permanent and largest office. In 2006 it accommodated around one thousand employees (some 15% of the total global staff and 34% of the expatriate staff) and accounted for a substantial proportion of the annual budget. It houses the material symbols of the institution, such as the memorial for staff who have died in service, the archives and a public media centre. Guided tours of the UNHCR building can even be arranged.[8]

Like embassies, when these territorialised spaces exist within a state jurisdiction, they acquire a particular status. UN norms stipulate that the state must recognise the inviolability of offices and the immunity of the agency's property. In this sense, they constitute territorial islands within which the UNHCR has complete freedom of action. The offices taken together can thus be likened to an archipelago of enclaves encapsulated within state jurisdictions, connected to one another by flows that are made possible by transport and telecommunications technologies.

Of the offices where I spent time or visited in Switzerland, Italy and Afghanistan (see Figure 3.3), only the Geneva Headquarters was purpose-built to house the UNHCR offices. In other locations the organisation adapts its set-up to the context, using available spaces which it organises according to its needs. Whether they are located on two floors of a residential building in Rome's Parioli district, in formerly prestigious mansions in central Kabul or in a small block in a mud-brick compound on the edge of the village of Bamyan, these spaces are taken over by the institution and thereby both separated from their surrounding environment and linked to one another. On entering them, UNHCR staff feel on familiar ground, 'at home', wherever in the world they are. Hard as it may be to ensure that UN principles are applied by states, these principles can shape practices and relations within the UNHCR's offices. The UNHCR's offices can be seen as its jurisdiction, a space where the organisation is free to shape the relationships within it. At the same time as asserting the UN's verticality and encompassment, the practices observed in these spaces and the principles underlying them help to create an autonomous translocal space.

When entering UNHCR offices, a number of features contribute to the impression of crossing a threshold and entering a UN space not subject to state authority. In order to enter UNHCR premises, it is necessary to pass through checkpoints. These resemble those of states: supervised barriers that can only be crossed with an entry pass. In Geneva and Rome, as in Kabul, offices are monitored by security guards and CCTV. Public access is restricted; entry is by appointment only. In Geneva, all staff have an electronic pass that allows them to go through the automatic security gates and the metal detector. Having gone in and out hundreds of times during my placement, I realised how difficult it is for people who do not work there to get into the central foyer at headquarters when I recently went to visit former colleagues. Visitors must wait at the entrance, with armed guards who watch over them until a staff member comes to fetch them. The restricted access reinforces the verticality of these spaces: global encompassment is not synonymous with free access for any inhabitant of the world.[9]

The UNHCR's blue and white logo (see Figure 3.4), often accompanied by the name of the organisation, is emblazoned in all of these spaces like a flag. It shows two hands joined to form a roof over a person. It reiterates the paradigm of the 'refugee problem': destitute people 'in need of protection'. This symbol gives UNHCR offices a common identity over and above the form they take in each context and their geographical separation from one another. In Geneva the logo and name of the organisation are inscribed in transparent letters on the glass frontage of the building. In Rome the UNHCR flag hangs at the third floor of the building, and the logo appears on the small plate by the doorbells, next to the name of the organisation in Italian (Alto Commissariato delle Nazioni Uniti per I Rifugiati (ACNUR)). In Kabul the logo is displayed in blue on the white entrance gate, next to the organisation's acronym in English and its translation in Dari (*daftar-e-muhajirina*).

Figure 3.3. Images of the UNHCR offices I visited. A) UNHCR headquarters in Geneva. http://media.unhcr.org. © UNHCR/Susan Hopper. B) Main foyer of the Geneva headquarters. http://media.unhcr.org/. © UNHCR/Susan Hopper. C) UNHCR Executive Office in Kabul, July 2007. Photo by the author. D) Main foyer of the Kabul Executive Office, July 2007. Photo by the author. E) UNHCR office in Bamyan, Afghanistan, October 2007. Photo by the author. F) UNHCR vehicles during a 'field mission' in Istalif district, September 2007. Photo by the author

Figure 3.4. UNHCR logo. © UNHCR, https:// creativecommons.org/licenses/by-sa/4.0/deed.en.

As Marion Fresia notes (2010), the figure of the refugee is a symbol of the institution's identity. This is further indicated by the frequent jokes that link the 'displacement' of refugees to that of UNHCR officers, who relocate regularly and are often out on mission.

UNHCR employees are familiar with these spaces also because these are all organised according to the same bureaucratic logic underlying the division of labour in the organisation. The division between the Protection and Operations departments and the senior management structures the distribution of workspaces at Headquarters, and is reflected in local offices, depending on the predominant activity there. In Rome, a staircase linked the lower floor, which housed the Communication and Fundraising department, to the upper floor where the legal Protection department, the administrative offices and the office of the Chief of Mission were located. In Kabul the Protection, Programme, Reintegration, Administration, Security, Logistics, and Data and Telecommunications units were overlooked by the most prestigious building, a lofty former palace that housed the Executive Office where the senior officers worked, surrounded by the Communication and External Relations departments. UNHCR offices are designed to be as self-sufficient as possible, both in terms of resource management (for example, they install independent electricity supply) and in the organisation of work. Most staff activities take place inside the offices, through exchanges between colleagues who are usually sitting in front of their computer.

The specific temporality common to UNHCR offices links them with one another and to other UN offices throughout the world. This temporality supports encompassment and verticality, and is manifested partly in a time difference in relation to the rhythms and institutions of surrounding contexts. For example, UNHCR holidays follow the UN calendar, which is guided by the principle of religious equality. The UN celebrates most major religious festivals of the main world religions. During my placement in Rome, without in any way expecting to, I celebrated the Muslim festival of Eid-al-Fitr, marking the end of Ramadan, while the city continued with a regular working day. Conversely, 1 May is always a working day at the UN, while for the rest of Geneva it is a public holiday. The UNHCR offices are also linked to one another by a common calendar whose tempo is set by the accounting year and marked by the bureaucratic procedures specific to the organisation. Furthermore, they share a temporality oriented towards the present and the near future, centred on the crises with which the organisation is currently dealing. I began my placement in Rome during the Christmas holidays in 2004: the tsunami had just hit Indonesia and Sri Lanka, and the Communications department was urgently seeking an intern. While outside a holiday atmosphere reigned, I stayed late at the office translating the updates coming from Geneva and posting them on the website, in an atmosphere of urgency and sadness about the tragedy. These time differences establish a distinction. They materialise the sense of belonging to a morally superior world that remains apart from the customs of the local country, celebrating equitably the main holidays of other countries of the world, and supporting humans in distress in distant crises.

UNHCR staff experienced this separation from the local context as rising above it, precisely because they felt free of national particularisms. For example, in the Kabul Branch Office, none of the female international employees covered their heads. Thus, the office constituted a sort of space apart where UN principles reigned. We were not entirely in Afghan territory, guests in a country whose cultural codes had to be respected. Here everyone was free to express their cultural belonging and all cultures were respected. Similarly, principles of gender equality and equality between nationalities underlay many practices and bureaucratic procedures. Prevention of sexual harassment featured prominently in the code of conduct and was the subject of specific training sessions; recruitment procedures incorporated national quotas.

What links these spaces concretely, in addition to the continual relocation of staff (see Chapter 4), is information technology. Whether they are connecting from a regular workspace at Headquarters or via a noisy generator in Kunduz, every UNHCR employee can, with a password, access the same virtual space, where time discrepancies are due only to differences in the time zone. The UNHCR's internal mail is a powerful means of communication that transmits messages and documents in real time. There is a permanent, high-volume flow of email. Whether one opens one's computer after a meeting or a period of leave, there is always a mass of email, a sign of the organisation's incessant, multisite activity. When I opened my inbox in Kabul in the morning, I would find messages from those who had been online late in the evening in Geneva or Brussels, or a message from Tokyo that had arrived during the night. The internal mail system creates a whole arena where decisions are taken and battles are played out. People throw themselves into the fray, expose themselves to others, get themselves noticed or commit terrible blunders. Certain codes need to be learned: how should you address the person you are writing to? Who should be included in list of addressees? Should they be included in the 'To' list or copied in? With time, you come to learn certain tricks, such as checking who has opened the message or recalling a message already sent. Although it is physically based in offices,[10] this space is effectively a virtual one. But staff are so consistently projected into it that it becomes very concrete.

The 'Field'

The UNHCR has no territory; it has a 'field'. While it must inevitably deal with states, it also needs to come into contact with its other source of legitimacy, the populations it is mandated to protect. While the political maps of the world in geography textbooks, with their flat, uniform areas of colour, represent impermeable jurisdictions, on UNHCR maps, state borders are usually marked on physical maps (see Figures 3.1 and 3.5). States thus appear permeable and possible to travel through. UNHCR offices serve as a base for travel within jurisdictions in order to reach places where the organisation's recipients find themselves and programmes are implemented. The UNHCR does not, then, have a territory it controls, but rather an open, unfamiliar 'field' across which it has permission to travel.

Whether the subject of fantasies, fear or proud claims on the part of UNHCR staff, the 'field' is key to the organisation's identity and is highly valued within it. The 'field' is conflated with proximity with recipients. The privileged place it occupied during the 2000s thus gave an idea of the expansion of the organisation's operational activity alongside its legal work. Representing itself as refugee-centred is a crucial mark of identity for the UNHCR, enabling it to set itself up as the only UN agency that intervenes directly with the recipients of its activity and at the heart of conflicts. Other UN agencies tend more to operate from the UN's coordinating centres and in state capitals. It is worth pointing out, for example, that in 2007 the UNHCR was the only body with thirteen bases in Afghanistan. The UNDP had many more employees there, but they were concentrated in the large UN complex in central Kabul. Glamorised in the relationship between staff and organisation, which always highlights delivery of aid and staff sacrifices in the field, for expatriate staff the 'field' represents a major rite of passage in establishing themselves in the long term in the organisation (cf. also Fresia 2010).

The 'field' is represented as a distant elsewhere, often difficult to reach, a place where staff stay temporarily, for the time it takes to complete their assigned task, whether that be a two-year posting to a field office or a half-day mission. It is defined in relation to a familiar space that serves as a 'base' and to which staff return. Depending on the context, this 'base' may be the office, headquarters, administrative centres or Western countries.

At the global level, some countries are more likely to serve as 'field' than others. This reflects the division between the legal side of the organisation's work, which is oriented towards state authorities, and the operational side, which is focused on recipient populations. The 'field' is where physical interventions take place. It is thus rare for European countries to be represented as the 'field'. In the UNHCR office in Rome, the 'field' essentially designated missions in Africa, Asia and Latin America. At a pinch, the term might be

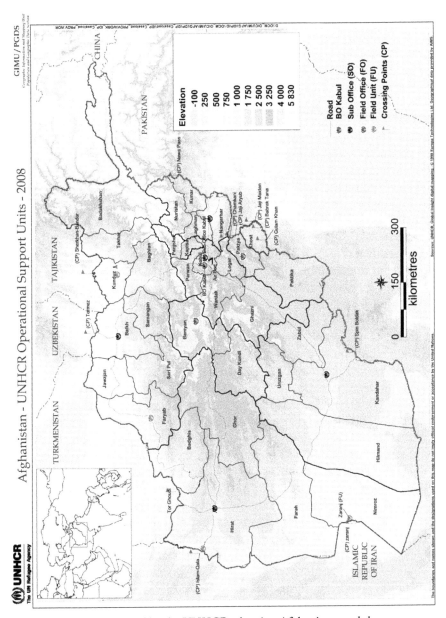

Figure 3.5. Map produced by the UNHCR, showing Afghanistan and the organisation's presence in the country in 2008. © UNHCR

used to refer to occasional missions to Italian locations where migrants were coming to shore, but most of the time, travel in Italian territory was for press conferences and meetings with local government bodies. As a context for intervention, Italy was seen through the lens of a legal system that needed improvement rather than a territory to be travelled through.

At the national level, the 'field' is contrasted with the offices and administrative centres in cities. Here again, the state's logic of verticality is apparent. The further one is from the urban centres where the central state authorities are based, the 'deeper' the field. One 'enters' the field on leaving metalled roads. The 'depth' of the field is thus measured in the number of hours and conditions of travel from administrative centres. Sites around the capital are the most frequently visited, both by internal staff and by outside visitors (donors and journalists). By contrast, very few UNHCR employees have gone to Kunduz, which is reached from Kabul by a long car journey through the Hindu Kush, or to Zaranj in the middle of the desert, which is only accessible by plane. And from Kabul, a visit to the transit centre for returnees just outside the city was not a 'field mission' in the same sense as a visit to the outlying districts of the capital for the purpose of finding out about the conditions in which returnees were living. The transit centre, located on the Kabul-Jalalabad road, was an easily accessible place with familiar bureaucratic structures: it was managed by the UNHCR in collaboration with the Ministry of Refugees, and here it was returnees who must conform in order to obtain repatriation aid. On a mission to the suburbs, on the other hand, as your vehicle inched its way through the alleys, you entered an unknown world where you had no point of reference.

Many studies of bureaucracy focus on the interface between users and institution, often materialised by the reception desk (Herzfeld 1992; Spire 2007). But the UNHCR is far from a 'street-level bureaucracy' (Lipsky 1980), that is, a bureaucracy in direct contact with the recipients of its policies.

The Headquarters, as well as many of the Branch Offices, are designed to interact with actors in the interstate arena, not with the UNHCR's people 'of concern'. These offices are therefore configured as towers with no opening onto the street, being accessible only from higher up. A telling example is the case of the asylum seeker who stayed outside the UNHCR building for a week during my placement in Geneva in 2006. He was not able to enter the building. There was no space provided for such an occurrence, nor was there any officer competent to deal with it. The security guards brought him food every so often, and from the inside someone took responsibility for referring him to the appropriate structures for dealing with his 'individual case', while every day hundreds of officers passed by him as they entered or left the building. In Rome the Protection department would only see asylum seekers or refugees in exceptional circumstances. And when in the spring of 2005 a few dozen Somalians arrived at the entrance to the building, the UNHCR staff were nonplussed. It was the Representative who eventually went down to the street to talk to them.

Sub-Offices are designed to enable the UNHCR to coordinate and supervise rather than directly executing aid programmes. The implementation of programmes is entrusted to 'implementing partners' who are funded by the organisation and thus become key intermediaries in its work with displaced populations. They are usually NGOs, of varying size, from major transnational bodies that specialise in emergencies and refugee aid, such as the International Rescue Committee and the Norwegian Refugee Council, to small local NGOs. They could be seen as the 'limbs' of the UNHCR. In 2007, in order to implement its programmes in Afghanistan, the UNHCR drew on the support of thirty-three international and Afghan NGOs that specialised variously in sanitation, construction, human rights, etc.[11]

While the relationship with 'implementing partners' (allocation of funds, monitoring and evaluation) is an integral part of the work of field offices, the NGOs have no part in shaping the UNHCR's operation. Because the UNHCR funds them, and because they recognise its expertise in matters of asylum on the global scale, it is rather they who 'follow' the UNHCR's systems and align their activities with the priorities and the frames of understanding of the UNHCR. It is the NGOs that apply to the UNHCR for funding and attend meetings at the organisation's offices. This chapter therefore focuses on other nonstate actors with a stronger influence on the UNHCR's presence in Afghan territory: the village councils and the Taliban. The concept of 'field' flattens all the contexts in which the UNHCR operates. Examining the way in which the UNHCR negotiates its legitimacy with actors who do not necessarily recognise its claims to neutrality, global encompassment and expert knowledge can reveal the multiple arenas of power hidden behind this concept.

The UNHCR and the *Shura*

I spent most of my time in Afghanistan in the UN-level circles of the UNHCR, moving between the agency's offices and its residential quarters. It was therefore with trepidation that, one winter morning in 2007, I joined a team from the Kabul Sub-Office on a 'field mission' to the Bagrami district, adjacent to Kabul district. Although NGOs act as intermediaries, it is vital for the UNHCR to evaluate the situation in the contexts where it operates and to monitor how it evolves. Sometimes the organisation decides to provide direct short-term aid. On average, the Kabul Sub-Office organised ten 'field missions' each week. The site to be visited was often a village or an outlying district of Kabul where returnees had settled.

That day, the mission was a 'need assessment'. The district had been on the frontline between the Russians and the Mujahideen, and had been very badly hit by the conflict: a large proportion of the population had left during the 1980s and returned after 2001. The aim was therefore to gain an idea of the situation regarding housing and water supply in the main villages of the district, in order to decide on allocation of shelters and water-related projects for 2008. The team consisted of four Afghan officers, who were to assess three villages between them.

In the car park at the UNHCR compound, I got into the vehicle with Salim, who was leading the mission. These missions are conducted from white 4x4s marked with the UNHCR's blue emblem on the two doors. The vehicles were a sort of mobile extension of the offices, dominating the road thanks to their size, highly visible with their big blue logos, and while seated in them the passengers remained in the UN space (see Figure 3.3). The city centre traffic gradually thinned out as we left the capital. In deference to the Afghan state, we stopped outside the office of the district chief on the main road in order to inform him of our destination and the reason for our visit. We set off again and the three vehicles separated. We left the metalled road. We passed alongside a large cemetery and then entered the village of Bot Khak. The 4x4 threaded its way along an alley that wound between the houses, some of them half-destroyed.

Salim had arranged a meeting with the members of the village *shura* (council), the assembly of notables and heads of family who represented the village in negotiations with the UNHCR.[12] In Afghanistan a meeting with the village council is an essential step in gaining permission to visit the site or interact with the people living there. We were met by a group of men who led us into a building at the centre of the village, and then into a small unheated room. Before entering, everyone took off their shoes. We sat in a circle on cushions and were served tea. Seven men were present, all swathed in blankets; all were bearded and wore a turban or a *pakol*[13] on their heads. The room was small and the walls were bare, except for a poster with a calligraphed sura from the Qur'an. Shortly afterwards, the village mullah joined us.

On every mission I joined,[14] when I got out of the UN vehicle I always had the impression of landing, of having been parachuted into another dimension, of being a stranger in a strange land. Like the vehicle-homes designed by Krzysztof Wodiczko, which enabled homeless people in New York to change their relationship with the city (Smith 1992), UN vehicles allow UN officers to 'jump scale', creating a bridge between sociopolitical orders that would otherwise remain impermeable to one another. Reference points disappeared and proportions changed. The 4x4s, an everyday sight in their space in the UNHCR compound or on the broad streets of Kabul, became incongruous on the unmade alleys of the villages where there were no other vehicles. Often there was nobody who spoke English. All of our interlocutors were men, making me abruptly and strangely aware of my belonging to a gendered order. Each time a field mission was planned, I made sure to wear loose clothing and bring a large shawl to cover my hair. Most expatriate women, even those who never usually paid attention to the way they dressed, pulled a scarf out of their bag as soon as they got out of the car. This gesture, whether considered or instinctive, marked the crossing of an invisible boundary: we were no longer in UN space.

For me, a young graduate in diplomatic relations, there was also a shift into an unfamiliar political landscape. In the *shura* hall, there were no representatives of the state. While some of the men worked for the local administration, it was not in this capacity that they were present. In this context, the rules of the game altered and matters were settled in a different way. These were no longer bureaucratic structures that operated on relatively familiar lines. I had no point of reference to situate these men, to understand their role and the legitimacy of their authority. The only way I could distinguish them was by the different kinds of hat they wore: as an Afghan colleague had explained, the turban indicates a higher status and the cloth hat a religious role. To begin with, I found it hard to conceive of these meetings as diplomatic encounters in their own right. Although we were not sitting in suits around a table as I had imagined during my studies, but rather on the ground, in *pashminas* and long sweaters, these meetings are fully functioning political arenas, where the modalities of distribution of UNHCR resources are at stake. The UNHCR bypasses the authority of the state, negotiating directly with power structures that carry more weight at the local level.

In the UNHCR's discourse and practices, these close interactions with bodies like the *shuras*[15] are often hidden and/or minimised, effectively reproducing the thinking centred on the state as national order. The *shuras* are not recognised as political interlocutors at the same level as state authorities; they are relegated to the depoliticised and remote space of the 'field', and associated with 'social' or 'cultural' rather than political dynamics. The UNHCR frequently emphasises its direct relationship with refugees, who are represented as an amorphous mass of people in distress amid a breakdown of social structure. In this case, the question of local intermediaries and the sociopolitical structures in which the recipients are embedded is completely overlooked. When the organisation mentions these interlocutors, it usually speaks in terms of 'communities' and their 'representatives' (cf., for example, UNHCR 2007u), as if to reduce local structures of power to the familiar logic of the national order and democratic principles. Moreover, in terms of the internal hierarchy of the organisation, it is the lower-ranking offices and staff who are usually delegated to deal with relations with the *shuras*. Yet, on the ground, the UNHCR recognises the existence and importance of these interlocutors; after all, it is UNHCR officers who go out to meet them. If necessary, the Sub-Office head himself travels to sit with the members of the *shura* – which implies adopting their way of sitting – despite the fact that most UN officers are not comfortable crouching barefoot with their notebooks on their knees.

Very often, the determining factor that establishes the legitimacy of the UNHCR is the aid it can grant. The members of the *shura* almost invariably sought to capture resources and to maximise the aid they could obtain from the organisation. I was struck by how explicit they could sometimes be. On one occasion, the UNHCR team was met with the demand: 'What have you brought? What is the good news?' The welcome ceremonies could thus be understood either as a *captatio benevolentie*, a rhetorical appeal for goodwill, or as a way of reiterating the UNHCR staff's status as guests and foreigners in relation to the *shura*'s authority. It was a sparring match: one side had to distribute aid in a way that conformed to the institution's systems, while the others tried to capture and orient these resources.

I observed that some were highly skilled in interacting with representatives of international organisations: the words 'priority needs of the site' were uttered confidently by members of the *shura* and repeated in exactly the same way by people interviewed during site visits. In other cases it was clear that the members of the *shura* were unaccustomed to interacting with aid organisations, did not understand their criteria for intervention and struggled to find their place among the international actors who arrived at the site and to formulate their demands in a way that the latter could understand. In either case, it was the aid already provided or that which might be granted in the future that was key to establishing the legitimacy of the UNHCR's visits to the village, to being received by the *shura*, to speaking with people, visiting houses, etc. Neither the legal status of the organisation in international law nor the UN values it represents were relevant.

Out-of-Reach Afghanistan

On the map of the UNHCR's presence in Afghanistan (see Figure 3.5), as in much of the UNHCR staff's discourse, Afghanistan was treated as a homogenous jurisdiction, a unit, the arena where the Afghan state exercised its sovereignty. In the Kabul Branch Office, this map was the official point of reference, always appended to funding applications. Another map, which had to be circulated with discretion, represented an entirely different reality. It showed, at the district scale, which parts of Afghan territory were accessible to UN staff. On this map, the southeastern part of the country was an almost uninterrupted red band that extended right up to the outskirts of the capital.

These regions were forbidden to UN staff, being considered too dangerous as they were under the de facto control of the Taliban.

The Taliban, which had been excluded from the peace process, had taken refuge in the tribal zones on the border with Pakistan. With the support of Pashtun tribal populations and transnational Islamist networks, they had re-organised and gradually resumed their fight in Afghanistan, counting on both the weakness of the government and the disappointed expectations of the population. The Taliban contested the legitimacy of the government in place and challenged it via attacks on its representatives and all those who collab-orated with it, using explosive devices planted along roads and kidnappings (Giustozzi 2007). The main targets were the Afghan armed forces and po-lice and the International Security Assistance Force (ISAF), but increasingly NGOs and international organisations were also being targeted.

The UN agencies hoped that the Taliban would not hamper their work, given the UN's long-established presence in the country and its potential role as mediator. UNHCR senior staff in particular counted on a degree of respect-ability they felt the organisation enjoyed thanks to its long-term presence and the aid it had provided since the 1980s to several million Afghans – including many Taliban, as some colleagues reassured themselves. Yet because the or-ganisation's identification with the UN associated it with the NATO foreign forces, UNHCR staff were placed in a delicate position vis-à-vis the Taliban. Bound by the decisions taken by the Secretary-General and other UN bod-ies, the UNHCR was aligned with the reconstruction process guided by the United Nations Assistance Mission in Afghanistan (UNAMA). This also im-plied being associated with the international military intervention and its ob-jectives, and providing unconditional support to the new Afghan government, whose legitimacy the guerrilla movement contested – hence the impossibility of negotiating with the Taliban in order to implement programmes.

Although part of Afghan territory according to international law, the south of the country was thus inaccessible to the UNHCR: the state's sovereignty was contested there and the UNHCR, trapped by its intergovernmental iden-tity, was unable to negotiate access. In order to cross Helmand province by car, neither the UN identity of the UNHCR, nor human rights, which the organ-isation championed, nor the fact that it had resources to allocate constituted sufficient sources of legitimacy.

In 2007, while security measures were omnipresent in Kabul (see Chapter 5), in the east and the south, the UNHCR offices were under siege. In Jalalabad, Gardez and Kandahar, staff were confined within high-walled com-pounds protected by barbed wire and armed guards. They reduced their travel to a strict minimum; their field missions were rare and were carried out in armoured vehicles, often with an armed escort. A journalist returning from Gardez described the complex where the UNHCR staff lived and worked as a 'camp'. For the Kandahar office, the siege situation had reached its height. On the red and green map, the city of Kandahar was virtually the only green point in the south of the country. International organisations' staff were confined in a space they could only leave by air. Staffing was reduced to a minimum and projects were evaluated by remote monitoring, via the few NGOs that had not left the region or the local administration.

This situation created major dilemmas for the operation's senior staff, who would have liked to intervene more in these regions, from which many returnees came and where clashes between the Coalition forces and the Taliban were leading many people to flee their villages. But the office's activity was so restricted that some wondered whether it would be better to close it. In the end the office was kept open: for the senior staff, closing it would have felt as if they were completely abandoning their mission and capitulating to the Taliban. The critical stakes of the debate on closing the office were brutally demonstrated in November 2011, when the Kandahar office was subjected to an attack that killed three UNHCR employees and injured two.

A Diffused Structure

The distribution of UNHCR offices corresponds to the organisation's need to interact with many different interlocutors in order to pursue its mission. These actors are the axes around which its deployment is shaped. The need to have 'connections' on multiple fronts is manifested in a presence that could be described as diffuse not only geographically but also in terms of the multiple arenas in which the organisation operates and negotiates its legitimacy: multilateral forums, state authorities in each country, nonstate actors, etc. Interactions with all these actors shape the UNHCR's bureaucracy, in the sense that the form and activities of the offices are designed to interact in one or other of these arenas. In addition to verticality and encompassment, a third principle of *diffusion* can therefore be identified in the spatiality of the UNHCR. The UNHCR's range of diffusion is more extensive and dispersed than that of states (whose administrations are focused largely on their own territories), of other international organisations (more concentrated within the interstate arena) and of NGOs (in direct contact with the recipients of projects, but less present in multilateral forums and interactions with governments).

Following UNHCR officers as they 'jump scale' in their work, moving from one political order to another, helps to identify the way in which the UNHCR understands the global political space and the nature of the political order in which it operates. Embedded in the interstate sphere, this UN order emerges in a subtle play of affirming and bypassing the principle of state sovereignty. For it is on the basis of representations of the verticality and encompassment of states, and thereby reasserting them, that the organisation defines a world-wide supranational scale that in its turn encompasses the role of states. In the UNHCR's system of representations, modelled on the interstate system, non-state interlocutors – described variously as 'nongovernmental organisations', 'local communities' or 'insurgents' – are of lower status and are not considered political actors in their own right in the same way as states. Yet it is often necessary to establish the organisation's legitimacy with these actors, who do not always recognise its claims to neutrality and universalism. While for the *shuras* the aid provided was an important source of legitimacy, in the case of the Taliban, an irresolvable conflict of legitimacy prevented the organisation from operating in half of the Afghan territory, despite the agreement of state authorities.

Notes

1. Since then, the size and area of activity of the UNHCR have grown still further: at the end of 2021, it had some 18,000 employees and 523 offices spread over 135 countries (UNHCR 2022).
2. In this case it is the UNHCR that is 'hosted' by the state.
3. For the model agreement, see UNHCR (n.d.). This refers explicitly to Article 35 of the 1951 Convention.
4. As happened in Uzbekistan in 2006: following the breakdown of relations with the Uzbek authorities, the UNHCR had to withdraw from the country.
5. The substantial flow of arms and funding from the United States was coordinated by the CIA, and then channelled by the Pakistani secret services, which were managing relations with representatives of the Afghan political parties (Centlivres and Centlivres-Demont 1999; Coll 2004; Rashid 2000; Roy 1985). The UNHCR's programmes in Pakistan offered a prime example of the dilemmas the organisation faced during the Cold War (Fielden 1998; Ghufran 2011; Grare 2003; Marsden 1992; Rizvi 1990; Schöch 2008).
6. At the time, the organisation had not yet started working on behalf of 'internally displaced persons'.
7. This situation changed during the 2000s, following a growing influx of asylum seekers into Southern Europe and the strengthening of border controls.
8. To 'visit the UN', the visitor must go to UN headquarters, the most visited location in New York. UN agencies are also often performatively represented by their buildings. On this point, see Beauguitte (2011), who notes that the objects most frequently represented on UN stamps are the buildings that house the organisation's main bodies, and that these places are always portrayed as isolated from their surroundings.
9. Guided visits to headquarters for tourists are conducted in groups and follow preset itineraries.
10. Only the computers in offices had access to the full range of functions.
11. In 2018, the UNHCR drew on the support of 800 NGOs throughout the world (UNHCR 2019).

12. Centlivres and Centlivres-Dumont describe the *shura* as one of the new social forms that, like Afghan NGOs, emerged during the 1990s when international organisations came to Afghanistan and encouraged the formation of pluralist and representative village assemblies in order to bypass the commanders (Centlivres and Centlivres-Dumont 1999: 957). During the 2000s, a new form of assembly, the Community Development Councils, was created under the National Solidarity Programme (Monsutti 2012).

13. A woollen hat.

14. The Kabul Sub-Office is the closest one to the Branch Office. During the year I spent in Kabul, I joined the Sub-Office team on fifteen field missions, including visits arranged for donors.

15. See, for example, the system of *malek*s (notables) in Pakistan, who organised the distribution of aid in the camps (Centlivres and Centlivres-Dumont 1999: 951; Edwards 1986: 319–20).

CHAPTER 4

The Institutional Career of the ACSU Project

Kabul, June 2007, the UNHCR Branch Office. The afternoon is given over to a big party in the grounds of the Executive Office. The hundred or so employees gather in a marquee set up in the garden, around a banquet of kebabs and fruit. This celebration marks a major rollover of staff, with five people leaving and four coming in. But above all, it marks a change of leadership. Saverio arrived a few months earlier (in February 2007) to head the Afghanistan Operation. It was he who decided to organise this celebratory gathering. And among those who are about to leave is the Deputy Head of Mission, who has been in Kabul for three years and is now leaving for Geneva. To replace him, Eric has just rejoined his partner as Deputy Head of Mission. Saverio introduces him enthusiastically to his colleagues. Since Eric arrived, spirits have been high in the Executive Office and the new Representative has attacked his work with renewed fervour. The knowing winks they exchange indicate not only their pleasure at seeing one another again but also their excitement that they do so in Kabul, with a status that gives them more authority to influence the organisation's policies.

This chapter follows the career[1] of the ACSU project within the UNHCR – how the strategy evolved and how it became established as its authors took up new roles and the institutional context also changed. We left them on the third floor at Headquarters, at the South-West Asia Desk. Their promotion to lead one of the organisation's most important interventions thus appears to indicate that their innovative strategy was being pursued with conviction within the UNHCR. However, as I will show, despite the support of senior managers at Headquarters, this vision did not yet enjoy a consensus or have a concrete impact on the everyday management of the Afghan Operation. In early 2007 Eric and Saverio were promoted to lead it. While their approach thus became more rooted in the field, opposition sharpened in the Tehran and Islamabad offices, while Saverio and Eric, faced with the priorities of the field and representing the UNHCR by virtue of the position they occupied, also came to somewhat modify their view.

By following the career of the ACSU project, we can examine the difficulties involved in translating this atypical strategy, which the UNHCR bureaucratic structure found hard to 'digest', onto the operational level. These difficulties derived both from the opposition of a number of internal actors and from the project's 'tailor-made' character, which departed from the standardised frameworks of understanding and management. The innovative potential of the ACSU project was thereby weakened. Considering the project's institutional career also offers the opportunity to examine the organisation's internal functioning. This incorporates powerful mechanisms of rationalisation and standardisation, such as internal hierarchies, staff rotation and formatted procedures for making reality legible, which are essential to an institution operating on a global scale. But this does not mean that the organisation functions mechanistically. Observing the multiple different perspectives that develop and come into conflict, depending on the trajectory and stance of each internal actor and the permanent processes of reconfiguration and negotiation that underpin the UNHCR's everyday activity, allows us to conceptualise its institutional space as an arena.

A Contested Approach

As noted above, when it was conceived, the ACSU project enjoyed a consensus that gave it a powerful legitimacy and led to the creation of the ACSU in 2003. The support of the then Representative in Afghanistan and some senior directors at Headquarters, who saw this approach as a reasoned and appropriate way of addressing the issue of Afghan refugees in the long term, despite its unusual character, were crucial in this process. But a dedicated unit and a strategic paper were not enough to make the new approach operational reality. In order for the strategy to influence the management of the programmes on the ground at all levels, it had to win over all the internal actors involved. However, not only did most of these actors have no hierarchical link with the unit created at Headquarters, they also had a different view of the problem and different priorities, depending on their position within the institution and the specific problems they encountered in their work.

In the distribution of tasks established in 2003, the Unit was simply juxtaposed with the work of the Desk,[2] and its two staff members were integrated into strategic discussions. They followed the evolution of the situation on the ground closely. They provided analytical support and catalysed internal strategic reflection, seeking to establish consistency between the three Country Operations in Iran, Afghanistan and Pakistan. Bolstered by their status as experts and sanctioned by the senior hierarchy, despite their lower rank, they participated in key decisions alongside senior managers from Headquarters and those in Tehran, Kabul and Islamabad. In the meantime, they also worked on setting long-term goals: they commissioned research on the labour market and migration flows, managed contacts with the IOM and the ILO with the aim of organising joint activities, and organised 'high-level strategic consultations' with representatives of the governments involved. These took place in Brussels in 2004, Kabul in 2005 and Islamabad in 2006 (AREU and Ministry of Refugees 2005; AREU and CSSR 2006).

Eric and Saverio hoped that in the long term, the strategy would be gradually incorporated into the local management of the three Country Operations and that the ACSU would merge with their leadership. Thus, once the strategy had been launched, the unit could be wound up and together the three Operations would follow the established tactical plan. This line of action seemed well in train during my placement in 2006, as Saverio had combined his position in the ACSU with the directorship of the Desk since 2005.

Nevertheless, the ACSU project encountered difficulties during its first three years. At Headquarters, colleagues in the Protection Department were hesitant or even anxious. During the weekly Desk meetings I attended, the delegate from Protection regularly expressed her concerns: would these long-term programmes focused on 'migrant workers' not detract attention from the concrete reality of the Afghans in immediate 'need of protection'? It would be better to concentrate on more immediate goals that could have a substantive impact for the population for which the UNHCR was directly responsible. They also felt the strategy's approach was over-intellectual and idealistic.

To some extent, these debates had their roots in the perennial tensions between the UNHCR's two major departments: Operations (of which the Desks are part) and Protection. The UNHCR's expansion during the 1990s laid the groundwork for an antagonism between the two, one of them focused on legal protection and the other on humanitarian interventions. The lawyers tend to feel that the compromises required to fund programmes weaken the organisation's capacity to fulfil its central mission, and even hijack this mission. But the concerns of the colleagues from Protection also related to a key element of the ACSU project: the holistic approach to migration flows. The Protection Department works tirelessly to define the legal boundaries of the specific category of persons for which the UNHCR is responsible, i.e. refugees – hence the difficulty of persuading them of the usefulness, for an organisation dedicated to refugees, of taking into account the entirety of the Afghan population in Iran and Pakistan.

These doubts were shared by the managers of the Country Operations, who were unreceptive or even opposed to the approach being advocated by Geneva. The Representative and their Deputy lead the UNHCR programmes in the field, with a status just below that of the senior management in Geneva (the directors of departments at Headquarters and the 'troika' comprising the High Commissioner and their two Deputies), and they enjoy a great deal of autonomy. The managers in the region put up resistance and expressed doubts about the viability of the ACSU project. Thus, during the initial years from 2003 to 2006, the unit's activity remained juxtaposed to the three Country Operations, and associated with Saverio and Eric as individuals. This was despite the fact that they had made frequent missions to the region and had collaborated with the management of the three Branch Offices in organising the 'strategic consultations', and that official documents (validated at the Desk level) had gradually incorporated the strategy's objectives. In practice, however, in the long term, the strategy was not followed with conviction in the field.

In Tehran and Islamabad the UNHCR managers, daily grappling with the Iranian and Pakistani authorities, were dealing with increasingly harsh conditions for Afghans and rising tension in negotiations. The senior staff of the Tehran Branch Office, for example, did not question the soundness of the strategy, but were very cautious. In their view, laying the foundations for a transformation of Iranian immigration policy would lead to a conflict of priorities that would be very difficult to manage – at a point when the UNHCR's room for manoeuvre was increasingly restricted as repatriation rates fell. Despite a few gestures, they felt that the Iranian government had no interest in following the project's long-term recommendations as put to them during the 'strategic consultations'. Their view thus aligned with that of the lawyers at Headquarters: in these circumstances, it was better to focus on more immediate goals that could have concrete effects for people who fell directly under the UNHCR's mandate.

In Kabul in the meantime, the former Representative who had encouraged the development of the ACSU strategy had been replaced. In his final mission before retirement, the new head was not enthusiastic about innovative approaches at this stage in his career. When I arrived at the Kabul Branch Office in 2007, I was surprised to find that staff knew relatively little about the content of the ACSU strategy, and at best it was seen as a somewhat nebulous approach cooked up at Headquarters in Geneva. The studies commissioned by the ACSU were displayed at the entrance to the Executive Office, but were tellingly covered with a thick layer of dust. The term 'comprehensive' was not understood by colleagues in the sense of strategy and did not arouse their curiosity; instead, it was ascribed, with a degree of mistrust, to a tactical and rather empty choice of language aimed at making the strategy attractive to donors and enhancing the image of the UNHCR as an innovative organisation.

The attitude of the three Representatives reflected the structural antagonism between Headquarters and the field. Officers based at Headquarters claim to have an overview, an encompassing position that allows them to stand back from the context of each Operation and hence take into account what is at stake for the UNHCR as a whole. This position justifies the relative hierarchical superiority of Headquarters, where the senior managers have their offices, and budgets, strategic orientations and field programmes are approved. As noted above, this encompassing vision is strongly evident in the regional and long-term approach taken by the ACSU. But it often meets with distrust from officers working in the field, who see it as too distant from the local, concrete operational realities with which any strategy must ultimately get to grips. At the Kabul Branch Office, staff working in the hushed corridors and well-appointed workspaces of Headquarters were often referred to as 'those who sit in Geneva'. From Kabul, Geneva is seen as the place of bureaucracy, where all people do is write reports and come up with new procedures and budget limitations; it is the place where people have time to focus on details (for example, footnotes and the consistent use of acronyms), to be sophisticated. In the field, on the other hand, there is no time to 'sit around'; staff are not in a position to get lost in nuances, because they are caught up in concrete, complex and contingent reality, and have to react to unforeseen events. Colleagues in Headquarters are often accused of disregarding local difficulties.

The strategy was also out of step at the administrative level. This project was a 'nightmare' for the administrative staff. The administration and accounting involved fell outside the norms for a structure accustomed to managing programmes on an annual basis (whereas the unit's project funding was supposed to run over two and a half years), operations targeted on specific countries (as opposed to this one with its regional scope) and with subordinate execution partners (while here the IOM and the ILO were equal funding partners for the project). Moreover, since Saverio had become Director of the Desk, management of the project had fallen to Eric, who was highly independent and impatient with bureaucratic formalities; he saw administrative requirements as less of a priority than the concrete pursuit of activities, and hence regularly aroused the irritation of colleagues in Administration.

This stalling of the strategy was beginning to shift. At the end of 2006, when the leadership of the Afghan Operation was due to be replaced, the managers at Headquarters decided to appoint Saverio and Eric to head it. The central leadership of the organisation had changed since 2003. António Guterres had replaced Ruud Lubbers as High Commissioner. The director of the Asia Bureau, Saverio and Eric's direct superior, was also new, and since his appointment, relations of respect and trust had been established. These new managers also agreed with Saverio and Eric's convictions and felt that 'comprehensive solutions' was the best approach. In the face of an increasingly alarming situation (the resumption of conflict in Afghanistan and growing pressure for return from the Iranian and Pakistani authorities), they decided to trust the authors of the long-term strategy. Given the growing complexity of the 'equation', their vision, however unorthodox and demanding, seemed the only one capable of overcoming major deadlock.

Thus, at the end of 2006, the Unit was wound up and Saverio and Eric took over the reins of the Afghanistan Operation. This was a substantial promotion for them, testifying to the trust placed in them. Saverio was the organisation's youngest Representative and was taking on leadership of the UNHCR's largest intervention. Eric, despite his short length of service with the UNHCR and his hitherto peripheral position as an adviser, acquired a position of responsibility and representation in the institution. Saverio, whose career had been more conventional (although young for a Representative, he had already had a long career with the UNHCR), remained nevertheless the live wire of the partnership: when he emailed me to tell me of his new posting, he said 'I'm taking Eric with me'.

Thus, the vision advocated by Saverio and Eric had the opportunity to be-come more rooted in the institution and influence the ongoing management of the Afghan Operation. For these two, it was an opportunity to come face to face with reality and take full responsibility for their recommendations. They recognised that the results remained hitherto modest and lagged behind the original time plan: the public declarations of the Iranian and Pakistani authorities had remained as inflexible as ever since 2001, despite the 'strategic consultations' and the research already undertaken. But they also remained fully convinced of the validity of their project. What was needed now was to get to grips with the UNHCR's internal machinery, to integrate the strategy more fully into the structure so that it could be pursued more consistently.

Staff Rotation

Before examining the challenges that awaited Saverio and Eric in Afghan-istan, I shall take a moment to consider the procedure whereby they were transferred from Geneva to Kabul, making it possible for the strategy to cir-culate within the organisation. This is the policy of staff rotation. As Saverio pointed out at the party in Kabul: 'In this job we're always welcoming and saying goodbye to colleagues.' Following a ritual I witnessed many times, the Representative says a public farewell to each member of staff who is leaving the office. In their remarks about the departing employee, they speak of the mission the employee has just completed and wishes them good luck for the following posting, before presenting them with a gift from the whole office.

Each departing employee also makes a speech, usually followed by speeches from their closest colleagues.

The life of the Kabul Branch Office, and the appearance of the offices, was punctuated by the rotation of expatriate staff. Spaces were perpetually rearranged and repopulated each time with new files, diagrams and photos. Thus, the gloomy space of the Executive Office in Kabul, where workspaces were installed for staff in transit, acquired an unusually solemn quality when Eric settled in there as he waited to take over the grand room reserved for the Deputy Head of Mission once his predecessor departed. And when a new post was created and a manager whose role justified a separate office arrived, the distribution of offices had to be completely revised. Dispossessed of the quiet outer room I had been sharing with a colleague who was only there in the afternoons, I found myself sharing the office of the Deputy Head of Mission's assistant. In this room, next to Eric's office, the constant comings and goings enabled me to participate more in the life of the office – but made it much more difficult to concentrate.

Staff rotation is a pivot of the UNHCR's bureaucratic machinery. Under this procedure, expatriate employees circulate between the agency's offices, on missions that last an average of two years. Rotation is based on the principle of interchangeability of expatriate staff and is designed to ensure that the most difficult postings are shared, and also to avoid the personalisation of relations with the organisation's interlocutors. It contributes to the high level of mobility of expatriate staff[3] and accounts for a considerable part of the institution's administrative work (especially on the part of the Human Resources department). This procedure is also found in other forms of bureaucratic administration operating over extensive territories, such as the diplomatic postings of foreign ministries, or imperial and colonial administrations (Anderson 2006; Aymes 2008). In these administrations as for the UNHCR, rotation of staff is an instrument of rationalisation and standardisation that enables the organisation to operate in a multitude of contexts while retaining global consistency (according to Weber, this is one of the principal interests of bureaucratic authority). Thus, this procedure fulfils an essential function of stability and reproduction of the institution.

For the protean, geographically dispersed machinery of the UNHCR, rotation of expatriate staff is a key element of consistency and internal cohesion. By way of their 'bureaucratic pilgrimages', to use Benedict Anderson's term,[4] UNHCR employees circulate around the UNHCR's context of intervention and functions. They mark the perimeter of the organisation's field of intervention, and renew relations between offices. Not only do they come into contact with many of their counterparts, fostering an esprit de corps, they also develop an awareness of the organisation as a whole. Thus, by virtue of their mobility, international officers form the hard core of the organisation; they embody its 'global' identity, transcending contextual interventions and are the agents of its epistemological, ideological and administrative consistency. On this point, Fresia (2010) describes UNHCR expatriates as an 'imagined community' that is close-knit despite its geographical dispersal. Moreover, rotation is also what distinguishes expatriate staff and sanctions their superior position in the hierarchy relative to both administrative staff in Geneva and staff recruited locally in countries of intervention. These employees do not rotate. Their localised and therefore peripheral position is underscored by hierarchical subordination.

Although at the level of the institution, rotation of expatriate staff is key to internal consistency, within each administrative unit, it limits continuity and acts as a brake on institutional activity. The federative function of mobility is in fact offset by the constant reconfiguration of teams. Officers – social actors each with their own background, personality and aspirations – are not as interchangeable as the bureaucratic ideal type suggests. Each rotation therefore entails a period of familiarisation, an individual and collective endeavour to integrate the new arrivals, and establishing legitimacy with one's colleagues. A new balance, including in relations of power, has to be negotiated each time.

The process of internal specialisation that took place within the UNHCR as it expanded led to a diversification of posts in terms not only of geographical context but also of tasks. A position in the Protection Department, for example, may take a completely different form depending on whether the person works at Headquarters drawing up directives or in the field coordinating aid programmes, in constant interaction with local authorities, refugee representatives and NGO staff. Thus, each time an employee changes post, they need time to familiarise themself with their new role. In addition to the specific tasks associated with the post, there are always quantities of new elements that need to be absorbed as quickly as possible in order to get to grips with the role, from the organisation's strategy in the country to the content of programmes, the names of provinces and of ministers, not to mention all the new acronyms to be remembered. The new arrival also has to integrate into a pre-existing socioprofessional group, which includes both new colleagues (expatriate and local) and external partners. Ultimately, it takes several months to become genuinely operational.

The set of knowledges and skills specific to the operational context is mainly acquired from colleagues in situ or from documents prepared by those who previously worked in the Operation. These modes of transmission imply strong dependence on colleagues already working in the context. Length of service in a particular posting gives officers a special authority with their colleagues. When I arrived at the Kabul office, I was welcomed by my line manager, who acted as my guide, outlining the programmes and pointing me towards key documents to read. At the beginning, she consistently checked the documents I was writing for external circulation, modifying terms, turns of phrase and the hierarchy of information. Asha had arrived for her first mission in Afghanistan after a long mission in Sri Lanka. She found herself head of an entire section at the Kabul Branch Office, while her juniors had been working in the Operation for much longer. Several months later, she still felt that she had not managed to catch up and free herself from her dependence on her colleagues. She relied heavily on Clara, who had been in Afghanistan for four years and had also been posted in the field in Herat for two years. Effectively, notwithstanding the hierarchy, it was Clara who led the section.

Subsequently, as the rotation continues, officers rapidly become 'experts'; long service is soon won. Barely ten months after I arrived, I was the one who welcomed, guided and supervised a new colleague joining the small Donor Relations section. Similarly, when a colleague arrived on a mission from Headquarters, we were his primary source of information, even those of us who had just arrived. This rapidly gained 'expertise' is precious in relations with colleagues but equally contingent, for it will be reset to zero at the beginning of the next mission.

It is now becoming clear what was at stake when Saverio and Eric arrived to lead the Afghan Operation. The time was counting down from their first day: this was 'their moment' to apply the direction they advocated to the organisation's policies in the field, knowing that they could not stay there indefinitely.[5] But before anything else, they had to familiarise themselves with the functioning of the Operation and, above all, to gain the trust of the teams already there. For Saverio, this was a return, since he had already been on mission in the region in 2002 and 2003. But his service in the field was not recognised as such by his colleagues in Kabul, because all the expatriate staff had changed since that time and because his job had been to maintain communications between the managers of the three Operations, and he had had little contact with the Afghan staff. For his part, Eric, on his many missions to Afghanistan, had been working for other organisations. Nor was the role of experts on Afghanistan that they had been credited with since 2003 recognised, as at the Desk they had interacted mainly with the managers they were now replacing. In the eyes of most of the staff posted to Afghanistan, Saverio and Eric were simply the new managers arriving in Kabul, who they hoped they would get on with.

The 'Briefing Kit' and Other Standardised Legibility Tools

Before examining how they took over the reins of the Afghan Operation, I consider another internal tool in the UNHCR's bureaucracy: the standardised frameworks for reading reality. This will help to highlight a significant element that made the ACSU an atypical project: its tailor-made character.

The diversity of operational contexts and the heterogeneous nature of UNHCR postings heightens the need for standardised points of reference that are easy to adopt and allow expatriate staff to move smoothly from one posting to another and quickly familiarise themselves with the contexts in which they are working. Thus, staff rotation goes hand in hand with formatted tools for reading the real-world situation, amplified by the culture of New Public Management (Jacobsen and Sandvik 2018). Faced with a heterogeneous and complex reality, the institution develops uniform, universal models of legibility and action that can be applied everywhere, enabling it to stabilise representations of reality and to take the measure of any situation and make it manageable. These models must be easily transposed and simple to handle. They therefore work more by analogy[6] and synthesis than through detailed knowledge of a context.

This feature is common to all bureaucratic institutions. James Scott (1998) analyses the procedures of rationalisation and standardisation developed by the state in order to convert the hieroglyph of reality into a legible and therefore manageable format. The need for standardised frameworks of understanding is even more acute in the case of the UNHCR because of the global scope of its activities. The organisation has not only to manage a multiplicity of specific contexts in a similar way (as in the case of a colonial administration or an NGO with projects in a limited number of countries), but to support all of the world's refugees. The UNHCR is thus continually engaged in the construction of a global order: the multiple contexts are seen as different sections of a coherent global system; local phenomena arise within the continuity of global phenomena; and local contexts are the multiple facets of the same 'refugee problem'.

The *Global Appeal* report offers a good illustration. Each year, this document gives an overview of the UNHCR's activity throughout the world (priorities, programmes, budgets and operational aspects), mainly with the aim of raising funds (UNHCR 2007m). An introductory section on trends in refugee affairs and the UNHCR's priorities in the world is followed by a description of each Operation in geographical order. The result is a coherent representation of the refugee phenomenon and the UNHCR's activity on a planetary scale. Contexts and activities are set within and harmoniously integrated into a global system, just as the UNHCR's global priorities are pursued at a local level. The information on Operations is produced by the Branch Offices, who are asked by Headquarters to fill in a template with preset fields. These files will be grouped by regions and then by continent. The introductory paragraphs on regions and continents are written by the editors. The resulting document describes a world that is entirely within the UNHCR's grasp.

The world is rendered legible for UNHCR employees primarily by the international episteme of refugees (see Chapter 2). The reading involved in this episteme allows migration phenomena and contexts of intervention to be classified according to easily mobilised concepts. It provides a key for comparing UNHCR postings, roles and programmes in such a way that staff are never at a loss in a new posting. Migrations are categorised as movements of 'refugees' or 'migrant workers', depending on people's reasons for departure. Countries are divided into 'countries of origin', 'countries of asylum' or 'resettlement' depending on their place in the migration journey. UNHCR programmes involve 'repatriation', 'reintegration', 'integration' or 'resettlement'. The concept of 'refugee situations' allows for comparison between flows and programmes.

Recurrent use is also made of 'portmanteau concepts'. These are not highly developed analytically; they simply need to be sufficiently elastic to be easily applied to various different contexts, in order to facilitate comparison and help identify common lines of action. They often reflect a new way of understanding or presenting the organisation's priorities rather than the result of detailed definition and conceptualisation. The concept of the 'protracted refugee situation' is one example of these amorphous ideas. This concept became widely used within the UNHCR during the 2000s, aiming to draw the attention of donors and the public to the political deadlock that was preventing the 'resolution' of many 'refugee situations'. The definition is quite flexible: the characteristic features of such 'situations' are the number of years they have continued, the number of refugees concerned and the absence of any prospect of solution.[7] Nevertheless, 'protracted refugee situations' are defined as a distinct phenomenon, with its own causes, effects and scale. Thirty-three such situations were identified in 2004, involving more than half of the world's refugees (UNHCR 2006a: 10). The concept quickly became a new key for comparative reading across situations, and a category among the UNHCR's global strategic priorities. In 2006 an entire chapter of *The State of the World's Refugees* report was given over to 'protracted refugee situations' (UNHCR 2006a: 105–77). In 2007, the concept was the central plank of understanding for the UNHCR's work in Asia, allowing for comparison between Afghans in Iran and Pakistan and the Karen in Thailand, the situation in Myanmar and the conflict in Sri Lanka (UNHCR 2007i).

The distribution of manuals and guidelines represents another way of producing and transmitting uniform, encompassing and transferrable cognitive frameworks and models of understanding. They are always produced by the central offices, with the aim of standardising the practice of subordinate offices. The Geneva Headquarters is therefore the primary producer. Manuals stabilise the interpretations circulating within the organisation and guide the actions of officers beginning a new mission. The best known is the one on criteria and procedures for determining refugee status (UNHCR 1992 [1979]), but there are many others, such as those on emergency contexts (*Handbook for Emergencies*) and on repatriation (*Handbook for Repatriation and Reintegration Activities*). When I arrived in Kabul, I was given a small handbook recently completed by the Protection Department in Geneva, entitled *UNHCR and International Protection: A Protection Induction Programme*. This was written for all employees in order to instruct them in the basics of refugee protection and communicate the current priorities and concepts to all UNHCR officers (UNHCR 2006b).

One of the key elements among the procedures for producing, organising and transmitting knowledge within the organisation is the 'briefing kit'. This is a file that brings together documents of various kinds (statistics, reports, maps, budgets, etc.), with the aim of providing concise but exhaustive key information on a given case, situation or context. The briefing kit is omnipresent. When I arrived at the Kabul office, my line manager drew up a list of colleagues who I should ask to brief me on the work of their offices, and also provided me with documents she deemed essential to read in order to grasp the context of the Operation and what was involved in my job. When a senior manager from Headquarters came on mission to the region, each of the three Branch Offices sent the Desk the key documents for their Operation. These were put together in a comprehensive file that the manager read on the plane, so that he could know what he was dealing with when he landed in the region.

My work consisted precisely of producing and updating briefing material – the documents that inform the UNHCR's external partners in Kabul about Afghan refugees and the organisation's programmes. I put together innumerable briefing kits, either in digital form or on paper. The preparation of the kit becomes an 'art', with the kit acquiring its own aesthetic: how best to put together the different elements that make it up (maps, statistics, narrative sections)? What is the most attractive format, the easiest and the most pleasurable to consult? What format is most appropriate to the person it is made for? I remember my disappointment when I realised that the material available would not allow me to present similar briefing kits to the various donors invited for a briefing – and the admiration I felt when my colleague from Jalalabad, on internal mission in the region, gave me a particularly well-crafted briefing kit on the UNHCR's action in the east of the country. Where had she got hold of those folders – did they come from Pakistan? When had she had the time to prepare it so carefully?

A pre-prepared and anonymous pack that packages reality in manageable, transmissible, ready-to-use formats, the briefing kit is one of the tools essential to the smooth functioning of UNHCR bureaucracy. It embodies the institution's bureaucratic rationality and its quest for consistency. Easy to produce and absorb, this procedure enables officers to move easily from one posting to another, to make reality manageable, to be interchangeable and always ready for action. Officers are spared the effort of reflecting and gathering for themselves the information that seems relevant to them. They have only to absorb the information selected by their colleagues.

Thus, global legibility is generated at the cost of simplification and even difficulty in grasping the specificities of the multiple operational contexts. While it makes it possible to intervene across vast territories, the bureaucratic framework is not equipped to deal with the incongruity and complexity of reality, or to grasp the historical, geographical and contextual aspects of phenomena. As Scott cogently explains (1998), bureaucracy tends to impose its own constraints on reality: the continual effort to maintain consistency that underpins its operation may even distort reality to make it conform to the needs of legibility and functionality. While they are essential elements of the flexibility that allows the organisation to operate on a global scale, these tools of legibility lead to a rigid understanding of reality and make it more difficult to adapt and take contextual specificities into account.

Take, for example, the knowledge held by longer-serving staff in a given Operation. This knowledge, the fruit of having spent longer in the place, does not necessarily equate to a deeper understanding of the sociopolitical context. It is usually an operational competence resulting from greater familiarity with the office procedures, its local partners and past programmes. This understanding is shaped by the institution and remains entirely compatible with a profound lack of connection with local reality (see Chapter 5).

Local languages do not feature among the set of knowledge to be acquired when an officer arrives in a new posting. The limited length of missions and the rarity of interactions between expatriate staff and locals give no incentive to invest time in studying them. In my job, speaking French was a hundred times more important than speaking Dari, since it allowed me to interact with European donors. Those who nevertheless make the attempt find once again that their learning is mediated by the organisation. My Dari teacher, for example, had previously taught several other colleagues. He taught me phrases – such as 'the head of mission is in his office' and 'the UNHCR is closed today' – associated with the bureaucracy of which I was part; the subjects were often his former students. In the end, owing to other priorities that determined my work, and lack of practice (given that English was always the language I spoke with my colleagues), I did not succeed in learning Dari despite my motivation to do so.

During my first placement with the UNHCR, I was surprised to discover that in order to build a career in the organisation, specialist knowledge of specific cultures, training in international law or knowledge of languages other than English and French were not as highly valued as personal qualities – charisma, quick thinking, relatability and adaptability – together with accumulated practical experience of working in the field of refugee aid. Building up missions was a major asset, enabling officers to master the key frames of reference and thus to acquire a mindset that allowed them to contain the complexity of the world. These frames of reference are acquired directly through practice, by working in the organisation. Thus, what matters is the number of missions accrued rather than a detailed knowledge of a specific context. 'I've done Darfur, Congo, Côte d'Ivoire...': each mission was not only a mark of distinction, but also added to the list signifies greater wisdom and expertise as a refugee aid professional.

In addition to offering an insight into the internal functioning of the UNHCR, this digression on standardised legibility tools helps to pinpoint a feature of the ACSU project that made it particularly hard for the institution to digest: the fact that it was tailor-made. Saverio and Eric worked with an approach they had matured over the years, through in-depth, context-specific reflection on the long-term issues of the Afghan refugee crisis. As noted above, Eric in particular was not preconditioned by the international refugee episteme or by operational requirements, but did have particular knowledge of the Afghan context. His approach resulted from years of work in Afghanistan in various capacities, from reading research on the issue, from continual monitoring of the current situation and from a rigorously regional attitude. This was an approach that took the history, economics and the social dimension of Afghan migration seriously, and situated them in a larger historical context. Such a relationship to a specific situation is very unusual in the UNHCR.

The result was a strategy that was repeatedly described as 'sophisticated' and even sometimes 'oversophisticated': sophisticated in the sense of 'coming from Headquarters', as noted above, where officers have the luxury of taking time to reflect, consult research studies and think on the grand scale – but also because of the frame of analysis and the concepts used, which were all different from those in the predetermined strategies. The concept of 'population movements', references to 'migrants' and to 'development' issues in the argument, for example, limited the document's legibility and made it hard to absorb. While it may seem paradoxical that Headquarters should support such an approach when it is there that standards are usually generated, it should be borne in mind that the senior managers who approved the strategy did not have to apply it themselves; their main concern was that the Afghan crisis should be well managed, even at the cost of making it an exception. Moreover, as noted above, the regional and long-term approaches corresponded closely to that of Headquarters.

How would officers in the field react? On top of the difficulty of grasping it, a bespoke project coming from Headquarters calls into question the role of offices in the field and their capacity to adapt the standard to the context.

Leading the Afghan Operation

To return to Saverio and Eric: when I arrived at the Kabul Branch Office in early April 2007, just a few weeks after Saverio had arrived, his change in status was striking. I had left him in his Geneva office as Desk Director. His workspace was more spacious than that of the other Desk staff, but he was only separated from his colleagues by plastic partitions with Venetian blinds. You could see when you passed through the corridor whether he was in his office or not, in a meeting or on the phone. He was always approachable: when I arrived and before I left, he had taken the time to have lunch with me. During my first day at the Kabul Branch Office, I did not see him at all – I merely heard his authoritative voice in the foyer as he gave final instructions to his secretary before getting into the car that his personal driver kept just outside the office. It was not until late in the evening that I dared to cross the now darkened office of his secretary, listen to see whether he was in a meeting or on the phone, and finally knock on his door to say hello. In the vast room that was now his office, he looked up from his files and greeted me warmly, but his eyes and hands were focused towards his computer, ready to dive back into his work.

In 2007 the Kabul Executive Office, where around twenty people worked, was the heart of one of the UNHCR's biggest interventions. It was the central cog in the administrative machinery of the Afghan Operation, directing all the activities of the Branch Office. There were around one hundred people working there, and it was responsible for the administration and coordination of all the Afghanistan Sub-Offices, accounting for a total of around six hundred employees. It was a nerve centre of power, linking levels of activity and reporting lines, and occupied a key position in the chain of bureaucracy. Within the space of a few seconds, the Representative's inbox might receive a Sub-Office's report on a mission in difficulty, a confidential message from the High Commissioner, an email from the head of UNAMA about the most recent Taliban attack, another from the Human Resources section about renewal of a contract and so on. Having arrived full of enthusiasm and energy, Saverio would not lose his charisma or his intensity and dynamic energy, but his drawn appearance was an irrefutable sign of a gruelling workload. The fact that he took no holiday, and the times when his emails were sent, offered evidence of how he sought an ultimate balance between his own needs and keeping a grasp on the machinery of the Operation.

Having started from a relatively peripheral position, the two authors of the ACSU project found themselves at the head of one of the central hubs of the organisation. But their new positions did not automatically translate into immediate pursuit of their long-term strategy. It was not this vision that would help them to establish their legitimacy as managers. Moreover, in order to bend it to one's vision, one must first have control of the mechanism. Thus, to begin with, while it remained on their strategic horizon, the ACSU strategy was not their priority: they first had to take hold of the reins of the Operation.

Having arrived with specific ideas about the long-term regional strategic orientation, the new managers quickly developed other views of priorities and the changes that were needed in internal organisation. As soon as he arrived, Saverio took hold of the Operation with gusto, aiming to re-energise and revitalise it, in order to foster greater cohesion between Sub-Offices and the Branch Office. Once Eric arrived, they embarked on a full review of the Operation. The comprehensiveness and rapidity of the changes shook up the habits of each and every member of staff, and inevitably aroused mistrust and resentment. Some criticised them for not even taking the time to assess the field and consult those who had been there for longer. The new priorities necessarily demoted programmes that had previously been considered priority, to the great disappointment of those leading them. This transition meant an increase in workload for everyone, even if it was only in adapting to the new priorities. The intensified work rate and organisational changes were particularly burdensome for colleagues whose missions were coming to an end.

Saverio and Eric, aware of the tensions their decisions might arouse, adopted a number of strategies to enhance their credibility, win the trust of the staff and build a close-knit team. First, they surrounded themselves with trusted collaborators. Just as Mr Gortani had done a few years earlier, Saverio invited colleagues with whom he had worked in the past to join him in key posts in Kabul (including as directors of the Branch Office Administration and Programme departments), as their previous missions came to an end. Second, they took care to establish links between the changes they were introducing and what had been done in the past. The Afghan Operation had the reputation of being particularly well managed, owing its success to the close-knit teams that had succeeded one another. As the third Representative since the Operation was set up in 2001, Saverio always presented his work as a continuation of that of his two predecessors. In the autumn he invited and welcomed Mr Gortani – who I recognised from having seen his photograph on the desk of his former secretary – to Kabul. A drinks reception was organised in the garden, during which several of the Afghan staff gave heartfelt speeches welcoming him 'home'.[8] Despite the changes they introduced, Saverio and Eric always showed the greatest respect for their predecessors and what they had accomplished.

Saverio and Eric also highlighted their longstanding links with the Operation and their understanding of the Afghan context. Saverio emphasised that he already knew several of the staff who were leaving, having met them during the time he had been working in Afghanistan. Shortly after his arrival, a photo of a much younger Eric, when he was in Herat during the 1970s, was circulated around the Kabul Branch Office, as a lighthearted reminder of his longstanding expert knowledge.

Over the months, Saverio won powerful legitimacy and was able to bring everyone behind him. His charisma, his devotion to his work and his drive, including the attention he gave to ensuring information was shared, quickly won him the trust of staff and established him as a popular leader.

With the change in leadership in Kabul, the ACSU project began to be integrated more into the everyday management. From this point on, all decisions taken by Branch Office senior staff were marked by this long-term vision. In this way, the content of the strategy was disseminated to the staff of the Afghan Operation. For example, in April 2007, during one of the first meetings of heads of Sub-Offices since he had taken up his post as Representative, Saverio declared 'we are following a vision', which he then proceeded to explain. The public documents produced by the office also emphasised the strategy more systematically. Thus, in a strategy document published in the spring of 2007, the establishment of a legal framework for regional migration appeared as one of the UNHCR's three major objectives in the region (UNHCR 2007b). For my part, in the weekly bulletins I was writing, I referred to it as often as possible, providing data on the frequency of cross-border movements and emphasising the need for a comprehensive approach to 'Afghan population movements' (UNHCR 2007p). Moreover, from the moment they arrived, Saverio and Eric had prioritised the relationship with the representatives of the European Commission Humanitarian Aid Office (ECHO) and the American Bureau of Population, Refugees and Migration (BPRM) (the organisation's key donors), and took care to ensure that their long-term strategy was understood and supported within the 'club', as Saverio called these gatherings.

Nevertheless, the place given to the ACSU project in the ongoing management remained relatively limited, confined to papers and high-level discussions. After several months, I could not help but note with disappointment that we were far from a radical shift of perspective among the staff in Afghanistan. Certainly, the vision was still clearly a strategic objective for the managers sitting in Kabul Branch Office, but their approach had changed markedly since they had arrived in the field.

The relatively peripheral place they had occupied in Geneva had allowed them to position themselves as unorthodox experts. Now that they were leaders, other priorities arose. First, the time they were able to devote to the strategy was much reduced, as their first concern was to run the Operation and, as will become apparent, to manage the successive crises. But there was also the question of how to introduce an atypical approach that was difficult for staff to take in when they were now representing the institution and concerned for its internal cohesion and smooth running. In their position as managers, they had to draw on standardisation tools that enabled them to direct the Operation (for example, the new standardised model for monthly reports from Sub-Offices that Saverio, unsatisfied with the previous model, instituted). A radical change of vision would be too costly.

The change of posting also partially altered Saverio and Eric's point of view because they were now in the field. In a reflective moment, Eric confided in me that once he was faced with his post in Kabul, he understood that his vision had remained detached from the problems of the field. He recognised that he had underestimated factors such as time schedules, the smooth progress of the reconstruction programme in Afghanistan (see Chapter 9) and the relative willingness of the Iranian and Pakistani authorities to negotiate (see Chapters 7 and 8). This explains why this phase of preparing the field and waiting for the right moment to finally push the ACSU project forward was extended indefinitely.

The Regional Front

In addition to the Afghan Operation, Saverio and Eric had another concern in Kabul: relations with the two neighbouring Operations. In the UNHCR's internal geographical organisation, the Operations in Iran, Afghanistan and Pakistan make up the 'South-West Asia' region,[9] which reports to a single Desk at Headquarters. Since the three Operations all focus on Afghan refugees and work in the same regional political context, the managers in Tehran, Kabul and Islamabad need to be aligned and consistent in their positions. The repatriation programme in particular requires joint negotiations with the authorities in the three countries, as well as continuous coordination between Sub-Offices on either side of the borders. While studies on humanitarian organisations generally focus on the vertical dimension – i.e. the relationship between headquarters and field (Atlani-Duhault 2005; Dauvin and Siméant 2002; Mosse 2005) – examining the horizontal dimension of relations between neighbouring Operations reveals a more complex play of internal connections and power relations.

At the point when Saverio arrived in Kabul, a process of decentralisation was under way in the UNHCR (and across the UN more broadly), aiming to create regional platforms to which Headquarters would grant greater decision-making and financial powers, in order to bring decision-making closer to the field and to foster greater cohesion between Operations dealing with the same crisis. From 2007, the Operations in Iran, Afghanistan and Pakistan were thus considered as 'the Afghanistan Situation' and were deemed to require a 'situational approach'. The Kabul office became the regional coordinating centre, and its Representative combined his role with that of 'Regional

Co-ordinator'. The regional approach of the ACSU project married well with this 'situational approach' promoted by Headquarters, and it is likely that this contributed to the decision by senior staff at Headquarters to entrust the leadership of the Kabul office to Saverio and Eric.

Yet tensions between neighbouring Operations were common. With the rates of repatriation falling, the situation in Afghanistan deteriorating and increasing pressure for return from the Pakistani and Iranian authorities, internal relations were becoming tense. It was difficult to reconcile the viewpoints of the Tehran and Islamabad Branch Offices, whose priority was to retain room for negotiation with the authorities in the 'host countries', and that of the Kabul office, faced with the urgent challenges of reintegrating returnees. For Saverio, becoming Regional Co-ordinator was also no easy matter. As noted above, the senior staff in Tehran and Islamabad had reservations about the long-term strategy, which they felt was not sensitive to their difficulties. Because of Saverio's age, they had even more difficulty in accepting his role and seeing him as not just a peer but above all a coordinator. Saverio was after all in his first post as Representative, whereas his opposite numbers in Tehran and Islamabad were older and well versed in their roles as managers.

These tensions were latent even before the crises of the summer of 2007 brought them out into the open. They were apparent when the Deputy High Commissioner for Operations came on mission to the region. This mission was organised down to its finest detail by the leadership of the Branch Offices, and occupied a large number of employees for several weeks. In each country, everything was put in place to ensure that the UNHCR 'number two' got the best possible impression of the Operation and its managers. His itinerary was planned down to the last detail. Saverio gave a trusted person the task of preparing her food (the instructions received from Headquarters specified that the 'number two' did not like to miss meals). The Representative in Islamabad went to the airport at 5 am to welcome her to the region. In a situation of latent horizontal tensions, the concern for each Representative was both to show how well he was managing his own Operation and could therefore be entirely trusted by Headquarters, and to make clear his point of view on the management of the 'Afghan Situation'. Each office therefore sought to impress on the top level of the organisation the main difficulties facing its Operation. For Saverio, for example, it was important to make clear to senior management the difficulties involved in reintegrating returnees – challenges that, in his view, should have been taken more fully into account when negotiating with the Iranian and Pakistani authorities. On returning to Geneva, the Deputy High Commissioner herself noted in her report that for the time being the 'situational approach' was far from established, since the three Branch Offices had very different visions and priorities.

The acid test for regional cooperation arose immediately after Saverio's arrival in Kabul in April 2007, when a first crisis erupted. The Iranian authorities began to expel tens of thousands of undocumented Afghans,[10] who thus found themselves stuck in desert areas on the Afghan-Iranian border, in conditions of acute distress. Never before had the Iranian authorities gone so far in terms of number of deportations and the conditions in which those expelled found themselves. A split emerged between the offices in Tehran and Kabul on how to manage this situation.[11] UNHCR managers in Tehran took a cautious approach. In a daily stand-off with the Iranian authorities, they were less inclined to take responsibility for Afghan deportees, or to adopt a public position by openly criticising the expulsion policy. Familiar with the unilateralism of the Iranian authorities, and working to alleviate repressive measures against Afghans holding a regular status in Iran, they feared that a confrontational stance would risk further reducing the UNHCR's room for negotiation.

The managers in Kabul took a different view. The escalation of deportations had generated a new situation: demonstrations in the street, the sacking of two ministers and so on. Never had the issue of Afghans in Iran received so much attention, both from the Afghan government or from international actors in Afghanistan. This attention put pressure on the UNHCR, which was clearly considered responsible for the deportees despite the fact that they were not officially 'refugees'. The organisation's reputation was at stake, at the same time as its legitimacy and its ability to work in the south of the country were being challenged by the Taliban. In addition, Saverio and Eric wanted to capitalise on this heightened attention to plead for one of the objectives of the ACSU project: the introduction of a bilateral regime to manage the migration of workers between the two countries (which would, among other things, protect Afghans from expulsion). From this point of view, while the UNHCR was not officially responsible for undocumented Afghans, the deportations were an indirect concern for the organisation. 'We can't wash our hands of this situation', Saverio declared emphatically at a meeting of Heads of Section where the expulsions were the subject of a long discussion.

Saverio and Eric thus favoured an interventionist approach aiming to assist deportees. Ultimately their point of view was endorsed by the Tehran office, following consultations with Geneva. At the same time, the issues raised by the managers in Tehran could not be ignored. It was therefore agreed that the UNHCR would act discreetly under the auspices of a multilateral intervention and would not officially take a critical position.

In this case too, the ACSU project shaped decision-making in the field more directly, even at a regional level. Nevertheless, the approach was still contested and its implementation always required negotiations with the managers of the neighbouring Operations. There was also an additional difficulty.

When Saverio and Eric were in Geneva, equally distant from the three Branch Offices, they could not be suspected of supporting one Operation more than another. Once they were in Kabul, it became difficult to hold the role of regional leader at the same time as heading the Afghan Operation, since it was even more difficult to recognise the difficulties Tehran and Islamabad encountered in their negotiations with the Iranian and Pakistani authorities from Kabul. Thus, at the very moment when the authors of the ACSU strategy arrived in the field, the horizontal understanding between Operations, so vital to the strategy, became more problematic.

The UNHCR as a Bureaucratic Arena

Even when they are investigating the reasoning and procedures behind the governance of bureaucratic institutions, many researchers tend to attribute greater coherence to institutions than they actually have. They also assume the existence of a single intentionality and way of thinking, which simply needs to be decoded before analysing how it is implemented. For example, Scott (1998) tends to view the state as a homogeneous actor that sees the world through a unified gaze – as the title of his book *Seeing Like a State* indicates. Ferguson (1994), in his study of a World Bank project in Lesotho, intelligently uncovers the conceptual apparatus of development while highlighting its depoliticising way of thinking. But he does this on the basis of a single document, the World Bank's 1975 Country Report on Lesotho. As for Barnett and Finnemore (2004), they seem to abstract the internal actors who design and implement the impersonal norms they view as the characteristic feature of international organisations.

Tracing the trajectory of the ACSU project within the UNHCR has shown that on the contrary, a bureaucratic institution cannot be ascribed a single gaze or even a unified voice. Many gazes coexist within the UNHCR (multiple resolutions and ways of approaching and understanding a given situation), and many types of documents are produced at the same time (from the *Global Appeal* report, with its standardised entries, to the ACSU project's strategic papers). Seen from the inside, the UNHCR is far from a monolithic institution operating mechanically and impersonally through its bureaucracy.

Max Weber (1968) saw bureaucratic administration as the form of power best adapted to large-scale interventions and to large populations. According to the ideal typical features identified by Weber, the legal authority that underpins bureaucratic operation rests, among other things, on a division of labour based on clearly defined areas of responsibility, on a hierarchy that monitors the activity of its officers, and on stable regulations that guide decision-making. These procedures make it possible to stabilise representations of reality, to make collective action predictable and to give bureaucratic power the universal potential to be applied to any kind of task, in any context.

Powerful procedures of rationalisation and standardisation are indeed at work within the bureaucratic apparatus of the UNHCR. The hierarchies and areas of responsibility laid down in the organisational structure (which attribute greatest power to the levels furthest from the field) are augmented by the circulation of officers, and cognitive frameworks that standardise the understanding of reality. Maintaining an overall consistency and a grasp of reality is all the more essential because the organisation has a global remit and intervenes in a wide range of political, cultural and linguistic contexts. These principles of rationality, hierarchy and transparency are evident in the architecture of the Headquarters building in Geneva (see Figure 3.3) – a massive, geometric structure within which each officer is given a workspace (containing at least a desk, a chair, a computer and a landline), the characteristics of which generally reflect their position in the hierarchy. The higher up one goes, the more elevated one is in the hierarchy, up to the offices of the 'troika' on the uppermost, eighth floor. Glass, as ubiquitous inside as it is on the outside, symbolises transparency.

But we have also seen that these procedures of rationalisation and standardisation are not sufficient in themselves to explain the UNHCR's internal functioning. I have noted, for example, the limits of the organisation's legal authority. The approval of the strategy by senior managers, and the appointment of Saverio and Eric to a position of power were not enough to establish the ACSU strategy, for in order to carry forward and realise a vision, its legitimacy has to be won and continually renewed with all the interests concerned. The post of manager involves a constant effort to establish one's authority. Each office fulfils a necessary function and establishes a unique position within the bureaucratic structure, and this interdependence relativises hierarchies.

Hierarchy and standardisation also come up against the plurality of perspectives that coexist within the institution – a plurality that the dominance of legal frameworks and rationalisation cannot of themselves bring into alignment. As I have noted, officers are by no means as interchangeable as bureaucratic rationality would wish. I have also noted that depending on its position within a particular arena, on its partners and specific difficulties, each office develops its own vision, its own way of understanding the organisation's priorities. These visions may be very different, if not irreconcilable.

The result is that the design and implementation of policies are continually contested and involve compromising with many different points of view. The UNHCR as institution can thus be seen from the inside as a *bureaucratic arena*: a field demarcated by bureaucratic rationality, within which many different actors interact and compete. These actors – offices and officers – effectively constitute hubs rather than cogs. Within this field, which is constantly reconfigured thanks to internal staff rotation, negotiation is permanent and relations of power are redefined over time. Accounts that suggest order and consistency (reports, organisational charts, etc.) testify not to an actual consistency, but rather to the constant efforts to organise and align within this arena. These efforts are thwarted both by the diversity of viewpoints that come into conflict within the organisation and by the specific details of each context of intervention.

This approach to the UNHCR aligns with a growing body of recent social science research on international organisations in general and international aid organisations in particular. This research reveals the plurality and diversity of the actors who interact within these organisations (officers, diplomats, experts, local staff, etc.) and their trajectories (Ambrosetti and Buchet de Neuilly 2009; Atlani-Duhault 2005; Bendix 2012; Dauvin and Siméant 2002; Fresia 2010, 2012; Mosse 2005; Pouliot 2006). They reveal an institutional space that is open and porous, at the crossroads between national and international fields, traversed by the transnational circulation of ideas, norms and knowledges, a place of negotiation between different understandings and interests (Abélès 2011; Cling et al. 2011; Decorzant 2011; Kott 2011).

Notes

1. In interactionist sociology, the concept of career designates an actor's sequence of moves within a given field over a given period. This concept seems appropriate here, as it allows the development of the strategy itself to be dynamically linked with the institutional context in which it was set. Drawing on one of the best-known studies that uses this concept, Howard Becker's study of 'deviant careers' (1963), here I show how the impact of a deviant strategy is diluted within the institution.

2. The administrative unit that acts as an interface between the offices in the field and Headquarters, and is part of the Asia Bureau, which in turn is a section of the Operations Department.

3. Within the UNHCR, some postings involve rotating between operations even more often; this is the case, for example, with teams deployed in emergencies. Internal missions are also very frequent.

4. Anderson describes the journeys of colonial officials in Latin America as 'bureaucratic pilgrimages', arguing that this mobility emerged as a secular counterpart to religious pilgrimages during the development of the administrative machinery of absolutist monarchies in the seventeenth century (Anderson 2006: 54–55).

5. Overall, their time there would last four years: Saverio remained Representative until the end of 2008, whereupon Eric took over the role until the end of 2010.

6. Aymes sees comparison as a central strand in the profession of provincial administrator in the Ottoman Empire, used by officials who found themselves in unknown lands and attempted to 'return to familiar ground' (2008: 7).

7. The UNHCR defines a 'protracted refugee situation' as a 'long-lasting and intractable state' in which after 'five or more consecutive years' of exile refugees have no prospect

of a solution to their situation and their 'basic rights and essential economic, social and psychological needs remain unfulfilled' (UNHCR 2004d).

8. A similar, but much less celebratory, atmosphere of remembrance overcame the Branch Office a few months later, on the death of the preceding Representative.

9. Depending on the context, Afghanistan may be attached to various different geographic units – Central Asia, South Asia, etc. For example, the US State Department locates the country in South Asia, a throwback to the geography of the opposing blocs during the Cold War. The UNHCR emphasises the geographical unity of South-West Asia in referring to the area circumscribed by Iran, Afghanistan and Pakistan. For the UNHCR, this unit makes sense because it brings together the 'country or origin' and the two main 'host countries' of Afghan refugees.

10. The issue of Afghans' status in Iran will be analysed in Chapter 7.

11. In this chapter the focus is on divisions between the Kabul and Tehran offices. In Chapter 8 I will consider those between the Kabul and Islamabad offices.

CHAPTER 5

The Insular Cosmopolitanism of Expatriate Staff

One day in Kabul, Asha, a permanent UNHCR employee, and I were getting coffee in our guesthouse. She had just spent a night in Zaranj, on the Afghanistan-Iran border, followed by several hours waiting in the airport at Kabul and an afternoon at an Afghan ministry. She told me that previously, she used to like her coffee with milk and sugar, but over the course of her career with the UNHCR – which had led her to live in Tuzla (Bosnia), Dushanbe (Tajikistan), Colombo (Sri Lanka) and Geneva, among other places – she had made herself learn to drink it black. She now only took it that way, even when milk and sugar were available. And she loved it. This is one example of how the profession becomes the base around which a permanent UNHCR staffer's life is organised, and of the way in which mobility is gradually incorporated, to the point where it influences the development and alteration of tastes.

As their bureaucratic peregrinations continue, the culinary practices and tastes of UNHCR expatriate staff evolve and shift between lack and abundance, make-do and access to luxury, adaptation and the potential for discovery, often out of step with the place where they find themselves. Being constantly on the move, switching rapidly from one sociocultural context to another, not knowing where they will live in two years' time, they learn to be at ease everywhere. But UNHCR staff are also subject to often frenetic rhythms that do not always allow them to take their time; you need practical habits. Instant granules, hot water and you have coffee. And, indeed, almost everyone had instant coffee in their store cupboard in Kabul. And everyone said that after all, there would surely soon be an opportunity to enjoy a real proper latte.

Through their travels and the multicultural environment in which they work, UNHCR expatriates have access to a wide variety of foods. They appreciate cultural diversity and take pride in it. I tasted more different kinds of coffee in Kabul than I had anywhere else. The machine my flatmate had brought from Denmark enabled us to make large quantities of very weak, North American-style coffee. I liked to drop in at the office of Danail, a Bulgarian colleague who guarded his Turkish coffee pot jealously. He never ran out of coffee – he stocked up when he went back to Bulgaria or asked another colleague to bring it back from leave in Sarajevo. I myself bought him several packets in Istanbul when I stopped over there.

Some tastes accompanied us and helped us to feel at home in a hectic life. Our Representative could not do without Italian coffee. In the Executive Office's small kitchen the housekeeping staff took good care of a stove-top coffee machine and two small cups. I also drank Italian-style coffee with my Italian colleagues, who had equipped the office they shared with a stove-top machine and an electric hot plate. For a few months, coffee became a ritual that added an element of intimacy to our conversations in Italian. One had a baby a few months old in Italy, the others had partners in Indonesia and Australia, but together we generated a comfortable feeling of family.

Numbering around a thousand in the early 2000s, the UNHCR's international staff form part of a cosmopolitan elite located at the intersection of the UN and humanitarian fields. 'Expats', as they call themselves, move casually through the world and are at ease anywhere, in Geneva just as in Kabul. Their high degree of mobility and the humanitarian nature of their work characterise a life they experience as out of the ordinary, distinguishing them from those who, both in their countries of origin and the countries where they work, are caught up in local or national systems.

This chapter considers the cosmopolitan culture and practices of UNHCR expatriates. It first examines their habitus and their movements, before considering the space-time of a mission in Kabul. By describing the materiality of a cosmopolitan life that is certain to be partially deterritorialised, but nevertheless always anchored in specific physical and social spaces, I will show that UNHCR expatriates are far from the 'free electrons' suggested by some studies that highlight only their privileged status (Bauman 1998). I identify the institutions that shape the mobility, the cosmopolitan practices and the worldview of UNHCR expatriate staff – the UNHCR itself, the interstate system and the institutional world of international aid, institutions that on one level open doors to a multicultural, mobile way of life and support their claims to universalism and moral superiority, and on another level are powerful forces structuring their practices and their view of the world.

Mobility and the Field as Foundational Experiences

The habitus[1] of UNHCR international staff is strongly shaped by the experience of mobility on the one hand, and the field on the other. In addition to consolidating their esprit de corps, these two foundational experiences raise them above the ordinary and project them into the elevated, morally superior, encompassing dimension specific to the UN space (see Chapter 3). Working for the UNHCR means being able to 'make a difference', to use a recurrent expression – in other words, to have a real impact on the most destitute populations of the world, to influence the policies of states, while at the same time living a more interesting, fulfilling and adventurous life than ordinary people. Nazim, for example, told me how shocked he was to hear people around him enthusiastically discussing the cheeses they had just bought at the supermarket at a tram stop in Geneva when he had just returned from an African country where salt was being distributed to a malnourished population.

UNHCR expatriates develop a strong feeling of themselves as distinct from all those whose lives remain restricted to the scale of nation, who go about their individual lives without wanting, or being able, to take an interest in the world's most urgent problems. Mobility and the field define a unique group, professionals ready to travel to where they are needed, where it counts, despite the dangers and their family attachments. Indeed, working for the UNHCR is not for everybody: being this ready to travel and working in difficult locations while remaining efficient and professional requires many resources, both intellectual and physical: lucidity, a cool head and adaptability to work in emergency or stressful conditions; excellent physical fitness to be able to step off a long plane journey fresh and ready to work despite the time difference; inner stability and a high capacity for concentration to spend long periods away from family, and stay focused on one's goals without being destabilised by one's itinerant life; and resourcefulness to be able to adapt to any situation.

The experience of mobility and of the field also generates a feeling of standing apart from the staff of humanitarian NGOs and other UN agencies. NGO staff also travel frequently and are often in the field, but UNHCR staff see them as having fewer responsibilities and less influence over major strategic orientations and state policies. In the UNHCR, on the other hand, staff have the feeling of combining fervent commitment to the victims of crisis with the weight of the UN's financial resources and political authority, enabling them to 'hold in [their hands] a strand of some important political process', as Max Weber describes the 'inner pleasures' of a political career (Weber 2004: 76). This sense of distinctness is bolstered by UNHCR officers' higher salaries and more comfortable travel. NGO staff have less leave and fewer financial resources for travel, and spend more time in uninterrupted postings. The difference from staff of other UN agencies is even greater: the latter carry out shorter missions in less arduous postings and mainly work in offices. Their high salaries allow them to live comfortably in the world's capitals.

I will consider these two foundational experiences in turn. Working for the UNHCR involves frequent travel, often on long-haul flights. This high level of mobility is not just due to the change of posting about every two years. There are very often internal missions – going off to meetings, or to visit the field. Some roles involve even more frequent travel, for example, in teams deployed in emergencies. The person sent by Headquarters in 2007 to oversee the development of a preventative strategy in case the camps in Pakistan were closed stayed in the region for three weeks, travelling between Kabul, Jalalabad, Islamabad and Peshawar, before writing his report in Kabul and returning to Geneva prior to taking on his next mission to Iraq. Then there is leave. Leave periods are more frequent for those posted to difficult locations, as compulsory Rest and Recuperation breaks are added to the annual leave entitlement. These compulsory holidays, every two months, are designed to enable expatriates to take a break from dangerous, isolated or stressful working conditions. In 2007 the organisation would fund travel as far as Dubai or Islamabad, which were considered safe and nearby destinations, but expatriates usually travelled onward, since their high salaries allowed them to go further even for just a few days.

The actual practice of mobility links expatriates to one another and creates common frames of reference. They share a familiarity with the airports, airlines and hotels they pass through on their journeys. 'Air miles' or the launch of a new airline are frequent topics of conversation, as are references to locations as geographically distant and distinct as a particular restaurant in New York, a hotel in Islamabad or a refugee camp in Sudan.

As they travel and stay for relatively long periods in countries with different cultures, expatriates accumulate references to expanded horizons linked together by their career trajectories rather than by national belonging. Thus, rather than acquiring familiarity with accents, physical features or the origin of family names on a national level, they accumulate much broader common points of reference – with 'skills' or 'regions of specialisation' that vary depending on each individual's career path. I developed the ability to detect a person's origin from their accent when they spoke English on the telephone – on the edge of the lips for French people, flat for Italians, the Germans' more withheld way of speaking, Afghans' open accent, the fluid accent of those from India and Pakistan, and so on. I began to notice the similarity between the accents of Azeri and Bulgarian colleagues, but still had trouble with Japanese and Thai accents. There were also those whose personal trajectory had given them a less obvious accent, if they had studied in an English-speaking country or married an English-speaker for example.

Mobility, coupled with professional responsibilities, is also part of constructing the elevated level to which expatriates feel they belong. Travelling over great distances, alternating between ground and air, they feel liberated from the scale of the nation, with its affiliations and institutions. They have a sense of transcending nation-states, of being above them. The national scale from which they have distanced themselves is first and foremost that of their country of nationality.

Indeed, the careers, affiliations and families of UNHCR staff are generally transnational. One example is Kanta: her family was Indian, but she held Malaysian nationality as she had been born in Kuala Lumpur, and she trained in the United Kingdom. Paradoxically, it was in her subsequent posting that she had the opportunity to live in India for the first time. Clara was an Italian national, but grew up in the Caribbean; she studied in the United States and was married to an Australian she had met in Afghanistan, and she wrote better in English and Spanish than in Italian. It is easy to see why the question 'Where are you from?' cannot be answered in terms of country of nationality. When asked this question, one permanent employee sighed before saying, in a brief summary she had repeated many times before, that on paper she was American, but that she had not lived in the United States for a long time.

Detachment from one's country of nationality plays out on both practical and moral levels. At the level of everyday practices, expatriates almost never live in their national territory (except for holidays). They often do not pay tax in their country; sometimes they do not vote in elections. On a moral level, working for the UNHCR implies adhering to – or at least being a spokesperson for – a moral community situated above states. The Code of Conduct with which every UNHCR employee must comply (UNHCR 2004c) stipulates that they must neither seek nor accept instructions regarding performance of their duties from any national government, including their own. Moreover, the 'refugee reason' championed by UNHCR staff is often in competition with the reason of state. Thus, refugees become a moral catalyst that can potentially replace nationality, even at the level of moral identification.

In addition, because state representatives are their principal interlocutors and because from a young age they are required to observe, critique and influence the action of states, state authorities and state power lose their aura. In Afghanistan the Italian embassy strove to consolidate an esprit de corps among Italians, for example, by holding receptions on Italy's national day. But notwithstanding the friendships that Italians might form among themselves, for us Italian UNHCR employees, the Italian embassy was primarily a funder. Thus, when it was pompously announced at the national unity celebration that a senior Italian official would shortly be arriving, for me it was simply a piece of information to be noted in the context of my work. Clara too remained unimpressed. However, she was deeply moved when Sadako

Ogata herself, the former High Commissioner, spent an afternoon at the Kabul Branch Office.

The field is the second foundational experience. First and foremost, it reinforces the sense of a unique profession and way of life. Having access, thanks to their status and by virtue of their responsibilities, to corners of the planet inaccessible to the majority, finding themselves at the heart of humanitarian crises where most people would prefer not to be, working in emergency situations, at a relentless, often addictive pace, the possibility of 'making a difference' for populations in distress that they come into contact with – all of this contributes to making theirs a unique profession.

The field is also a key point of initiation for the youngest, as Marion Fresia notes (2010). An employee's first experiences in the field allow them to prove their worth and show they have the capacities required to exercise this profession. My first stay in Kabul and my experience in a shanty town in Kenya certainly helped me obtain an internship with the UNHCR. Once I was in the field, I would often find myself admiring the ingeniousness of a colleague who could skilfully manipulate the cables of a dusty old computer and finally get it to work, or the cool head of another who managed to remain lucid and professional when confronted with scenes of suffering. The pressure to show I was up to the job stimulated me to work to develop these skills, so that I could be recognised as a member of the team in my own right and increase the chances of my contract being renewed.

Finally, the field also constitutes a matrix of socialisation. Whereas in Geneva the separation between private and work life is a block to socialisation, in the field this distraction fades away. Sharing an unusual daily routine and difficult moments, working side by side in out-of-the-way places, can create deep bonds and consolidate an esprit de corps that outweighs professional rivalries and hierarchies. Within the organisation, networks of this type override affinities based on national or cultural belonging, as evidenced by the network of 'Afghan' expatriates – that is, staff who have undertaken missions in Afghanistan.

During my stay in Kabul, in addition to the team based there, I met dozens of other colleagues. Because of its centrality in the bureaucratic machinery, the Kabul office was a major transit point.[2] Social interaction and familiarity with colleagues on mission or in transit were immediate, irrespective of hierarchies, because we had communicated by email or because we had heard about one another, or even if we had never come across one another before. During my internship at Headquarters, Janet, a member of the administrative staff at the Desk, had been cordial but fairly reserved and distant; when she came on mission to Kabul, her attitude was more relaxed and our conversations were more personal. On meeting a colleague for the first time, you always asked where they undertook their previous missions and who they had worked with. When you met someone who worked in a mission or with colleagues you knew well, there was even greater familiarity: is this or that person still posted there? How is that programme going, which wasn't working at all at that time? Say hello to so-and-so. In any case, there is never any shortage of subjects of conversation: the frequency of 'recuperation leave' in a given posting, the colleagues you work or have worked with, flight connections and so on. Familiarity is quickly reinforced by a shared meal that generally unleashes more edgy exchanges. It is then that conflictual relationships within offices emerge, long discussions on the size of the cockroaches in UNHCR apartments around the world, or on the High Commissioner's pulling techniques when on mission.

The UNHCR as a Pivot of a Rotating Life

Focusing purely on the frequent and multidirectional mobility of the UN-HCR's international staff neglects the role of the organisation. At the same time as making this mobility possible and necessary, the organisation frames it. Moreover, in setting itself up as the base of an itinerant life, the organisation becomes an important point of reference for its staff, and also shapes their identity and their view of the world.

The career trajectories of expatriate staff are inevitably shaped by staff rotation, both in space (within the framework of UNHCR postings throughout the world) and in time (depending on the length of missions and leave). It is primarily owing to this mobility, with its fixed stages, that a career in the UNHCR becomes a life project. Rotation determines the way in which UNHCR staff see the spatiality of the world. All roads, for example, lead to Geneva. New York remains an important centre, but in the context of the decentralisation process under way throughout the UN, Bangkok and Nairobi are becoming equally important hubs. The emergence of crises, and the setting-up and withdrawal of programmes, punctuate both the history of the organisation and the lives of its employees.

Trajectories are strongly linked to the progress of the employee's career within the organisation. International staff apply for a number of vacant posts, stating their order of preference. Each person makes up their list in line with their own priorities, weighing up the advantages and disadvantages of each posting and estimating their chance of obtaining the post requested. As noted above, experience in the field is essential for all staff and can be very helpful in building networks. But anyone who stays for too long in an out-of-the-way posting risks being marginalised. From this point of view, in late 2001 Afghanistan was an attractive posting: well funded and well staffed, it offered the opportunity to demonstrate one's capacities and get oneself noticed. At a dinner in Kabul, Arnold remembered it as the first major mission that his network had helped him secure, following which he had risen meteorically up the hierarchy. Nazim, on the other hand, recalled his frustration when he had been asked to join the team. He would desperately have liked to join straight away, but his line manager had kept him 'stuck in Bosnia'.

Living conditions and security measures in the field can become oppressive sooner or later. A mission to Headquarters then represents an ideal breathing space: the temperate climate and nearby ski slopes make it an oasis of tranquillity. Since living conditions in Geneva are so good, many employees have bought houses there. When they are on mission, their partner and children, who are enrolled in school, wait for them in Switzerland. Time spent in Geneva, or in another key centre, is also essential to create contacts or update one's network. Because of the principle of equity applied in assignment of postings, those who seek a transfer to Geneva or a similar posting have a better chance of obtaining it after a mission in a difficult posting.

Staff rotation clashes with employees' need to reconcile private and professional life, career imperatives and family needs. The relatively high number of single people and divorce rates among UNHCR staff offer telling evidence of this (Wigley 2005: 76). Postings are classified either as 'family duty station' or 'non-family duty station', to which the employee may not bring their family. In any case, school-age children are difficult to reconcile with staff rotation. All the postings in Afghanistan were 'non-family duty stations'. Separation, palliated by Skype and Interflora, was particularly hard for mothers. In order to stay in the organisation and in the hope of obtaining an easier posting before too long, Christine, a mother of four, had left her family in Nairobi to work in Kabul. Fatma, who had returned to Geneva after a year in the field in a 'non-family duty station', was struggling to recover a stable relationship with her teenage son.[3]

The most stable couples often consist of partners who work in the same international milieu, sometimes both in the UNHCR. Couples and families are thus founded on periods of distance alternating with periods of proximity, like Danail, who had reunited his family in Kabul between two separations. In Geneva, I met couples where one partner had expressly given up a career in order to follow their partner or provide a stable home life for their children.

The compromises inherent in a career with the UNHCR mean that the profession is also often experienced as a sacrifice. Sacrifice, associated particularly with staff rotation and postings to 'non-family duty stations', is one element of the esprit de corps of UNHCR staff, which places devotion to the refugee cause above all else. The commitment of staff is always highlighted and presented by senior managers as one of the organisation's great strengths, the crucial element that enables it to achieve concrete results.[4] This notion of sacrifice is also apparent in the administrative jargon relating to the compensations designed to reward staff, such as 'hardship allowances', 'compensation' and 'rest and recuperation leave'.

While the UNHCR's mode of operation undermines family structure, the organisation becomes a fundamental point of reference for its permanent staff. Since the employee's entire life literally revolves around the UNHCR, the organisation is not just an employer, but also represents a source of stability and a vital anchor for social life and identity. The employee's relationship with the organisation is the most constant element in an itinerant life, giving coherence to their experience and lifestyle. Significantly, Headquarters is known as 'the House', and some UNHCR staff often describe themselves as members of one 'family'. Although they are scattered through the world, permanent UNHCR staff almost all know one another either personally or by reputation. Thus, when you arrive at an office, you immediately have the sense of being in a familiar place, among your peers. Clara told me that when she arrived in Geneva, she not only renewed deep friendships formed during postings in the field, but was also surrounded by a multitude of familiar faces she had encountered at one point or another in her career.

I also observed a process of collective identification with the organisation's mandate and the refugee paradigm. This is revealed, for example, in frequent plays on words that establish a parallel between the mobility of refugees and that of UNHCR employees. Thus, when he came on a visit, the former Representative in Afghanistan described himself as a 'returnee', while expatriates in Afghanistan often joked about being 'displaced'. The refugee paradigm underpins this world of shared meanings and constitutes expatriate UNHCR staff as an epistemic community. This phenomenon is analysed by Marion Fresia (2010), who sees adherence to the common refugee cause as one of the principal elements structuring the close interconnectedness and forming UNHCR expatriate staff into a solid community despite their geographical dispersion.

As employees accumulate years of work with the UNHCR, it becomes more difficult to separate from it. Once they have come to terms with staff rotation, the organisation becomes a pivot that provides stable employment and other benefits and privileges, which increase substantially with promotion. On a pragmatic level, salary levels are higher than those of any other NGO, making the UNHCR, along with the International Committee of the Red Cross, the most financially attractive employer in the humanitarian sphere. Moreover, the status of UN official comes with benefits and preferential treatment, such as immunity or exemption from taxes. The organisation looks after its employees and their families, becoming the prime provider of social services: health insurance, medical services, psychological support and so on. The medical department at Headquarters even takes care of vaccinations. In the field, the organisation sometimes takes charge of the entire life of expatriates and their families, including their physical security.[5]

In return, personal commitment may generate substantial expectations of the institution, or indeed be a source of resentment and frustration if it is not acknowledged or valued. Before she secured the long-desired posting in Geneva, Clara had been offered one in Central Asia. But even though it would come with a promotion, she did not want to accept a non-European post. After missions in East Timor, Ethiopia, Ivory Coast, Iran and Afghanistan, she was no longer prepared to take a posting in the field; she was physically exhausted and also wanted to start a family. The fact that the organisation did not understand her situation and refused to offer a compromise provoked a crisis in her relationship with it. How was it possible that after all she had given the UNHCR, it was not prepared to make an effort to retain her? When she was finally allocated a posting in Geneva, she heard through a call from a colleague, for it was already late in Kabul when the list was posted by Human Resources in Geneva. She received other congratulatory calls from colleagues posted throughout the world, who were delighted that she would be staying in the organisation.

This strong bond with the organisation distinguishes UNHCR staff from the elusive elites and multiple affiliations analysed by Wedel (2009). The latter, and the networks they form, cross between institutions (universities, state bodies, international organisations, think tanks, etc.), and their allegiance is to their networks, not to the institutions to which they are attached. Only a minority of UNHCR staff can be likened to these elites: some of the influential senior staff, such as António Guterres (President of Portugal who became High Commissioner and then UN Secretary-General) or Mr Gortani, who after directing another UN agency was appointed to the UNHCR as a member of the 'troika'. Consultants too, like Eric, circulate between institutions, as do those who do not manage to join the organisation and construct an alternative career for themselves instead. But those who succeed in securing a permanent contract develop a strong bond with the organisation, which becomes a catalyst in their lives. Once they have obtained this post, they establish an allegiance with the UNHCR and the 'refugee reason'. They want the UNHCR to prosper, if only because it is a guarantee they will always be needed. Leaving the organisation is often experienced as a disappointment, and joining government bodies or NGOs as a fallback solution.

The International Backstage and the National Stage

There is a second institution that shapes the mobility and habitus of UNHCR expatriates – the interstate system. As noted above, this habitus is defined partly by the idea of detachment and indeed emancipation from the national scale on material, spatial and moral levels. Yet even though this cosmopolitan elite claims to be beyond national particularisms, its professional culture and modalities of travel remain enmeshed in the system of states: they are defined in relation to this system and ultimately reassert the national order they are supposed to supersede. Distance from the state serves less to define a world in opposition to states than to mark an 'international' dimension located 'behind the scenes' with respect to states and enmeshed with them. The same tension can be observed between emancipation and affiliation, a contrast and a confirmation of the tension noted in the relation between UN institutions and the system of states. Ultimately, the state sphere represents not an obstacle to be overcome, but the driving force behind the UN sphere. I will now examine some aspects of this enmeshment.

It is the principle of state sovereignty that defines external and internal, above and below, categories on the basis of which expatriates see their position as one of distance and superiority. The spatiality of UNHCR expatriate staff is anchored in the national order: the state field is the stage, while they see themselves as working behind the scenes. The term 'expatriate' also relates to the idea of a country of origin from which the person has departed: as Hindman notes (2007: 157), expatriates move around the world as an embodiment of their country of origin.

Nationality influences the modes and criteria for recruitment to the UNHCR. A certain number of posts are directly funded by donor states, with the aim of promoting access to UN institutions for their nationals, potentially circumventing the nationality quotas. In the recruitment programme for Junior Professional Officers, for example, candidates are selected by national committees. Having a large number of nationals among permanent UN staff is a source of prestige for the country and may offer the possibility of exerting some influence on these institutions. From this point of view, the tension between reason of state and refugee reason lessens. The refugee cause is no longer a moral cause defined in opposition to states, but rather an international field of expertise within which states conduct a struggle for influence. It also becomes clear how interstate strategies and power relations shape the composition of UNHCR staff. For example, there are more nationals of Western countries, especially in the most senior positions. Citizens of the United States, the organisation's principal funder, are particularly well represented, and it is customary for one of the two Deputy High Commissioners to be a US national.

Moreover, in order to have a career with the UN, one needs cultural and linguistic skills and aptitudes that are essentially a matter of inherited social and cultural capital – what Anne-Catherine Wagner, in her studies of social classes under globalisation, calls 'international capital' (Wagner 2007). Citizens of rich countries, or those with the most internationally prestigious education pathways, have the advantage. Conversely, it is often only the members of elites in the less wealthy countries who have the opportunity to develop these skills. Kanta and Clara, for example, the two colleagues mentioned above, each had three native languages and studied at prestigious universities, in the United Kingdom and the United States respectively. The hierarchies that are apparent on the national scale thus influence access to UN jobs and contribute to erecting the barrier that makes the interstate sphere inaccessible and opaque to all those without the aptitudes required to access it.[6]

It is worth noting too that within the UNHCR, nationality is the main criterion of classification of employees. When I arrived in Geneva, I was immediately introduced to several Italians. Before I arrived in Kabul, I was told I would be working with 'a very strong Danish woman'. The first evening, someone offered to put me in touch with a 'very nice Italian colleague' to help me acclimatise. Nationality is also a factor in internal groupings and socialisation, offering the pleasure of speaking one's mother tongue and coming back to shared points of reference that would otherwise be passed over, such as places, food or national politics. National stereotypes are often the source of jokes – for example, about the 'Italian mafia' in the Afghan Operation.

Finally, the mobility of UNHCR expatriates fully respects state sovereignty. While state authorities that wish to obstruct an international organisation's activities sometimes impose restrictions, UN officials are usually able to move smoothly between states, which recognise their right to travel and facilitate their passage across international borders. When I lost my passport during a week's leave in Spain, I went anxiously to the Italian consulate. Initially it seemed that it would be impossible to get a new one in less than a week. When the person I was talking to understood that I worked for the UN and my flight for Kabul was leaving in three days, his attitude changed completely and I had a new passport two days later.

In return, UN officials' mobility conforms rigorously with interstate regulations. UN institutions provide their staff with an additional travel and identity document that supplements the national passport: the UN Laissez-Passer. For senior staff, this is a genuine permit that confers diplomatic immunity and privileges. When they show their documents at borders, when they queue at airports – in short, when they submit to the discipline of interstate regulation of movement – international officials reassert the national order. Although their lives are marked by expatriation, they rely on a territorial and national conception of identity and politics, in which mobility and the lack of a strong link with one's country of nationality are perceived as 'abnormal', an exception. Thus, the backdrop to the mobility of expatriates and that of refugees is the same. We can therefore consider refugees' and UNHCR expatriates' mobility as opposite mobilities within the national order – the *problematic* mobility of refugees, and the *exceptional* mobility of expatriates that is necessary to the normalisation of refugees' situation. In both cases, the norm is a sedentary national order.

The Cloistered World of Expatriates in Kabul

Having considered the cosmopolitan life led by the UNHCR's expatriate staff, I now turn to the space-time of a mission in Kabul. In the Afghan capital, as in most other postings in Afghanistan, UN expatriates lived in a situation of acute segregation, removed from the local context. Although the particularly strict security regulations made Afghanistan an extreme case, their mode of presence was similar to that of humanitarian workers in other cities or countries: Banda Aceh (Smirl 2008), La Paz (Eyben 2011), Kathmandu (Harper 2011; Hindman 2007), Dhaka and Ho Chi Minh City (Rajak and Stirrat 2011), northern Kenya (Hyndman 2000), postings in Sudan (Duffield 2010), Burundi (Redfield 2012) and other African countries (Pouligny 2004). Examining the spaces frequented by expatriates, the social life that took place there and the professional culture of the work in Afghanistan reveals the extent to which the UNHCR and the institutional world of international aid shape their expatriates' way of life and view of the world.

UNHCR expatriates' smooth movement through the world contrasted with the confinement to which they were subject in Afghanistan. Their travels were channelled and minutely regulated by the organisation, which also managed the organisation of the spaces where they lived and worked down to the last detail. The organisation took care of all aspects of their life in Kabul and was by their side day and night. It thus represents a total institution, exerting a disciplinary power over its employees who must demonstrate their 'willingness to obey' (Weber 1968: 338; Foucault 1995) so that the organisation can protect them against kidnapping and attack. Like the disciplinary power analysed by Foucault (1995), the security rules and detailed monitoring of all daily activity created a relationship of docility-utility between employees and institution that provided it with a labour force in the country. While expatriates might find this confinement burdensome, they experienced it as one of the ordeals of the field, or as the price to be paid for working in a war-torn country.

The channelling of UNHCR expatriates' mobility began even before they arrived in the country. Since Afghan airlines were not considered sufficiently secure by UN standards, the last part of the journey was made on UN planes, leaving from Terminal 2 at Dubai Airport. In the departure lounge, you began to recognise a few faces and see some blue laissez-passer. After flying over the Persian Gulf, the plane continued over the Iranian desert and a good part of Afghanistan. The desert changed to mountains. Little cultivated rectangles could be seen in the valleys, following winding grey rivers. Before descending into Kabul, the plane almost grazed the Hindu Kush. For most passengers, these were the only moments when they could see the country with their own eyes. In the plane I often tried to overlay the landscape unfolding beneath me on the maps of the country that I already knew by heart. But seen from above, international and administrative borders disappear in the physical continuity of the terrain. I therefore found myself systematically disoriented.

Within the country, the life of UN expatriates was regulated by security measures centralised at the UN level, and implemented in the UNHCR by the Security and Administration departments, sometimes with the assistance of local private companies. The rules tightened between 2007 and 2008, with the rise in the number of suicide attacks, including in central Kabul. Breaking the rules was subject to heavy sanctions, which could go as far as dismissal. These security measures governed expatriates' relationship with the country: they constituted a substantial barrier, with staff living shut away in 'bunkerised' spaces,[7] limiting their interactions with the surrounding context to a minimum.

The centre of Kabul was radically altered by the arrival en masse of military personnel and staff from embassies, international organisations and NGOs between the end of 2001 and 2002. These institutions enlarged, re-established or established their offices and rented housing for their staff, creating a sort of enclave in the city centre to which access was controlled and regulated by a series of checkpoints. Within this perimeter, officers travelled from one office to another in UN or diplomatic vehicles. Many expatriates lived in the Wazir Akbar Khan district, between the airport and the city centre, in marble-floored villas endowed with *bukhari*[8] and gardens, which belonged to the Kabul middle class during the 1960s and 1970s and were now rented out for thousands of dollars.

Any house occupied by expatriate staff had to meet the UN security criteria. These included the height of enclosing walls, the presence of barbed wire, anti-blast window film, bars on the windows and an underground bunker. All houses had a watchman, who lived in a small lodge within the compound, and at least one armed guard stationed outside, near the entrance. As the place where staff spent most of their time when they were not at work, houses were designed as self-sufficient spaces. They were provided with cable TV (often connected to the BBC or Al Jazeera), computers, books and DVDs; in one of the compounds, a gym had been installed in the basement. Expatriates often employed a chef who took care of the shopping and the evening meal. The office was also fortified: it had only one entrance monitored by armed guards. In order to enter the office compound, you had to go through a barrier and wait for the guard to open the gate. You then entered an antechamber surrounded by blast walls where guards checked underneath the vehicle for hidden explosives, using a mirror. There was a special entrance for pedestrians, who had to pass through an X-ray scanner. It was rare for people to go out on nonwork-related trips: lunch was usually taken at the office, prepared by the housekeeping staff or delivered.

Since they were not allowed to walk in the city, expatriates always travelled by car, in UNHCR 4x4s, in permanent radio contact with base. At the same time each morning, a shuttle circulated around the compounds to bring staff to work. The journey took five to ten minutes, depending on the traffic. You passed the NGO emergency hospital and the DHL office, and in front of the Iranian embassy. The journey was always the same, every day, summer and winter – and I therefore felt euphoric each time a meeting or a field mission enabled me to glimpse other streets in the city, albeit still through the windows of the 4x4. In the evening, the same shuttle took staff back to the residences. After 7 pm armoured vehicles were used. The curfew was 11 pm, which was also the time for a radio check-in.

UN expatriate staff were not authorised to enter any establishment that did not meet UN security criteria, severely restricting the public places they went to. Sometimes at the weekend, collective expeditions were organised to shop at the large stores designed for expatriates, which sold a vast range of imported products, from cornflakes to gorgonzola. Otherwise the public places that UN expatriates went to outside of work were limited to a dozen or so restaurants. Since 2002, following the influx of hundreds of expatriates, several restaurants serving an international clientele had opened in Kabul. The Security section regularly visited them to check security standards. Thus, after work, you could choose between a plate of assorted French cheeses served at l'Atmosphère (which had a swimming pool and Wi-Fi), a pizza at Vila Velebita (opened by a Croatian who cooked Italian food), an enchilada at La Cantina, the Mexican restaurant, gazpacho at Gandamak and so on. None of the restaurants that were accessible to expatriates was Afghan.

Set up and run by expatriates, with exorbitant prices in a country where you could eat for two dollars, these restaurants catered specifically to expatriates. Access to some of them was explicitly forbidden to any person of Afghan nationality. Consumption of alcohol also marked them out in a country where the law forbade serving it to Afghans, and gave rise to disputes between the restaurants and the Afghan government. The condition 'Foreign passport only' was displayed at the entrance to l'Atmosphère. At one point, the UNHCR Representative had organised a relaxed work dinner with donor representatives. Mahmoud was one of those invited, but as he had come in *shalwar kameez* and with his long beard, he was asked for his documents. As an Afghan, he was not allowed to enter, despite Saverio's insistence to the restaurant owner. After a few shocked remarks, the evening continued as if nothing had happened.

At the weekend, the other favoured destination for UNHCR staff was the Hotel Serena. Located right in the city centre, the capital's luxury hotel had a modern gym, a restaurant and a bakery serving renowned cakes. In summer the main attraction was the open-air swimming pool. A few hours spent at the Serena were an opportunity to break out of confinement, to relax and to release stress. The mismatch between the spaces frequented by expatriates and the surrounding reality was particularly striking from the Serena swimming pool. Located right at the heart of Kabul, it was separated from the noisy, teeming capital by a single wall. The pool was enveloped by the noise of traffic and the smell of the city. Women in swimsuits sipped their cocktails while on the other side, women in *chadari*[9] did their shopping.

Relations with the Afghan population were extremely limited, being restricted to interactions with Afghans who provided services (drivers, housekeeping staff and restaurant employees) and a few traders (carpet sellers and grocers in the Wazir Akbar Khan district), for whom expatriates constituted a particularly profitable clientele. But socialisation remained very limited, even with Afghan colleagues. The possibilities of meeting outside of work hours were restricted by the security measures. At the office, relationships were largely structured by professional hierarchies and hampered by the language barrier. Within the office compound, there were spaces used exclusively by Afghans, like the mosque and the cafeteria. As Peter Redfield (2012) notes in relation to MSF expatriates in Burundi, they are 'materially heavy and socially light': they have substantial financial resources (what they earn and what they spend there), but develop only very weak links there.

Linked to one another by 4x4 journeys, all the spaces in which expatriates lived and travelled were protected enclaves. As expatriates themselves remarked from time to time, it was as if they lived permanently in a bubble, a closed vessel without access to local life. Distances were paradoxically redefined: the Sri Lankan coast, with its tropical climate, and even New York – despite the long hours of travel, there was only one stop – were easier to get to than an Afghan colleague's house. Expatriates were conscious of this gulf between them and the Afghan context. Their way of life in Kabul also sometimes made them ill at ease. But at the same time, they believed they deserved the escape offered by the restaurants and luxury hotels. The sacrifices of the job and the pace of work justified the need to relax, to have a social life, even if it did not fully respect local customs or led them to show off their privileged situation.

Social Life in a Closed Circle

The segregation of the spaces frequented by UNHCR expatriates went hand in hand with an intense social life. As they shared the same residences and these were located close to one another, they spent most evenings and weekends together. When colleagues passed through on mission, large dinners were organised to welcome them. These occasions, as noted above, consolidated the esprit de corps and made the field a place of intense sociality. But social life extended beyond bonds between UNHCR colleagues.

In the mid-2000s, the expatriate community in Kabul numbered several thousand, including staff from the UN, NGOs, embassies, private companies, journalists and intelligence agents. There were always opportunities to party, hook up and flirt over drinks and music: in addition to the restaurants, which were always very busy, there were salsa nights on Wednesdays in a large UN complex, and the embassies regularly sent out invitations to events you could slip into with the help of a colleague of the right nationality. There were also the goodbye parties for friends leaving the country, and colleagues from the Red Cross often organised all-night parties in the basement spaces of their residences. An electronic newsletter, to which everyone was automatically signed up on arrival, announced the forthcoming events and published photos of past parties.

Spatial concentration made the expatriates in Kabul a tight social group: after a few months, you began to know everybody; when you ate at a restaurant, you observed others and knew that you were being observed; rumours spread rapidly. The boundary between private and professional life became blurred. Institutional relations were often bound up in highly personalised relationships. My colleagues and I spent a lot of time with the representatives of the European Commission Humanitarian Aid Office (ECHO), including playing sports together in the garden of the UNHCR offices. Susanne from ECHO and Mitch from the Bureau of Population, Refugees and Migration (BPRM) had become very close to colleagues with whom I was sharing a house. Because of this, I often had dinner with the partners I was mostly working with, and I was regularly invited to gatherings they organised. In this way, you might spend an evening together and see one another again the next morning at a meeting. This proximity greatly facilitated professional relationships: a simple phone call could resolve administrative conundrums – for example, we could decide together how to arrange matters to satisfy both our respective headquarters.

At moments when the support of donors was particularly important, or when Saverio wanted to explain to them what was going on behind the scenes in negotiations with the Iranian and Pakistani authorities, or to find out informally how much money could be released for emergencies, he would ask me to summon the 'club'[10] to a restaurant or organise a dinner at his apartment. These dinners allowed them to talk in a relaxed atmosphere. Questions linked to programmes and funding were interspersed with personal exchanges. These situations consolidated bonds within the club, for each person felt less subject to the oversight of their own institution.

In addition to their shared involvement in the field in Kabul, the bonds between the members of the 'club' were also strengthened by the fact that they had long belonged to the same professional networks. Eric and Éloïse, from the European Commission, had known one another for a long time, having worked at the Commission together. Saverio and Susanne, from ECHO, had never met before they got to know one another in Kabul, but had undertaken missions in Congo at roughly the same time, and had thereby developed similar knowledge and experience. At one dinner at Saverio's apartment, a batik hanging on the wall, which Susanne immediately recognised as Congolese, sparked a lively conversation about furniture and decorative items brought back from missions. The BPRM representative impressed everybody when he told us he had decorated each room of his Washington DC home in the style of a different Asian or African country.

The meetings of the Kabul 'club' closely resemble those of the 'upper spheres' of the institutional world of aid (the directors of the major UN agencies and embassy staff) described by Rosalind Eyben (2011). Eyben argues that this sociability has an important function in reproducing and consolidating the now globalised institutional culture of the world of international aid, of which the community in La Paz that she analyses constitutes a local cell. Through this intense social life, policies deemed appropriate are reproduced, and social life bulwarks this culture against the contradictions and disruptive elements that might be introduced by the local context (see also Harper 2011). A similar analysis can be applied to the way in which sociability functions in the closed community of expatriates in Kabul to create and reproduce a shared vision of the international intervention in Afghanistan.

A Depoliticised Understanding of the Afghan Context

At the start of my mission, I was always woken by the *muezzin* at the Wazir Akbar Khan mosque, and I was curious to know what he was saying in his impassioned sermons. I said to myself: when I've learned Dari, I will understand. Similarly, I would jump any time I heard the rumble of a plane – military exercises, a visiting head of state, Karzai leaving his palace? I said to myself: once I have got to know more about the political life of Kabul, I will understand. I had also brought with me several books to help me gain a better understanding of the country in which I was to live. But all my attempts to acquire a broader perspective came to nothing: overtaken by deadlines to meet and the need for rest, I had to resign myself to the impossibility of learning more about anything that did not relate directly to my professional tasks, which demanded all my concentration and energy. After some time, my failure to understand the surrounding context became ordinary and my forced estrangement normal.

Expatriates move in a social and cognitive world that is unreceptive or even impermeable to the local context. Interactions with it are structured and codified exclusively by work. Work provides ready-to-use frames of understanding that help aid professionals to stabilise their perspective, give a coherent meaning to their mission in Afghanistan and endow each officer with a specific place in the enterprise – perceived as urgent, huge and important – of reconstruction in Afghanistan. The intense sociality among expatriates helps to protect and reproduce this shared interventionist professional culture. For UNHCR expatriates, two interlocking institutional layers frame the perception of time and of the Afghan context: the UNHCR Operation, and the UN reconstruction project in Afghanistan.

For any UNHCR expatriate, the dominant world of reference is the organisation's mission in the country, of which they are a part. Grasping its multiple dimensions (programmes, internal organisation, partners, etc.) is essential and takes time. Thus, everything that happens outside the organisation often remains beyond their purview. The temporal frame is dictated partly by administrative timescales and the short timeframes of projects, which are funded on an annual basis, and partly by the rhythm of staff rotation. A mission in Afghanistan is generally considered an unattractive posting, for which its benefits (potential interest of the work, higher salary, frequent leave, potential positive repercussions for one's career) nevertheless compensate. At the beginning, you have to familiarise yourself quickly with your role. Subsequently, expatriates are often completely absorbed by the relentless pace of work, which they must strive to complete as well as possible, since their manager's evaluation is a determining factor in future promotions. Time, patterned by meetings and deadlines, passes in constant tension and with the challenges of being efficient and holding course day after day. As the end of the mission nears, departure must be prepared in advance.

The second frame of reference is that of the reconstruction project launched by the UN in late 2001. In order to contextualise our presence in the country, we would refer to the 'legal framework', citing the Afghanistan Compact – the international agreement that renewed the Bonn Agreement – and the Afghan National Development Strategy, the national development plan put together by donors, international organisations and the Afghan government. In this larger context, the domain and responsibilities of the UNHCR are restricted to the displaced persons' sector. The speed with which information and new reports circulate, the multiplicity of sectors into which international activity is divided, the number of bodies involved, the innumerable abbreviations and acronyms create an impenetrable bureaucratic forest, making it impossible to gain an overview of the project's institutional apparatus, its evolution and its effects. This is even more true of trends and developments on the military-political level, on which less information is available. The density of this institutional world also adds weight to the impression of being part of a huge, legitimate world, engaged in an urgent and important work, and the feeling of participating in a crucial moment in the history of Afghanistan, in which the future of the country is being played out (see Chapter 9).

There are at least two myths that are maintained at the heart of these two institutional worlds and underpin the professional culture of expatriates in Afghanistan. Both are solidly anchored in the paradigm of modernisation. The first myth is the need for international intervention in a backward Afghanistan. Work documents and the discourse of expatriates reveal a mechanism of dehistoricisation and exoticisation of Afghanistan, made possible by expatriates' lack of knowledge of the sociopolitical reality and of the country's history.[11] Afghanistan is abstracted from contemporaneity and relegated to a past conceived along the lines of the history of Western countries. In a process similar to those described in the case of the 'South' (Comaroff and Comaroff 2012), the 'Orient' (Saïd 2003 [1978]) and 'Africa' (Ferguson 2006), Afghanistan is read through the prism of the West and seen as a country that needs to be transformed in order to catch up, to overcome its shortcomings. The year 2001 is therefore considered a sort of Year Zero, inaugurating Afghanistan into the modernity of which expatriates are the messengers and benevolent agents.

Thus, expatriates would say that Afghanistan had 'remained in the Middle Ages', that here things did not 'yet' work as they should: the country had not 'yet' experienced industrialisation, the sexual revolution, etc. This attitude could take a negative tone: Afghanistan is a country that exhausts expatriates, dominated by corruption, where male-female relations are extremely unequal. Conversely, it could take the positive form of fascination for a different world, primitive and unindustrialised, where the beauty and power of nature were intact, where both the sense of hospitality and tribal solidarities were very strong, and it was possible to relive the age of explorers and adventurers. Even danger could be idealised in this way: war is something that no longer happens in 'civilised' countries.

The second myth is that intervention works. Senior managers always emphasised progress and results achieved, and the importance of the UNHCR and the UN's activity in the country. In 2007 the Kabul Branch Office became an important regional coordinating centre, and the Afghan mission was revitalised. This was completely out of step with the development of the conflict, in which the power of the Taliban was rising, there was growing distrust of international organisations and reduced access to the field. The work of the senior staff in Security, which is conducted in great secrecy, plays an important role in producing the illusion that 'everything is going well'. Both the statistics regularly emailed to all UN staff and the updates to security measures reinforced the idea that there was no need to worry, as the security issue was 'sorted' by other colleagues so that we could work. The process of staff rotation also stopped people from imagining that the international project might fail in the long term, making it difficult, for example, to gauge how much more restrictive the confinement conditions had become over the years.

As well as giving meaning to their presence in the country, these two myths helped to normalise the mismatch between expatriates' living conditions (with electricity, hot showers and water to keep a garden in bloom) and those of Afghans. The UNHCR's mandate and the reconstruction project provided an interpretative framework based on a differentiation of roles (the 'beneficiary' and the 'aid worker') that reified the unequal relationship, while at the same time rendering it acceptable and normal. Comparison with their own conditions was beside the point, because expatriates were there to help, liberate and ultimately improve the living conditions of Afghans. The energy they devoted to their work, the sacrifices they made and the risks they ran were the proof of their goodwill and their commitment to justice. Moreover, revealing themselves to be too affected or subject to feelings of guilt would not be appropriate: in order to do this job, you need to demonstrate cool-headedness and know how to manage your emotions. Thus, in the eyes of expatriates, Afghans, despite the fact they shared their same locality, lived relegated to another world characterised by a lack of modernity that expatriates were there to remedy.

Even so, from time to time, an event would shake up expatriates' depoliticised everyday life. For a few moments the myths teetered, the contradictions surfaced and the constructed normality wobbled. But the way in which these episodes were managed – as 'incidents' – exposes the mechanisms of depoliticisation that quickly re-established routine, rebuilt the walls of the bubble and resubstantiated the myths.

In winter, ice or snow could lead to the cancellation of flights, and there was nothing to be done: the chain of stopovers was broken and the hope of spending Christmas with the family crumbled all of a sudden. Electricity blackouts regularly threatened to erase 'urgent' emails, 'important' documents that you were in the middle of writing. The alarm that announced the start-up of the generator accompanied the anger and despair of those who had lost their documents. 'Welcome to Afghanistan,' would be the remark on these occasions: such inconveniences were ascribed to the backwardness of the country, which required staff to show patience and flexibility, or indeed a spirit of sacrifice. The generator and substitute flights were considered our due, because of our own priorities and those of the organisation. The fact that most Afghans could not legally leave their country or saw a few hours of electricity as a luxury did not even cross our minds.

Yet it was the episodes associated with the conflict that revealed most strikingly the fragility of the bubble within which we lived. It would happen when we least expected it. It is 7.30 am, I am writing up my field notes in the dining room, someone is making tea in the kitchen, someone else is taking a shower, and the others are preparing to board the next shuttle. A dry, deep explosion booms, very close by. It is followed by several moments of complete silence. Then the sound of sirens. Everything stops, the routine is broken.

We get together in the dining room. One of us is in radio contact with base at the office. We are told that there has been a car bomb in the district. The shuttle service is suspended. We are asked to stay in the residence and await further instructions. It is the first time that a suicide attack has taken place in the expatriate district.

James, who arrived a few days earlier, has a spike of adrenalin and paces up and down with the radio in his hand. Beatrice stays seated on the sofa, her cup of tea in her hands, staring into space. Mary has seized the moment, taking a photo of the cloud of smoke above the roofs.

Such episodes expose the contradictions underpinning the presence of UN expatriates in Afghanistan. That presence is embedded in power relations that go well beyond the efforts to coordinate and competition between international organisations that absorbed our attention in the everyday. These episodes reminded us that we were working in a situation of immanence, not exteriority, with regard to the Afghan context. Not only were we renting houses from people we described as 'commander' in UN reports, but above all we were also involved parties in the ongoing conflict. Aligned with NATO policy, we thereby expressed a specific opinion as to who might legitimately govern the country. When the Taliban targeted us, they were genuine *attacks* and not simply 'incidents', as colleagues from Security termed them. This violence laid bare the question of the legitimacy of our presence and the way in which we and the reconstruction project were perceived by the local population (Donini 2006). Furthermore, suicide attacks forced us to place ourselves on the same level as all those who shared this locality – in other words, the Afghans who were or could have been at the site of the attack. Such episodes also led us to radically review our sense of the supposed centrality of the reconstruction project.

After an hour, the Security division informs us that order has been restored and the shuttle service is resumed. Although they were sometimes experienced as irksome, observing the security rules structured our everyday routine. While they were the most obvious indicator of the paradoxes and contradictions of our position, the rules became reassuring points of reference and encouraged us not to question the legitimacy of our presence. And then, you could not allow yourself to be too disturbed, you had to measure up to the situation.

Thus, such episodes paradoxically helped to reinforce rather than challenge the myths outlined above. The belief in the need for segregation was reinforced, as was the idea of a dangerous and unpredictable outside that contrasted with the secure and predictable spaces in which we lived. The organisation came to seem like an institution that protected and ensured the safety of its staff and to which you could quietly yield. As such, these episodes were quickly absorbed and became part of the routine as 'incidents', on a par with everyday annoying events. Deadlines and diaries were the best allies for reimmersing yourself in the rhythm of work. As soon as we are told that order has been restored, I get on the first shuttle. At the office at last, I hurriedly switch on my computer to make up for lost time.

An Insular Interstate Cosmopolitanism

The standard representations of UNHCR expatriates often emphasise their privileges, their bravery and the power they exercise, while the weight of the UN bureaucracy of which they are part – what makes them bureaucrats, ultimately – is generally obscured. My aim here is, on the contrary, to understand the institutions (the UNHCR, the interstate system and the international aid system) that shape their mobile way of life and the modes of their presence in the field. I have noted that even though these institutions foster their high level of mobility, give them responsibilities and support their universalist claims to moral superiority, they also powerfully shape their practices and their view of the world.

The UNHCR as an organisation emerges as a powerful disciplinary device that provides a base, in terms of life paths, social belonging and prism of understanding of life. We saw how much the interstate system shapes the mobility of UNHCR expatriates and supports their claim to occupy a morally superior, encompassing sphere. We also realised the extent to which their relation to the contexts in which they intervene can be restricted and codified by a professional culture of international aid, underpinned by the paradigm of modernisation. While UNHCR expatriates undeniably belong to an economically and politically privileged group that moves easily around the world, as professionals they also have to demonstrate docility towards the institutions to which they have chosen to belong, accepting the resulting material constraints, and make the cognitive frameworks of these institutions their own.

Some researchers argue that international aid professionals cannot be considered cosmopolitan, owing to the ghettoised spaces in which they live and work as well as to their monoculturalism, closed to new epistemologies (Rajak and Stirrat 2011). Or they describe this cosmopolitanism as provincial (Eyben 2011) and contrast it with other social groups more open to other cultures (Harper 2011). My own view is that UNHCR expatriates can be called cosmopolitan. According to Ulf Hannerz's definition (2004), they embody a cosmopolitanism that is both cultural (if only because of the diversity of their geographical origins, the products they consume and the places they travel through) and political (to the extent that 'refugee reason' is anchored in UN cosmopolitanism). They also have the feeling of being at home anywhere in the world.

Nevertheless, this cosmopolitanism needs to be situated and qualified. Here I follow approaches that suggest there are multiple 'vernacular cosmopolitanisms', that is, many ways to be cosmopolitan, that can be reconstructed by studying practices, trajectories, belongings, views of the world and the potential political projects that underpin them (Hannerz 2004; Rajak and Stirrat 2011; Tsing 2000). From the Nepali health professionals described by Ian Harper (2011) to the rich Chinese families involved in the 'Pacific shuttle' described by Aihwa Ong (1999), from the North Africans in Southern Europe studied by Alain Tarrius (2002) to Janine Wedel's 'shadow elites' (2009), each of these groups is, in its own way, cosmopolitan.

Identifying the institutions that shape the cosmopolitanism of UNHCR expatriates suggests at least two ways in which it can be qualified. First, this is an 'interstate' cosmopolitanism. Despite the fact that it is characterised by opposition to the system of states and the national order, this cosmopolitanism is strongly anchored in that system. Second, it can be described as insular. This oxymoron articulates the institutional processes that give rise to frequent movement in many directions, but traced along imposed trajectories and temporalities, to time spent in many different countries, but inside a bubble, and to a professional culture of humanitarian intervention that claims to have universalist values, but remains self-referential and closed to other worldviews.

Notes

1. I use the term 'habitus' to designate a set of lasting dispositions, norms, categories and structures. Born of a specific apprenticeship associated with a group to which one belongs, they are internalised to the point where they become a component of personal identity and matrices through which individuals interpret the world and act in it (Bourdieu 1977).

2. In March 2008 alone, the Travel Section made seventy flight reservations to or from Kabul. Directors of Sub-Offices travelled to Kabul once every three months to meet with the Operation's senior staff, submit their reports and receive instructions; staff posted to Sub-Offices had to travel via the capital in order to enter and leave the country for training or holidays. Colleagues from Headquarters also came to Kabul on mission.

3. The difficulty of maintaining family life in the field is one of the reasons why, although the field is highly valued in the organisation, posts in Sub-Offices are often occupied by 'juniors' on short-term contracts who hope to join the organisation and do not yet have family ties.

4. For example, in his end-of-year message to staff in his office, one senior manager wrote: 'I thank ... each and every one of you personally for your tenacious work, your incredible commitment and dedication, which have enabled us to achieve so much over the course of this year.'

5. In the field, UN staff are integrated into the UN's security system rather than that of their embassy. In the event of an evacuation, these staff are evacuated by the UN, whereas other expatriates depend on their national systems.

6. This subject merits a study of its own, which might draw on Yves Dezalay's writings (2004) on the internationalisation of elites and the articulation between the national and international fields. In Delazay's work, the 'international' field is loosely defined as any space that extends beyond the national field, whereas in my work the 'international' (in the sense of 'interstate') field does not exhaust the range of fields that extend beyond the national field.

7. While in Kabul this segregation corresponded to a genuine danger of attack and kidnapping, Mark Duffield (2010) observes very similar living arrangements in countries where no such risk exists. He describes a phenomenon of 'bunkerisation' of aid actors that aligns with a distance from the field. According to Duffield, this phenomenon results in part from internal changes in the aid sector (central offices taking over, the development of communications technologies), and in part from changes brought about by globalisation (the spread of risk culture and ghettoisation of the privileged classes).

8. A wood-burning stove.

9. Or *burqa*, a garment that covers the woman from head to toe.

10. Set up by Saverio when he arrived in Kabul, the 'club' brought together the senior UNHCR staff and representatives of the main funders of the Afghan Operation.

11. The UN's welcoming Briefing Kit included a timeline that began in 1979, the year of the Soviet invasion, which was generally perceived as the moment when the 'problem' began. There were books that circulated, such as Barnett Rubin's study (1995), which the head of mission gave one new arrival, for example, and could also be consulted in the library at the residence. But in general they were not read.

CHAPTER 6

Afghan Staff, the Brokers of the Intervention

The village of Bot Khak, winter 2007. Salim is talking with the members of the *shura* in Dari, breaking off from time to time to inform me of the main points of the discussion. This relates to living conditions in the village, particularly housing and water supply, as the Kabul Sub-Office has to decide which are the most 'vulnerable' of the villages housing returnees and which will be funded in the following year. To avoid setting up expectations, Salim does not reveal that this is an 'need assessment', pretending he is simply looking for feedback on projects carried out this year. After the meeting, he insists on a tour of the village, in order to corroborate the information provided by the *shura*, who Salim suspects of resource tapping. His suit and shirt, his uncovered head and his well-trimmed, relatively short beard contrast with the *shalwar kameez*, blankets and long beards of those he is speaking with. Although he is holding them discreetly, he is the only one with a notebook and pen. On return to the office, he will write up his report in the Sub-Office's bureaucratic language of indicators.

The functioning of the UNHCR is based on the articulation of two distinct groups of staff: expatriates (or 'international staff") and staff recruited locally ('national staff'). The former are recruited centrally, from among all nationalities, and circulate from one posting to another. The latter are recruited in the country where the UNHCR is intervening, remain there, and are associated with the organisation only for the duration of its presence there.[1] The respective distribution of the two groups within the organisation is complementary. In 2007 over 30% of 'international' officers were concentrated in Geneva, and of the thirty expatriates in the Afghan Operation, nineteen worked at the Branch Office. Away from Headquarters 'national' staff are substantially in the majority: 80% of the organisation's employees were local, spread across the various missions. In Afghanistan about 90% of the staff were 'nationals'. Half of the Afghan staff were drivers, cleaners and other service personnel. The other half were 'professionals' who supported the expatriate staff in managing programmes.[2]

These simple figures give an idea of how important 'national' staff are in rooting the UNHCR in the locations where the organisation intervenes. Yet little attention is devoted in the literature to staff recruited locally by aid organisations. The few studies on this subject (Ong and Combinido 2018; Redfield 2012; Roth 2012; Shevchenko and Fox 2008) focus mainly on the inequality between expatriate and local staff, and the way in which this inequality plays out and is managed and indeed reproduced within humanitarian organisations. This division is very evident in the UNHCR and for me, as I note below, constituted a significant methodological barrier. But while it is important to analyse this division, in order to study the UNHCR's action in Afghanistan, it is equally important to consider the role of Afghan staff in the concrete implementation of programmes and the social transformations that go alongside them.

Development anthropology offers useful tools in this respect. Norman Long and the authors who follow the line of his work (Arce and Long 1993; Bierschenk et al. 2000; Lewis and Mosse 2006; Long 1989) have drawn attention to the interface between local populations and aid institutions, as a key terrain for studying the social processes and power relations that are an integral part of aid projects. Taking an interactionist perspective, they analyse the various meanings given to interactions depending on the position of the actors, the way in which meanings and identities are produced and negotiated in interactions, the strategies of actors and the role of intermediaries. Attention is focused primarily on 'local development brokers', actors established in a local arena who represent the local population in interactions with external funding structures. Researchers have emphasised the strategies deployed by these brokers to capture and redistribute external resources, which often go hand in hand with strategies for social and political self-promotion (Bierschenk et al. 2000; Blundo 1995). The role of *malek*s (notables) in the camps in Pakistan in the 1990s (Centlivres and Centlivres-Dumont 1999: 951; Edwards 1986: 319–20), and the constitution of the *shura*s in Afghanistan (Centlivres and Centlivres-Dumont 1999) are examples of this configuration.

In this chapter I will show how, by virtue of their position at the interface between Afghan society and an international organisation, the UNHCR's Afghan staff too were caught up in an equally crucial role of brokerage. Although within the organisation it is seen as no more than a simple job of linguistic translation and relaying international norms, this brokering role is much more complex. It performs an essential function for the organisation, preserving the consistency of its programmes in a country in which its rationale is little understood, challenged and indeed contested by part of the population. I will first consider the relationship between Afghan and expatriate staff in the Kabul office, and will then situate the Afghan employees in Afghan society and show that their engagement with the UNHCR formed part of strategies for survival and sociopolitical promotion in an uncertain context. I will then turn to the function of mediation at the heart of their work in order to see what it consisted of, what tensions were inherent within it and what functions it performed for the UNHCR's action in the country.

The Gulf between Expatriate and Afghan Staff

The articulation between two categories of staff with a complementary relationship to the contexts of intervention is fundamental to the operation of the UNHCR's apparatus. It enables the organisation to intervene in many geographically, culturally, linguistically and politically distinct contexts while retaining an overall level of consistency. The 'international' staff form the pivot of the organisation, as bearers of its institutional culture, its purportedly universal frames of reference and norms – the hard kernel that holds the fragmented mechanism together and guarantees its unity. The 'national' staff enable the organisation to adapt to heterogeneous contexts, to anchor itself locally and to carry out its activities in these diverse contexts.

The Afghan agents, bulwarks of the UNHCR in Afghanistan, anchored the organisation in the country, guaranteed its institutional continuity there and became the brokers of its activity. With the language barrier and the travel restrictions to which expatriates were subject, their role expanded during the 2000s. Everyday follow-up of programmes was thus in fact conducted mainly by Afghan officers. Depending on their role, they interacted directly with the organisation's Afghan interlocutors in the country: local political leaders, administrative authorities, media, local NGOs and so on. For their expatriate colleagues, they were essential intermediaries to the accomplishment of their mission.

Yet despite the complementarity of their roles, there was a clear hierarchy between the two categories of staff. Managerial posts were occupied only by expatriates, whose salaries were also far higher. Discussion of the most important decisions and debates on the most sensitive questions were always conducted exclusively among expatriates. The opinion of Afghan officers might be more or less highly valued, depending on the degree of trust they had established with their closest expatriate colleagues, but they were still hierarchically subordinate. Whatever their age or their length of service, every two years they had to account to a new expatriate. Unlike the 'international' staff, they were not deemed to be posted to a 'hard duty station', with all the ensuing benefits in terms of enhanced salary, housing provision, etc. The procedures for evacuation in situations of extreme danger applied only to the expatriate staff.

The 'international' staff's superiority also played out on the cognitive level. Expatriates were the holders of the expert knowledge that is most highly valued in the organisation (see also Roth 2012; Shevchenko and Fox 2008), on the refugee paradigm, the functioning and institutional culture of the organisation, international refugee law and funders' priorities. Knowledge of the local context and proximity to the field – the expertise that 'national' staff were acknowledged to have – was of course important and gave them some authority, but it was less highly valued. This knowledge was supposed to enable the 'national' staff to apply and relay the organisation's policies, not to question their relevance or appropriateness to the local context. Expatriates and 'nationals' often emphasised the benefits in terms of 'learning' that Afghan employees gained through this UN employment. Expatriate employees often felt they had an 'educator' role in relation to their Afghan subordinates, for whom numerous workshops were also organised. For the organisation, the aim of these sessions was primarily to train its local staff, but also to reduce inequality between the two categories by giving temporary staff a skill set that would help them in their future careers.

This hierarchy is fully accepted by the organisation and its expatriate staff. Within the UNHCR, as in many other aid organisations, this difference in treatment derives from the high value placed on expatriates' distance from the context where they intervene. 'International' staff can thus claim to guarantee the organisation's objectivity and 'neutrality': since they come from outside and stay for a limited time, they are deemed to be above local power relations and to have no personal interests in the local context.[3] From this point of view, the allegiance and neutrality of staff recruited locally, who are caught up in local power relations, is always in doubt. In the Branch Office, expatriates often expressed a degree of distrust towards their Afghan colleagues – they worried about potential diversion of resources, following criteria that did not conform to those of the organisation. There were rumours in the office that several Afghan colleagues had been dismissed for misappropriation of funds.

In the Kabul office in 2008, this hierarchy and these disparities were materialised in a dense social barrier between expatriate and Afghan staff. This division was the strongest marker of alterity within the office, and obstructed socialisation between the two categories of staff. The spatial separation described in Chapter 5 was reinforced by administrative arrangements that limited the opportunity for interaction still further. The hierarchy of posts meant that it was rare for an expatriate and an Afghan to share an office. There were two Human Resources departments and two separate email distribution lists. The measures Saverio took to reduce this barrier – increasing the number of meetings of all staff and encouraging expatriates to use the cafeteria – did little to change the situation.

Among expatriates, one of the consequences of this social barrier was a fixed perception of their Afghan colleagues en masse as 'prototypical Afghans'. This image, which was consistent with the role assigned them in the organisation, was reinforced by expatriates' segregated accommodation and the language barrier, as 'national' colleagues were often the only Afghans with whom expatriates had the opportunity to talk. Thus, Afghan colleagues were considered the experts on Afghanistan and its history and culture, and became the spokespeople for a world that remained largely unknown to expatriates. At the beginning of my mission, I often asked my Afghan colleagues' advice on whether foreign women should cover their heads: did they recommend I should? In which situations? Over time, I realised that assigning them this role, while at the same time failing to understand their social position in Afghan society and the effects of the barrier between expatriate and Afghan colleagues, could lead to deceptive simplifications. Was the driver who invited me to leave my head uncovered not in fact giving me a message about his own beliefs? Viewing the veil as unimportant is a marker of belonging to an educated and 'progressive' urban social class. It is also a way of presenting the country to foreigners as on the path towards 'civilisation', stating a view consistent with the expectations of expatriates. And how could my Afghan colleague tell me he was in favour of the headscarf in the field when a woman who ranked above him, who was present in the room, did not wear one?

For their part, Afghan colleagues readily lent themselves to playing the 'authentic Afghan' and the 'well-versed local'. Such assigned roles were often accepted and even claimed, sometimes going as far as identifying with the entire Afghan population, for whom they made themselves spokespeople. For example, at farewell ceremonies for expatriate staff, the 'national' staff often spoke in the name of the 'Afghan people' to thank the departing member of staff for helping the country. Adopting this role can be seen as a way of establishing one's authority in accordance with institutional criteria: since expert knowledge of the context of intervention is precisely what justifies the importance of 'national' staff, playing this role was a way of defending their autonomy and their scope for action within the organisation. This analysis aligns with that of Peters (2016) in her study of local staff in Angola: conforming to the expectations of the institution is a way of retaining a job that has many advantages.

The bureaucratic divide between 'international' and 'national' adds to broader sociopolitical differences that go beyond the organisation. These inequalities become meaningful on the global political stage, a stage that the organisation itself materialises through its UN cosmopolitics, and by bringing together individuals from contexts far removed from one another. Thus, expatriates embodied a privileged 'global' elite (first-class citizens of the world), while their Afghan colleagues became the representatives of a subaltern population (second-class citizens of the world). This polarisation deepens the gulf, making it still more unbridgeable.

Two forms of inequality frequently emerged in exchanges with colleagues and in office life. The first was the experience of violence. Speaking with an Afghan colleague about their life, you would immediately realise that they had direct experience of war (violence personally experienced, the loss of close family members, etc.). It was often through colleagues' stories that I was able to get a more concrete picture of the phases of the conflict, which I had only read about in books. Of course, a number of expatriates had also experienced violence in the contexts where they had intervened, but in their case they experienced it in the context of their work, as the consequence of a professional choice. The other inequality was the extremely limited legal pathways for Afghan employees to emigrate, whereas international mobility is second nature to expatriates. This inequality was recurrently manifested even in work: organising foreign missions for Afghan staff was often extremely complicated. Despite their status as UN employees, as Afghan citizens their mobility was strictly contained: travel to the countries concerned was authorised only for the event they were to attend and sometimes they were not even allowed to leave stopover airports.[4]

These inequalities affected relations between colleagues and often made it impossible to establish links beyond the context of work. For expatriates, the awareness of belonging to a privileged class reinforced their determination to train colleagues, to help them through administrative procedures and even to sponsor them financially, creating paternalistic relationships. This awareness could also generate a feeling of discomfort that paralysed the relationship. Among Afghan employees, I noted a tendency to see expatriates as representative of 'foreigners' – 'foreigners' to be made aware of the subaltern condition of Afghanistan and its people, or to be 'exhibited' as prestigious guests at weddings.

I got a measure of the depth of the gulf between expatriates and 'nationals' when a car bomb hit the expatriate district. When I arrived at the office profoundly shaken and thoughtful, I realised that it was very difficult to talk openly about this event with my closest Afghan colleague. Indeed, he seemed almost embarrassed by my state: what was I worried about? I could leave whenever I wanted. And in case of a major security issue, the UN would evacuate me. I also realised that for someone with personal experience of the civil war, who was regularly threatened by the Taliban and had already had his house looted twice, it was incomprehensible that I should be so upset by simply hearing an explosion.

The division between Afghan and expatriate staff, and the play of preconceptions that arose with it, had powerful methodological repercussions for my fieldwork and the first stages of my analysis. Any interaction with Afghan employees was strongly influenced by our respective status. My status as an 'international' employee led me to develop a victimising perspective on Afghan colleagues, reinforced by the inequalities of which I was strongly aware and that I found unsettling, and also by the way in which my colleagues themselves presented themselves to me. In these conditions it was difficult to ask myself (before asking *them*) how working for the UNHCR changed their subjectivities and their view of the world, for example.[5]

In addition to providing information on social relations within a UNHCR office in the field, recognising this deep division and the way in which it shapes relations between employees shows how the diffuse bureaucracy of the UNHCR, which stretches over social realities far removed from one another, is shaped from the inside by inequalities that operate worldwide. But analysis needs to go beyond these observations. Seeing Afghan employees purely through the lens of their relation with their expatriate colleagues fixes them in a power relationship and fails to take account either of their relation to the organisation or of the important role they play in the implementation of programmes. In the remainder of this chapter, I will focus on another interface – that between foreign aid workers and Afghan society, and the way in which the UNHCR's Afghan staff operate in this context.

Which 'Locals'?

The UNHCR's Afghan staff comprised individuals of diverse geographical origin, ethnicity and political orientation. Some of them were or came from families that had been close to the communist regime and had spent time in Russia; others were or came from families close to the Mujahideen and grew up in Pakistan. What characterised the UNHCR Afghan staff in Kabul in the 2000s (and also linked them to some other Afghans employed as 'national' staff by international organisations) was that they belonged to an educated urban elite, in contact with foreigners, in a country where education is not widespread and the rural world remains very remote from international organisations, and indeed distrusts them. In the scene I described at the start of this chapter, Salim wears the symbols of urban technocratic power (his clothing, his hairstyle and his ballpoint pen), contrasting with the council of a rural village. The social class to which the UNHCR's Afghan staff belonged was an intermediate elite. While they were clearly distinguished from the recipients of UNHCR programmes, they were also separate from the high political and economic elite, which consisted of men of power who occupied key positions in the state administration, and of those who controlled drug trafficking.

Within the UNHCR, Afghan employees were assigned and adopt the status of 'local', in recognition of their supposed familiarity with the context of intervention and their proximity to the 'field'. Yet most of them were not 'local' in the literal sense of the term. Paradoxically, very often the immediate reason for their presence in the field was precisely their employment with the UNHCR. Most of them had not always lived in Afghanistan, the conflict having led them to leave the country for shorter or longer periods. Some of them did not come from Kabul, but moved there when they were appointed; others lived in the Central Region and returned to their families at weekends. Furthermore, many of them retained an outward focus: their families were often transnational and working for the UNHCR was, as I will note below, generally considered a springboard that would enable them and subsequent generations to leave Afghanistan.

Salim came from Kabul and studied civil engineering there. During the communist period, he worked for the government; the Taliban then removed him from his post, and he found employment with an NGO. But the Taliban continued to harass him, particularly because the NGO was grounded in a Christian ideology. Fearing arrest, he left for Pakistan, where he lived for years working for other NGOs. After 2001, he returned to Afghanistan, attracted partly by the opportunities offered by construction companies and UN agencies. After a year with Action Against Hunger, in 2003 he was recruited by the UNHCR as Field Officer. Soraya was a young Pashtun woman from an important family in eastern Afghanistan. She came from a younger generation, but her career path had been similar. She grew up between Kabul and Jalalabad, and then left Afghanistan under the Taliban regime in the mid-1990s. After studying in Peshawar in Pakistan, she started working for NGOs. In early 2002 she returned to Afghanistan, where she was soon taken on by the UNHCR.

In most cases, belonging to relatively well-off kin groups did not spare the Afghan staff from the war, but gave them more options than those available to the vast majority of the population. Their socioeconomic resources also enabled them to make the most of exile. Many of them have lived in Pakistani cities – mainly Peshawar, Quetta and Islamabad. In addition to gaining a secondary education, they learned English and IT skills there, two fundamental assets for working in an international organisation. Very often they had prior experience working for NGOs in Pakistan. It was thus natural for them to follow the new epicentre of international aid programmes, reinvesting the linguistic and professional capital acquired in exile.

The arrival en masse of international organisations after 2001 resulted in a high demand for English-speaking Afghans with IT skills, preferably with experience working for NGOs. Working for an international organisation thus became an attractive possibility – some even returned with the intention of finding a job under the auspices of the international reconstruction project. In other countries, their skills would not be valued to the same extent, as the experience of family members living in America or Europe showed: despite their qualifications, they were working as drivers or petrol station attendants, or, in the best case, had started a small business.

Given the mobility and careers of the UNHCR's Afghan employees, it is difficult to describe them as 'local' in the sense of a permanent presence in the country as natives. But the term acquires meaning when contrasted with the 'international' staff and if we take into account the 'gravitational force' that the Afghan context exerted on their field of possibility. Unlike their expatriate colleagues, who were freed from the sociopolitical context of their country of origin, their choices and strategies continued to be impacted by political developments in Afghanistan (conflicts, reconstruction project, resumption of conflict, etc.). Unwilling or, much more often, unable to radically detach themselves from their origins, their strategies for geographical, social and professional mobility remained linked to the Afghan political context. Even if they were to migrate to Europe, the recognition of their refugee status (virtually the only possible route to legal immigration) would depend on the situation in Afghanistan. As Redfield (2012: 360, 365) notes, what characterises 'national' employees is the 'gravity of local attachment': while expatriates, 'materially heavy and socially light', are 'swept away by distant concerns', 'national' staff, who are 'materially light and socially heavy', remain 'stolidly set, a repetitive actor in local history'.

A Job That Opened Doors

While in 2002 the geopolitical context made returning to Afghanistan and a UN job attractive prospects, the evolution of the conflict gradually altered the situation. Certainly, for most Afghans who had lived through the civil war, the Taliban regime and the US air strikes, the period from 2007 to 2008 was relatively stable. But the rising power of the Taliban placed all those Afghans who were cooperating with international organisations in a difficult position. With the escalation in violence in the country after 2005, they had become the targets of brutal acts (murders and kidnappings) and intimidation[6] (Giustozzi 2007: 105–35; United Nations General Assembly 2008: 3). In 2007 the situation was less oppressive in Kabul than in the south of the country, but UNHCR staff were also affected. The risks were so real that paradoxically, employees of humanitarian organisations were among those eligible for refugee status, under the category 'Afghans associated with international organisations and the security forces' (UNHCR 2007c: 72–73). Present insecurity was compounded by future precarity: in the event that the Taliban returned to

Kabul, they would immediately find themselves on the 'wrong side'. Unable to leave, they would have to suffer the consequences.

Nevertheless, a job with the UNHCR offered a number of ways to deal with uncertainty. In this sense, engagement in the organisation's work was one of the strategies deployed for survival or for social advancement. It was not only the desire to work for a cause (the future of the country, the reconstruction process and the fate of refugees) that motivated Afghan employees, but also the necessity of meeting their everyday needs and the uncertainty of the political context, as well as the aspiration towards social and/or political advancement. There were four main resources that a UN job offered 'national staff': financial security, the possibility of involvement in politics, a professional capital that could be drawn on in the future, in Afghanistan or elsewhere, and routes to leaving the country. I will now consider these four resources in more detail.

In the first place, these jobs were particularly attractive from a financial point of view. They offered a regular salary well above the average, in a country where the normal income on the informal market was three dollars a day. UN salaries were approximately twice those offered by NGOs and bore no comparison to those in the national administration. As an indication, in 2007 the director of a provincial office of the Ministry of Refugees received a salary of $130 a month, while a cleaner employed by the UNHCR earned almost twice that. Such a salary was a means of financial advancement for that person and their family. The money was often redistributed among family and community members, enabling the UN employee to acquire an important status in these circles and consolidate their solidarity networks. The money was also invested in children's education in order to facilitate family advancement through the generations. Salim, for example, encouraged his eldest son to go to India, where he would be able to fund his university studies and enable him to find work easily when he returned to Afghanistan. This money also constitutes a safety net in the event of the resumption of hostilities, making it easier to emigrate. The disadvantage is that such people become the target of the organised criminal networks that have proliferated in the cities, who engage in looting and kidnapping for ransom, often with impunity. Many of the UNHCR's Afghan employees had been victims of armed robbery: Tahir, for example, told of how one evening, armed men had burst into his house, tied him up in front of his wife and his mother, and taken all they could find.

For some of the UNHCR's Afghan employees, the job was also a way of making a commitment to the future of their country and/or for the benefit of the Afghan people. A number of colleagues told me they wanted to contribute to the reconstruction of the country. The differing cases of two young female employees sensitive to the condition of Afghan women show both that the terms and modalities of this commitment could vary widely depending on the person (their social position, values, position in the organisation and so on) and that such a commitment did not necessarily equate to total adherence to the organisation's values and aims.

Hadija was a young woman who worked in the Administration department at the Branch Office in Kabul. She was from an urban family in Herat and had grown up in Pakistan. She was always in full make-up, wore tight jeans and bright colours, and did not cover her head when she was at the office. These clothing choices did not go without saying: even in her social milieu, her style of dress, coupled with the fact that she worked, expressed her claim to belong to an educated and progressive Afghan elite, and were also ways of laying claim to a new place for women in this environment. Her male colleagues, some of whom were unused to seeing women dressed this way, formed part of her audience, for they had to interact with her professionally and show respect for this woman in the workplace.

Soraya was a young Pashtun woman who worked in the Kabul Sub-Office as Field Officer. She saw her job as a commitment to the Afghan people, particularly the women. She felt it was vital that they had access to education. She always kept her head carefully covered and wore loose, dark-coloured clothing – a style that many expatriates, who see the veil as a symbol of the oppression of Afghan women, would describe as very 'traditional'. But for Soraya, the headscarf was essential to her fight. She wanted to show those she interacted with in the field that being an educated woman, who worked and interacted with 'foreigners', was not incompatible with being a respectable Muslim Pashtun woman. She wanted the most conservative village leaders not to be afraid for their daughters to become like her. She therefore presented herself as a positive and acceptable model.

As well as offering financial capital and an opportunity to contribute to their country, working for the UN also enabled people to acquire a professional capital – what could be called 'international capital' – that could open doors in the near or more distant future. Working in English, in constant contact with expatriates, and following training and language improvement courses offered by the organisation opened the door to spending time in international and multicultural environments, acquiring language skills and also understanding the reasoning of international organisations (the rudiments of international law, the terminological and conceptual registers of the world of international cooperation and familiarity with international standards). They also acquired a technocratic knowhow in bureaucratic procedures and administrative management, as well as brokering skills that I consider below – in other words, the capacity to act as intermediaries between Afghan interlocutors and foreign agents. These skills combined with a social capital constituted by the relationships they formed with a large number of expatriate colleagues.

The fourth and final resource that a job with the UNHCR could offer was the chance to move out of the country in the short term. Many of the UNHCR's Afghan employees aspired to this, particularly the younger ones and those most exposed to danger. The outside world, especially Europe and the United States, exerted a strong attraction. Walking around the Branch Office, you would come across the CD of a German course a colleague was following at the Goethe Institute, and then hear another repeating a few basic phrases in Polish. Others were taking language courses at the French embassy. With the exception of the young women waiting to join their husbands in Europe under the family reunification programme, for most this aspiration faced the obstacle of the very limited number of legal channels for leaving the region. Contact with expatriate colleagues could then become a precious resource, sometimes manifested in access to information, as was the case with the watchman at my residence. An American colleague had told him about the US visa lottery, and then helped him to write and submit his application. I was asked several times about the procedure and criteria for obtaining Schengen visas. For the watchman Jaweed, the support of UNHCR managers was key to his success in obtaining a visa.

For a minority of Afghan employees, promotion to the status of 'international' staff, which was highly competitive and subject to very stringent conditions, became the means to escape the weight of the local context and radically alter their field of possibilities. From this point of view, employment with a UN agency represented an important springboard. Tests were regularly organised internally, and the skills acquired combined with the support of expatriate colleagues were often crucial factors in passing them.

Studies of the internationalisation of elites prove fully relevant to the case of Afghan employees of the UNHCR. Certainly, the studies by Wagner (2007) and Dezalay (2004) focus on the upper echelons of national elites, and in the Afghan context the central focus is on pragmatic survival strategies rather than deliberate tactics for accumulating power. Nevertheless, here too, the internationalisation of Afghan employees of the UNHCR – first through privileged expatriation and then through employment with an international organisation – is a determining factor in the formation and reproduction of a privileged class. The capital acquired through the first expatriation gave them access to their current employment, which will furnish resources for the future, regardless of whether or not they stay in Afghanistan.

Bridging the Gap between Disconnected Worlds

Located at the interface between Afghan society and an international organisation, the Afghan employees of the UNHCR acted as mediators between these two worlds, each with its own universe of meaning, such that mediation involved constantly juggling between different registers and understandings. But the relation between these two worlds was also a power relation, for during the 2000s, international organisations held a great deal of sway in Afghanistan. The language barrier extended the Afghan staff's mediating role, since in fact the organisation delegated the concrete negotiation of its legitimacy, its reputation and its local policies almost entirely to them – particularly to the employees entrusted with interacting with its Afghan partners.

The most salient feature of the interface between these two worlds was the breadth of the distance between them. Edwards and Centlivres emphasise the incommensurable difference between the humanitarian ethos – egalitarian, individualist, secular and depersonalised – and the Pashtun ethos, grounded in self-determination, social reciprocity, a code of honour, the religious ethics of Islam and bonds with lineage groups (Edwards 1986; Centlivres 1988). Centlivres also points out that mutual aid in Afghanistan is not based on the principle of humanity, but works on a more localised scale, according to different rationales:

> for Afghans, humanitarian aid sits outside of the charitable precepts that govern the Muslim community and beyond the rules of solidarity and tribal assistance. (Centlivres and Centlivres-Dumont 1999: 958)

Afghans, particularly in rural areas, often find it difficult to understand the bureaucratic rationality of international aid bodies. Prior to 2001, the concepts of human rights, humanitarian aid and development were alien to Afghanistan. Furthermore, given the limited presence of the state across the territory, in the early 2000s the people were not used to interacting with bureaucratic institutions. Notwithstanding the quantity of external actors, their modes of operation, criteria for intervention and objectives remain obscure for a large part of the Afghan population. Several Afghan Field Officers told me that the majority of the rural population 'puts all foreigners in the same box'; in other words, they cannot distinguish between military and humanitarian personnel, between government bodies and NGOs, between the UN and NGOs, and so on. These bodies are all designated by the single term *mu'asisa* – organisations. The gulf was deepened by the generalised mistrust and even hostility towards foreigners. History teaches Afghans to distrust interventions from outside. This goes back to the arrival of the British and their abortive attempts to conquer and colonise the region in the second half of the nineteenth century. Since the Soviet invasion in 1979, everything that has come from outside has been associated with conflict: military invasion and external aid have often gone hand in hand. In 2007 air strikes were deeply unpopular, reinforcing the disappointment generated by the lack of concrete results from development projects (Donini 2006). The people wondered how the billions of dollars disbursed to the country had been spent, when they had seen so little change in their everyday lives. The presence of NATO forces was often likened to an 'occupation' dominated by US interests, a reminder of the Soviet occupation (Daulatzai 2006: 304). Some colleagues told me that when they went to the villages, they were seen as spokespeople for the Americans, and that in other very remote villages they were even taken for Russians. The PR officer, who often appeared on television and was well known in Kabul, told me that his friends often jokingly called him a 'slave of the United States'.

Distrust of foreigners was also apparent at the level of values. Aid programmes are rooted in a desire for social change, based on principles of democratisation and the fight for women's rights, which can be misinterpreted in a country where Islam informs all aspects of social and political life (Centlivres and Centlivres-Dumont 1999: 953; Daulatzai 2006; Roy 2004). The most sensitive areas were women and *sharia* law. Foreigners were seen as the bearers of incompatible values, if not corrupt customs, in terms of the position of women and the consumption of alcohol, for example.

I have already addressed several aspects of the UNHCR's ways of thinking. Here I will emphasise two points. The first is the fact that the values and norms of refugee law are conveyed via the intervention of a managerial and bureaucratic logic comprised of allocation criteria ('vulnerability', 'needs', 'high-return villages'), objectives to be achieved and schedules – precisely the kind of logic that was unknown in rural Afghanistan in the 1990s. Second, this logic, used by expatriates, does not lend itself to negotiations of substance, requiring only to be *applied* in the field. For expatriates, its legitimacy derives from the interstate sphere and the presumed universality of the values upheld by the UN. It goes alongside an eschatological understanding of international refugee law: where it is not 'yet' applied, the aim is to disseminate it. These norms are not set on the same level as those that govern the life of much of Afghan society (lineage solidarity, codes of honour, etc.), which are reduced to 'cultural' or 'social' practices.

Afghan employees operated at the crossroads between these two worlds. They navigated the interface between international aid and Afghan contexts, and their work consisted precisely of bridging the gap between them. The difference between the two worlds generated tensions that the Afghan staff had to contend with directly.

It often happened, for example, that the expectations of the population conflict with the UNHCR's allocation criteria. Afghan employees then had to explain why the organisation could not provide the expected aid. This could be very delicate, especially in the case of people who, despite their manifestly distressed situation, did not 'fall within the mandate' of the organisation. Such was the case in very poor villages that had not received enough returnees, or

Afghans who, owing to their undocumented residence in Iran or Pakistan, could not be considered 'returnees' even though they had spent very long periods outside the country.

This gap between international and local norms became powerfully apparent during the crisis over expulsions from Iran in April 2007, when the UNHCR's position provoked total incomprehension, and indeed anger and outrage, in the Afghan media and among the Afghan population: why was the UNHCR not coming to the defence of deportees, who in Afghanistan were considered 'refugees' (see Chapter 7)? Nourullah, the PR officer, was on the front line, especially during the first few days when the UNHCR's official position had not yet been determined and the media were hysterical. Constantly interrogated by journalists, he faced often aggressive and accusatory questions. He had to be very careful in the statements he made in order to untangle the unintelligible situation that had arisen and defend the organisation's reputation, while showing sensitivity to the objections. One day, returning from a press conference, he told me he had been deeply shaken by one explicitly moral question. As he was explaining that, from the point of view of international law, the Iranian authorities had the right to deport these Afghans, he was asked: 'As an Afghan, are you not angry at the treatment of the deportees?' He had stood dumbfounded in front of the microphone for several seconds.

The UNHCR's Afghan staff repeatedly had to defend the organisation's legitimacy within local arenas of power, when the organisation's very presence destabilised the balance of power. Aid could become a stake in conflicts between solidarity groups and notables, and the organisation's activity could also contribute to weakening the legitimacy of a given actor and provoke his hostility. Hassan, for example, worked as Protection Officer at a UNHCR Sub-Office. His role was to report human rights violations. He told me how he had often been threatened by local commanders or had been prevented from entering a particular area or village. He recalled, with still visible agitation, the time when he unwittingly interviewed a commander known for having perpetrated atrocities during the civil war, who had introduced himself as a member of the *shura* and whose identity he had discovered only afterwards.

The tapping strategies of the UNHCR's Afghan interlocutors also had to be regularly managed. The leaders of a group might absorb what they had observed to be the criteria for allocation of international organisations and NGOs, and attempt to obtain aid, or more aid, using tapping strategies well understood in development sociology. They would highlight the 'vulnerability' and 'needs' of their location, or point out widows or sick people during visits by organisations. We observed this in the village of Bot Khak when Salim went there on mission, where the members of the *shura* inflated the number of returnees and emphasised the gaps and therefore the inadequacy of projects implemented up to that point. In these contexts, UNHCR staff have to demonstrate lucidity and diplomacy: they need to be able to construct a realistic overview that will be recognised as such by their colleagues and make it possible to allocate funding to the villages in accordance with the organisation's criteria, while maintaining relationships with the village leaders, whose collaboration is essential in order to complete projects successfully.

There was a further challenge in presenting themselves as credible and respectable actors to interlocutors who were distrustful or even hostile towards international organisations. Their proximity to 'foreigners' often sparked challenges and suspicions of both financial and moral corruption. This was even more the case for women: working for an international organisation equated to putting one's respectability at risk not only in the field, in the context of work, but also in daily life. Some female colleagues told me of the strong social pressure they felt: even those in their close circle regarded them with distrust and sometimes contempt. Persistent rumours circulated in Kabul that Afghan women were all required to uncover their heads when they entered international offices. Soraya refused several proposals of marriage from men who asked her to stop working for the UN.

What was at play in these situations often went unnoticed by expatriate colleagues. When they arrived in the field, the expatriate had the impression that attention is focused on them, whereas it was the behaviour of the Afghan staff that made the difference. Whether the expatriate officer covered her head or took off her shoes in the village meeting room can be much less important than where her female Afghan colleague was seated in the car. If she sat next to a male colleague – an immoral proximity according to local codes – it might affect not only her reputation but also that of the expatriate colleagues accompanying her, the UNHCR as an organisation and, by extension, all international organisations in the country.

Intervention Brokers

The typical situations described above show that the role of Afghan staff cannot be reduced simply to that of translating or relaying information that the organisation assigned to them. It was a much more crucial and complex role of brokering that required specific skills and a considerable personal commitment. The skills Afghan employees demonstrated went well beyond simple linguistic competence and familiarity with the context that the organisation valued them for: in order to manage the kind of situations described above, they needed tact, diplomatic skills and, above all, the capacity to continually change register depending on whether they were speaking with expatriate colleagues or the organisation's Afghan interlocutors. Jonathan Ong and Pamela

Combinido (2018) point to a 'mental mobility' and an 'epistemological openness' that expatriate colleagues lack. The responsibilities that Afghan employees effectively took on were also important ones, since they had to negotiate the reputation and legitimacy of the organisation on the ground. Finally, while expatriates were sometimes doubtful about 'national' colleagues' loyalty to the organisation, it is clear that whatever their personal values, they demonstrated serious commitment, since they embodied the organisation, imposed its way of thinking and established its power in Afghanistan, presenting themselves individually as its representatives, and thereby putting their reputation and sometimes even their safety on the line.

A consideration of the UNHCR Afghan staff's brokering role opens at least two fertile avenues for analysing the UNHCR's activity 'in context' (Fresia 2009b): the functions this brokering role performs for the UNHCR as an institution, and for its intervention in Afghanistan.

First, the institutionally undervalued activity of brokering by the Afghan staff helps to reproduce and mitigate the gap between the two worlds they straddle. David Lewis and David Mosse's edited volume (2006) shows that rather than putting two worlds of meaning in direct communication, the translation operations inherent to the implementation of aid projects tend instead to reproduce the gap between them. It is by reproducing the disjunctions that translation holds incommensurable worlds in connection and thus helps to preserve the coherence of a given project. This is a heuristic thesis. In fact, most of what happened in the field, managed by the Afghan staff and then translated into the institution's language, did not filter through to most expatriate colleagues, and hence to the organisation's official accounts that the latter were in charge of.

Afghan staff's brokering thus preserved the ignorance of the expatriate staff (for whom the Afghan context and the stakes involved in programmes remained to some extent opaque), and prevented the distrust, incomprehension or indeed opposition to the organisation's rationality that might arise on the ground from challenging the UNHCR's programme in Afghanistan or its global project. When they talked in terms of 'vulnerability' or 'international law', Afghan employees helped to stabilise projects and disguise the gap between Afghan society and aid organisations. This effectively helped to disconnect the organisation from the Afghan arena and thus to preserve its central rationality. In this way, the organisation could represent its programmes as coherent, in accordance with the 'needs' of the population and successful in their objectives, even if the rationale behind these programmes was not always understood or accepted locally.

This thesis is corroborated by the cushioning role that, as I have shown, Afghan staff often played – a role that goes hand in hand with brokering, but to which less attention is paid in development sociology. The friction between these two very different worlds generated tensions. Whether as targets of violence or intimidation from the Taliban, in the daily management of distrust, or when they defended the UNHCR's criteria for resource allocation in the face of incomprehension, the UNHCR's Afghan employees absorbed these tensions, playing a cushioning role. In my research I was not able to assess the extent to which, in addition to being suffered as an 'occupational hazard', this gap was something the 'national' staff actively sought to preserve, since having the monopoly on managing the interface was also a source of power and influence in the Afghan arena.

Second, the Afghan staff's brokering role invites reflection on the effects of the UNHCR's activity in the country. This focus on the organisation's Afghan employees has begun to show how these effects go well beyond the isolated impact of programmes. Changes in the labour market, the training of a middle-level elite with financial and professional capital, the introduction of new paradigms, repertoires of political action, criteria for resource allocation – the UNHCR's presence was an integral part of the processes of social reconfiguration and political competition in post-2001 Afghanistan. Even though the Afghan arena remained largely illegible to the organisation, the changes these processes instigate in Afghan society are substantial.

The methodological obstacles due to my status as an expatriate (and to the ignorance typical of this status) prevented me from researching both interactions between the UNHCR's Afghan employees and its Afghan interlocutors, and the Afghan employees' relationship to the organisation (what kind of loyalty to the organisation, its way of thinking and its values? How did they take on, interpret and elaborate this way of thinking and these values? What impact did this job have on their subjectivities?). The example of Soraya, who combined her commitment to improving the condition of Pashtun women with her work as Field Officer, shows in any case that in addition to strategies for advancement, there are ways that people re-appropriate the organisation's rationality, and that processes of social and political reconfiguration, in which Afghan staff played an integral part, played out in the interactions between them and their Afghan interlocutors.

Notes

1. The administrative staff employed in Geneva have a separate status and therefore constitute a third category: they are also recruited worldwide, but remain permanently posted at Headquarters.
2. It was with the latter that I had most interaction and this chapter focuses on them.
3. Silke Roth (2012) argues that this reasoning is a justifying myth, rightly remarking that expatriates are not necessarily neutral by virtue of coming from outside, for they surely arrive with preconceived ideas about what should be done.

4. There was one particularly striking case: a colleague who had obtained a Schengen visa, at the request of the UNHCR, to participate in a training in Italy was arrested at Islamabad airport, on suspicion of holding a false visa. It was only when the UNHCR and the embassy that had issued the visa intervened that he was able to continue his journey, after spending a night in detention.

5. In order to study these questions in depth, I would have had to stay in Kabul beyond the end of my contract or return as a researcher some time afterwards, which was unfortunately not possible.

6. 'Night letters' were the most widespread form of intimidation – generally thrown into the house's compound during the night. They discouraged those targeted from working with the 'invaders', sometimes threatening their addressees with death, and thus making it clear that they had been identified and were being watched.

CHAPTER 7

Selecting between Non-nationals

Negotiating the Status of Afghans in Iran

Kabul, early May 2007. The sudden increase in deportations of Afghans from Iran has generated a political crisis. The deportations have become the central concern among politicians and in the media, provoking heated debate. Under pressure from the Afghan Parliament, the Minister of Foreign Affairs and the Minister of Refugees are sacked, having been deemed incapable of dealing with the situation. The UNHCR office in Kabul is caught up in this political storm. Like the Afghan government, the organisation is under powerful pressure, being held responsible for the fate of those deported. It is also continually bombarded with questions from both journalists and delegations from international organisations and funders seeking information. In this tense atmosphere, those deported are described in the most varied ways: 'deported refugees', 'illegal migrants', 'illegal refugees', 'returnees', 'undocumented', 'migrant workers' and so on. The UNHCR office struggles to calm the mood, despite repeatedly asserting that these deportees are undocumented 'migrant workers' who do not fall within its mandate and whose deportation cannot be contested.

Article 1A, Paragraph 2 of the Preamble to the 1951 Convention defines a 'refugee' as:

> any person who ... owing to well-founded fear of persecution for reasons of race, religion, nationality, membership of a particular social group or political opinion, is outside the country of his nationality and is unable or, owing to such fear is unwilling to avail himself of the protection of that country.

The states that have ratified the Convention are committed to applying the principle of nonrefoulement of those who meet this definition. The application of the 1951 Convention therefore involves first and foremost identifying those non-nationals who are 'eligible' for the treatment established under this treaty – that is, those who fulfil the necessary conditions to claim it. In each situation, then, a decision has to be made as to whether non-nationals should be considered 'refugees' and, if so, precisely what treatment they should receive. As such, the labelling process is a crucial stage in the application of international refugee law.

Here I want to go beyond the normative approaches, which reify refugees. The term 'refugee' is often used as if it designated individuals, a phenomenon or a problem with their own discernible ontological existence independent of institutions. It thus becomes possible to state that 'refugees are one of the most serious problems of our age' (Harrell-Bond 1986: xi), despite the fact that refugees were not constituted as a public issue prior to the First World War, or indeed to observe that the number of refugees has increased or fallen, without taking into account how this population is understood and counted by the UNHCR and states. But a social fact only becomes a public issue once it has been interpreted and categorised. Institutions produce classifications and labels, the main aim of which is not to describe or explain reality, but to organise public policy (Becker 1963; Gusfield 1981). They categorise humans as a focus of institutional action. After the Second World War, once the category of refugee had become the central criterion for determining which migrants could claim special treatment from states, the term can no longer be used independently of its labelling function as a synonym for people fleeing violence and conflict.

Many anthropologists have shown that the category 'refugee' has no descriptive or analytical significance in and of itself: 'the refugee experience' or 'refugeeness' does not exist as such (Bakewell 2000a; Black 2001; Malkki 1995a; Richmond 1988: 20; Turton 2003: 7) and can only be understood in the context of relations between migrants and institutions. Social history studies reveal the historically situated nature of processes of identifying 'refugees'. For example, Karen Akoka's study (2020) of the development of OFPRA,[1] the French body responsible for evaluating asylum applications, shows how this institution's use of the category 'refugee' has been reconfigured over time, depending on the background and social trajectory of its officers, and the organisational procedures they follow, which are themselves articulated with specific public policies.

In this chapter I examine what was at stake in the categorisation of Afghans in Iran between 1980 and 2007, drawing on internal UNHCR reports on their legal situation. I first consider the negotiations between the Iranian authorities (which under international law hold the ultimate power to determine the status of these non-nationals) and the UNHCR, which, as the moral entrepreneur of international refugee law, seeks to influence the criteria and modes of awarding status of those it considers 'in need of protection', so that they may be recognised as refugees. I note how, notwithstanding the universal significance conferred on the concept 'refugee' by the UNHCR and the frequency with which it is used by a wide range of actors, it remains too vague once a specific population or country is concerned. Concrete procedures for determining the status of people fleeing conflict vary depending on the state concerned (its legal system, its cultural models and the political context at the time) and are the by no means certain result of negotiations between the UNHCR and states. Despite the UNHCR's expertise in this area, in this case the confrontation with the Iranian authorities was greatly to the organisation's disadvantage, and the treatment reserved for Afghans was determined by the interests of the Iranians. Categorisation and award of status took place outwith international norms, and the distinction between 'refugees' and 'nonrefugees' that the UNHCR itself ultimately upheld did not reflect the 'protection needs' criterion.

After examining the procedure for labelling and assigning status through the lens of the deportations, I then move on to consider the consequences of this procedure for Afghans themselves, who had very little input into the negotiations concerning how they were to be labelled. Resituating this classification in the legal-institutional framework established by states to govern migration, I address the violent effects of the boundary erected between 'refugees' and 'nonrefugees'. In the absence of any other system of protection, the refugee regime becomes a preferential regime that protects those designated 'refugees' from deportation, while legitimising the deportation of others. Applying international refugee law effectively means promulgating a regime of dispensation, the exception that proves the rule – the rule being the 'deportability' of non-nationals. Thus, in effect, the UNHCR's activity contributes to reinforcing the division of human beings into nationals and non-nationals, and the legitimacy of a system in which states effectively have the discretionary power to legitimise movement or – more commonly in the case of Afghans – to render it illegitimate.

Understanding this context helps to highlight the key innovation of the ACSU project – its holistic approach. But it also gives a sense of the significant obstacles the project faced. It was not only the Iranian and Pakistani authorities who had no interest in introducing the system recommended by the UNHCR; it came up against the unequal legal and institutional framework of 'international migration governance'. This inequality is consciously promoted by many states because it enables them to be selective in their application of international human rights law. They can thus pay lip service to the most visible protection regime, while retaining substantial discriminatory power over the management of non-nationals.

The UNHCR and the 'Refugee' Label

The determination and the actual award of status are prerogatives of the state. The UNHCR's role is to monitor state procedures and try to influence the criteria and methods, first by encouraging states to sign up to the 1951 Convention and the 1967 Protocol, and then by defining the ideal process for determination and monitoring whether state practices conform to it. Over time, the UNHCR has thus developed substantial expertise in this area. The organisation's Protection Department regularly produces new standards to guide state officials in interpreting how the 1951 Convention applies to current cases.

These directives lay down, for example, how the definition of a 'particular social group' applies to current real situations (UNHCR 2002), or discuss the applicability of the 1951 Convention to specific groups such as 'migrant victims of trafficking' (UNHCR 2006e). The organisation also produces directives on eligibility criteria depending on country of origin (*Country of Origin Information*), assessing the situation in a given country and giving its own interpretation of the applicability of the Convention's provisions to the nationals of that country. For example, in the directives applicable to Afghan asylum seekers at the end of first decade of the twenty-first century (UNHCR 2007c), the UNHCR, on the basis of observations by its own staff in Afghanistan and NGO and media reports, identified twelve 'categories at risk'[2] among the groups that might have 'protection needs'.

The UNHCR also issues directives on the actual process for determining status. Ideally, this involves establishing 'refugee status determination procedures' – judicial-administrative procedures for examining individual applications for asylum. Thus, the *Handbook on Procedures and Criteria for Determining Refugee Status* (UNHCR 1992 [1979]) lays down the standards to which examination of asylum applications should conform in order to ensure that applications are 'examined properly and duly ... in the context of fair procedures'. These criteria include the requirement for a hearing, legal representation of the applicant, the possibility of appeal, and so on.

The UNHCR thus aspires to shape the process of identification of 'refugees' across the planet. Ideally, this process would be uniform throughout the world, once administrative and judicial procedures that conform with the UNHCR's directives have been introduced in all countries. But in practice, its guidelines have to be reconciled with the specificity of each state jurisdiction and with the perspective of the state authorities, who have many other priorities that very often impinge on the award of status to foreigners. Moreover, it is the state authorities who decide whether or not to sign up to an international treaty, and how they will execute it in practice. In international law, none of the UNHCR's directives on 'determination of status' has any legal standing.

Eligibility criteria for refugee status thus vary from one country to another, primarily in relation to the international treaties applicable. The first question is whether or not a state has signed up to the 1951 Convention. Pakistan, for example, has not (see Chapter 8). The next issue is whether the state in question has signed up to the 1961 Protocol, which removes the conditions that limited the 1951 Convention to migration resulting from the Second World War in Europe. Turkey, for example, has ratified the Convention but not the protocol: international refugee law is not applicable to any migrant, including Afghans, who arrive in the country.[3] By contrast, African countries that have signed up to the Organisation of African Unity's Convention, which adopts an 'extended' definition of 'refugees', embrace not only migrants fitting the definition of the 1951 Convention but also those who can be shown to be fleeing conflict and public order disturbances.[4] After this, the conditions for determining status vary depending on how each state transposes the provisions of the 1951 Convention into its national legal system and concretely implements them. These processes vary widely depending on whether they incorporate hearings, interviews, collective or individual decisions and so on. In addition, the legal and bureaucratic, formal and informal practices involved in the assessment of applications have to be taken into account.

It is thus clear why the issues around status, and the friction between states and the UNHCR on these questions, take different forms for different states. For example, European countries already have protocols for assessing individual asylum applications; in this case, the UNHCR's role is to monitor and improve them.[5] In other countries, such as Iran and Pakistan, where the size of the concerned population makes it impossible to assess cases individually, there are no such procedures; here the UNHCR's role is to negotiate the treatment of the Afghan population in its entirety.

The Status of Afghans in Iran (1979–2001)

From the beginning of the conflict in Afghanistan, and despite the fact that international organisations, researchers and the media referred to all Afghans in Iran as 'refugees', the determination and award of status to Afghans in Iran had been conducted purely on the basis of Iranian law, entirely out of step with international law. However, while initially this discrepancy did not pose a problem for the UNHCR, the organisation subsequently moved to intervene more directly and began to call for a change to the national immigration system, with the introduction of screening procedures designed to categorise groups in relation to 'protection needs'.

Iran ratified the 1951 Convention and the 1961 Protocol in 1976, but the treaty was not incorporated into domestic law. Some regulations introduced in 1963 include a definition of 'refugee' drawn from Article 1A(2) of the 1951 Convention and govern the issue of the status to be granted to individuals recognised as such. But this status (*panahande*)[6] was only exceptionally granted and only one thousand Afghans have benefited from it.[7]

During the 1980s, the Iranian authorities took a benevolent attitude towards Afghans, a generosity that aligned with the national interests. Iran was in fact benefiting from the Afghan workforce and was able to reinforce its role as the leader of Shi'ism by demonstrating its solidarity with a majority Shi'ite population. This approach was not informed by the provisions of international asylum law: the Iranian authorities presented the welcome they offered to Afghans as a matter of religious solidarity with brother Muslims in difficulty (as prescribed in Qur'an 59-9) rather than of international law.

During this period, Afghans were either governed by ad hoc measures adopted within the framework of national laws applying to foreigners in general, or managed (or rather not managed) entirely informally, with no official legal status but having the de facto possibility of entering, living and working in the country. Since 1979, all Afghans who presented themselves to the Iranian authorities had received Blue Cards confirming their status as *muhajir*,[8] and granting them the right to remain and substantial entitlements to education, healthcare, employment and freedom of movement. Subsequently, Iran gradually stopped granting these residence permits, but thanks to the porosity of the border, Afghans were in fact able to enter the country and live there informally (Abbasi-Shavazi et al. 2008; Rajee 2000; Stigter 2005a).

From the point of view of international law, this management of Afghan immigration did not accord with the 1951 Convention, since the treatment of Afghans was not determined by the application of the treaty. However, until the mid-1990s, the UNHCR judged the situation relatively satisfactory. This was because of the welcome offered by Iran, which:

> has successfully provided international protection and assistance to millions of Afghans during successive periods of conflict and instability in their country. (Internal document, 2004)

In international circles, this situation quite easily slipped into the generalised categorisation of all Afghans in Iran as 'refugees', regardless of whether they were living in camps or in cities, when they arrived and so on. The UNHCR saw the reception offered by Iran as a form of *prima facie* collective recognition without case-by-case assessment. This generalised consensus that all Afghans in Iran were 'refugees' was based on the convergence of a number of factors: the situation in Afghanistan was unquestionably one of prolonged conflict and showed no sign of improvement; the host countries provided a basic positive treatment; they had an interest in the introduction of aid programmes for

Afghans; and in the context of the Cold War, donor countries were disposed to spend the necessary funds.

But during the 1990s the climate became much less welcoming, despite Iran's tense relationship with the Taliban (Abbasi-Shavazi et al. 2008; Adelkhah and Olszewska 2006; Rajee 2000; Stigter 2005a). The Iranian authorities stepped up deportations and placed more restrictions on residence. Restrictions on employment reached a peak in 2000, when, complaining of high unemployment, Iran substantially tightened its legislation on foreign workers and began to apply it more strictly. The Afghan population was portrayed as a factor in social and economic destabilisation, linked to the economic crisis, criminality and drug trafficking. The Iranian government asserted that favourable reception and treatment were no longer justified and Afghans were no longer designated as 'refugees', but rather as 'economic migrants' (Safri 2011; Turton and Marsden 2002: 14).

In the face of this change of attitude at a time when there was no prospect of any marked improvement in conditions in Afghanistan, the UNHCR undertook intensive negotiations with the Iranian government, with the aim of establishing individual screening procedures to identify Afghans 'in need of international protection' under the 1951 Convention. This was to ensure they had a formal status that would protect them from deportation and guarantee them a minimum standard of treatment. Negotiations and pilot procedures were interrupted by the 9/11 attacks and subsequent events.

In the aftermath of 2001, the UNHCR persisted in its attempts to establish individual assessment procedures. There was internal agreement that in the new context it was no longer possible for the UNHCR to consider Afghans settled in Iran as a homogeneous and undefined population: the situation in Afghanistan no longer justified generalised and systematic 'international protection', and in any case the Iranian authorities were clearly no longer disposed to offer it. Nevertheless, the changes in Afghanistan were not such that it could be deemed that persecution no longer occurred. The time had therefore come to introduce distinctions within the Afghan population in Iran:

> An important priority is to ... differentiate between persons moving for economic, commercial or social purposes and refugees ... It will be important to identify who is moving and why. (UNHCR 2007a: 9)

The UNHCR's priority in this process of differentiation was to identify 'persons in need of international protection', and to ensure that they were not forced to return to Afghanistan and enjoyed satisfactory conditions of residence in the host country. The introduction of selection procedures was thus a key component of the migration regime recommended by the UNHCR in the 2000s: in the context of the much less welcoming attitude to Afghans, the

UNHCR promoted the introduction of procedures for identifying the 'refugees' among Afghans in Iran, to ensure they received a treatment it deemed appropriate and in conformity with the Convention.

The Keystone of Iranian Sovereignty (2001–8)

Becker (1963) points out that labels are used to establish relations of hegemony: power struggles involve clashes on definitions. The designation 'refugee' itself involves a confrontation between the UNHCR and the state in question for governments are guided by priorities other than those of protecting non-nationals. And as the principle of state sovereignty gives them the last word in attributing status to non-nationals, the UNHCR is always negotiating from a position of weakness.

Randeria's notion of the *cunning state* (2007), which emphasises the central role of states in transposing global norms to the national arena, can be appositely applied to Iran: this is a state that draws selectively on international law, depending on its interests. The UNHCR is authorised to retain a presence there and is seen as a partner in the repatriation programme, but otherwise has a very limited influence on how Afghans are treated in Iran. This situation also confirms the thesis that states are still the most powerful actors in the application of international refugee law (Bhabha 1998; Dauvergne 2008; Sassen 1996), demonstrating their role as a filter in the application of international norms throughout the world.

Between 2001 and 2008, the UNHCR struggled to shake Iranian unilateralism on the criteria and procedures for attribution of status to Afghans. This status was determined on the basis of national interests, primarily with the aim of benefiting from the situation at the lowest possible cost while retaining a lever of influence in Afghanistan. Iranian legislators always opposed any UNHCR involvement in drafting laws, and the organisation was not generally consulted in political decisions relating to foreigners. Iran's policy remained largely unpredictable for the UNHCR: repression alternated with relative laxity, and actions were not always in line with declared intentions. The UNHCR was only called upon when its recommendations coincided with government policy – in other words, mainly in the context of the repatriation programme.

In particular, the Iranian authorities showed no interest in introducing screening procedures based on 'protection needs'. Since the 2001 regime change in Afghanistan, they saw all Afghans as former 'refugees' who, given the new geopolitical situation in Afghanistan, could no longer justify any 'protection need'. The UNHCR faced insurmountable difficulties in introducing a screening system. In fact, apart from the exceptional award of residence permits under the 1963 asylum regulations, Iran had never officially introduced such screening procedures, nor had it recognised the UNHCR's prerogative to do so. The organisation itself sporadically conducted a 'refugee status determination' under its own refugee mandate, solely for those who apply direct to its offices. In exceptional cases, it provided a certificate, but the Iranian authorities did not recognise it as valid.[9]

I now consider in more detail how Iran managed Afghan non-nationals in the 2000s unilaterally, through ad hoc measures based on the general Iranian law on foreigners. In 2001 the Iranian government unilaterally revised the administrative status of Afghans. All previously issued residence permits were declared invalid and a census of all Afghans living in Iran was conducted: in total, some 2.3 million Afghans were counted. All were given a card called the *Amayesh* card,[10] which recognised their status as 'foreigners' under the remit of the BAFIA and granted them temporary residence in Iran. All the Afghans who had been registered were thus deemed ordinary foreigners, no longer persons deserving asylum (*panahandegan*), or persons for whom religious solidarity justified favourable treatment (*muhajir*). Aside from residence, they had very limited rights – for example, the *Amayesh* card entitled them to work in only a limited number of sectors of the economy (primarily manual occupations) and did not allow free movement between provinces.

It appears that rather than protecting Afghans and regularising their situation, the census was aimed at 'bringing the Afghan population to the surface' in order to channel them and encourage repatriation. Throughout 2003 and 2004, the Iranian authorities substantially toughened their policy towards holders of the *Amayesh* card, with the unconcealed aim of making residence in Iran less attractive, and thus maintaining a high level of repatriation. This helped to reduce the number of Afghans entitled to claim rights definitively and in a way that was recognised internationally as legitimate (since return terminated the validity of the *Amayesh* card). In 2003, when the cards were due for renewal, the number of Afghans holding it dropped to 1.46 million, falling to 920,000 in 2005.

After 2001, no other means of obtaining a residence permit was introduced; Afghans who arrived subsequently in Iran had no official status, and under Iranian law were therefore considered to be illegally present in the country.[11] Yet migration from Afghanistan remained steady and substantial throughout the 2000s: the Iranian labour market was still attractive, the border porous and the situation in Afghanistan difficult. The Afghans illegally resident in Iranian territory lived in still more precarious conditions, working on the black market, without any protection and for very low pay. They were also constantly at risk from the Iranian police's regular deportation raids. As the number of returns under the repatriation programme dwindled, Iran took a harder line towards undocumented foreigners. The restrictive regulations introduced in 2003 were also aimed at Afghans who were illegally resident,[12] and available data show a rise in deportations since 2002, from around 40,000 in 2002 to 150,000 in 2006. In 2005 the number of deportations overtook the number of repatriations and in 2006 the UNHCR reported 5,000 'assisted returns' and 150,000 deportations.

Yet this attitude was combined with a tendency to turn a blind eye towards the entry and presence of undocumented Afghans in the country and on the labour market. Moreover, the deportations never completely eliminated the illegally resident population. Rather than openly seeking to get rid of them, it seems that the aim was to establish a climate of insecurity and precarity.[13] This policy effectively enabled Iran to benefit from an Afghan workforce, which, being inexpensive and ready to accept jobs and working conditions that are generally rejected by Iranians, helps to stabilise the labour market.[14] In this context, the deportations ensured turnover of the workforce, maintaining a politically weak working population and giving Iran a lever for increasing its influence in Afghanistan. This dynamic, whereby states seek (often intentionally) to maintain an undocumented population for whom entry and residence are rendered difficult, but not entirely prevented, has been highlighted in relation to Iran (Adelkhah and Olszewska 2006; Majidyar and Alfoneh 2010; Monsutti 2005), but also in many other countries (de Genova 2002; Gibney and Hansen 2003: 439; Joppke 1998). Thus restrictions and deportations may be applied flexibly and more or less rigorously, depending on the fluctuations of states' political and economic requirements.

The sudden intensification of deportations in April 2007 thus appears to be linked to the state of international relations, which were marked by growing tensions between Iran and the Western powers, particularly the United States, over Iran's nuclear programme. In addition, it was rumoured that Iran was supporting the Taliban by supplying them with arms. In this context, the stepping-up of deportations can be interpreted as a manifestation of Iran's desire to show the international community that it was able to exert influence in Afghanistan.

Faced with Iran's decision to conduct a census of Afghans in 2001, the UNHCR found itself in a delicate position. While regularisation meant less unstable residence conditions for all those registered, the criteria for regularisation did not include assessment of 'protection needs'. In early 2002, during discussions prior to the signing of the Tripartite Repatriation Agreement, the UNHCR repeatedly emphasised that there might be 'persons in need of international protection' among the undocumented Afghans. But the BAFIA, the Iranian Interior Ministry body in charge of issues related to foreigners, resolutely refused to review the criteria for granting residence permits, or to establish this distinction.

The UNHCR attempted to alleviate the situation by demanding the right to screen deportees in order to determine whether there were persons 'in need of protection' according to international standards among them. This screening was the subject of lengthy discussions at meetings of the Tripartite Commission.[15] The UNHCR never succeeded in getting it included as a clause in the official agreement. Informal agreements between the BAFIA and the UNHCR allowed the organisation access to Afghan deportees. But the actual implementation of the programme was always highly problematic. This question was therefore avoided, so as not to compromise other negotiations.

The UNHCR faced an implacable reality: the Afghan population in Iran was for all practical purposes divided into those who held the *Amayesh* card and the undocumented. And Iran only recognised the UNHCR's mandate with regard to Afghans who were officially registered. The organisation therefore had to acknowledge the distinction in the immediate present, and subsequently attempt to modify it by working for this population to be reclassified according to other criteria. This was the complex issue at the centre of the UNHCR's work in Iran in the 2000s.

Thus, on one level, the distinction between holders of the *Amayesh* card and undocumented Afghans inevitably underpinned the UNHCR's activity. It was on behalf of *Amayesh* cardholders that the organisation put pressure on the Iranian government; Afghans without residence permits were outside of its prerogatives. On another level, the UNHCR was urging its recommendations for altering this situation and introducing new criteria and measures for classifying the Afghan population in Iran. But it was in vain that it contradicted the Iranian declarations and argued, with the backing of data, that political conditions in Afghanistan were not yet sufficiently stable and that the Afghan workforce was valuable to the Iranian economy; it came up against the unilateralism of the Iranian authorities. Moreover, it needed to ensure it did not compromise negotiations and retained space for manoeuvre in order to defend the interests of *Amayesh* cardholders.

Five years later, the introduction of concrete provisions for selection of Afghan migrants according to the criteria proposed by the UNHCR remained a distant goal and existed only on paper. Iran had not established procedures for individual assessment; nor had it adopted the other provisions recommended by the UNHCR. The organisation was still in the position of promoting a vision, caught between the ideal situation it had envisioned and the reality of the facts on the ground.

Who Are the 'Afghan Refugees in Iran'?

The UNHCR, governments, the media and researchers all often talk of 'Afghan refugees in Iran' as if they formed a discernible entity. But to whom are they actually referring? Given that the label 'refugee' is contested, since national and international law are not aligned, its semantic value is unstable. The expression 'Afghan refugees' cannot tangibly refer to a defined group of individuals, or to a relation to state laws, or to a mode of migration, living conditions, etc. The term is used differently depending on who is using it, the normative framework they refer to and their claims about how Afghans should be treated in Iran.

The vague and fundamentally ambiguous way in which the UNHCR and the Iranian authorities use the term 'refugee' demonstrates that there is no consensus between them over the choice of which Afghans have the right to remain in Iran. The formulation adopted in the Tripartite Agreement clearly reveals this absence of consensus.[16] It was agreed that the repatriation programme would be targeted at holders of the *Amayesh* card, but they are identified not as 'refugees', but rather by the more vague expression 'refugees and displaced persons'. Iran would have no problem with describing them as 'refugees', but the UNHCR cannot recognise technical equivalence between those who hold the *Amayesh* card and 'Afghans in need of protection', since the procedure for granting the cards does not involve assessing 'protection needs'.

Even within the UNHCR, the term 'refugees' was used ambiguously in referring to Afghans in Iran. At least two registers coexisted, depending on whether those using the term worked in the more technical context of experts negotiating status or whether they were speaking more generally of the population 'of concern' to the UNHCR. On the one hand, in technical and strategic documents and discussions, UNHCR officers expressed a desire not to amalgamate *Amayesh* cardholders with those who should be considered 'refugees'. The use of the term 'refugee' was thus restricted: people either aimed for clarity and precision by referring to 'holders of *Amayesh* cards' or used expressions covering the whole of the Afghan population in Iran such as 'displacement from Afghanistan', 'population movements' or 'Afghan population in asylum countries' (UNHCR 2003a, 2004a, 2007a). The aim was effectively to show that the population was not homogeneous and that it was important to understand which among them could be considered refugees. The same was true of studies commissioned by the UNHCR, the final version of which was carefully monitored by Eric.

On the other hand, in the statistics and all documents for public dissemination the term 'refugees' was extensively used, usually in reference to holders of the *Amayesh* card, although this was not explicitly stated. Thus, for example, the *Global Appeal* reported that 'there are 920,000 Afghan refugees in Iran' (UNHCR 2008a: 27). Only those who knew where this figure came from understood that in fact it referred to the population 'of concern' – the population recognised by Iran. This usage was also very common within the UNHCR among staff who were not directly involved in negotiations over status. Yet the status associated with the *Amayesh* card was a matter for the Foreigners Act (rather than asylum regulations conforming to the 1951 Convention) and did not involve assessment of 'international protection needs'. A tension therefore existed: the UNHCR needed to talk about its work and its 'population of concern', despite the fact that the 'persons in need of protection' had never been specifically identified. Thus, when it referred to *Amayesh* cardholders in its account of 'refugees', the *Global Appeal* concealed both the gap that remained between Iranian national law and international refugee law after 2001, and the absence of consensus between the Iranian authorities and the UNHCR over the treatment of Afghans in Iran.

Substantial ambiguity is also evident in the use of the term 'refugee' by researchers, the media and other organisations. The expression is very widely used with reference to Afghans in Iran.[17] But it soon becomes obvious that there is no common agreement as to the precise definition of the term. It is often used without any reference to the conflict between the UNHCR and the Iranian authorities over the issue of determination of status, and with varying awareness of the national and international legal provisions involved. Thus, if the author does not explain the use of the term in describing Afghans in Iran at the outset, it emerges on reading the text that the word is used: (1) as a simple descriptor for 'a person who has had to flee his country of origin in order to escape danger (war, political or religious persecution etc.)';[18] (2) as a generic term for the whole of the Afghan population in Iran;[19] or (3) to refer to holders of the *Amayesh* card, thus reflecting the UNHCR's use of the term in its publications.

A Preferential Regime

For individuals, whether they are designated 'refugees' or not is a matter of crucial importance. What is at stake is not merely access to a given public service, but the right of residence in the state territory concerned, and the enjoyment of all other rights – in other words, to borrow Hannah Arendt's expression (2017), the 'right to have rights'. Zetter (1991) was the first to point out the 'disturbing distinctions' made between refugees and nonrefugees, demonstrating the vulnerability of migrants to the labels imposed on them. Heyman (2001) highlighted the violent effects of the practice of classification of migrants by the US Immigration and Naturalization Service on the US-Mexican border.

Considering the stakes involved in the process of identifying 'refugees' through the lens of deportations sheds light on the violence inherent in the application of the label 'refugee' and, by extension, in international refugee law. In the absence of any other international regime for the protection of migrants, the refugee regime amounts to a process of dispensation, the application of which justifies preferential treatment for non-nationals labelled 'refugees', at the same time as legitimising the exclusion of others. With no other route to legalising their residence, the latter are by definition relegated to illegality – a condition that, as Nicholas de Genova notes (2002), is essentially characterised by 'deportability'.

I now look in more detail at the way in which organisations with a presence in Afghanistan (UNAMA, UNICEF, the WFP and the IOM) reacted to the deportations of undocumented Afghans during the summer of 2007. In 2007, at least 360,000 individuals were deported.[20] To begin with, representatives of these organisations approached the UNHCR Branch Office for clarification about the status of the deported Afghans. When it had been explained to them, all these bodies recognised the validity of the distinction between Afghans who held the *Amayesh* card, who fell under the remit of international refugee law, and undocumented Afghans to whom this law was not applicable. They quickly integrated this distinction into their thinking and their language, and began to consistently describe the deportees as 'illegal migrants'. None of them contested Iran's right to deport Afghans without a valid residence permit.

However, prompted by the UNHCR, these international organisations contributed to a multilateral intervention on the Afghan side of the border. UNAMA launched an emergency appeal that enabled the UN Office for the Coordination of Humanitarian Affairs (OCHA) to make three million US dollars available. Reception capacity at the border was thus expanded and the aid provisions established: all deportees would receive basic assistance at the border, transport to their destination in Afghanistan, and a material aid package on arrival. The international bodies also decided to monitor the way in which deportations were conducted and require the Iranian authorities to respect the 'human dignity' of the deportees (not separating families, giving people time to put their belongings together and so on). To this end, the Afghan Human Rights Committee, a body set up in 2002 with the support of UNAMA and based in Kabul, was invited to set up a base at the border.

These organisations thus drew on international human rights law not to contrast it with the deportation policy or to challenge that policy, but purely in order to monitor the conduct of deportations and provide deportees with mitigating aid designed to facilitate settlement in Afghanistan.[21] Only Afghans holding the *Amayesh* card – in other words, those the UNHCR deemed subject to the international refugee regime – were protected against deportation. And, indeed, the Iranian authorities hastened to stress that no Afghan in possession of an *Amayesh* card had been deported (which was essentially true). This situation, of mass deportations conducted in full view of UN agencies, arose because there was no international norm with sufficient authority, or any international moral entrepreneurs with sufficient influence, to oppose them.

In fact, beyond signing up to the 1951 Convention, states have proved reluctant to commit themselves to multilateral agreements designed to protect the rights of other classes of migrants. The priority of governments is to control migration rather than protect migrants. The 1990 UN Convention on Protection of the Rights of All Migrant Workers and Members of Their Families stipulates equality of treatment in employment between national workers and foreigners employed in the same state. Thus, in recognising that every migrant has individual rights, it establishes the principle of equal treatment between all migrants, whether documented or undocumented. But this is also the instrument of international human rights protection with the fewest state signatories.[22]

Other instruments of international human rights law could be applied here. But these provisions do not have enough authority to supersede state law. Article 13 of the 1948 Universal Declaration of Human Rights stipulates the right to move freely and to choose one's place of residence within a state. But this text, which is merely declarative, does not even have the status of an international treaty. Moreover, in Articles 12 and 13 of the International Covenant on Civil and Political Rights, an agreement that has the status of international norm and has been ratified by a large majority of states, the formulation changes, speaking not of the right to freedom of movement, but of the right to 'leave any country' and to 'enter [one's] own country'. Furthermore, by limiting its applicability to those who are lawfully within the territory of a state and subject to 'national security, public order, the protection of public health or morals', the article clearly articulates the subordination of this international treaty to state laws and, ultimately, to their criteria for legitimisation of international migration.

This lack of interstate consensus was also manifested in the absence, in the early 2000s, of any organisation of the UNHCR's size or influence that could act as a moral entrepreneur on behalf of other categories of migrants. The two bodies most directly concerned were the IOM and the ILO.

The IOM is not strictly speaking a UN agency, does not have an international normative frame of reference like the UNHCR and is funded by contributions to its projects. Because of this, it is subject to heavy monitoring by donor states and its programmes vary widely, depending on the context and the funding available. As Antoine Pécoud's review of various studies shows (2018), the IOM's programmes are more explicitly focused on control than on protection of migrants. The organisation itself states that its mandate relates to 'migration management' or 'orderly migration' rather than the 'protection of migrants'. The UNHCR's attitude towards the IOM oscillates between a degree of contempt for an organisation of lower moral stature and pragmatic collaboration in certain sensitive areas – typically the transport of returnees and deportees in their country of origin. Under the division of responsibilities established in the multilateral intervention in Afghanistan in 2007, the IOM was tasked with transporting deportees from the border to their final destination.

The ILO, on the other hand, is a specialised agency of the UN. Set up in 1919 to develop and promote standards relating to work throughout the world, it was the first genuinely multilateral body to operate in the field of international migration. In 2007 it had 182 member states. Migration has always been at the centre of its work, through protection of migrant workers' rights, which are the subject of many agreements promoted by the organisation. Nevertheless, seeking renewed legitimacy amid shifts in the global economy, in the early twenty-first century the ILO was not in a position to insist on placing the issue of migrant workers at the centre of debate (Standing 2008). In Afghanistan in 2007, the ILO, which had only a small office in the country, was not involved in the multilateral operation to support deportees.

Only the NGO Human Rights Watch issued a statement condemning Iran's actions, and also criticising the UN for not having done more to prevent the deportations (Human Rights Watch 2007). But the organisation carried little influence with states. The Iranian authorities were unconcerned by its accusations, particularly given that UN bodies had indirectly supported the deportations. Indeed, Human Rights Watch had backed up its criticism of the UN with data produced by the UNHCR, the only international organisation present at the Zaranj border crossing.

In other contexts, organisations that defend national or international human rights law contest the deportation of migrants who are not designated 'refugees'. But in most cases they do not succeed in preventing these deportations. In France, for example, organisations defending non-nationals' rights, such as CIMADE and the Groupe d'information et soutien aux immigrés, Immigrant Advice and Support Group (GISTI), protested in vain against the organisation of charter flights to return Afghans to Kabul. The individuals concerned can become their own moral entrepreneurs, as in the demonstration organised in Cairo in late 2005 by those Sudanese declared ineligible for refugee status – which ended in tragedy. While UNHCR representatives deemed them 'economic migrants', they demanded the right to be 'refugees' to avoid deportation to Sudan (Moulin and Nyers 2007).

The Iranian deportation of undocumented Afghans in the summer of 2007 shows how crucial an issue determination of status is for individuals. Even though conditions for *Amayesh* cardholders were becoming substantially more restrictive, the card did still ensure them relatively better treatment by at least protecting them from deportation. Figuring among the population subject to international refugee law and the UNHCR's mandate was thus the only way to be protected against deportation. Similar situations are to be found in most other countries, varying in relation to the applicable legal and administrative frameworks. Since the 2000s, states have classified most migrants in one of two groups, destined to receive very different treatments. On the one hand, there are the 'refugees', who exceptionally have the right to enter and are granted a residence permit. On the other hand, there are the 'migrant workers', or simply 'migrants' who cannot claim such legitimate motives and whose only alternative, if they wish to stay, is illegality, with the accompanying risk of deportation. Thus, in effect, lacking the possibility of obtaining an alternative legal status, the only way an Afghan can be legally present in a foreign country is to be recognised as eligible for 'international protection'.

In the absence of any alternative system of protection, asylum therefore emerges as a preferential regime that operates by distinguishing which among the set of all migrants may aspire to favourable treatment in accordance with international law. The fact that the abovementioned Sudanese demanded to be classified as 'refugees' rather than 'economic migrants' is significant in this respect. Identifying 'refugees' amounts to drawing a line dividing those included from those excluded in the only form of international protection available to non-nationals. As the rights of non-nationals are by definition limited within state jurisdictions, to defend the interests of 'refugees' is to promote the opening of a valve that prioritises the passage of one category of people. It indirectly legitimises the exclusion of nonrefugees, whether they are Afghans without an *Amayesh* card or 'failed asylum seekers' in other countries. With no other possibility of legal residence in the state jurisdiction, they immediately find themselves in a situation of illegality and 'deportability'. In this sense, the application of international refugee law offers a clearer understanding of the illegalisation of migrants (de Genova 2002), since the rationale behind illegalisation is largely shaped by this law.

Reflecting on the refugee label from the point of view of those not considered eligible for international protection under the 1951 Convention reveals the dispensatory nature of the international refugee regime during the 2000s. Given the way in which asylum is presented both by the UNHCR when it requests favourable treatment for 'refugees' from state authorities, and by the states themselves when they grant it, it constitutes an exception to the principle of state sovereignty. And, as ever, the exception proves the rule. Despite the fact that its application implies a conflict between the UNHCR and the state, which apparently renounces its sovereignty, granting a particular status as an exception effectively comes down to reasserting state sovereignty as the ultimate and arbitrary power. Like the 'sanctity' of the nation-state, the hierarchy between nationals and non-nationals is taken as read in a world where sovereignty is the ultimate authority legitimising human movement and where national difference takes precedence over human similarity, which may be invoked only with reference to certain individuals – a world in which, to return to Arendt's phrase, the state is the only real guarantor of the 'right to have rights'.

But here a hierarchy is established not only between nationals and non-nationals, but also among non-nationals. 'Failed asylum seekers' could be seen as the ultimate 'residual', 'surplus' population who, lacking the support of a strong state, do not fall under the mandate of any regime or specialist international institution, and are thrown against the wall of state sovereignty. They, then, not the 'refugees' vaguely and abstractly defined as those for whom an international protection regime was created, are the ones truly 'excluded from humanity', deprived of the 'right to have rights' within the system of states. Once classified as a 'refugee', a migrant has access to preferential treatment. The exclusion of others is legitimised by the same process. Thus, a hierarchy is established among migrants, between those whose deviance can exceptionally be redressed by decision of a sovereign state that respects international refugee law, and those who remain illegitimate.

The fact that the dividing line between those qualified as 'refugees' and others is always to some extent uncertain and arbitrary accentuates the violence of the labelling process inherent in the application of international refugee law. In the case of Afghans in Iran, they have been attributed status under procedures that have varied over three decades – procedures that, moreover, have almost never included the assessment of circumstances of leaving that the UNHCR recommends. Afghans had access to Blue Cards if they had arrived in Iran during a certain period (the 1980s or 1990s); they were able to obtain *Amayesh* cards if they had been able to present themselves to the authorities during the 2001 census, and during the renewal procedures in 2003 and 2005. From 2001 onwards, Afghans newly arriving in Iran had virtually no possibility of obtaining a residence permit.

This arbitrary dimension also pertains in countries where applications for asylum are assessed individually. Recent studies show that these decision-making structures are governed by understandings and mechanisms that applicants are powerless to affect (Akoka 2020; Greslier 2007; Ramji-Nogales et al. 2007; Rousseau et al. 2002; Valluy 2009). This is evident from the substantial disparities in rates of award of status to applicants of the same nationality in different European countries.[23] Finally, the arbitrary nature of these procedures is heightened by the specificity of this kind of judgment, which concerns events that occurred in another country (to which the applicant cannot return to obtain evidence) and by the fact that the judges have no witnesses to question.

Differential Access to Legal Movement

In the 2000s the regime established by international law with regard to migration rested on a clear opposition between two types of migrants: 'refugees' (or 'forced migrants'), who could benefit from the provisions of the 1951 Convention, and other migrants (often termed 'voluntary migrants', 'migrant workers', 'economic migrants' or simply 'migrants'), who could not claim this treatment. 'Asylum' and 'migration' were considered (as they largely continue to be considered today) as two distinct areas of international public policy: on the one hand, a consolidated, institutionalised regime centred on the 1951 Convention and a UN agency; on the other hand, a more undefined and institutionally fragmented regime largely made up of bilateral agreements between countries. The distinction between the 'forced' migration of 'refugees' and the 'voluntary' migration of 'migrant workers' had become common understanding, and was widely invoked by the media and researchers.[24]

This was not always the case: this binary classification gradually sharpened after the Second World War, as the 'asylum' and 'migration' sectors developed, becoming firmly established towards the end of the 1990s. This process occurred in a political context where many Western states were introducing restrictive immigration policies in response to migrations from the Global South, the UNHCR was expanding substantially, and other international organisations had little mandate over migration. It is worth pausing briefly to consider the historical development of the domains of 'asylum' and 'migration'. Between the two World Wars, the distinction between political and economic aspects of migration was not drawn as it is now. Resettlement of those who fled conflict was evaluated in close relation to the issue of unemployment: the Nansen International Office for Refugees, in collaboration with the ILO, sought to ensure that resettlement benefited the newly arrived and host counties equally (Loescher 2001a).

As Karatani shows (2005), the distinction between 'refugees' and 'migrants' was established at the end of the Second World War, mainly as a result of the dispute between the United States and the ILO over how to manage the great migration flows caused by the conflict. The ILO, with the backing of the UN, proposed to create a single comprehensive regime under its oversight. In the ILO's view, this would be a step towards achieving peace and social justice. However, the United States was concerned that its immigration policy would be obstructed by international regulation. It therefore proposed a plan that emphasised the functional distinction between migrants and between the international bodies that would take charge of them, each of which would have a specific mandate. With the United States now a world power, its plan won the day. As a result, two new organisations were created. Protection of 'refugees' was entrusted to the UNHCR, while transport was entrusted to the Provisional

Intergovernmental Committee for the Movement of Migrants from Europe (PICMME). The ILO was thus led to focus on 'migrant workers'.

After PICMME had become the IOM, and as the UNHCR expanded over the second half of the twentieth century, these separate regimes were consolidated. In the absence of any other entrepreneur holding an authority comparable to that of the UNHCR, this was an unbalanced process: international refugee law was developed and more consistently applied than other forms of protection of migrants' rights. Moreover, amid a generalised toughening of states' immigration policies through the 1990s, the UNHCR vigorously defended the population under its mandate to ensure that they were not also subject to these restrictions. While the UNHCR had worked to extend this population as far as possible, by broadening the applicability of the concept of refugee, this concept now demarcated the population with which the organisation was concerned. In order to strengthen its demand for the application of international refugee law, the UNHCR was more and more explicitly presenting 'refugees' in opposition to other migrants, pleading for exceptional preferential treatment, on the grounds that refugees had more legitimate motives than others for claiming legal entry and residence. This dynamic helped to cement the opposition between 'refugees' and 'migrants', and encouraged a compartmentalised approach to migration.

I have considered the case of Iran: the toughening of policy towards Afghans during the 1990s led the UNHCR to promote the introduction of screening procedures designed to separate Afghans 'in need of protection' from other migrants. This tendency is particularly evident in Europe. While restrictions on immigration have led many migrants to apply for asylum, a development that has subsequently been used to justify restrictions on asylum, the concept of 'mixed migration' has emerged to describe migrations in which people 'in need of protection' mingle with those 'not in need', and the UNHCR has itself started to plead for preferential treatment for the former.

It is also worth noting that the UNHCR is increasingly emphasising the concept of 'forced migrants' rather than 'refugees'. This development can be related to the UNHCR's desire for expansion, mainly into the humanitarian sphere. Having increased in size and operational capacity, and now present in conflict situations, the UNHCR sought to extend its mandate to the 'internally displaced', reconfiguring itself as the UN's humanitarian agency.[25] This has helped to entrench the distinction between 'voluntary' and 'forced' migrants that was so significant in the 2000s.

Whether it uses the term 'refugees' or 'forced migrants', the UNHCR is now deeply committed to defending the specificity of the recipients of its policies – people 'forced' to leave their place of origin to save their lives and escape persecution – compared to other migrants, who 'choose' to leave simply to improve their living conditions. While on rare occasions the UNHCR has also appeared to concern itself with other migrants – for example, when it asserts that the human rights of all migrants should be respected or when it proposes opening legal immigration channels (UNHCR 2000a: 26; 2007n: 5) – the starkly oppositional approach that prevailed in the 2000s was indifferent to the consequences of the refugee regime for other migrants. Some of the UNHCR's statements explicitly supported the claims of states with regard to the illegitimacy of certain migrants' movements. Take, for example, the following remark:

> UNHCR is especially mindful of the need to ensure that the provision of protection and asylum to refugees and other people of concern to the Office does not compound the difficulties that states experience in controlling more generally the arrival and residence of foreign nationals and in combating international crime. (UNHCR 2007n: 2)

Thus, when High Commissioner Lubbers asserts that 'we have to be clear about who is a refugee and who is a migrant, and not sacrifice one to keep out the other' (UNHCR 2004e), the question is whether the recommended approach achieves precisely the opposite result.

In particular, the UNHCR Executive Committee's position on repatriation of 'failed asylum seekers' explicitly risks harm to migrants deemed 'not in need of international protection': 'efficient and expeditious return of persons found not to need international protection is key to the international protection system as a whole'.[26]

Although these people do not come under the organisation's mandate, it still concerns itself with their fate when it declares their deportation advisable. Deportation is deemed desirable because it guarantees the credibility of selection procedures.[27] This is a good example of the way in which the UNHCR, seeking to promote the application of international refugee law, supports the rule, giving it greater legitimacy in order to promote the exception.

Evidently, then, promoting the application of international refugee law involves the selective application of international human rights law. Backed by a moral entrepreneur that wields authority, the principle of nonrefoulement enshrined in international refugee law is effectively defended more strongly than other rights such as freedom of movement. Here state sovereignty is involved not only in making case-by-case decisions on non-nationals, but also in the creation and modification of international organisations, and the application of international law. Here states pursue common interests that are as likely to restrict as to open space for multilateral regimes.

In this case, the imbalance between the relative robustness of the international refugee regime and the legal and institutional fragmentation of existing protections for other migrants works to the advantage of all states that receive large numbers of migrants. It allows them to make a choice in each case as to how they will address the issue of non-nationals, and to decide on differential access to legal movement. For a minority of migrants, states negotiate the concrete application of a dispensatory regime with the UNHCR, giving the appearance of yielding to their obligations under international law, but in fact remaining largely in control of how it is applied. They take a more unilateral approach to other migrants: the goodwill shown in the case of 'refugees' subsequently legitimises the exclusion of others from legal status.

Aware of the consequences this selective application of human rights law can have for migrants not considered 'refugees', a number of human rights NGOs and other international organisations such as the ILO and the International Committee of the Red Cross have attempted to qualify the sharp distinction between 'migrants' and 'refugees', as I showed in my examination of the position taken by the ILO and some NGOs during the 2001 Global Consultations on International Protection (Scalettaris 2007). A number of researchers and experts have also highlighted and/or criticised this situation: some indirectly, questioning the analytical relevance of the distinction between 'voluntary' and 'forced' migration and whether it can be concretely applied to migrants (Richmond 1988; Turton 2003), and some more directly, in the context of debates and proposals for reform that proliferated among international organisations at the turn of the millennium, prompted first by the UN Secretary-General and then encouraged by the Global Commission on International Migration. Some authors have suggested that priority should be given to ensuring the right to free movement (Carens 1987, de Gutchteneire and Pécoud 2008; Teitelbaum 1980). Others have called for greater coordination in the 'governance of migration', for example, by setting up a single agency responsible for overseeing the 'governance' of international movement (Bhagwati 2003; Ghosh 1995; Helton 2003; Martin 2001, 2004). Still others have proposed new categories such as 'survival migration' (Betts 2010a), as a way of going beyond the compartmentalised understanding and management of migrants based almost exclusively on the 1951 Convention.

The Originality and Limitations of the ACSU Project

The ACSU project took an innovative position with regard to these debates. The specific parameters of 'persons in need of protection', and the need to identify them to ensure they benefited from preferential treatment, were not questioned. However, the strategy did not limit itself to distinguishing 'Afghans in need of protection' from the entirety of migrants. Afghans 'under the mandate' of the UNHCR were considered 'within a broader policy framework for displacement' (UNHCR 2007a: 1). This strategy adopted a holistic approach, placing forms of migration on a continuum, identifying four types of migrants ('Afghans in need of protection', 'future returnees', 'longstaying Afghans' and 'migrant workers'), and putting forward a range of provisions adapted to each.

The ACSU project, rightly termed 'comprehensive solutions', thus envisaged a global migration regime within which forms of protection would be distributed between different categories of migrants in a balanced way. The strategy thus implicitly recognised that policies concerning different categories of migrants were closely linked and influenced one another, and that they should be designed as a whole and harmonised. If alternative forms of protection existed alongside those provided for 'refugees', the selection of persons 'in need of international protection' would have less drastic consequences than deportability for those considered ineligible for refugee status.

This concern was clearly evident in the ACSU strategy when it sought to postpone individual selection for as long as possible: immediate selection was not desirable because its consequence would be to leave all those declared ineligible 'without cover'.

The aim was therefore to move to selection only after the Iranian and Pakistani governments had accepted solutions for those not eligible for international protection. The IOM and ILO were called upon to become involved as moral entrepreneurs on behalf of the migrants under their mandate.

This holistic approach was evidently at work during the summer of 2007, in the UNHCR's reaction to the deportations. Saverio, who was by then Representative in Kabul, took it upon himself to promote, both internally and in representations to the international organisations in Kabul, an interventionist approach to ensure that the deportees received aid. And, indeed, ultimately the UNHCR played a central role as a behind-the-scenes catalyst for the multilateral intervention. In addition, Saverio took advantage of the attention generated by the deportations to promote the vision of 'comprehensive solutions', including the recommendations for a bilateral regime for 'migrant workers', at every meeting and press conference. It was also no accident that, at the UNHCR's suggestion, the formal leadership of the multilateral intervention was entrusted to the IOM. This role had a major symbolic import, indicating that these migrants, although they had not been recognised as coming under the UNHCR's mandate, also had rights that needed to be protected. It was also a way to make the IOM accountable in order to ensure that it actively concerned itself with these migrants.

But the events of 2007 around the deportations also reveal the formidable obstacles faced by the ACSU project, raising the question of whether it was actually possible to establish a 'comprehensive', balanced system with regard to Afghan migration between Iran and Afghanistan in the existing institutional configuration. The limited results achieved by the strategy between 2003 and 2007 are evidence of this. In 2007, when the Tripartite Agreement was renewed, the Iranian authorities consented to add a clause based on the work permit system, and to grant 250,000 visas for seasonal work – but only on condition that the families concerned all returned to Afghanistan. Apart from this concession, and a few informal allusions to the possibility of guaranteeing more stable residence for specific categories (specialist professionals or veterans of the Iraq war), the Iranian authorities' reluctance to question their immigration policy was manifest.[28]

Saverio and Eric themselves were to be directly faced with this serious conflict of priorities in the autumn, when the Iranian authorities announced their intention to forbid residence in other Iranian provinces to all Afghans, including *Amayesh* cardholders. Efforts to contest this harsher policy took up all their attention, while the deportations and the introduction of a system for 'migrant workers' were relegated to the background.

This was in fact a highly ambitious initiative for the UNHCR, for it required a delicate balancing act between concern for people 'formally under its mandate' and pleading for other migrants. It thus risked unbalancing the organisation's centre of coherence (the 1951 Convention and the figure of the 'refugee'), which underpins its justification for existing and is its primary source of legitimate authority in relation to states. Moreover, in the light of increasingly restrictive immigration policies, it proved impossible to defend both 'refugees' and other migrants. And pleading in favour of 'refugees' increasingly equated to demanding exceptional favourable treatment.

Notes

1. Office français de protection des réfugiés et apatrides – Office for the Protection of Refugees and Stateless Persons (trans.).
2. The categories are as follows: Afghans perceived as criticising factions or individuals who exert control over a zone; government officials; members of minority ethnic groups in certain zones; Muslims who have converted to another religion; women with specific backgrounds; unaccompanied minors; victims of serious trauma; individuals at risk of or victims of harmful traditional practices; homosexuals; Afghans associated with international organisations and the security forces; property owners; Afghans associated with the Democratic People's Party (UNHCR 2007c).
3. Here it was the UNHCR itself that in the 2000s secured authorisation from the Turkish government to determine status so that they could then resettle those whom the organisation recognised as 'refugees' in other countries.
4. The 1969 Convention of the Organisation of African Unity, which governs issues relating to refugees in Africa, extends the definition of refugee to any person who has left their country by reason of 'external aggression' or 'foreign domination', or 'events seriously disturbing public order in either part or the whole of his country of origin or nationality' (Article 1).

5. See, for example, the UNHCR's comments on procedures in Greece (UNHCR 2008d).
6. The word *panahande* comes from the root *panah* – refuge, shelter, asylum (Lazard 2000: 80).
7. The status applied to students of religion, disabled veterans of the Iran/Iraq war and the families of 'martyrs' of that war, who received renewable passes that are still currently valid.
8. The concept *muhajir* (plural *muhajirina*), which has the same Arabic root as *hijrat*, Mohammed's exile in Medina, refers to a religious exile who has left a territory where it is no longer possible to practise Islam. During the 1980s (the years of the Soviet occupation of Afghanistan), this concept was very widely used in relation to all those who had left Afghanistan. See Centlivres 1988; Centlivres and Centlivres-Dumont 1999; Edwards 1986; Masud 1990; and Shahrani 1995.
9. The number of people awarded a certificate by the UNHCR since 2001 is negligible, of the order of one hundred each year. UNHCR observations indicate that even if they are not valid as a residence permit these documents have been effective in protecting people against deportation.
10. The Farsi word for census or registration. The term derives from the root *âmâr* (statistic) (Lazard 2000: 8).
11. The only exception was visas, although these are very rare, very expensive and valid for only a few months.
12. The new provisions strictly forbade Afghans without a residence permit access to government services, the right to belong to cultural, political or social parties or groups, to open a bank account or to take out any kind of insurance. They also prohibited Iranians from letting accommodation to Afghans, and toughened the legal action that could be taken against employers who took on Afghans without work permits (Abbasi-Shavazi et al. 2008).
13. The fact that the 2003 regulations targeted undocumented foreigners reveals the ambiguity of Iran's attitude towards this population and proves that the state was aware of its size.
14. The Afghan workforce thus plays a fundamental role in the Iranian economy. Citing a local source, Monsutti notes that during the 1990s, Afghans contributed 4.4% of Iran's GDP (Monsutti 2004: 168).
15. The repatriation agreement led to the creation of a Tripartite Commission between Iran, Afghanistan and the UNHCR, which met periodically to oversee the programme.
16. Article 1 of the Tripartite Agreement, renewed in 2005, states that: 'The term "Afghan refugees and displaced persons" shall – for the purpose of defining the scope of this Joint Programme only – mean any Afghan citizens in Iran who were registered in the Amayesh registration exercise undertaken by the Iranian authorities in 2003.'
17. For example, to take only academic publications, the titles of the following articles all use the expression 'Afghan refugees': Fielden 1998; Kronenfeld 2008; Macleod 2008; Maley 2001; Novak 2007; Rizvi 1990; Schöch 2008; Turton and Marsden 2002; Zieck 2008.
18. Definition from the *Petit Robert* French dictionary.
19. For example, the NGO Médecins Sans Frontières, which runs aid programmes targeted at the Afghan population in Iran, says it assists 'Afghan refugees in Iran', thus

suggesting that it identifies all Afghans in Iran as 'refugees', regardless of their legal status (Médecins Sans Frontières 2006).

20. This figure includes only the deportations recorded by the UNHCR.

21. This aid was too limited to really make a difference to the fate of deportees, beyond briefly alleviating a situation of distress at the border. Field reports indicated that the package was of little help in supporting settlement in regions where many people had lost all reference points and that were still ridden by conflict.

22. It came into effect in 2003, twelve years after it was adopted by the UN General Assembly and following a long period of negotiation. By the end of 2020, only fifty-six states had ratified it, the majority of them countries from which migrants originate, who were concerned to ensure their fellow citizens were protected in other countries.

23. Afghans in particular are among the nationalities with the most varied levels of acceptance across the EU (Donini et al. 2016).

24. As is indicated by the flourishing domain of Refugee Studies and the many publications that approach the global phenomenon of migration from the standpoint of the difference between forced and voluntary migrants (see, for example, Martin 2001).

25. An ambition that materialised in the 'cluster' approach adopted when the UN was reformed in the late 2000s.

26. Conclusion on International Protection No. 96 (LIV). Return of Persons Found Not to Be in Need of International Protection, 10 October 2003, p.1.

27. However, it is worth noting that with regard to Afghan failed asylum seekers, in 2007 the UNHCR made a final proposal, on the basis of 'humanitarian considerations' (UNHCR 2006d). This document lists categories of persons who, despite not being recognised as deserving protection, are in a situation such that the UNHCR judged that return would put their safety at risk. The organisation asked states not to deport them for the time being.

28. See Macleod's overview (2008).

CHAPTER 8

Confronting State Sovereignty

Camp Closure in Pakistan

Spring 2007. Among UNHCR officers in Kabul, the sixth year of the repatriation programme opens in anxious mood. Four refugee camps in Pakistan are scheduled to be closed this summer, including Jalozai and Kacha Gari. According to census data, these camps, which sprang up in the early 1980s, are the largest and fourth largest in the country respectively. Jalozai alone, situated about 30 kilometres from Peshawar, houses 110,000 legally resident Afghans, and is thus effectively a town in its own right, with markets, shops and permanent infrastructure. Kacha Gari has become a neighbourhood incorporated into Peshawar.

Worry can be sensed in the air, and filters through half-open doors in the evening, as senior staff hold sombre discussions in the almost-empty office. One evening in April, at a group dinner, the Deputy Head of Mission receives a call from Geneva. Everyone falls silent when his voice on the phone turns serious. He then tells his colleagues that three Afghans have died in one of the camps due to be closed. All automatically assume an intervention by the Pakistani security forces, fearing that the inevitable has already begun: 'It's started already.' The dinner continues, but everyone is pensive. The following day, we discover with some relief that no, 'it has not yet started': the incident was an internal dispute in the camp.

Clearly, the recent issue of residence permits to some three million Afghans is not going to diminish the pressure for repatriation. In early June, at the last meeting of the Tripartite Commission, the Pakistani delegation presented its plan for the three years to come. With an average of over 800,000 returns each year, this roadmap effectively amounted to the total elimination of the Afghan presence in Pakistan by 2009. The Pakistani authorities went as far as suggesting that residents in the camps should be 'encouraged' to go back to Afghanistan.[1] This time it seems the Pakistani government is determined to go right to the end. Officials from the Ministry for Frontier Regions (SAFRON) have communicated to UNHCR senior staff in Pakistan that the Prime Minister's office has made closure of the camps a priority. The fate of the Afghan camps in Pakistan is once again caught up in global geostrategic issues. The 'war on terror' launched by the United States following the 9/11 attacks, and Pakistan's ambivalent policy with regard to it, have created a new context. President Karzai has repeatedly accused Pakistani President Musharraf of providing the Taliban with refuge and strategic bases. Musharraf has retorted that Afghans living in Pakistan are contributing to the rise in power of militant Islamists and the Taliban movement. He promotes the closure of the camps as a national security priority and a sign of goodwill towards the NATO countries that have chosen Pakistan as an ally in the 'war on terror'. The Jalozai camp, which was one of the main support bases for the Mujahideen during the 1980s, is depicted as a place heavily influenced by militant Islamists.

The UNHCR, for its part, has firmly stated that the Pakistani authorities' objectives are unrealistic, if Afghans' freedom of choice and Afghanistan's 'absorption capacity' are to be respected. At the Tripartite Commission meetings, UNHCR delegations had repeatedly pointed out that the residents of the camps were mainly women, children and older people, and that the closure of several camps in 2005 had not slowed the rise of radical Islam in Pakistan's frontier regions. In addition to emphasising the unstable conditions in Afghanistan, they had also pointed out that the best way to prevent Afghans resident in Pakistan from joining the ranks of the Taliban was to forestall situations that made them vulnerable – for example, forced return to Afghanistan. But these arguments cut no ice with the Pakistani government, which was determined to ramp up the rate of repatriation.

Researchers have approached the repatriation programmes from two main angles. Some have sought to explain at the macrolevel why repatriation has become established as the 'preferred solution' since the 1980s, for reasons that include geopolitical changes since the end of the Cold War, the adoption of restrictive immigration policies by donor countries, and the UNHCR's financial crisis (Barnett 2004; Black and Koser 1999; Chimni 2004). From a different point of view, a number of researchers have criticised some repatriation programmes for violating the principle of voluntary return (Barnett 2004; Bialczyk 2008; Blitz et al. 2005; Crisp 1984; Harrell-Bond 1989; Strand et al. 2008; Takahashi 1997; Zimmermann 2009). In these analyses the UNHCR is depicted either as being at the mercy of power relations between states or as an agent of oppression, often owing to errors or poor judgement on the part of its officers. The issues involved in the concrete implementation and the operation of these programmes, and the dilemmas faced by UNHCR staff, are rarely addressed.[2]

In this chapter I offer a detailed examination of the negotiations between UNHCR staff and the Pakistani authorities around the future of the Kacha Gari and Jalozai camps in the summer of 2007. Taking the approach to power outlined in Chapter 1, I consider the UNHCR and the Pakistani state as two 'overlapping sovereignties' and unpick their confrontation. In addition to exposing the inadequacy of normative perspectives for understanding this relationship, this approach allows me to examine the articulation between the two, the resources and tactics each deployed, and to situate this confrontation within the context of broader power relations (including, but not limited to, relations between states) in which it is set. I thus reveal the extremely constricted position in which the UNHCR found itself, unable to counter the Pakistani authorities' pressure for return. Notwithstanding serious internal tensions, the organisation sanctioned the international legitimacy of closing the camps and of the related repatriations, thus participating in a mechanism that placed a heavy burden on Afghans living in Kacha Gari and Jalozai, aimed at *emplacing* them in Afghanistan.

The Economy of Repatriation

When it began in 2002, the repatriation programme formed common ground between the UNHCR and the Pakistani authorities. Being fully aligned with the interests of the Pakistani government, its establishment had given the UNHCR substantial room for manoeuvre, since the organisation's contribution was fundamental, both financially and logistically, to the implementation of the programme. In addition, as guarantor of the 'voluntariness' of the returns, the organisation lent them international legitimacy, and the Pakistani government was keen for the repatriation to be seen as a legitimate process.[3]

The ACSU project aimed to capitalise on this advantageous position to plead for more stable residence conditions for those Afghans who had no intention of returning, and for migrant workers. The hypothesis was that at some point, the balance would tip and enough Afghans would have left for Pakistan to show a more benevolent attitude to the minority who remained. The plan was therefore to wait until the flow of returns had reduced this population to a 'politically digestible number'. In the meantime, the return of a proportion of the Afghan population in Pakistan would need to continue. Repatriation would thus act as a balance in the search for Pakistan's tolerance threshold. It was the variable that could never be reduced to zero if the 'equation of Afghan displacement' was to be solved.

But after two years, and following the return of some two million people, rates of repatriation began to fall but the Pakistani authorities were clearly not yet satisfied and gave no sign that they intended to follow the UNHCR's recommendations. On the contrary, the fall in repatriation rates from 2004 prompted increasing pressure on Afghans to return. Their residence conditions were markedly deteriorating: they could no longer officially own property or access public services. By 2002, most returnees had left the cities. The Pakistani authorities then turned their attention to the camps, with the stated intention of closing several of them.

The dwindling rate of returns gradually eroded the UNHCR's power in its relationship with the Pakistani authorities. The organisation then faced a difficult dilemma: should it attempt to maintain the best possible relations for collaboration, in the hope that the Pakistani authorities would eventually agree to its recommendations, bringing lasting benefits for a large number of Afghans? Or was it preferable to show firmness by formally noting the pressure for return and the deteriorating residence conditions suffered by the whole of the Afghan population in Pakistan, at the risk of offending the government? The worse the situation became, the harder it was to say nothing about it. The last resort would be to condemn the violation of the principle of 'voluntary return' and suspend the programme. But such a decision could not be taken lightly, because keeping the repatriation channel open was still the (increasingly weak) base from which the UNHCR had been negotiating other solutions over the years.

In 2004 this shifting relation of power had given rise to the process known in the UNHCR as 'camp consolidation'. Faced with the Pakistani authorities' firm intention to close some of them, the UNHCR had taken it upon itself to evaluate conditions in these camps and the 'inclination to return' of the people living there.[4] It was therefore agreed that some camps that had arisen near the border more recently, between 2001 and 2002, to house people fleeing the military campaign against the Taliban should be closed. These camps, which were heavily overcrowded, were located in very inhospitable places to which it was difficult to transport aid. UNHCR staff thought that the Afghans living there might be inclined to return. The organisation therefore agreed to these camps being closed, but on condition that the residents were allowed to move to larger, more accessible camps.

But by the following year, things were almost at breaking point: the UNHCR was on the brink of suspending the repatriation programme. Dissatisfied with the rate of return in 2004, the Pakistani government had tried to boost repatriation by announcing its intention to close all camps in the Federally Administered Tribal Areas (FATA). This time the camps identified for closure were not recent; some had been established as far back as the 1980s. But they were also located in border regions where the Taliban

Census of Afghans in Pakistan : Top 35 Camps by Province of Residence
Feb 23 - Mar 11, 2005

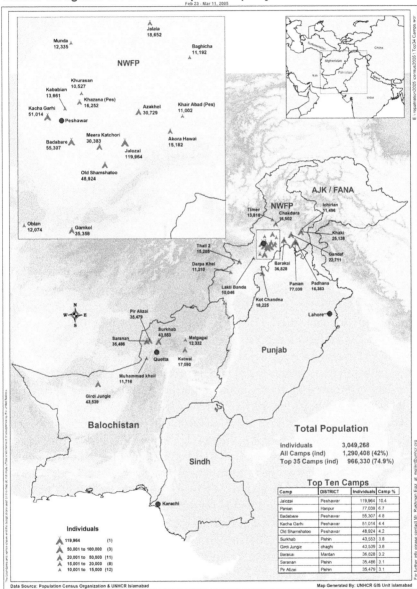

Figure 8.1. The 35 largest refugee camps in Pakistan in 2005 (SAFRON, NADRA, UNHCR 2008: 38) © UNHCR

was regrouping, and to which the UNHCR had no access. All of this made it difficult and delicate for the organisation to argue against closure. It therefore drew up assessments of each of the camps concerned and insisted on the need for all residents to have the opportunity to relocate in Pakistan. Relations between the UNHCR and Pakistan became tense, and the closure of thirty or so of these camps accounted for around one-third of the 450,000 returns that year. This episode, which the UNHCR treated with great discretion in its public statements, nevertheless had a major impact internally, leading the organisation to adopt more confrontational and explicit language in the following years. In early 2007 the UNHCR's public documents spoke of a 'critical juncture' (UNHCR 2007b: 1), and warned of pressure for return, citing 'attempts to engineer large scale return' (UNHCR 2007a: 1).

A Framework of Principles
(and the Limitations of Normative Approaches)

In order to counter the pressure from the Pakistani authorities, the UNHCR established a framework of principles to which the repatriation process should conform, setting limits on the exercise of Pakistani sovereignty. The basic principles were articulated in the 2003 Tripartite Agreement between Afghanistan, Pakistan and the UNHCR, which was renewed in almost identical form in 2006: the voluntary nature of return, graduality, safety and dignity. In Article 11, the two governments recognised the UNHCR's supervisory role and established it as guarantor of the respect of these principles, with the organisation 'monitoring the voluntary repatriation ... in order to ensure that repatriation is voluntary and carried out in conditions of safety and dignity'.

As the closure of the FATA camps in 2005 had been conducted under the aegis of the Tripartite Agreement, the UNHCR made its in-principle agreement to the closure of the Kacha Gari and Jalozai camps conditional on three further stipulations: first, the 'absorption capacity' and security conditions in people's regions of origin had to be taken into account; second, Pakistan should offer camp residents a viable option for relocation within Pakistan; and, third, camps would not be closed after the summer, the last point when returnees could resettle in Afghanistan before the winter. These principles were approved by the Pakistani authorities at the meeting of the Tripartite Commission in 2006.[5] In early 2007 the three delegations had confirmed all the above principles and had also agreed that the closure of the four camps scheduled for 2007 should be conducted 'peacefully'.[6]

It was important to the UNHCR that these principles were formalised, and thereby constituted written engagements on the part of the Pakistani government that the UNHCR could invoke. However, they had little legal standing.

The conclusions of Tripartite Commission meetings formalised specific decisions about the management of the programme, but did not have the status of an international treaty. Since Pakistan has not ratified the 1951 Convention, the only international agreement applicable was the Tripartite Agreement that Pakistan had concluded with Afghanistan and the UNHCR. But the UNHCR's supervisory role, as articulated in that agreement, had no power of coercion. The treaty gave the UNHCR no means of sanction should it deem that Pakistan had failed to respect the principles of the agreement, and there was no third organisation with power of sanction to which the UNHCR could appeal in such an event.

'Covenants, without the sword, are but words, and of no strength to secure a man at all', said Hobbes. This adage seems entirely apposite to the Tripartite Agreement (and by extension to international refugee law as a whole). As many analyses have emphasised, international law is generally characterised by a lack of coercive power. In the absence of any possibility of sanction by force, the norms of international law are like words without a sword. But this approach that sees the law (covenants) and force (the sword) as the principal manifestations of power is highly reductive as a way of understanding the relationship between the UNHCR and the Pakistani state. The focus is solely on what is missing: legally enforceable norms. In this view, both the bureaucratic practices and the negotiations between the UNHCR and the Pakistani authorities are merely a matter of what political scientists and lawyers often call the 'informal'. But my aim here is to grasp the relation of power between the UNHCR and the Pakistani state by opening up the black box of the 'informal' and examining the resources, strategies and techniques deployed by each to influence the other's actions.

This entails going beyond the normative, state-centred conception of power as expressed purely through force and the law, in order to grasp the more varied and complex ways in which authority is exerted. Foucault, in his dismantling of the myths of the state and the law, showed that the law is just one of the forms through which power is manifested. He argued that the law is a 'terminal form' (1979: 92), one of the diverse configurations that relations of power can take. This approach resonates strongly with the notion of 'overlapping sovereignties' introduced by Hansen and Stepputat (2005), as a way of acknowledging the sovereign prerogatives of bodies other than the state and grasping the heterogeneous ways in which authority is exercised.[7]

When the UNHCR talks about the repatriation programme in Afghanistan and its own relationship with the Pakistani state, it always refers to the 'legal framework' – that is, Pakistan's immigration laws, the Tripartite Agreement on repatriation, and the Conclusions of the Tripartite Commission meetings. Many political scientists do the same, as if these legal texts by themselves could give a sense of the nature of the programme and the relationship. They thus reproduce the myth of the state and of state (and international) law, despite the fact that these norms in and of themselves provide no detail on the operation of the programme or about the relationship between the UNHCR and the Pakistani state. In my view, this 'detail' emerges from the stakes, the reasoning, and the procedures and tactics of the game – a game with unwritten rules and no referee – in which the UNHCR and Pakistan engaged when they negotiated the repatriation programme. The power relation between them was not determined or framed by legal norms, but was constructed on a line that shifted depending on the constraints structuring that relation and the way in which each of them made strategic use of the resources at its disposal, took advantage of the other's weaknesses and played the game day by day.

Letting go of the normative approach means that legal norms no longer constitute explanatory frames of reference. It also means that their role in this confrontation needs to be examined. These legal norms in fact prove to be one of the means essential to the tactics and conducts at issue here, around which they crystallise, and on the basis of which they can be observed. By focusing attention on the modes of production and application of these norms, their manipulation and interpretation, the way in which they were implemented and circumvented, and the way in which various actors used them and invoked them, it becomes possible to grasp the relationship at issue here.

To give one example: at the Tripartite Commission meeting in June 2007, the Pakistani delegation expressed a wish to remove the term 'gradual' from the definition of the return process in the text of the Tripartite Agreement, proposing that it be replaced by the terms 'orderly' and 'phased'. The question remained unresolved: the Afghan and UNHCR delegations sought official comments, but this request held up the renewal of the agreement. This is an example of how the confrontation between the UNHCR and the Pakistani authorities was played out in the formulation of legal texts. Not having been at this meeting, I cannot fully analyse this initiative (was it a show of power to mark the beginning of the repatriation season, or a well thought-out strategy to prepare and cover themselves in the event that Kacha Gari and Jalozai were closed?). In any case, this was clearly an aggressive manoeuvre through which the Pakistani authorities were attempting to dismantle the framework of principles established by the UNHCR.

The vagueness of the principles articulated in the treaty and at the Tripartite Commission meetings should also be borne in mind. The timeframe of the principle of graduality was not specified in terms of a maximum number of returns per year. The sustainability of return to regions of origin and of the options for relocation in Pakistan was not defined. Even the principle of 'peaceful closure' remained vague because there was no definition of precisely what would be considered use of force: cutting off electricity and water? Demolishing homes? The use of physical force against individuals?

Conformity with these principles, on which the international legitimacy of the returns rested, therefore depended on the interpretation and evaluation of them by the officials concerned. What was the nature of the reasoning at work in these evaluations, and how were graduality and sustainability measured? With these questions in mind, I examine how, from May 2007 onwards, the UNHCR took on the Pakistani authorities who were apparently determined to close the Kacha Gari and Jalozai camps before the end of the summer.

Kabul and Islamabad: Two Irreconcilable Points of View

In May, the Deputy Head of Mission of the Pakistan Operation came on mission to Kabul. A big meeting was held in the Branch Office meeting room, attended by Heads of Section and Heads of Sub-Offices. The officer on mission from Pakistan spoke about the context there. He painted a gloomy picture of growing political instability, where feelings of distrust towards Afghans were exacerbated by tensions between the two countries, and the issue of Afghans was inextricably linked with President Musharraf's ambiguous policy towards Islamic militants. He also spoke of the difficulty his office had in operating in this sensitive context: the possibilities for containing pressure on Afghans were dwindling, since the higher echelons of government were determined to 'close the chapter on refugees'. He reported that despite almost daily attempts to establish a constructive dialogue and encourage the Pakistani authorities to take a more realistic view, it was extremely difficult for the Islamabad office to wield any influence. Openly referring to the ACSU strategy, he also emphasised that the Pakistani authorities did not seem in any way inclined to grant adjusted status to Afghans who were 'in need of protection', durably settled or migrant workers. While the Pakistani government had agreed to launch a development programme in some areas with a large Afghan population (which might be a step towards accepting longer-term residence of Afghans in the country), it was still manifestly reluctant to question its immigration policy.

The impersonal tone taken by the officer from Islamabad when he addressed the closure of the camps contrasted with the note of concern the Kabul office staff were used to hearing from their own managers. When the Islamabad Deputy Head of Mission reminded people of the deadlines and listed the relocation sites identified, the closure of Kacha Gari and Jalozai was presented as a fait accompli, a decision already taken that was not subject to review. All that remained to be seen was whether the government would actually manage to close the camps that year. Closure was presented as an unassailable fact that sealed the relationship between the UNHCR and the Pakistani government, a *sine qua non* of their dialogue. The priority was for it to take place 'without incident'.

This report was followed by an oration from Saverio, who put forward the Kabul office's perspective in a much more impassioned tone. The repatriation of hundreds of millions of people was not a prospect to be taken lightly. In addition to the now extremely limited 'absorption capacity' of many regions in the south and east of Afghanistan – the regions from which the majority of those in the camps originated – confrontations between the international forces and the Taliban were causing civilian casualties and flight. In this context, the UNHCR's capacity to assist the repatriated population was extremely limited. The memory of the closure of the FATA camps in 2005 weighed heavily on the Afghan Operation, and its legacy was still visible. Saverio reminded people that entire projects were still dedicated to the reintegration of some groups repatriated from the FATA, who were still unable to provide for their own subsistence two years later. He also pointed out that the crisis around the deportations from Iran was ongoing. The UNHCR's work was in the spotlight: its credibility in Afghanistan was at stake in the way in which the closure of the camps was managed. And while the deportations from Iran concerned undocumented Afghans, in the camps, those in question were Afghans officially under the UNHCR's mandate, holders of residence permits valid until 2009, whom the UNHCR had fought to keep in Pakistan.

The friction between the two Operations had been amplified by the arrival of the new leadership in Kabul. Saverio, newly in post, brought to the management of the Country Operation and the Regional Situation not only the ACSU project, but also a renewed idealist fervour. He did not want to see the repatriation programme as a henceforth established mechanism that would be automatically reproduced year after year in order to satisfy the Pakistani authorities. He argued that even in a very difficult situation, there should be no concessions on questions of principle. Every camp closure should be considered an exception, and they should be careful not to create precedents. He wanted more specificity, at least internally, on the criterion of 'peaceful closure' and the limit beyond which the UNHCR would not go. But this 'idealist' vision of repatriation was viewed with scepticism (if not a degree of hostility) by the managers of neighbouring Operations, particularly since it was difficult to reconcile with the pragmatic approach and the inclination towards short-term compromise recommended by the ACSU project. In fact, during the summer of 2007, the closure of the camps became the dominant issue in the Kabul office, and the long-term ACSU strategy moved into the background, even in the minds of its instigators.

In my interactions with colleagues from External Relations in Islamabad working on the weekly information bulletins, I noted that the discrepancy in tone was not only among the managers, but also influenced the way in which all staff expressed themselves: nuances of vocabulary, emphasis on one fact rather than another. These bulletins were the source of skirmishes between the Kabul and Islamabad offices, provoked by the differences in tone and by divergent conceptions of the confidentiality of information: the Islamabad staff were more tight-lipped and more attentive to not using phrasing or language that might displease the Pakistani authorities. They did not appreciate the Kabul office mentioning what was happening in Pakistan and demanded 'copyright' on the information they had communicated to the Kabul office. In any case, they claimed the right to approve the final version. I was sometimes ill at ease with my counterpart in the Islamabad office, for she altered text that had already been approved by my manager. On a few occasions the Deputy Head of Mission in Islamabad reprimanded me in person, prompting a blunt response from his opposite number in Kabul.

The heated tone of the discussion died down only when the meeting ended and the formalities of welcome and hierarchy took over again. Saverio underlined, with barely concealed asperity, the importance of cooperation between the offices. But the reality appeared very different. Each office was engaged in its own struggle, leading to a 'standoff' between Operations within the organisation. The Islamabad office was in daily negotiations with an unpredictable government on an issue sitting at the intersection of internal and international political stakes that were well beyond the scope of the UNHCR. The Kabul office, on the other hand, faced a different kind of impasse owing to the situation in Afghanistan – a country that was not ready to receive thousands of returnees each year. This internal tension thus reflected the external difficulties facing the organisation, torn between two contexts that were both intractable and irreconcilable.

The UNHCR's Arsenal

The UNHCR had four arms at its disposal in its confrontation with the Pakistani authorities. The first was the framework of principles described above, which the UNHCR had constructed previously to counter pressure from Pakistan. The second was 'contingency planning', an exercise in 'risk anticipation' in the event of a mass return. This plan, developed under the leadership of the Kabul office with the help of an expert from the organisation's Emergency Preparedness and Response Section at Headquarters, envisaged possible future scenarios in order to make logistical preparations and maximise capacity for support to returnees. The aim of this process was to contain uncertainty around the intentions of the Pakistani authorities and create a network of 'allies' in Afghanistan, consisting of donors and NGOs (all involved in developing the plan) whose collaboration would be needed in any large-scale emergency intervention in the event of a mass return.

The other two weapons that the UNHCR deployed in early 2007 were a communications strategy and a system for monitoring returns. While the deployment of these resources was shaped and indeed often hampered by the underlying tensions between the Kabul and Islamabad offices (which led to the two offices carrying them out independently within their respective countries), they were nevertheless means deployed tactically in order to mount a better defence.

One of the changes Saverio introduced from the spring concerned his office's external communications, which he wanted to be more forceful and more transparent in terms of what they said about the constraints and dilemmas facing the organisation. This was one way of raising awareness and keeping the representatives of the UNHCR's external partners (donors and NGOs) informed of how events were developing, and thus ensuring they were cognisant of the Pakistani authorities' manoeuvres, so that these might affect Pakistan's international reputation. It was with the same intention that the weekly bulletin for which I was responsible was instituted at the beginning of the summer. Sharing the latest developments with donors and international organisations in Afghanistan was a way of ensuring attention stayed focused on the closure of the camps and keeping alert 'allies' on side. In line with the 'committed' approach Saverio promoted at the meeting, the importance of respecting the principles of voluntary and gradual return, and the impossibility of a repatriation that was both voluntary and en masse, were key points in this communications strategy. The managers regularly articulated these principles in public at both meetings and press conferences. This was also the first time it had been so explicitly stated that that security conditions in Afghanistan were not conducive to return: the need to emphasise this fact prevailed over concern for how such sensitive statement might be received by donors.

The fourth weapon deployed by the UNHCR was a system for monitoring returns, rolled out through its multilocal infrastructure that gave the organisation a translocal presence in both Pakistan (in the camps, in Peshawar and in Islamabad) and Afghanistan (in Kabul, at its Encashment Centres[8] and in the regions).

The most comprehensive observations came from the Peshawar Sub-Office, whose staff made regular visits to the camps and managed relations with representatives of both refugees and the Commissionerate for Afghan Refugees (CAR), the Pakistani agency responsible for the administration of the camps. The Peshawar office regularly sent reports to Islamabad, who forwarded them to Kabul. According to these reports, the process of closing Kacha Gari had begun in early spring. Public announcements called on the population to dismantle their houses and leave. The CAR demanded a list of the first families prepared to be repatriated, threatening detention if this was not forthcoming. Supplies to the camp's shops were suspended, and those on the main road were demolished. Elders asked for an extension of the deadline, but the CAR would not step back. The UNHCR office in Peshawar asked for assurance that water and electricity would not be cut off before the camp was definitively closed and reasserted that the UNHCR would not accept the use of force. There was a continuous but limited flow of people leaving the camp under the repatriation programme. None of them showed any interest in relocating in Pakistan. However, many refugees left the camp during the night, and it was gradually emptying.

As summer arrived and the situation continued uncertain, Saverio set up a monitoring system on the Afghan side of the border, in order to track the Pakistani authorities' moves, but also to shift the balance of Kabul's dependence on information from Islamabad. He made interviews at the Encashment Centres a priority, so as to have a reliable gauge of the repatriation process. An experienced member of the Protection Department was tasked with taking on, reinforcing and coordinating this monitoring system. UNHCR officers interviewed returnees, asking about the reasons and circumstances that had led them to return, and the conditions of their journey. With this information, the UNHCR was able to take the pulse of the flow of returns and to keep a watchful eye – albeit indirectly and after the fact – on the Pakistani authorities' actions with regard to Afghans.

Whereas previously the choice of information to be sent to the Branch Office had been left to the discretion of the Sub-Offices, the system was now centralised. The key questions to be put to returnees were specified and standardised, with the help of all the Heads of Office and senior managers of the Pakistan Operation. Staff at the Encashment Centres were instructed to conduct more systematic and intensive interviews.[9] Each evening the Sub-Offices compiled and consolidated the data received from Encashment Centres in their region and sent them to the Protection Department at the Branch Office, where they were in their turn compiled, analysed and forwarded within the Operation. Thus, each day there was an immediate report on the previous day's repatriations: the total number of returns and the number per Encashment Centre; the place of departure in Pakistan; the destination in Afghanistan; a separate section on the situation in the camps scheduled for closure; and safety on the journey. Day after day, this information was attentively monitored by the senior staff and guided their thinking. The information was also relayed to the offices in Pakistan so that they could follow up on their side of the border.

The accounts gathered from Kacha Gari residents at the Encashment Centres more or less aligned with the information reported by the Pakistan offices, but they offered a more detailed insight into the camp residents' decision-making process. All of them knew of the option to relocate in Pakistan, but none of them felt this was viable owing to the lack of job opportunities, the lack of basic services and, above all, the requirement to build a new house in a remote location that they would in all likelihood have to leave once their residence permit had expired, or when Pakistan decided to close that camp in its turn. The real alternative to repatriation was rather what within the UNHCR was called 'self-relocation': leaving Kacha Gari to settle elsewhere in Pakistan independently. But the returnees interviewed could not avail themselves of this option because of the bribes demanded by the police and the increase in rents around Kacha Gari. It appeared that the government had encouraged private individuals not to rent property to Afghans.

A Summer of Waiting

Once the 15 June deadline had passed, events speeded up. The Peshawar office reported that at Kacha Gari, the CAR had given those still living in the camp ten to fifteen days to evacuate, and announced that any houses still standing after that point would be demolished. Water and electricity were now only available at night. The CAR had agreed with the elders that at least 500 families must leave the camp each day. Returns increased, reaching a peak in early July.[10] The Peshawar office reported only one moment of tension, when rumours that a private house was to be demolished prompted vociferous protests. The Head of the Peshawar Sub-Office had stepped in to discourage the CAR from taking this action. Apart from this incident, information from Islamabad indicated that there had been no violent confrontations.

It was the Peshawar Sub-Office, via the Islamabad Office, that vouched that the process was conforming with the principles and that there was no use of force. The Pakistan offices had the authority to assess the acceptability of the conditions of closure of Kacha Gari, and they monitored returnees' accounts of it. Kabul recognised their authority on this. The fact that almost all the returnees seemed to be going back to their villages of origin in Afghanistan helped. There were only a few groups stranded in the east of the country, having no place to go, which the Jalalabad office seemed capable of managing. These kinds of settlements were a source of anxiety for the senior staff in Kabul, because they showed that there were 'non-integrable' returnees who were difficult to incorporate into national development plans; in all likelihood, these settlements would remain dependent on humanitarian aid.

From Kabul, what was happening in Kacha Gari remained hazy: the information they received was an impersonal echo of distant events. The UNHCR seemed to have everything under control. Islamabad also reported that 'the Afghans are dismantling their shops', that 'the Pakistani police is not using force and demolitions are not contested' and that 'the refugees have taken all their merchandise with them and not mounted any resistance', until the point when, on 26 July, it was announced that 'the camp was closed without incident and without violence'. The Islamabad office sent a copy of the official document in which the CAR testified that the camp was empty, the infrastructure had been dismantled and the immovable properties had been taken back by the provincial authorities.

It was on the basis of this set of reports that the Kabul office produced its official account of the closure of Kacha Gari for its external partners. After a long series of weekly bulletins that had tracked the gradual emptying of the camp, the closure of Kacha Gari merited only one laconic paragraph in the final issue:

> On 26 July the Kacha Gari camp was officially closed after three years of negotiations. Close to 40,000 Afghans repatriated out of the 65,000 residents registered at the beginning of 2007. The remaining population of Kacha Gari reportedly relocated within Pakistan. (UNHCR 2007k: 1)

In subsequent bulletins, the word 'reportedly' disappears. The closure is reported to have taken place 'peacefully'. At a meeting with donors Saverio took stock of the closure of Kacha Gari, saying that it had passed off 'reasonably well': the Sub-Offices were in the process of evaluating the situation in Afghanistan, and for now only a few families in the eastern region had nowhere to go. In the absence of accounts contradicting that of the UNHCR (for example, from NGOs, which had been present during the closure of the FATA camps, or from actual residents of the camp), the closure of Kacha Gari passed into history as a legitimate act.

After the closure of Kacha Gari, all eyes turned to Jalozai. According to information communicated by the Islamabad office and gathered at the Encashment Centres, representatives of the camp residents were asking for the closure to be postponed, but the CAR's representatives were standing firm on the deadline of 31 August. The CAR issued public announcements calling on Afghans to leave the camp, traders not to order any more merchandise and to leave their shops, and announcing that shops would be demolished after the deadline. A checkpoint was set up at the main entrance to the camp. The CAR was checking that families leaving the camp had demolished their homes, and demanded an increase in the number of families repatriated. Yet negotiations continued, and the general feeling was that the government was not sending signals that the camp would definitely be closed. There were persistent rumours that the closure would be postponed. According to the Peshawar Sub-Office, uncertainty was rising among the population of Jalozai. The number of returns remained very low, at around 500 individuals per week.

The growing political instability in Pakistan added to the uncertainty around the closure of Jalozai. Musharraf's position was increasingly weak.

He also seemed to be getting more and more bogged down in his policy towards the Islamists, whose attacks on Pakistani soil were intensifying. Having launched a military attack on Lal Masjid in Islamabad, which had been seized by the Islamists, Musharraf was now preparing another military offensive in the FATA (Abou Zahab 2010). UNHCR officers wondered whether, in this context, the closure of the camps was still a priority.

The Kabul Branch Office remained on alert, following events day by day through eager, meticulous reading of reports. The future remained uncertain. Nobody could predict whether the camp would be closed or not. This might be the calm before the storm, except that nobody knew whether there would ultimately be a storm. On the one hand, the more the days passed, the more closure became unlikely. But on the other hand, experience of previous closures indicated that camp residents tended to wait and see until the last moment, then rush en masse to the repatriation centres if there were clear signs of definitive closure. The spectre of an influx of 50,000–60,000 people thus loomed, on the verge of winter.

The Afghan offices prepared for the worst-case scenario. All Sub-Offices that might have to deal with returns were on full alert. A member of the Emergency Preparedness and Response team was ready to leave from Geneva; some employees of the Afghanistan Operation were prepared to be temporarily transferred to Jalalabad to reinforce the staff in the eastern region. Armoured vehicles and additional portable computers were ordered. The Programme Department in Kabul was ready to initiate procedures for requesting an increase in its budget. Interchange with donors and partner organisations intensified. Each day that passed made the waiting and the tension more acute.

On 15 August, two weeks before the deadline, only around 5,000 people had departed from Jalozai. Some of the population had left the camp discreetly, but the majority remained. Senior staff in Kabul were increasingly uneasy in this limbo situation. Faced with the real risk of a massive influx, limiting themselves to stating that the UNHCR would not support closure activities after 31 August was increasingly unsatisfactory. Demands for information from donors and partner organisations were becoming insistent.

The tension of uncertainty and waiting generated more spats between the Kabul and Islamabad offices. To the senior staff in Kabul, the Islamabad office seemed stingy in sharing information that they eagerly awaited. The reports from Encashment Centres were also a source of internal tension. The managers in the Islamabad office seemed to take Kabul's analyses of the interviews as a personal attack, as if Kabul was indirectly criticising their office's policy and its weakness in relation to the Pakistani authorities. In their view, disproportionate attention was given in the interviews to the way in which returnees from the camps had made their decisions, and they demanded that other issues should also be raised, such as safety during the journey and returns from the cities. The tone of the emails became very sharp when the Kabul senior staff reiterated that the interviews at Encashment Centres were a key element of the UNHCR's protection work that the Afghan Operation was not prepared to give up.

The weekly external bulletins were also a source of tension. The Islamabad office continued to object to the Kabul office reporting about the situation in Jalozai, and argued for a clear division of areas of competence: if Kabul's donors wanted to know what was going on in the camps, all the Kabul office had to do was distribute UNHCR-Pakistan's information bulletin. But for the managers in Kabul, communication with donors and partner organisations was crucial and could not be put off; on the contrary, it needed to be stepped up and focused on the situation in Jalozai. Once they had been alerted, they needed to be kept updated about developments as the crucial weeks began. Saverio reclaimed his power of final approval of all documents issued by his office.

From 20 August – ten days before the deadline – reports from Peshawar suddenly took on an alarming tone. Some 700 members of the Pakistani security forces had been deployed around Jalozai. The troops had encircled the camp, but for the time being were not patrolling within it. The CAR was continuing to insistently reiterate its categoric message, demanding that a thousand traders close their shops or face demolition. According to the head of the Peshawar office, the situation was developing more quickly than foreseen, and the possibility of complete closure loomed ever larger. He stressed that the closure of shops would have serious implications, because Jalozai was a long way from other markets. In his view, panic was beginning to rise among the population. Indeed, there was a considerable rise in returns, which tripled within a week, reaching a level of almost a thousand on 21 August alone.

The Head of the Peshawar Sub-Office reported that he had called an emergency meeting with the CAR representative and had secured an assurance that shops selling basic necessities would not be closed. The director of the CAR agreed to push back the deadline to 2008 and confirmed that the provincial authorities were also in agreement with this. But he also stated that the decision to suspend closure of the camp was beyond his authority. He gave to understand that there was a power struggle within the federal government. In view of the panic he saw spreading through the camp, the Head of the Peshawar Sub-Office felt it necessary to take a clearer position with regard to the population in Jalozai. He could no longer limit himself to saying that the UNHCR would not support closure after the deadline. His report called on the Islamabad office to step up to the mark – this was the moment to intervene and take a stand, or it would be too late.

In the Kabul office, the report from Peshawar immediately ramped up the tension. The deployment of security forces around the camp with the largest population barely ten days before the deadline, on the verge of winter and just before the beginning of Ramadan, was seen as a move openly incompatible with the principles articulated in the Tripartite Agreement. It was of paramount importance that this should not set a precedent. Pakistan's gesture, the tone of the report from Peshawar, the number of people concerned and the spectre of potential consequences in Afghanistan led the managers in Kabul to cross a line. They were no longer prepared to remain mere passive observers until 31 August: these returns could not take place as if they were nothing out of the ordinary, portrayed as voluntary returns conducted under the aegis of the UNHCR. In their view, it was time to take a public stand.

But the Islamabad office was more inclined to manage the situation by negotiating with the Ministry of the Interior and trying to approach the presidential cabinet. The viewpoints of Kabul and Islamabad clashed irremediably. Tension between the two offices around the crucial question of whether or not to take a public position reached a peak. It was time for Geneva to intervene. On the evening of 21 August, a teleconference between Peshawar, Islamabad, Kabul and Geneva took place, during which a shared position was adopted and a plan of action was drawn up. The Islamabad managers accepted a public intervention, with the UNHCR demanding that closure of Jalozai be postponed, on condition that this came from the highest level. It was therefore decided that the press release should be issued by Headquarters in Geneva, and that the High Commissioner would meet with the Pakistani ambassador there and then communicate directly with the Pakistani President, through an official letter.

Speaking out

The UNHCR reacted, deploying its key weapon. The text of the press release was hurriedly sent around all the offices concerned to be edited and approved. It was published the following day, 22 August (UNHCR 2007g). The UNHCR called for a temporary suspension of the closure of Jalozai. The press release noted that the UNHCR:

> is deeply concerned that at this late stage of the repatriation season, tens of thousands of Afghans are being pressured into leaving in a manner that will lead to a humanitarian crisis this winter ... UNHCR considers that given the very short deadline before the end of the month, it will now be impossible to manage a safe, voluntary, and sustainable repatriation operation from Jalozai.

In the face of Pakistan's show of force, the UNHCR reacted with words. The deployment of troops was met by a press release. Up to that point, contacts had been managed through 'private' negotiations between the UNHCR and the Pakistani authorities, within the framework of the Tripartite Commissions and the contacts the Islamabad and Peshawar offices had with their respective interlocutors. The UNHCR ended this negotiation and made the situation public, bringing the closure to the attention of other states and international organisations. The various levels of parallel negotiations and the multiplicity of interlocutors were instantly thrown up in the air by this official stance on the part of the organisation as a whole. The UNHCR was using all the cards in its hand, playing on Pakistan's international reputation and at the same time unleashing a serious blackmail threat – the most extreme gesture the organisation can make – that it would condemn the returns as forced and abandon the programme. This statement was all the more incisive because it was initiated from Geneva: the shockwaves from the UNHCR's stance and the visibility of the Pakistani authorities' move reached delegations in Geneva, not just those in the region.

Because the UNHCR was risking everything it had, it needed to use its words wisely, gradually, in such a way as to leave room for manoeuvre. For the time being, Pakistan had not been accused of instigating forced return. The press release reiterated the principles agreed in the Tripartite Agreement and at the Tripartite Commissions, and pointed to the residence permits issued at the beginning of the year. For the time being, it merely deplored the 'risk' that these principles would be violated if the closure was not suspended. It made no reference to the troops encircling the camp or to the interviews at the Encashment Centres. Moreover, the warning was expressed in positive terms:

UNHCR believes that such a strong humanitarian gesture ahead of the holy month of Ramadan and winter would underline once again the extraordinary generosity and hospitality of Pakistan towards the Afghan refugee population.

The repressive attitude that had now been adopted by the Pakistani authorities remained hidden; Pakistan was instead offered the possibility of making a 'humanitarian gesture' that would confirm its 'generosity'.

During the days after 22 August, a diplomatic process was set in motion, deploying the full range of levers available to the UNHCR's translocal bureaucracy. The plan of action developed at the teleconference specified concerted action to be taken at all levels and in all the places concerned: depending on its position, each office was tasked with relaying the UNHCR's request to its own interlocutors, adapting it according to the context. The press release was translated into Urdu and Pashto. In Jalozai, the Head of the Peshawar office met with representatives of the camp residents to explain the UNHCR's position. He asked residents not to demolish their houses unless they had already signed up for repatriation, and not to sign up if they did not want to return immediately. In Peshawar the Head of Office met with the CAR representative. They agreed on a maximum number of people who could leave the camp each day, and to stop the demolition of any further homes. In Kabul the senior managers of the Afghan Operation met with the Pakistani ambassador and offered their support for any action by the Minister for Refugees and the Minister of Foreign Affairs. They even met with President Karzai's team in order to bring the matter to the attention of the presidential cabinet. In Geneva, the Assistant High Commissioner supported the High Commissioner's initiatives by writing to the Pakistani Ministers of the Interior and for States and Frontier Regions (SAFRON) and to the governor of the North-West Frontier Province.

UNHCR managers in Islamabad were now in an extremely delicate position. SAFRON and the Interior Ministers reacted coldly to the press release; they clearly had not wanted matters to reach this point. It may be reasonably supposed that they had not had any intention of resorting to force, but wanted nevertheless to do all they could to evacuate at least part of the camp. The two ministers agreed to extend the deadline until March 2008, on the condition that the residents of Jalozai agreed to leave the camp in the spring. But like all the Pakistani authorities at all levels, they pointed out that the deadline for closure could only be modified by decision of the President's office.

Once the UNHCR had spoken with one voice, the internal tensions were forgotten. All the offices were working towards the same goal, strictly aligned with one another. The structure was compact, tensed with effort and concentration. Swamped by the flood of reports, I and the Communications team were aware that everyone was under pressure: the Head of the Peshawar office went to Jalozai every day, despite the poor security, to check that the agreed number of returns was not exceeded; senior staff in Islamabad were conducting delicate negotiations; senior staff in Kabul were holding difficult meetings; colleagues in the Sub-Offices were working in overcrowded Encashment Centres; and the eyes of Geneva were trained on the region.

The UNHCR's aim was to secure an official announcement of suspension of the closure as soon as possible. According to the representatives of SAFRON and the CAR, the postponement of the deadline had been unofficially agreed at the federal level and communicated to the provincial authorities. Nevertheless, the order to withdraw the troops and put back the deadline had to come from the President's office – and he, for the time being, 'was not there'. It became clear that no immediate announcement was to be expected. This was clearly an intentional delaying tactic, aiming to take advantage of last-minute departures and prevent those who had just left the camp from returning there. The dominant view in the UNHCR was that the Pakistani authorities were hoping to bring the question down to the level of bilateral relations. Musharraf seemed to be waiting for Karzai to contact him directly.

Given the tense relations between the two governments, a request for suspension of the closure on humanitarian grounds would amount to a sign of weakness, and the suspension could thus be presented as a favour Pakistan was doing for its neighbour.

In any case, the delaying tactic was achieving the desired result. According to reports from Peshawar, confusion and panic reigned among the residents of the camp, who were receiving contradictory messages. It appeared that the pressure was being maintained: more shops were closed, and water and electricity were cut off in some parts of the camp. The UNHCR's reassuring declarations were countered by messages suggesting the opposite. The local media gave out distorted or baseless information. The rumour spread that the security forces would enter the camp on 31 August, demolish all the buildings and arrest all those remaining in the camp. According to other rumours, UNHCR aid payments would be suspended from 31 August. The elders were becoming increasingly mistrustful and no longer knew who to listen to or what messages to communicate to the population. The flow of returns swelled to a mass, with over 200 families per day. Returns had already been planned up to the first week of September.

Despite the pressure from the UNHCR for Pakistan to define the conditions of closure, under threat of a further, more aggressive public statement, the official announcement of the new deadline of 15 April 2008, and the withdrawal of the security forces, came only on 7 September. Subsequent news from Peshawar reported that the situation in Jalozai was gradually stabilising: there were no more demolitions, some people were rebuilding their houses, shops were reopening and schools were starting back up again. A total of some 30,000 people had left the camp under the repatriation programme. According to the UNHCR's estimates, taking into account those who had left the camp at their own initiative, the population of Jalozai had halved. But this was only a brief lull, as the camp would be definitively closed and demolished the following spring.

The Bureaucratic Production of 'Voluntariness'

A number of those who have researched repatriation programmes have questioned whether the returns involved were voluntary (Barnett 2004; Bialczyk 2008; Blitz et al. 2005; Crisp 1984; Harrell-Bond 1989; Strand et al. 2008; Takahashi 1997; Zimmermann 2009). Many of these authors have concluded that the repatriation was forced, or that the UNHCR put undue pressure on refugees to return, and have criticised the organisation on these grounds. Agata Bialczyk, for example, analysed the bulletins distributed by the UNHCR to Afghans in Pakistan in the mid-2000s, and concluded, using the organisation's own words, that repatriation was not just 'facilitated' but 'promoted' (Bialczyk 2008). Similar observations have been made with regard to the return of Rohingya refugees from Bangladesh to Burma in the early 1990s (Barnett 2004). Barnett's analysis is more fully explicated, but although his stated intention is to examine the bureaucratic procedures involved in the implementation of the programme, he does not extend this approach to 'voluntariness', which he sees as a sacrosanct and universally applicable principle to which the programme should have conformed, and against which the substance of the UNHCR's actions is to be judged.

Asking whether the repatriations that took place under UNHCR programmes were *genuinely* voluntary or not implies adopting and reproducing the logic of the programme rather than interrogating it, as if the 'voluntary' (or forced) nature of the return was an objective feature of the journey. It seems to me that this approach implies taking up philosophical questions about freedom of choice, or debates on the opposition between agency and structure in the sociological theory of migration (Bakewell 2010; Richmond 1988). The researcher who insists on determining whether the return took place willingly or by force finds themself in the same position as the UNHCR: what is the criterion for assessing 'voluntariness' (the use of force? the number of returns? the opinion of the returnees?) and what is the methodology? Bialczyk bases her conclusions on her own evaluation. Barnett draws on NGO reports (mainly from Human Rights Watch), but without explaining why these reports should more accurately represent the true nature of the returns than those of the UNHCR. There is a high risk of entering into a vicious circle, as the following phrase suggests: 'UNHCR officials used a definition of voluntariness that violated the traditional principle of voluntary repatriation' (Barnett 2004: 106).

My aim here is rather to understand the reasoning underpinning the principle of voluntary return and to examine the bureaucratic procedures through which this principle is made operative, as well as the factors determining how it is evaluated by UNHCR officials. This helps in terms of understanding how the international legitimacy (or illegitimacy) of repatriations is produced, as measured by 'voluntariness'.[11]

The reasoning underpinning the principle of 'voluntary return' derives from the logic of the 'refugee problem'. The voluntary nature of return is the logical response to the pressure assumed to be the cause of departure and is the corollary of the principle of nonrefoulement.[12] In European countries, the forced nature of departure is generally evaluated at the point when the person arrives in the national territory, through 'refugee status determination' procedures (see Chapter 7). Assessment of an asylum seeker's situation therefore takes place within a legal process that assumes the judgment of individual cases on the basis of case files and interviews (or hearings). In this context, the

UNHCR produces directives and often participates directly as judge or observer. However, the Pakistani state has not established any such procedures. The principle of nonrefoulement is instead rendered operational through the UNHCR's evaluation of the 'voluntariness' of the returns. This evaluation is not carried out on a case-by-case basis, but rather collectively.

The norm of 'voluntary return' is translated bureaucratically in the title of the programme, which was identified precisely as a 'voluntary repatriation programme'. These programmes, which have become standardised since the 1990s, are structured by the concern to ensure and evaluate this voluntariness. A set of measures has been designed to widen the range of choices available to migrants. Logically, when one has a choice, this means making a decision. One example is the Mass Information programme, under which the UNHCR produces and distributes to Afghans in Pakistan regular bulletins that are supposed to provide exhaustive information on the situation in Afghanistan; others include the residence permits obtained following the census, the option of relocating in Pakistan imposed as a condition of the closure of the camps, and the additional time the UNHCR wanted to give refugees when it pressed for the deadlines for camp closures to be put back. The wish of the returnee is formally certified, as in order to obtain a repatriation card, all returnees must sign a declaration confirming their 'voluntary return' that appears at the bottom of the card.[13] This document ensures that the individual can never claim to have been 'forced' to leave. All of these features allow the repatriation programme to be described as 'voluntary', as the UNHCR officially terms it. This in its turn means that the return of all those who take advantage of the programme can be defined as voluntary, since it has taken place under a programme expressly designed to guarantee voluntariness. Returnees have signed a declaration confirming it. Unless something jams its mechanism, this programme will continue to produce 'voluntary returns'.

I identified two criteria used by UNHCR officials to assess conditions of return, enabling them to decide whether to continue or interrupt the programme. They both result from the balance of power with the Pakistani authorities. The UNHCR's weakness raised its officers' threshold of acceptance. The fact that the aim was redefined as a 'workable and human compromise' (UNHCR 2007a: 1) points to the awareness of the heavy cost for refugees. While this power relation affects all the officers concerned, as noted above, they viewed the situation differently depending on whether they were posted to Islamabad or Kabul. In Islamabad the central concern was to keep a diplomatic channel open. In Kabul it was rather the sustainability of returns to Afghanistan that determined how reports from Islamabad and Peshawar, and the data from interviews, were analysed and evaluated.

Indeed, in practice, the criterion used by senior staff in the Kabul office to evaluate and determine the acceptability (and hence the international legitimacy) of the Pakistani authorities' actions was that of sustainability. The central concern of the managers of the Afghan Operation was not so much to guarantee freedom of choice for individual Afghans as to ensure that those who returned to Afghanistan found the means of subsistence there and were 'resorbed' into the Afghan jurisdiction, without creating a 'surplus' (such as groups of landless migrants who might generate camps of 'internally displaced people'). The importance of thinking in terms of sustainability emerged in internal discussions and in the concepts that became increasingly present in the UNHCR's language: 'absorption capacity' and 'sustainability of returns'. More and more logical links were made between 'voluntariness' and these factors in UNHCR-Afghanistan's discourse.[14] Thus, the August press release raised the problem of the onset of winter and the risk of a humanitarian crisis in Afghanistan, rather than that of failure to respect the wishes of camp residents.

In the end, the UNHCR did not challenge the legitimacy of the returns. Even the press release speaks only of the 'risk' of forced return. The discrepancy between this official position, legitimised by the bureaucratic mechanisms of the return programme, and the awareness within the organisation that the situation was highly problematic, was quite evident. During the summer of 2007, within the Kabul office I several times heard people say, in a tone of discomfort and bitterness, that 'strictly speaking these are not voluntary returns'. It became increasingly difficult for UNHCR staff in Kabul to use this term in the conceptual sense comfortably and with integrity, and to match the programme's bureaucratic title, which theoretically justified describing all the returns as voluntary, with the heavy constraint created by the closure of the Kacha Gari and Jalozai camps, which the organisation was unable to prevent. This ambiguity was clearly evident even in the Islamabad office's announcement of the closure of Kacha Gari (UNHCR 2007j). The text strove to convey both the powerful intensity of the event and its international legitimacy. The result was a contradictory mixture. On the one hand, the announcement reiterated that the decision to close the camp was taken by agreement between the Pakistani government and the UNHCR, that the option to relocate in Pakistan had been offered and that the closure of the camp occurred peacefully. On the other hand, the document discreetly refuted the grounds of the official reason for closure ('security reasons') and emphasised that the reason no Afghans had opted for relocation was because the designated sites were extremely inhospitable. The text also painted a distressing picture of Afghans demolishing their own houses, and even quoted a woman who stated openly that she did not want to return to Afghanistan but was forced to do so.[15] This situation testifies to the increasingly difficult position in which the UNHCR found itself.

The Pressures on the UNHCR Bureaucracy

Examining the interaction between the UNHCR and the Pakistani government over the fate of the Kacha Gari and Jalozai camps offers a way to delve into the relation between these two overlapping sovereignties. Here we have a state and an international organisation, heterogeneous bodies with distinct projects of government, and different ways and means of exerting authority. They overlap to the extent that both their projects of government concern Afghans in Pakistan. They are bound to one another in a close relationship, since the UNHCR is an interstate organisation and its mandate acquires its meaning within the system of states. This connection means that the two institutions share the perspective of Afghans in Pakistan as non-nationals whose exceptional situation has to be managed. But their goals are different, and this is why their interaction takes the form of a confrontation. The UNHCR's priority is the wellbeing of Afghans in Pakistan, which it pursues in part by pleading for their incorporation into Pakistani jurisdiction. The Pakistani state has other priorities (on which I have been able to touch only briefly), such as reinforcing the nation-state, managing its internal conflicts and exerting influence in Afghanistan – priorities that in all cases imply keeping its Afghan population in a precarious situation.

The UNHCR did not have the means to exert legitimate physical force, or a territory to offer Afghans, or even the power to punish any violations of the Tripartite Agreement. As noted above, it nevertheless had a series of arms and tactics: the framework of principles the organisation had constructed, the 'risk anticipation plan' established at the beginning of the summer, the monitoring system based on its translocal presence and the interviews conducted at Encashment Centres. Its authority to evaluate the legitimacy of returns aligned with its capacity to produce accounts that were authoritative at the international level. It could thus make use of words, which could have an openly offensive power if the organisation was to use them to condemn violation of the Tripartite Agreement and influence Pakistan's international reputation – as it did, using the penultimate card in its hand, in the press release. These words are not those of the law, but they could nevertheless have a power of attack, even though they were not accompanied by a sword.

But the confrontation with the Pakistani state was an unequal one: despite the tactics it deployed, the organisation was unable to offer any significant counter to the pressure to return. The uncertainty that prevailed in the Kabul office throughout the summer was the clearest sign of this. It was very difficult for the UNHCR to control the future, and the spectre of Pakistan using force and of an unmanageable flood of returnees remained a likely scenario until the last moment.

The articulation between the UNHCR and the Pakistani state helps to explain the subordinate position ultimately taken by the UNHCR. As an interstate body, the UNHCR is obliged to recognise the ultimate power of the Pakistani state. Born out of the system of states, the UNHCR is by its very nature bound by the duty to recognise and respect the founding principle of this system, state sovereignty – the principle that underpins the organisation's very existence. And the national order that structures the system of states legitimises the primacy of national interests. Thus, the Pakistani government's stated grounds for closing the camps, 'national security reasons' was a principle against which the UNHCR was largely powerless.

In fact, the power exercised by the Pakistani state is by no means as absolute as the principle of sovereignty (and the normative, state-centred conception of power) suggest. Certain material conditions are necessary for it to be exercised in practice: in order to strike, the sword needs first to be sharpened, unsheathed and borne. The Pakistani state too is a vast bureaucracy composed of bodies with their own agendas. In order to proceed with the closure of the camps, the Pakistani government needed, for example, the cooperation and coordination of all the national administrative bodies involved, such as the Ministry of States and Frontier Regions, the Commissionerate for Afghan Refugees, the provincial authorities and the security forces.[16] I also discussed above how the Pakistani state sometimes deployed its weapons strategically, measuring out the use and threat of force tactically, as indicated by the delaying tactic adopted in early September 2007, and more generally the precarious situation in which the Afghan population was kept. Although they were permitted to reside in Pakistani territory, these people were living in deteriorating conditions and faced an uncertain future. Nevertheless, for the UNHCR, Pakistani state sovereignty was effectively an ultimate power, without the state needing to unsheathe its sword, but simply by virtue of the conventions on which interstate relations are based.

In addition to the 'keystone' of state sovereignty (Lochak 2002), there was a second factor explaining the UNHCR's weakness. Its relationship with the Pakistani state was strongly influenced by the broader set of power relations within which its activity was set. This context was shaped by the 'war on terror' that had been instigated in 2001 by NATO, headed by the United States, in the region. This was the background to the Afghanistan reconstruction project funded by these same countries, the fight against Taliban forces, and NATO's alliance with Pakistan – an alliance that the latter, seeking to maintain strong influence over Afghanistan, but suspected of nevertheless providing support to the Taliban and internally plagued by the rising power of militant Islamists, was pursuing with some ambivalence.

This context tested the UNHCR severely. As a transnational bureaucracy present in Afghanistan and Pakistan as well as in New York and Brussels, the organisation found itself straddling all of these relationships. The UNHCR operates in many arenas, which are at once independent and enmeshed with one another. In order to pursue its mission, it must establish collaborative relationships with all of these actors, some of whom are also its main funders. I analysed above the contradictions inherent in participating in the Afghanistan reconstruction project in close collaboration with NATO, whose campaign against the Taliban guerrillas was rendering huge regions inhospitable to returnees and inaccessible to the UNHCR, as well as damaging the organisation's local legitimacy. Similarly, it was difficult to oppose Pakistani pressure on the camps when Pakistan could claim that this was a way of honouring its commitment to NATO, and the majority of the UNHCR's donors supported the continuation of the repatriation programme.

In Kabul, relations between the UNHCR and NATO countries were structured by the donor–service provider relationship. In the case of the United States, for example, the organisation interacted with Mitch, the representative of the Bureau of Population, Refugees, and Migration (BPRM), a US State Department body concerned with international aid, which is one of the UNHCR's principal donors. Mitch, like Suzanne from ECHO, was very cooperative and sensitive to the situation, and followed developments in the camp closures closely, but he also hinted at the tensions he himself faced daily in his attempts to raise awareness of the closure of the camps within the US administration, where suspension of the closures was far from a priority. Moreover, since 2001, donors had viewed the repatriation programme in a very positive light, since it legitimised international presence in Afghanistan and the reconstruction process.[17]

The BPRM and ECHO finally made exceptional funding, on top of their annual contributions, available to finance any necessary humanitarian aid interventions with returnees in Afghanistan. NATO also made known its willingness to provide logistical support in zones where access was more difficult. But this support for a potential emergency operation on the Afghan side of the border contrasted with the lack of support for the UNHCR in its relationship with the Pakistani authorities. For all that the donors followed the negotiations closely, none intervened directly in support of the UNHCR. Cooperation within the Kabul 'club' was a local niche, in the context of a very specific institutional structure that defined and demarcated the scale at which problems could be addressed and the means available to do so. The niche had some power, provided that the club did not go beyond the limits of the remit assigned to it. Thus, when Saverio brought up the closure of the camps with Mitch and Suzanne, NATO policy and its relationship with Pakistan never entered the discussion, and nor did the issue of security in the camps.

The UNHCR bureaucracy was thus entangled within a complex set of power relations that limited the organisation's scope of action. As the powerful frictions between the Kabul and Islamabad offices demonstrate, these power relations created strong internal tensions and severely restricted its space of manoeuvre. The dilemmas and internal tensions faced by the UNHCR during the summer of 2007 reveal the degree to which the organisation is restricted and stifled. The UNHCR deployed its tactics, despite internal disagreement and with much unease, and almost reached the point of playing its final card. But ultimately all of these steps were insufficient to counter the pressure for return exerted by the Pakistani authorities. The result was merely palliative; in the end, the UNHCR was only able to mildly attenuate the pressure.

The UNHCR and Re-emplacement of Afghan Refugees in Afghanistan

How did the negotiations between the Pakistani state and the UNHCR ultimately affect the residents of Kacha Gari and Jalozai? And what was the UNHCR's role in governing them? Giorgio Agamben's concepts of the state of exception and bare life (1998, 2005) have been widely applied to the international government of refugees, and they are indeed attractive. They convey well the powerlessness of individuals in the face of a machinery of power that reduces them to biological existence. This view helps to explain the Pakistani government's policy towards Afghans. While several camps had become places of lasting settlement, the Pakistani authorities persisted in viewing them as temporary sites of exception. Through the threat hanging over the fate of the camps, and the concrete actions that sometimes followed these threats, the Pakistani authorities thus kept the Afghan population in a state of precarity (performing a similar function to the deportations in Iranian policy). Caught in this liminal position, Afghans were pawns in Pakistan's internal and external politics. The concept of bare life also matches with the UNHCR's concern to guarantee at least the sustainability of return to Afghanistan – that is, the possibility of survival and basic subsistence.

But these concepts become problematic when thinking in terms of overlapping sovereignties, because they do not account for the power relations within the camps. In fact, the Pakistani state and the UNHCR were not the only actors with influence; their policies were not the only forces in the political field. Their relationship was just one of those that contributed to shaping the field of possibilities within which camp residents forged their strategies. As several researchers have noted (Agier 2011; Moulin and Nyers 2007; Turner 2005, 2006), there are other political agencies at work in a refugee camp. In his study of refugee camps in Africa, Michel Agier shows how refugees appropriate humanitarian language to make demands and contest the systems of the 'humanitarian stage', troubling the victim role imposed on them in this context. Simon Turner (2005, 2006) examines how in the Lukole camp in Tanzania, a group of young refugees produce authority, partly thanks to that delegated to them by state and international bodies, and partly in the interstices in the authority exercised by these bodies.

Thus, in their inability to recognise the agency of camp residents, and their capacity to put in place strategies to protect themselves and even circumvent the Pakistani state's measures, the concepts of state of exception and bare life fail to grasp the full range of power relations that shaped the field of possibilities open to camp residents during the summer of 2007. Because they describe only the reasoning of the national order and the humanitarian order, as if these were the only ones at work, these concepts risk reproducing a victimising view of refugees.

This is confirmed by the history of the camps concerned: it was these same camps that served as a support base for Mujahideen resistance during the 1980s. The Pakistani state struggles to exert its authority in these regions, which were historically governed indirectly and were becoming Talibanised in the mid-2000s (Abou Zahab 2010). The military campaigns and the actions of militant Islamists greatly hampered UNHCR access to the camps. But the very diverse situations to be found among the camp residents should also be taken into proper consideration.[18] The Pakistani authorities' actions were felt to be more or less harshly depending on the resources available to each individual, or more usually each group. It can thus be hypothesised that the closure of the camps was the deciding factor for some (because it led them to make the choice of survival), but less so for others who had managed to put in place strategies that protected them from Pakistan's pressures, or to limit their dependence on UNHCR initiatives. For example, around 30% of the residents of Kacha Gari left the camp to relocate in Pakistan,[19] most of them in Peshawar. This option required social and financial resources, to pay the bribes demanded by the security forces at the exits from the camp, to cover the cost of transport and rents in the city (which were rising in the context of the camp closure), and to have access to urban networks that could facilitate relocation.

But recognising refugees' capacity for action should not blind us to the extremely restrictive measures that fundamentally shaped the range of possibilities open to residents of the two camps, regardless of their resources. The number of returns proves that the summer was decisive for tens of thousands of people. Because they had been durably settled in these sites, everyone (the UNHCR, the media and also often the Pakistani authorities) now referred to these people as 'residents' of Kacha Gari and Jalozai rather than 'migrants'. They had to leave these places and see them erased from the face of the earth.

As an example, take the returns from Jalozai during the first week of September. Residents of the camp responded with panic to the Pakistani authorities' delaying tactic, designed to evacuate as much of the camp as pos-sible. It may be assumed that the vast majority of those who signed up to the repatriation programme at that point had a very narrow range of possible options: they had stayed in the camp until the last minute, before choosing, on the eve of winter, to give up the residence permits they had obtained only a few months earlier. The fact that they signed the declaration confirming their 'voluntary repatriation' – a procedure that was required in order to ob-tain aid on return and hope for assistance from humanitarian organisations in Afghanistan – aligns their situation with those of potential deportees (Cleton and Chauvin 2019). The space of manoeuvre open to Afghans appeared mini-mal; it seemed that the authority exercised by the Pakistani state had left only 'interstices' that were too narrow to slip through.

The closure of the camps, and the conditions in which it took place, give a heartbreaking demonstration of how undesirable non-nationals are forced to adapt to the national order that structures the policy of states and inter-national organisations. These policies can be violent and oppressive. The na-tional order assumes a spatial distribution of the world's population according to the principle of nationality, and attributes to states the power to deter-mine the legitimacy (or illegitimacy) of cross-border movement. Under this regime, non-nationals may even be subject to the use of force by states that wish to expel them from their jurisdiction. International refugee law was cre-ated precisely to protect non-nationals whose situation does not allow them to live safely in their country of origin from such extreme treatment. However, I showed above how, as the UNHCR's space of manoeuvre shrank, the repatri-ation programme gradually became the linchpin of a process of re-emplacing Afghans in Pakistan in their country of origin.

The repatriation programme was indeed the keystone of this process, and the bureaucratic production of 'voluntariness' was central to its functioning. It was in the context of this programme that the difference – crucial on the conceptual level, much more labile at the bureaucratic level, as I have shown – between freedom and constraint, between internationally acceptable and un-acceptable actions on the part of the Pakistani authorities was established within the UNHCR. I noted that this 'voluntariness' was determined by the bureaucratic mechanisms of the programme, which were shaped in their turn by the restrictive power relations in which the UNHCR was enmeshed. In these conditions, the programme became an outlet for legitimate constraint exerted by the Pakistani authorities on Afghan non-nationals. Thus, year by year, more camps were closed, the living conditions of the Afghan popula-tion in Pakistan deteriorated, and these pressures led to a continuous flow of returns to Afghanistan, their legitimacy sanctioned by the repatriation programme.

Admittedly, the reason why the repatriation programme became the keystone of a process of re-emplacement in Afghanistan was ultimately the pressure exerted by the Pakistani authorities. But this was a process that the UNHCR had been involved in creating and sustaining. The organisation was, indeed, at the heart of the process, certifying the legitimacy of repatriation, which it always presented as the 'preferred solution', the route that would help to normalise the situation of Afghan refugees, who could finally 'go home'. Although the UNHCR and the Pakistani authorities had different objectives, and their relationship was genuinely confrontational, they in fact formed a single system. They participated together in maintaining and operating the programme. The UNHCR struggled with the Pakistani state, warned it and came almost to the point of taking its action of last resort. It was riven by the powerful tensions, frustration, anxiety and anger that gripped its officers. But, in fact, the UNHCR's room for manoeuvre was powerfully shaped by the broader relations of power in which its international bureaucracy is enmeshed. It had no choice but to stay in the game. The difficulties were resorbed and cushioned within the organisation, while externally they were highlighted in order to call for more support, more resources for the repatriation and reintegration programmes – in other words, to perpetuate the re-emplacement process.

Notes

1. Anonymous official source.
2. With the notable exception of Long's work on the history of refugee repatriation (Long 2013).
3. An anonymous official source explicitly told me of the concern to respect international commitments and not to incite criticism from the UN, human rights organisations or the international community.
4. Here the UNHCR had promoted the criterion of 'region of origin', deeming certain regions (such as Kabul and Nangarhar province) stabilised and habitable, and others highly inhospitable.
5. *Conclusions of the 12th Tripartite Commission Meeting*, Geneva, 17 January 2006.
6. *Conclusions of the 13th Tripartite Commission Meeting*, Dubai, 8 June 2007.
7. For a more detailed discussion on this, see Chapter 1.
8. Points of entry into Afghanistan located on the main routes in, where returnees could receive aid for resettling in the country.
9. To give an idea of the extent of this activity, from August to October, a total of 1,569 interviews was carried out, corresponding to 15.8% of the repatriated families.
10. In the order of 5,000 returns in the last week of June, 9,000 the following week and 8,000 the week after that.
11. My approach is analogous to that of Cleton and Chauvin (2019), who study how the return of potential deportees from the Netherlands came to be interpreted as 'voluntary' through the bureaucratic work of government workers. While Cleton and

Chauvin analyse the forms of soft coercion employed by 'street-level bureaucrats' in individual cases, the UNHCR officials under consideration here operate at a different level, because they manage large numbers and their main interlocutors are the Pakistani authorities.

12. A genealogy deriving from Western political and institutional history, where individual freedoms and free choice are central values, is also evident in this principle (cf. Long 2013).

13. 'I, the undersigned, declare that after due consideration and entirely of my own free will, request repatriation to Afghanistan for myself and my family.'

14. The concept of sustainability was closely linked to the voluntary nature of return, which was presented as an essential condition for sustainability. For example: 'Ensuring the voluntary nature of return is also extremely important to ensure sustainability [of returns] and minimise human distress' (UNHCR 2007a: 4). 'The Tripartite Agreement ... provides important legal and practical guarantees against unsustainable rates of return' (UNHCR 2007a: 6).

15. 'We did not want to go back but had to dismantle our house ... I decided to repatriate because we could not afford to rent a house in Peshawar' (UNHCR 2007j).

16. It was indeed the lack of coordination between these bodies that led to the closure of Kacha Gari, scheduled for 2005, being postponed year after year.

17. On this point, see Turton and Marsden (2002).

18. Here I refer to studies by Saito (Saito 2007; Saito and Hunte 2007) and by the Sustainable Development Policy Institute (SDPI) (2006), which examine how Afghans made their decision about possible return. These studies analyse the factors that weighed in the process of deciding between the possible options, including living conditions in Pakistan (access to services, job opportunities, etc.) and the perception of how they might evolve, the perception of the situation in Afghanistan, the collective reasoning and strategies of the group to which they belonged, etc.

19. According to the UNHCR's estimates.

CHAPTER 9

Emplacing Returnees in Afghanistan

November 2007, Beni Warsak, Afghanistan. Leaving the tarmac road and driving on over sandy terrain, you might be forgiven for doubting whether you are really travelling towards any inhabited place. The sites that have sprung up to accommodate landless returnees are all characterised by their isolation and the absence of vegetation. As you draw nearer, greenery disappears and rivers take another route. Then hamlets under construction begin to emerge, the same colour as the desert landscape that surrounds them. This place, which a year ago was an empire of dust, is now the focus of an ambitious drive to transform it into a place where life is possible. The mud-brick buildings now form a small hamlet around a wide street. There are signs of new plots marked out, the foundations of other houses and piles of bricks drying in the sun. The plain is scoured by a strong wind that raises clouds of dust. The land that extends as far as you can see around the site is not cultivable or suitable for pasture. The only shop is a little corrugated iron shack, where a young man is selling tins of tomatoes, washing powder and cigarettes. It is hard to imagine that any form of subsistence is possible in this inhospitable region of Afghanistan.

By the logic of the 'refugee problem', return to Afghanistan means that the problem has been solved. As far as the nation-state order is concerned, Afghan state jurisdiction is the legitimate place of Afghans. The displaced are finally in the right place, their place. But entry into Afghan territory is not in itself enough to solve the problem. The aim of the UNHCR's reintegration programme is to support returnees to settle in Afghanistan by making survival and subsistence possible. One arm of this huge programme, which concerns around one-fifth of the country's entire population,[1] involves constructing shelters and water supply points in the returnees' provinces of origin; the other consists of supporting the Ministry of Refugees to take responsibility for the protection of returnees itself.

This chapter examines the UNHCR's activity in Afghanistan from the point of view of one strand of its reintegration programme, the Land Allocation Scheme, which allocated land in partnership with the Ministry of Refugees and aimed to reintegrate or 'resorb' into Afghanistan the most problematic returnees – those who had no land. I first examine the rationale behind the UNHCR's project in the country, which was aimed at setting the Afghan state back on its feet in order to support durable settlement of returnees in the country. The place that the UNHCR was attempting to establish for returnees was both physical and political, created by forging a dual link with the territory and with the state. To this end, the organisation sought to connect return-ees to the territory and the state, in line with the principles of the nation-state and a liberal-democratic regime. They were to become citizens integrated into the polity of a nation-state, and the state itself was to be rebuilt so that it was capable of protecting its citizens. As I will show, this process was set within the context of the reconstruction and political transition project that NATO and the UN had been conducting since 2001, which prioritised 'statebuild-ing', a straightforward engineering of the Afghan polity that aimed to implant the liberal-democratic model in the country.

In the second part of the chapter I draw out the contradictions inherent in this project of 'statebuilding'. Many researchers have observed and analysed the contradictions and limitations of the international intervention that began in Afghanistan in 2001, and lasted two decades (Barfield 2010; Coburn 2016; Rubin 2006; Suhrke 2011). I focus on three of these limitations that apply equally to the UNHCR's activity. First, I show that aid aimed at remedying the 'weakness' and 'incompetence' of the Afghan state overlay a hegemonic project of normalisation that turned Afghanistan into a subaltern country in which surplus refugees could be 'accommodated'. Second, the imposition from outside of the model of the liberal-democratic nation-state failed entirely to take into account the local political culture, preventing those implementing it from evaluating the changes and political tensions their intervention gener-ated in the Afghan political arena. Finally, I show that international action did not transform Afghanistan into a country capable of providing for the survival and subsistence of its population. Despite the efforts made to settle returnees, migration remained the only solution for countless families.

Reintegrating Landless Returnees

The Land Allocation Scheme consisted of selling land at low cost to re-turnees who had none, enabling them to settle in their region of origin. The programme was launched by the Ministry of Refugees in 2005. In 2007 the Minister presented it as the Ministry's flagship programme. The Ministry had received hundreds of thousands of requests and had established ambitious plans to create hundreds of new municipalities.

In the UNHCR offices, this initiative was the subject of heated debate throughout 2007. On the one hand, the principle of allocating plots of land had enormous potential. The UNHCR's inability to intervene at the level of land was one of the greatest obstacles for its reintegration programme: without the legal capacity to influence the political economy of land, the organisation could not aid returnees who had none.[2] While other returnees could be assisted in their villages of origin through dedicated programmes and by being included in plans for national development, how were those who had no physical place to return to be 'resorbed' into Afghanistan? UNHCR officers feared that 'spontaneous settlements' might arise on contested land, completely dependent on humanitarian aid. And UNHCR staff in Kabul, caught between the pressure from neighbouring countries and the instability in Afghanistan, were ready to explore all options. American, European and Australian donors were also showing a keen interest in the programme, for the same reasons.

Yet, on the other hand, the way in which the programme had been inaugurated by the Minister was a source of anxiety, with regard to both the sites designated and the methods of management. In early spring, visits to the first sites under construction revealed that the plots were situated in isolated areas, in arid terrain, with no access to water, and some subject to flooding or contestation of ownership. It turned out that these were lands that the Ministry of Agriculture could make no use of, and had therefore ceded to the Ministry of Refugees. Moreover, the profile of the recipients clearly did not match the selection criteria specified in the programme description. Some Sub-Offices reported that plots had been marked out, but no houses had been constructed. In other cases the houses were empty, while groups of returnees were living in tents or under thin survival blankets not far away. All of this suggested corruption and land investment operations that aroused the anger of UNHCR staff.

The UNHCR could have distanced itself from the programme and criticised the Minister's manoeuvres, but opposing this initiative by its main Afghan partner would inject an element of discord, weakening the Minister's credibility with international actors and leaving him free to continue down the same road. In the end, the UNHCR management decided to fully involve the organisation in the programme, in order to rein it in and bring it into line with standards of sustainability and equity. From the point of view of the Branch Office, the aim was to 'correct the shortcomings'. Taking advantage of donors' interest in the programme, the UNHCR brought with it resources, visibility and NGOs, and thus increased the chances of making the programme viable – and these elements were appreciated by the Minister. But in return he would have to commit to respecting certain standards in its execution.

Thus, following a technical evaluation of the viability of the sites, it was decided that only five would be developed in 2007. Beni Warsak, a desert location north of Kabul, was one of them. In early April, the Ministry had resettled several families originating from Parwan province, who had been squatting in a school in the capital that the Ministry of Education wanted to take back, at the site. Since the site had been judged viable and was in a 'high-return' province, a simple group of scattered tents 'in the middle of nowhere' (UNHCR 2007h) was reconfigured as an expanding pilot site, with a capacity of 10,000 plots, destined to accommodate landless returnees originating from Parwan and neighbouring Panshir provinces. By September, the ministry had already received 35,000 applications for allocation of land. A total of 6,000 families had been chosen by the selection committee and 3,000 plots had been marked out (see Figure 9.1).

Empowered by the funding and international legitimacy it conferred on the programme, the UNHCR took up the reins. The decision to participate in this ambitious plan, aimed at creating villages in isolated desert areas of the country (the only ones available) illustrates above all the limitations that

Figure 9.1. The Beni Warsak site, January 2008. Photo by the author.

now weighed on the 'reintegration' of returnees. This poor, war-torn country, of which only 12% is cultivable, could not 'resorb' returnees in decent conditions. As there was no setting that could provide for their subsistence, the UNHCR had to bring one into being by developing sites where life was feasible at any cost.

Furthermore, because it was trying to create villages from scratch, the UNHCR's approach to reintegration is particularly visible in this programme. The measures taken by the organisation to develop a place for returnees reveal how it understood decent living conditions. In line with the rationale behind the international reconstruction project, the UNHCR sought to develop a place for Afghan returnees by creating links between people, territory and state that resembled those of a liberal-democratic nation-state. In the next two sections, I will examine the UNHCR's work with returnees and with the Ministry of Refugees.

A Liberal Democratic Nation-State under Construction

The hypothesis underlying the UN-led international project in Afghanistan was that transforming the Afghan polity into a liberal-democratic state was key to the reconstruction of the country. 'Statebuilding' was effected through the intermeshing of a multitude of organisations and programmes at all levels, from ministry offices to schools, and from cultivated fields to houses. It included the US-sponsored reform of the army (Pinéu 2009), the promotion of democracy in the villages via the National Solidarity Programme (Monsutti 2012a), and the gender component aimed at changing relations between men and women, which was incorporated into all programmes (Daulatzai 2006). Whether it was the explicit aim of a programme or inherent in the way in which projects were implemented, all initiatives promoted by donors involved the establishment of basic elements of the liberal-democratic state: democratic institutions, the law-based state, a rational administration distributed through the territory, a state-based society, human rights, social justice, secular education and so on.[3]

Land allocation programme sites like that at Beni Warsak were thus effectively a microcosm of the wider construction project established by aid organisations in Afghanistan after 2001. In order to settle returnees in the country and provide them with the means of subsistence, a functioning state jurisdiction needed to be constructed around them – the 'envelope' of a state operating on the model of liberal democracy – and they needed to be incorporated into it. What was 'under construction', then, was the relationship between population, territory and state. Alongside agents of other aid organisations, UNHCR staff inserted themselves into this relationship in order to

instil principles that would guide it in the 'right' direction. They then monitored the situation to ensure that this bond was forming and developing as a
democratic link between governors and governed. In the case of Beni Warsak,
the task was to transform a desert site into national territory, returnees into
citizens resident in this territory, and to do so in such a way that it was the
Afghan state that governed them.

Part of the UNHCR's work was therefore with the new residents of these
sites, aiming to encourage them to become a population of governed citizens,
holders of titles to their plots, users of public services, subjects of bureaucratic identification procedures, and required residents to respect state law.
The UNHCR therefore supported a process of nationalisation of the returnees, to use Gérard Noiriel's term (2001), which was particularly visible here.

Take, for example, the fact that in order to settle on the site, residents of
Beni Warsak had first been subject to administrative identification procedures
that certified and formalised their relationship with the Afghan state. First,
possession of a repatriation certificate was the basic eligibility condition for
the programme. Thus, in order to apply, returnees had to show a *taskira*, an
identity document certifying their identity and their province of origin. All
of them had also passed before the selection committee that had confirmed
their eligibility, issued them the title of ownership of the plot of land, and
registered them as residents of Beni Warsak. These documents were carefully
kept by the returnees and were displayed to visitors.

UNHCR staff also took a pedagogical role with returnees, who were 'educated' in how to fulfil their status as Afghan citizens. UNHCR officers wanted
them to understand that while as returnees they could claim special treatment
from the state, they also had obligations and rules to comply with. I noted
this, for example, at a meeting held in the late summer in Beni Warsak, which
was called because the families relocated from Kabul were refusing to pay the
price for their plots. The UNHCR Field Officer supported the request of the
ministry's representative and strongly urged the families to respect the laws
and authority of the state by paying the full price for the plot (this was extremely low – it was the symbolic value that mattered). The UNHCR and the
Ministry spoke with one voice, proclaiming the importance of legal ownership of land, and were inflexible: if ownership titles were not in order, the land
would be confiscated. There was no alternative: *qanun ast* (that is the law).

Under the UNHCR's influence, the Beni Warsak site underwent a huge
transformation over the course of 2007, against a backdrop of widening state
control. Guided by the UNHCR's vision, the Afghan state moved to extend its
activity to a territory and a population it had not previously concerned itself
with. An isolated, unproductive area had been transformed into an administrative unit integrated into Afghan state jurisdiction. The UNHCR worked to
create the vertical and encompassing dimensions of the state, and to render

them operational. In the view of the organisation, the state should be the main point of reference for this territory, defining the modes of spatial, social, political and administrative cohabitation. Verticality was established through the citizen's dependence on state activity, and submission to its law. A hierarchy was created between national order and local order. Encompassment was measured through the integration of Beni Warsak into the Afghan state's administrative structure. In the spring, there was no road; by autumn, a tarmac road linked the site to the district capital of Parwan and to Kabul. This road, and the traffic that flowed along it (mainly from institutions delivering services), created a hierarchical relationship between places, marking the centre and periphery of Afghan jurisdiction.

Setting the Ministry of Refugees to Rights

As well as working with returnees, the UNHCR worked on the Ministry of Refugees. As in the case of a number of other international organisations and their Afghan institutional partners, the relationship that the UNHCR had maintained with the Ministry of Refugees[4] since the end of 2001 had been based on 'capacity building'. UNHCR senior staff repeatedly described the Ministry as a 'weak, but necessary partner' – necessary because a strong ministry was considered an essential condition for the reintegration of returnees and the sustainability of returns, but weak because it was judged to be completely inadequate to its functions: inefficient, disorganised and lacking skills. The UNHCR's aim was therefore to transform the Ministry into a functional institution and then to gradually transfer management of the reintegration programmes to it. Once the Ministry had taken over, returnees would enjoy the long-term protection of a state institution responsible for looking after them. The Ministry would thus serve as guarantor of the protection of the Afghan state, being seen as the natural provider of protection for Afghans and of their incorporation into the Afghan state polity.

In 2007 this objective was far from achieved, despite the reforms UNHCR staff had led in 2002 and 2003,[5] in collaboration with the Independent Administrative Reform and Civil Service Commission, the body tasked with coordinating the reform of Afghan public administration. In the view of UNHCR management, one of the most problematic elements was 'corruption'. The merit-based system promoted by the UNHCR clashed with the logics of cronyism and patronage that, in the view of UNHCR officers, dominated staff recruitment and thus compromised the Ministry's competence. Another problematic element was the relations between the central Ministry and its provincial departments. The UNHCR wanted a centralised administration, but felt that the provincial departments were being managed in an individualistic fashion by departmental directors appointed by provincial governors according to the same systems.

The Minister himself was, in the view of UNHCR senior staff, the very example of a civil servant unfit for his role. Appointed by President Karzai in early 2006, he was the third to have occupied the post since 2002. He aroused the suspicion and distrust of UNHCR senior staff, who saw him as an incompetent and irrational official, unpredictable and recalcitrant, guided by his aspirations for power, which led him to take ill-considered initiatives without worrying about the sustainability of programmes or about diplomatic relations with neighbouring countries. According to UNHCR staff, he had still not taken on board the codes of international relations and the principles of international law that they were attempting to instil in him.

In October 2007, for example, the Minister travelled to Geneva for the annual meeting of the UNHCR Executive Committee.[6] Rather than going with his UNHCR-appointed advisor, he decided to have his nephew accompany him. Rumours filtering through from Headquarters spoke of a 'disastrous' mission. His speech had been carefully prepared by the UNHCR management in Kabul, a well-crafted address, in perfect English, in which he would assert that he spoke in the name of the Afghan government and people. He would thank the international community, emphasise the importance of the principle of voluntary and gradual returns, and remind Iran and Pakistan of their deep-seated neighbourly relations. Yet, in the end, the Minister did not attend the meeting.

During the Jalozai crisis, the UNHCR employee tasked with advising the Minister told me with exasperation that he had not even understood the principle of 'voluntariness' of returns – a basic principle for all UNHCR staff and the linchpin of the Kabul office's strategic argument. He told me that according to the Minister, all Afghans should come back to Afghanistan because he saw the number of returns as an indicator of the success of his ministry's work.

For UNHCR staff, the Land Allocation programme consolidated all of these problems: the Minister's quest for visibility, corruption in the selection of recipients, management that had little concern for the sustainability of sites, and the central Ministry's inability to control its provincial departments. When UNHCR staff took representatives of funders to visit the new villages, it had a ready response to their surprise: 'the ministry creates disasters, and we do our best to resolve them'.

The idea of the Ministry's 'incapacity' justified the UNHCR, empowered by its substantial funding and the international legitimacy it brought to the Ministry, taking its place and monitoring it, like a powerful sponsor. It was in fact UNHCR employees who were actually designing national policy on returnees, running the programmes officially emanating from the Ministry and closely monitoring the activity of Ministry officials.

The Ministry's programmes corresponded to the UNHCR's main programmes (repatriation, shelters and water), and were designed and funded by the UNHCR. Under the guise of its role as 'political adviser', the UNHCR management in Kabul wrote or reworked all official documents. At international conferences, it prepared the discussion topics it wanted the Ministry representative to address. Thus, in the spring of 2007, in preparation for the Afghanistan/Pakistan/UNHCR Tripartite Commission meeting, UNHCR-Kabul managers suggested to the Minister the arguments and tone he should adopt. It was they who decided how the arguments should be distributed between delegations so as to make them more effective and incisive as a whole. Similarly, that same spring, the substance of the strategic plan for 'refugees, returnees and internally displaced people' that would be integrated into the National Development Plan[7] took form on the screen of the UNHCR Deputy Head of Mission, who himself drew on the organisation's most recent policy paper (UNHCR 2007a). Since the official author of the strategy was the Afghan government, references to the UNHCR were removed and some paragraphs were reformulated in order to adjust the point of view. But, in fact, the national strategy was simply the state version of the UNHCR's analysis and strategy. The words were those of the UNHCR, the maps and statistics likewise. Moreover, the UNHCR's precepts were faithfully transposed, as were its reasoning in constructing problems and objectives, and its criteria for transparency and resource allocation.

This 'political advice' was accompanied by close monitoring of the key Ministry officials, called 'technical assistance' – training, institutional support and advice. The UNHCR funded 'advisors' each year, which it recruited and trained itself. The programmes were jointly run. UNHCR staff had a training, supervisory and monitoring role, aimed at gradually transferring their tasks to ministry employees.

These two features – of substitution and continuous monitoring – were also evident in the Land Allocation Scheme. Once the UNHCR management had decided to commit UNHCR funds to the programme, the administrative structure was entirely reorganised. Management of the scheme was entrusted to a dedicated unit within the Ministry created for this purpose; its duties and responsibilities were defined by the UNHCR, which also recruited and paid its director. UNHCR staff rewrote all the administrative procedures governing the programme, introducing principles of equity in the selection of recipients, protection of the returnees' human rights, and accountability. For example, in order to prevent corruption and land speculation, the Committee responsible for allocating plots had to adopt procedures that guaranteed equity, integrity and transparency. Selection criteria and reasons for refusal had to be communicated in writing, and each meeting of the committee had to be minuted. In addition, a new post of Land Allocation Officer was created at the

Branch Office, tasked with close monitoring of the Ministry's work. In addition to participating in coordination of the programme, he also accompanied Ministry staff on site visits, and stayed with them to observe their activity and instil a sense of responsibility in them. For example, on a visit to Beni Warsak, I saw him point to the numerous plots empty of construction or occupied by vacant shelters. He strongly urged the head of the Parwan Department for Refugees to concern himself with this, encouraging him to organise regular door-to-door inspections and confiscate plots that remained uninhabited for more than three months. If he did not, the UNHCR would withdraw from the programme.

All of this explains the ambivalence that had marked the relationship between UNHCR offices and officials of the Afghan Ministry of Refugees since 2001. For all the influence that the UNHCR continued to exercise, there was frustration and unease that despite the long-term work to 'build the capacity', the Ministry's performance was disappointing, and it was still one of the weakest and most marginal ministries in the Afghan government. Thus, the paternalist relationship persisted in the long term. In the two following sections I will examine this ambivalent relationship by highlighting two aspects of it: the dominance inherent in the way in which UNHCR officers worked, and their failure to understand the local political culture.

Extraversion and Normalisation: A Hegemonic Project

The international project in Afghanistan was marked by the *extraversion* of the Afghan state: since 2001, the legitimacy of those in state government, the use of force, the resources that enabled the Afghan state to exist and the content of public policies had been shaped by external actors as never before.[8] As the main providers of funding and international legitimacy for the government in office, they had substantial authority that gave them free rein in establishing priorities and budgets.[9] Moreover, at the same time as the international statebuilders were seeking to strengthen the Afghan state, they were substituting for it and constructing a parallel administration. Most of the international funding did not pass through Afghan institutions, but was paid into the country through a myriad of programmes funded and run by international actors. Monsutti (2012a) and Petric (2005) describe the condition of a state under an aid regime like that in Afghanistan as a 'globalised protectorate'; Ferguson (2006) uses the term 'non-governmental state', and Donini (2010b: 3) talks of a 'fissured 'protégé' state'.

This extraversion is clearly evident in the case of the Ministry of Refugees. As noted above, the national strategy on refugee matters was drawn up by UNHCR senior managers in a language of which the Ministry had no command. In order to become official, it would be submitted for donors' approval. It is striking that this document, officially issued by the government, highlighted that government's weakness, and included 'strengthening' its own 'capacities' through international support among its primary objectives.[10] The involvement of the UNHCR in the Land Allocation Scheme drew in the further involvement of a number of international organisations and NGOs, and above all the overseas governments that funded the project. The latter, as members of the supervisory committee, gave or withheld their approval of the programme's policy directions and budgets. Simply walking around the Beni Warsak site made this clear. At the entrance to the site, visitors were greeted by a sign promoting CESVI, an NGO that had constructed housing funded by Cooperazione Italiana, and one for Action Against Hunger, which had built wells with funding from the French Foreign Ministry (see Figure 9.2). It was these notices publicising external organisations that told visitors that they were indeed at Beni Warsak, Bagram district, Parwan province, Afghanistan. Looking closely, each house had a metal plaque attached with the acronyms of the body that had constructed it and the funding organisation. Logos and acronyms were also present, more or less discreetly, inside the houses – for example, on the children's textbooks. As throughout Afghan territory, Beni Warsak was scattered with innumerable flags and logos that formed a sort of aid signage system.

Historically, external factors have acted on each successive form of political organisation in Afghanistan, restricting their room for manoeuvre. This dates back to the premodern era, when Afghanistan lay in the contested zone between empires based in India, Iran and Central Asia (Barfield 2010). The country's current borders were established in the late nineteenth century, defined by external powers without regard for geographical or ethnic configuration, and still less for the country's material resources. These borders were traced in order to create a buffer zone between the Russian and British Empires. Although Afghanistan was never colonised (the British only managed to make it a protectorate), like many other non-European countries, it was integrated into the interstate arena in a position of weakness. It was incorporated into a pre-existing order where the rules of the game had already been set and where those governing it depended on external alliances to stay in power and rule.

The extraversion of the Afghan state thus meant that it was strongly influenced by regional and global geostrategic situations, and the fluctuating interests of the great powers. For long periods, these powers displayed their lack of interest, and the country was forgotten. But when they rediscovered their geostrategic interest in Afghanistan, its territory and population came to serve as a theatre of confrontation for them, or even as a laboratory for political projects outside their borders. Thus, during the 1980s, Afghanistan became a contested site of bipolar competition, and a stage for Saudi Salafists' attempt

Figure 9.2. Aid signage at returnees' sites. AAH sign at Beni Warsak. BPRM plaque at Sheik Misri. Photos by the author.

to take the lead in a transnational *jihad*.[11] Following the Soviet withdrawal, the great powers lost interest: Afghanistan returned to being an inoffensive country with little strategic importance. Thus, during the 1990s, the country was abandoned to civil war and then to the Taliban regime, which the United States and its allies saw no particular reason to challenge (Coll 2004; Rashid 2000; Rubin 2006). After 11 September 2001, the pendulum swung back the other way. Afghanistan returned to the centre of interest for Western powers and once more became the theatre of conflict for an overseas project – this time the 'war on terror'. But the US strategy had changed: rather than conducting a proxy war, it intervened directly, deploying soldiers and diplomats on Afghan terrain.

Although the Afghan state had been dependent on the external world in terms of its economy, it had always managed its internal affairs independently. With the exception of the British attempt at conquest and the Soviet invasion, external powers had never intervened directly in the internal government of the country. However, the United States was now accompanying its military project (eliminating centres of Islamic terrorism and preventing them from being rebuilt) with a project to transform Afghan sociopolitical institutions. It was in this context that a multitude of international experts arrived in the country, alongside the soldiers and diplomats. From this point of view, the year 2001 marked a major turning point. External powers were now pursuing a deep intervention into social and political institutions. Thus, within a few years, Afghanistan became pervaded by concepts, logics, principles and values derived from international law and/or liberal-democratic polities that were not part of the country's history and until then had been foreign to it.

The implantation of liberal-democratic principles in Afghanistan thus formed part of the security strategy conducted by the United States and its allies, aimed at taming this hitherto uncontrolled, unfamiliar, different country and bringing it under control, placing it under liberal influence so as to neutralise it. The 'statebuilding' project pursued by the UN and other international aid bodies was directly connected to this security programme. A number of studies have shown that in the context of the Cold War, 'statebuilding' sat at the nexus of the United States' security interests and the UN's new agenda. From the 1980s onwards, the UN took the view that as a source of political instability, 'failed states' or 'fragile states' constituted a danger for the international community, and that effective liberal-democracy is the best guarantee of sustainable humanitarian and development interventions (United Nations 1992). The focus was therefore on strengthening 'fragile states' by instilling liberal-democratic principles, which were seen as the recipe for progress, development and modernisation. This view made it possible for UN agents to be co-opted into Western countries' security agenda, a hegemonic project of putting the world in order and making it secure.[12]

A number of authors have noted that, under cover of a benevolent, emancipatory rhetoric, interventions by many international and humanitarian organisations contributed to supporting and even moving forward the hegemonic project of contemporary liberal democracies, which instrumentalise democratic principles and human rights in the context of a postcolonial imperialist project (Agier 2003, 2011; Donini 2010a, 2010b; Duffield 2001; Guilhot 2005; Hindess 2002; Paris 2002). Oliver Richmond has described this post-Cold War configuration, which sees 'statebuilding' deployed throughout the world in a form of postcolonial hegemony, as 'liberal peace' (Richmond and Franks 2009). This project of dominance is justified by, and lays claim to, altruistic, benevolent principles – a 'will to improve' (Murray Li 2007) or a 'civilising mission' (Paris 2002) – that hark back to nineteenth-century imperialist reasoning, with those intervening proclaiming that their ultimate goal is the wellbeing and progress of remote, 'backward' populations.[13]

While the statebuilders imputed its problems purely to internal factors, some of the structural factors that explain Afghanistan's lack of resources, its lack of influence in the interstate arena, and the conflicts and devastation the country had undergone during the 1980s and 1990s had their origins in global power relations. By failing to question these relations of power, the 'statebuilding' project helped to reproduce them. Although the country features at the top of all the UN lists, by virtue of alphabetical order, it was subject to an international intervention that consigned it to the global margins – a state to be improved.

This hegemonic project was set up primarily as a process of normalisation, transformation to conform with a model. While during the colonial era the ethnocentrism underpinning the civilising mission was based on racial factors, it was now a political ethnocentrism based on the supposed superiority of the liberal-democratic model (the White Man had become Liberal Man). The model of the liberal-democratic state had become the new standard for civilisation. The political and institutional journey of Western states was set up as the model, and the situation of other states was read in terms of how far they conformed with this model. It thus mapped a moral and political geography of the world that put Western countries at the centre, immediately creating a hierarchy between countries where this model had emerged, and that therefore had the expertise to propagate it, and the countries that needed to learn it. The world was divided into those who understood international law, human rights and democracy, and those who knew nothing of them, between those who democratised, and those who were to be democratised. The principles of liberal democracy and human rights thus served as techniques of government, since interventions were designed to implant these principles (organising elections, reforming administration and society in line with their model). This made it possible to keep Afghanistan in a position of weakness, on the margins. And even if the model was to 'take', its realisation would always be less advanced, and the countries concerned would remain morally indebted.

Michael Merlingen (2003) emphasises the power relations inherent in the normalising activity of international organisations, which operates in part through education and incentivisation. This attitude was apparent in the UNHCR staff's relationship with the Afghan Ministry of Refugees. The Minister's 'poor' and 'inadequate' understanding of the concepts of international law offers an example. According to UNHCR staff, he got everything backwards: when he should have protested against returns (for example, when the Jalozai camp was closed), he failed to do so, but when the returns were legitimate, he reacted without thinking, as he did twice in 2007. At the end of April, following the rise in deportations from Iran, representatives of the Ministry described the deportees as 'refugees'.[14] The UNHCR staff's attempts to explain that these were 'undocumented migrants' were simply translated by the use of the term 'illegal refugees'. In the autumn, when Sweden was on the point of deporting a group of Afghan 'failed asylum seekers', the Ministry made an official protest without consulting the UNHCR. UNHCR staff then mobilised to ward off a diplomatic crisis with Sweden, one of the main donors to the reconstruction project. The Minister's reaction was systematically ascribed to a clumsiness that called for endlessly repeated explanations of the founding principles of international relations and the 'correct' definitions for migrants.

But another reading is possible. Describing Afghans who were being deported from other states as 'refugees' could be seen, on the contrary, as a way of appropriating international refugee law, in order to advance specific demands in terms of the (better) treatment Afghans deserved in other countries. This implies contesting the legitimacy of deportations, entering into debate around the labelling of Afghans in other countries, and contesting the classification criteria defined in negotiations to which the Afghan government had not been party. Seeing this reaction as clumsiness thus indicates a lack of awareness of these demands, a failure to accept them as such. Dismissed as 'errors', 'ignorance' or 'incapacity', they are thereby silenced. The problem, then, seems not to be the incompetence of Afghan institutions, but rather Afghanistan's subordinate position in interstate relations – in this case, in relation to Iran and Sweden. The Afghan government lacked the political weight to lend authority to its claims and therefore had to resign itself to accepting the designations assigned by other institutions.

For the UNHCR and other UN agencies, liberal peace is a trap situation. Certainly, these agencies can prosper and have scope for substantial activity and expansion, but this comes at the price of adhering to a universalism based on a specific political and moral model, which is also the expression of a sociopolitical ethnocentrism. They thus risk legitimising these hegemonic projects while giving them a semblance of benevolence, and contributing to the depoliticisation of global power relations.

Failing to Understand the Local Political Culture

International statebuilders (including the UNHCR expatriate staff) held precise, fixed assumptions about the way in which public life works, and should work, in Afghanistan. They saw their own model as the best, most appropriate system. Their teleological, evolutionist view was that implanting a liberal-democratic nation-state was the key to achieving 'modernity' with all its benefits. The actual sociopolitical relationships played out in Afghanistan were read purely through the lens of this model. And because the Afghan state did not conform to it, their resulting view was negative and condescending: the Afghan state was seen as 'weak', 'failed', 'incapable', 'corrupt' and 'backward' because of the persistence of 'traditional' ideas and practices such as cronyism, tribalism and the importance of Islam. It was precisely these elements that they sought to eradicate and replace. This view, centred on a confrontation between tradition and modernity, was powerful, not only pervading evaluation reports produced for the reconstruction project but also widely disseminated by the media, think tanks[15] and a number of researchers, including some who were otherwise critical of the reconstruction project.[16]

The problem with this view is that it is enclosed in self-referentiality. Those who hold it refuse to take Afghan political culture seriously.[17] The statebuilders refuse to place their model and other forms of political organisation that operate in the world on the same footing. They are unable to see the liberal-democratic nation-state as just one among all the possible forms of political organisation, a model that implies a particular view of society and politics, arising out of historical, political, social and institutional processes specific to a particular region of the world. Because the international statebuilders did not bother to understand the power structures and forms of political legitimacy at work in Afghanistan, they risked remaining blind to the deep shifts in the political field caused by their sudden arrival en masse in late 2001, and hence being unable to analyse the impact of their programmes. By introducing resources in a context where they were scarce, and by imposing new criteria for distribution and political legitimacy, international aid led to major changes: processes of political reconfiguration (competition, appropriation, contestation, etc.)[18] and highly destabilising effects within the state administration.

Contrary to the received ideas of international statebuilders, the Afghan state is much older than European nation-states. In its earliest form, it dates back to the thirteenth century, when Ahmed Shah Durrani, a Pashtun from the Popalzai tribe, created the emirate of Kabul, a Pashtun tribal confederation that extended from Kandahar to New Delhi (Barfield 2010; Roy 2004). Moreover, the state was remarkably stable until the communist coup d'état in 1978. The power of the central state still owes a great deal to Abdur Rahman, the ruler who embarked on a great internal military conquest and established a multilevel administration throughout the territory. But the political legitimacy of the Afghan state rested neither on the monopoly of force nor on nationalist ideology, as was the case in Europe. In this region of Asia, ethnicity and nationalism have never been linked: multiethnic states and empires were experienced as the norm rather than a historical injustice (Barfield 2010). Thus, in Afghanistan it is thanks to other factors that this assemblage of territories, populations and state 'holds together'.

Although on one level a degree of extraversion enabled those in government to tap into external resources, helping to maintain internal legitimacy and avoiding conflicts around taxation, the crucial issue for the Afghan state has always been to affirm its power in relation to infra-state actors. It was at this level that the construction of effective loyalty networks, the circulation of resources and the exercise of force and justice were played out (Roy 1985). The central state, not being able to position itself as the main provider of security and resources, did not seek to supplant or alter social organisation. Rather, it imposed itself through a politics of negotiation, pressure and encouragement, working through intermediate figures like local notables, and always seeking an internal balance between the state political-juridical order (*hukumat*) and local customary institutions. It presented itself as the essential mediator and key donor, offering protection, resources and positions in the administration. The state thus tended to exercise its authority indirectly and never systematically provided social services at a local level, particularly because unlike many colonised countries, the Afghan state administration had never been subject to Western-style rationalisation. To return to Gupta and Ferguson's notions of verticality and encompassment, here the state defined itself neither as encompassing nor as a hierarchical superior; rather, it formed an 'umbrella', or a conveyor belt between the local and global levels.

The UNHCR staff's paternalist and didactic approach, based on the assumed 'incompetence' and 'corruption' of the Ministry, infantilised the Minister, denying him all rationality, at the same time as demonising him and only seeing his defects. Yet if we consider the way in which the Afghan state has long operated, and the nature of the resources brought in and the changes imposed by the statebuilders, a different reading is called for: first, a rationale of appropriation can be detected in the Minister's decisions; and, second, it is clear that the Afghan Ministry for Refugees was caught in a destabilising dual-language situation

In his study of the National Solidarity Programme, a vast rural rehabilitation programme funded by the World Bank, Monsutti (2012a) highlights the strategies for appropriation of international aid established at the national and local levels. This logic of appropriating resources reveals a clear rationality in the way in which the Minister managed his relationship with the UNHCR. The notion of the cunning state (Randeria 2007) – in this case the cunning minister – is once again useful in explaining in what circumstances and why the Minister decided to go along with the UNHCR's precepts and when he instead decided to go his own way. The UNHCR was a source of precious resources for the Ministry. It was the key to accessing donor funds, and conforming with UNHCR precepts was essential for this. It provided the Ministry with a ready-to-use, internationally legitimate 'package of policies'. It also ensured that the returnee sector was central and visible in national public policy. All of these resources could be put to use in interministerial competition.

In the aftermath of 2001, international aid became a key factor in ensuring status and funding for ministries.[19] The Ministry for Refugees was not one of the central ministries. Very peripheral, it was housed in bare offices in a dilapidated Soviet-style building. It was therefore unsurprising that the Minister saw a high number of returns, and hence of clients for his ministry, as an advantage for it, particularly in a context where the UNHCR itself was asserting that return was the 'preferred solution'. From this point of view, it was the attitude of the UNHCR that was ambivalent.

We can now realise the stakes involved in the Land Allocation Scheme for the Minister, in terms of visibility and the importance of keeping the UNHCR in the programme. The practices that the UNHCR described as corruption for the benefit of local strongmen and notables also become more intelligible. While the concerns of UNHCR staff are entirely comprehensible, we can also understand that in order to acquire land in a country where it is an extremely scarce resource and where the administration of state power and access to jobs have for centuries been played out through negotiation with local forms of power, in order to intervene and govern at the local level while taking ownership of a resource as precious and contested as land, the state administration had to engage in negotiations – and potentially in practices of redistribution – with local actors.

Thus, the Ministry, like the rest of the Afghan state machinery, was torn between contradictory injunctions that were hard to reconcile – between new criteria for legitimacy and distribution imposed by donors on the one hand, and indigenous criteria on the other. The Afghan state was performing a balancing act, split between two languages, creating powerful tensions and permanent instability within its administration.

Hamid Karzai is an emblematic case in point here. The Americans chose him from among the few Afghan leaders who had the linguistic capacity and the background necessary for interacting with diplomatic circles. Moreover, as a scion of the Ghilji lineage of the Durrani, the Pashtun tribal confederation to which all Afghan rulers have belonged since the eighteenth century, he had the pedigree to lead the country. However, he was the first elected leader in the country's history: in 2004, presidential elections confirmed his status as President. But as Barfield notes, the relationship between the elections and Karzai's entitlement to occupy the role of president was seen in different ways. While in the view of international actors his legitimacy derived directly from the elections, for Afghans these simply marked the beginning of a quest for legitimacy that Karzai would acquire depending on how he fulfilled his role (Barfield 2010: 300).

The logic Karzai adopted in appointing the members of his cabinet and other state officials clashed violently with the criteria specified by his international sponsors. He distributed jobs and resources on the basis of his personal judgement, guided by the concern to maintain a balance between regions, solidarity groups and political factions, working to co-opt powerful men in order to secure their support. He then established a rotation among officials and redistributed jobs to prevent them gaining too much power within one ministry or province, and in order at the same time to neutralise potential competitors (Barfield 2010: 284; Roy 2004). Beyond his desire to ensure his own political survival, he was attempting to build an administration that would 'hold', anchored in the territory and satisfying both local and external criteria for legitimacy.

Thus, after 2001, two categories of officials could be identified within the Afghan state. On one side, there were the technocrats in intermediate political positions, who had usually lived abroad and received a Western education. They formed an emergent state elite that was more receptive to the values and behaviours promoted by international donors – not only because they spoke English, but also because they had mastered the language of international organisations, and behaved and dressed in Western style: they wore suits, kept their hair and beard well groomed, shook hands with female foreigners and so on. The Deputy Minister for Refugees was of this group, and UNHCR senior managers always preferred to deal with him. On the other side, there were the Afghan notables chosen in accordance with local political and ethical criteria: these were powerful men (regional notables and commanders), either jihadists whose legitimacy rested on the Mujahideen resistance or Taliban sympathisers. These men were less obliging with foreigners, and international actors found it much more difficult to come to an understanding with them. The then Minister fell into this category. A Pashtun from Paktia province, he had been a Mujahid and supported the Islamist party Ittehad

Islami (the Islamic Union for the Liberation of Afghanistan). He did not speak English. It was not his style to behave accommodatingly with foreigners, and I always saw him dressed in a traditional blanket, his hair dishevelled.

In his efforts to create a viable administration in Afghanistan, Karzai was torn between internal power plays and the new criteria and concepts imposed by aid agents. The risk he ran was that he would satisfy no one. The international actors were dissatisfied: indifferent to the local sociopolitical systems, they saw Karzai's decisions as manifestations of cronyism and corruption, precisely what they were attempting to replace with the merit system they wished to introduce. They were irritated at having to deal with officials they deemed incompetent. At the same time, popular support diminished as Karzai demonstrated his subordination to the Americans and recruited commanders who had committed atrocities during the conflict into the administration. Moreover, the administration's local grounding was eroded by the rotation imposed on officials, while local notables still played a major role in mediating between the population and the state administration.

Thus, it is clear that failure to understand the local political culture prevented the international 'statebuilders' from grasping the effects of their interventions, and ultimately the reasons these failed. While they admitted the reconstruction's shortcomings, this did not lead them to question their hypotheses. They assumed that the failures were due to insufficient action being taken, and to underestimating the difficulty of the problem to be resolved. Thus, for example, the failure to establish a monopoly of force in Afghan territory was ascribed to insufficient military commitment. This justified the deployment of more funds, more personnel and more foreign troops to construct the Afghan state. Responsibility for the failure of the reform of public administration was attributed to the weakness of the Commission tasked with coordinating the reform, and it was itself subjected to reform (Lister 2006: 2). The failure of 'capacity building' in the Ministry of Refugees was imputed to insufficient reforms having been introduced up to that point. Thus, in late 2007, when Karzai appointed a new minister, the UNHCR staff decided to embark on a new reform of the Ministry – a 'radical restructuring'. The Ministry was once more reshaped in the belief that the new administrative moulds would generate substantive changes.

Violence and Utopianism in Re-emplacement

Notwithstanding the UNHCR's intervention, when I left Afghanistan in 2008, the fate of Beni Warsak and the other villages under construction that had sprung up across Afghanistan remained highly uncertain. There were countless logistical and coordination problems with the basic services, including water supply and sanitation. The land around the sites was un-productive and the lack of public transport hampered any prospect of employment. Making these places habitable for returnees still seemed to require 'magic' (UNHCR 2007h). At the UNHCR, the programme continued to generate dilemmas and internal tensions. In the autumn, the expert recruited by the organisation had resigned because he no longer had any faith in the programme. Each time a donor or a Branch Office employee visited a site for the first time, the optimism inspired by reading documents describing the project was shaken. How could humans live in such a place? Later reports confirmed that most of the sites failed to become established (Macdonald 2011; Majidi 2013).

According to the nation-state order, the arid plain on which the Beni Warsak site arose was suitable for returnee settlement. Displaced Afghans were finally in their rightful place there. These sites that sprang up from nothing across Afghanistan, out of a need to create a place where life would be possible for returnees, represented an ultimate attempt to establish a place in the national order for a surplus population, and to implant them there. The UNHCR committed to this ambitious programme in the hope of solving the 'equation for the resolution of Afghan displacement' by increasing the 'absorption capacity' of this mountainous state, where only 12% of the land was cultivable, which had one of the highest birth rates in the world and was one of the least developed economies. But this was a bold experiment in the quest for an unlikely equilibrium. The Land Allocation Scheme required colossal and utopian engineering, involving a battle against nature and the transformation of a political system.

Embedded in the context of the international reconstruction project in Afghanistan, this utopian programme was part of a project to dominate the country and its migrants. *Emplacement* of returnees was sought at any price, despite the fact that the international intervention had failed to stabilise Afghanistan or to substantially alter its economic situation. On the contrary, it had solidified the marginal and subaltern position of the country, which was once again serving as the arena for external actors and projects. Because the Afghan state did not have enough weight or strategic advantages to be able to ensure favourable reception of its citizens in other countries, what was offered to landless returnees was the margin of the margins – the land most unsuited to human life in one of the most inhospitable countries in the world. They were supposed to find a way to survive there.

In these conditions, one thing was certain: that movement would continue to be a crucial survival and subsistence strategy for returnees, despite being criminalised (see Chapter 11). Several studies conducted at Beni Warsak in 2007 showed that at this time, most of the men living there walked several hours a day to paid work in Kabul, and that money transfer from relatives abroad also constituted a crucial support for the survival of families living there. More generally, the persistence of substantial migration flows in the region and the emergence of new migration routes to new destinations testify to the utopian nature of the project of lasting emplacement of Afghan returnees in Afghanistan.

Notes

1. In 2007 the Afghan population was estimated to be between 20 and 30 million. Some four million Afghans had returned to Afghanistan under the repatriation programme launched in 2002.
2. Land issues were at the heart of the conflict, during which land was seized by warlords. After 2001, even nonproductive land was subject to appropriation and property speculation. Moreover, the superimposition of several legal systems (national, ethnic, religious, etc.) generated contestation of ownership. All of these issues presented obstacles to the UNHCR's involvement in land issues. For an analysis of the complexity of land issues in Afghanistan, see Adelkhah (2013).
3. The objectives of the Afghan National Development Strategy clearly reflect this (with the exception of the religious element): 'By 2020, Afghanistan will be (1) a stable Islamic constitutional democracy at peace with itself and its neighbours, a worthy member of the international family; (2) a tolerant, united and pluralist nation that honours its Islamic heritage and its deep aspirations toward participation, justice and rights for all; (3) a hopeful and prosperous society founded on a solid economy led by the private sector, on social equity and environmental sustainability.' Retrieved 3 May 2013 from http://www.afghanexperts.gov.af/?page=AboutUs&lang=en.
4. This ministry was set up in the late 1980s by the Afghan administration supported by the Soviet Union, with the aim of encouraging national reconciliation. In 1988, when the Geneva Accords approved the withdrawal of the Soviet Union, the UNHCR opened its first office in the country and the first repatriation programme was launched. The Ministry's role was then to manage the return and reintegration of repatriated people in collaboration with the UNHCR. After Kabul was taken by the Mujahideen in 1992 and the Taliban arrived, the Ministry of Refugees was cut and restructured (first being downgraded to a department and then merged with the Ministry for Martyrs and Disabled Veterans), while the repatriation programme was suspended. In late 2001 it was restored to the rank of a ministry and fundamentally restructured under the aegis of the UNHCR. In 2007, the Ministry had some 1,100 employees (almost twice the number of UNHCR staff in Afghanistan), distributed between the central Ministry and the thirty-four provincial departments.
5. This reform incorporated material assistance and institutional restructuring, leading to a review of the Ministry's mandate and organisational structure, the division of responsibilities, and training for staff in management, international refugee law, IT skills and English.
6. At the time, Afghanistan had observer status on this committee. It has been a member since 2014.
7. Islamic Republic of Afghanistan, *Afghanistan National Development Strategy* (ANDS), *Refugees, Returnees & IDPs Sector Strategy 2008–2013.*

8. On the concept of extraversion, which can be defined as outward orientation, see Bayart (1996).

9. The Afghan state did not have the monopoly on legitimate violence within its territory: the International Security Assistance Force (ISAF) was responsible for national security. The Afghan state was also not the principal provider of goods and income: in 2006–7, Afghanistan received more than $4 billion in foreign aid, equivalent to seven times its own GNP.

10. This paradox was highlighted by one donor's comments on the draft strategy, when he remarked that there were still too many references to the UNHCR: 'Even if the Ministry of Refugees does not have the capacity to write this document, it should be worded in a way that clearly indicates that the policies articulated originated with the ministry.'

11. Like the imperialist competition of the nineteenth century, the opposing ideologies of this period (socialism versus capitalism, or Islamism versus atheism) bore little relevance to Afghanistan, either in terms of the aspirations of ordinary Afghans or in the political life.

12. This convergence is evident in the book *Fixing Failed States*, of which I found several copies in the library at the UN headquarters in New York. Its introduction is a manifesto for 'statebuilding', which is described as the solution to all the world's evils: 'They simply want their states, economies and societies to function … it is the dysfunctional state that stands between them and a better life … This problem – the failed state – is at the heart of a worldwide systemic crisis that constitutes the most serious challenge to global stability in the new millennium … A consensus is now emerging that only sovereign states – by which we mean states that actually perform the functions that make them sovereign – will allow human progress to continue' (Ghani and Lockhart 2008: 3–4).

13. If we replace 'White Man' with 'Liberal Man', Kipling's poem about the 'white man's burden' is strikingly topical: it speaks of a generation of people in exile (expatriates working for international bodies and NGOs), 'in heavy harness' (now equipped with computers and vehicles), who watch over local populations seen as 'half devil and half child' (an attitude that, as noted above, aptly describes that of UNHCR officers towards the Afghan Ministry of Refugees), in order to 'serve [their] need' (for example, through 'capacity building').

14. For example, the representative of the Ministry of Refugees in the frontier province of Herat criticised Iran for 'its treatment of Afghan refugees' (*Afghan TV*, 27 April 2007).

15. Fund for Peace (2011).

16. See, for example, Nixon (2007).

17. Those with the most in-depth knowledge of the Afghan context have repeatedly noted the lack of knowledge, and indeed the failure to understand it, shown by international experts. Barfield, for example, argues that Afghanistan is 'one of those places in the world in which people who know the least make the most definitive statements about it' (Barfield 2010: 274). Monsutti shows that the National Solidarity Programme, the programme that sought to educate and train Afghans in political participation, was designed with a striking lack of understanding of local social structures, starting with the definition of the 'family unit' and the criteria for territorial demarcation of villages (Monsutti 2012a). Roy warns of the risk of destabilisation arising from aid

programmes based on the desire for social transformation without taking the specific nature of the Afghan context into account (Roy 2004: 56).

18. Monsutti demonstrates this, pointing out the new habitus that Afghan agents employed in the programme acquired when they participated in workshops and interacted with international experts. It was also evident in the emergence of a new sociopolitical and economic class of employees of international organisations and NGOs, as I discussed in Chapter 6.

19. Describing the contrast between the headquarters of the Ministry of Agriculture, Irrigation and Livestock and that of the Ministry of Rural Development, Monsutti (2012a: 582–83) shows how they were treated differently depending on the importance ascribed to them in the context of the reconstruction project.

CHAPTER 10

The Authority of Expertise

Jalalabad, December 2007. I have organised a field visit to the east of the country for two ECHO officers. They are here not only to check in on UN-HCR programmes, but also more generally to evaluate the situation on the ground after the end of the repatriation season. Donors are entitled to make a field visit at any time, but as they have no presence outside Kabul, it is often the UNHCR that provides access to the field, taking charge of transport (in the organisation's vehicles) and accommodation (in its residences). UNHCR teams also reserve the right to choose the itinerary – in line with the donor's wishes, of course, but also depending on the messages they wish to communicate. The two ECHO representatives are therefore accompanied and guided in the field by a succession of UNHCR staff.

Being based in Kabul, I had the overall view of the country: during the journey from Kabul to Jalalabad, I placed the programmes, and the issue of returns to the east, in the general context of Afghanistan. Once we arrived at the Jalalabad office, the ECHO officers were briefed by the Head of Sub-Office, who sketched an outline of the region, summarised the current situation and offered guidance on how to interpret returns and reintegration. To help with this, they also received the Sub-Office's briefing kit containing maps, statistical data and descriptions of projects. The Field Officer then took over to escort them to the sites, where he showed them around and helped them talk to the local leaders and recipients of the projects. The Head of Sub-Office took up the baton again to facilitate a meeting with the deputy governor, and at dinner talked with the visitors about what they had seen. UNHCR staff thus planned the route and showed the way, preparing the representatives for what they would see and discussing it afterwards. In the field, UNHCR staff stepped back to allow them to observe freely what was happening around them, but were always at hand to explain what they were seeing, translate what was being said, help them to interact with people and answer their questions. Ultimately, while the UNHCR was not the only source of information for these ECHO officials, it played a major role in the construction of their observations and analyses.

Through their 'updates' and their 'explanations', UNHCR staff framed the way in which its partners saw Afghan migration, and how it was and should be governed. The impact of this 'information' thus went well beyond simple monitoring of what was going on. UNHCR officers explained to their partners 'what is happening', 'how things are' and why, how they should be and how to make them as they should be. The organisation conceptualised and defined phenomena and processes, established relationships between cause and effect, and on the basis of these analyses expressed opinions as to the best way of intervening in reality. In doing so, it powerfully influenced the way in which its partners grasped that reality. Although it has no territory and no coercive force, the UNHCR does have discourse and the production of knowledge at its command, and through these shapes the perspectives of others on migration and how it should be governed. The organisation deploys its discursive resources continuously, and the resulting narratives are often taken as authoritative: it is to the UNHCR that people turn for the most reliable, 'official' data and analysis on the subject of refugees.

One of the central themes of Michel Foucault's thought is the correlation between knowledge and power. Knowledge both conveys and produces power:

> [P]ower and knowledge directly imply one another: ... there is no power relation without the correlative constitution of a field of knowledge, nor any knowledge that does not presuppose and constitute at the same time power relations. (Foucault 1995: 27)

Foucault uses the example of the birth of criminology following the reform of the French penal system to demonstrate this: the new science posited the 'criminal' as the object of a new way of addressing and sanctioning crime (Foucault 1995). The action of governing implies the production and mobilisation of specific knowledges that constitute individuals as governable subjects. Through her analysis of the way in which the UNHCR represents refugees, Lisa Malkki (1996) shows that the destitute, dehistoricised and voiceless victims portrayed by the organisation embody the ideal subject of the 'solutions' it is able to offer. Similar observations could indeed be made with regard to the way in which the UNHCR depicts Afghan returnees: the accounts, quotations, images and statistics that the organisation deploys help to create infantilised victims who are finally able to return to their country, but need help to reconstruct their lives. But more generally, drawing on Foucault's analysis, the international refugee regime can be seen as a field of power-knowledge within which the UNHCR wields a very particular authority, to the extent that its narratives are considered especially reliable, or indeed read as truth.

A number of authors have pointed out that the authority of the UNHCR and other international organisations is located largely on the cognitive and normative level (Barnett and Finnemore 2004; Chimni 1998; Douglas 1986; Fouilleux 2009; Malkki 1996; Nay 2012, 2014; Pécoud 2015; Valluy 2009). Barnett and Finnemore emphasise that the 'power of social construction' – framing the questions, defining the meaning and nature of social actors, establishing policies and identifying the key issues in negotiations – is the main form of power exercised by international organisations (Barnett and Finnemore 2004: 7–9). Jérôme Valluy describes the UNHCR as the 'principal 'collective organic intellectual' in the forced migration sector' (Valluy 2009: 161). But few researchers explain how these representations are actually produced, what characterises them, how they are used and why they hold influence.

This chapter is based on the set of narratives on Afghan migration produced by the UNHCR between 2001 and 2008, and on my own experience of writing some of these texts as an officer of the organisation. I first show that for the UNHCR, producing expert knowledge and deploying it strategically is a key way of exercising its authority – an authority that is exerted both over migrants (who are thereby constituted as governable subjects) and over the various partners who see the analyses and data produced by the UNHCR as significant or even as the truth. I then examine the factors that make the UNHCR's accounts convincing and attractive, including their technical specificity, their internal consistency and the legitimacy they draw from the UNHCR's links with the academic world. Third, I show how these factors operate as mechanisms of depoliticisation, concealing the fact that the organisation's cognitive repertoire is itself shaped by the power relations within which it is embedded as a UN agency. The nation-state order and the power relations between European countries and countries of the Iran-Afghanistan-Pakistan region in particular determine what can be conceived within the UNHCR – including the content of the ACSU project – and are thereby naturalised and reproduced by the organisation's statements.

The Power to Frame Perspectives on Migration

Through my work as Donor Relations Officer in Kabul, I realised that the relationship the UNHCR has with donor countries cannot be seen as one of unilateral dependence. In Kabul the donors also needed the UNHCR. They needed analyses, reports and data to guide their own analyses, decisions and positions, which only the UNHCR was in a position to produce. For specialist donor bodies like ECHO and the BPRM in particular, the ability to act as a wise astute donor depended on the 'raw material' of accounts produced by the UNHCR. Other donors also turned to the UNHCR Office for 'information' or 'clarification' on current questions, the situation in the field, or simply 'the Afghan refugee question'. My job was to continually explain all of this, both in writing and verbally. There was a constant flow of narratives from the UNHCR to donors – in the phrase often repeated in the office, we had to continually 'feed' them.

Most of the time, this was done through a combination of various types of written material. Funds were sourced through calls for donations or applications for funding. At the end of a funding period, activity reports would have to be written. Each week, I put together a Weekly Update, reporting on recent developments. At meetings with donors, a briefing kit containing the latest statistics and information brochures would be prepared for each participant. Then I had to respond to all the individual questions that came by email or telephone: here I would adjust the level of detail in accordance with the donor's familiarity with these questions, often supplementing my answers with statistical data and forwarding brochures and key strategy documents. The volume of reports sent to donors gives an indication of the UNHCR's influence on the perceptions donors have of reality. By disseminating its own interpretation guides, the UNHCR sets itself up as an essential cognitive intermediary.

In addition to accounts for donors, a great deal of time and resources were devoted in the Kabul Branch Office to the production of data, and the writing and dissemination of reports. Some posts were entirely dedicated to this work – for example, the Head of the Communication Unit or the officers who worked in the Data Section. The senior managers formulated the strategic orientations, which they would present as 'policy papers', 'concept notes' and so on, depending on the context (meetings, workshops and conferences). Thus, from 2001 onwards, a substantial and unequal body of knowledge on Afghan migration between Iran, Afghanistan and Pakistan, produced by the UNHCR, took form. It was made up of strategy and analytical documents (UNHCR 2007a), statistical data (UNHCR 2007d; UNHCR, SAFRON, and PCO 2005), bulletins (UNHCR 2007h, 2007p), press releases (UNHCR 2007g), brochures and prospectuses (UNHCR 2007q), requests for funding and activity reports, and directives on the assessment of asylum requests from Afghans (UNHCR 2007c), not to mention the many studies commissioned and partially funded under the ACSU project.[1] Similar observations could be made with regard to the activity and publications of Headquarters in Geneva.[2]

All of these documents were very widely disseminated through a dedicated strategy. Because they were published and issued online on the UNHCR's website and other sites, and translated into several languages (Dari, Pashto, and where appropriate the languages of donors), these texts were immediately accessible to NGOs and officers of international organisations, as well as to researchers. Statistics were updated each month, disseminated to a lengthy distribution list and published on the UNHCR website. Studies funded by the UNHCR could be found on Google Scholar, and being in electronic format had a potentially wider circulation than academic articles.

This body of knowledge about Afghan migration produced and disseminated by the UNHCR inhabits and occupies the discursive arena, thereby structuring how the question is framed and how it arises for a wide range of actors – the media, NGOs, funders and researchers. The accounts and representations produced by the UNHCR constitute an important reference for them, an authoritative or even 'official' source that they can draw on to validate, justify or contextualise their own analyses and/or actions. And, indeed, all the publications about Afghan migration, including academic articles, cite UNHCR data at least once.

As Mary Douglas points out (1986), the authority of institutions is located principally on the cognitive plane: they 'think for us', influencing our categories of thought, our clarification processes, the way in which we construct the spaces of meaning within which we put and define questions and problems. They provide a set of interpretative tools that allow actors to decode and attribute meaning to the events they encounter. In the case of the UNHCR, this consists in conceptualising and producing cognitive frameworks and narratives around the phenomenon of migration and the way in which it is and should be governed. This explains the breadth of resources (financial and intellectual, in terms of staff) devoted to discursive production within the organisation.

Thus, without territory, armed forces, financial autonomy, legislative or judicial power, the UNHCR nevertheless has the authority to produce discourse and knowledge. When it provides definitions, produces analyses, accounts and recommendations, it can be seen as possessing a form of freedom, a creative power that can claim to be 'final', and sometimes does succeed in imposing itself as such – creative because the organisation produces accounts that did not exist before and would not exist without it, and thus shapes the epistemic space of the refugee regime, and final because the UNHCR speaks as the principal authority on the subject. This is clearly evident in the style of its documents: their tone is assertive, stating facts, describing processes with certainty and allowing no space for any objection. It is also normative; these accounts 'fall from on high', like 'revealed truths'. They are also often self-referential: there is no reference to sources other than the organisation's own data and analysis.

Douglas Holmes highlights the performativity of statements by institutions, analysing the 'ever-changing ecologies of discourse by which the economy is created and articulated' (Holmes 2009: 411) by central banks; it is these discourses that create the context and the analytical framework for other actors. They thus create the economy itself as a field of communication and an empirical fact. The UNHCR does not have an authority or a monopoly over discourse comparable to that of a central bank, but the performative effect of its discourse persists. It is principally on the basis of the statements and concepts promoted by the UNHCR that policies concerning refugees are created and negotiated by those involved in their design and implementation.

The crisis over deportations from Iran shows that it was often the analyses and positions of the UNHCR that structured debate. In late April 2007, following a sudden rise in deportations, the UNHCR was the first port of call for the media, funders and NGOs that were uncertain as to whether the deportees were 'refugees' or not. An emergency meeting was called, with representatives of the main Afghan ministries and international organisations present in the country. Most of those present did not know how to interpret this unprecedented development. It was the UNHCR Representative who contextualised the events, put them in perspective and, on the basis of data produced by UNHCR Sub-Offices at the border, explained their significance and what was at stake, thus defining the terms of the problem to be resolved. The NGOs working on reintegration of the returnees drew extensively on the data, definitions and classifications formulated by the UNHCR ('high-return regions', 'vulnerable returnees', etc.) in developing their programmes.

The UNHCR's cognitive influence also shapes the thinking of those not directly involved in the government of refugees – public opinion, the media and researchers throughout the world. Take, for example, the distinction between 'refugees' and 'migrants', of which the UNHCR is the primary arbiter: the classification is now accepted as a 'natural' and appropriate distinction by many journalists, researchers and a much wider public. There is also the way in which many people in the world think about Afghan migration: the post-2001 return (quantified by UNHCR statistics and pictured in images of returnees crammed into trucks) has become established as the most significant aspect, and the word 'return' is often taken as synonymous with the UNHCR's repatriation programme.

The UNHCR does not have the monopoly on representations of migration. State authorities, NGOs, local leaders, researchers and sometimes migrants themselves intervene in this political, cognitive and discursive arena. And there is often a lack of consensus among these actors as to the way in which migrants should be conceptualised and governed. This was clear in the case of the deportations from Iran in 2007 (see Chapter 7). Some NGOs also sometimes express divergent opinions. In 2007, for example, the Norwegian Refugee Council (NRC), an NGO, published two reports condemning the closure of the camps in Pakistan and the deportations from Iran (NRC 2007). These reports were also quite critical of the role of the UNHCR (despite the fact that the organisation was the source of almost all the data on which they were based). The organisation immediately reacted in the same tone, retorting that many of the reports' assertions were erroneous and inaccurate.[3] The UNHCR thus eroded the authority of the NRC's reports, at the same time reasserting its own authority to produce the most influential and reliable accounts on the subject.

Discourse as a Weapon

The influence of the UNHCR's accounts varies depending on the context and who is engaging with them (see also Garnier 2014). In relationships with funders, NGOs, the Afghan authorities, other international organisations and the public at large, the authority of the UNHCR's discourse to define, classify and explain is powerful. However, as noted above, it is much more difficult for the organisation to impose its vision when it comes to influencing the way in which states, particularly interior ministries, deal with foreigners in their territories. Even faced with the arbitrariness of states' migration policies, the UNHCR's expert discourse still remains the main weapon at its disposal. Whether in the form of legal directives (see Chapter 7), press releases (see Chapter 8), strategy documents (see Chapter 2) or studies, the accounts produced by the UNHCR constitute the organisation's arsenal for promoting its objectives. This arsenal is created and deployed strategically.

This is clearly apparent in the extreme care and attention devoted to the formulation of texts for public dissemination. Making a public statement that will be examined and perhaps cited by other authors, these texts have a very different status from internal documents. They must all be 'cleared' by a superior. Thus, Saverio or the Deputy Head of Mission read, approved and sometimes edited all the documents that the Communication Officer and I prepared. Indeed, they made this a priority, despite their heavy workload. At the beginning of the summer, the senior managers of the Afghan Operation drew up a communications strategy, which was circulated within the Branch Office and to all Sub-Offices. It specified precisely the messages and certain key phrases that should always feature in external communications.

These included, for example, the concept of 'absorption capacity'. Prior to 2007, this phrase had only rarely appeared in the UNHCR's accounts and never in reference to Afghanistan or any other country of origin. It was introduced in 2007 by the senior managers in the Kabul Branch Office when pressure for return from the Iranian and Pakistani authorities and the worsening situation in Afghanistan was making the situation increasingly difficult. The phrase began to be used systematically by all the UNHCR offices in Afghanistan (see, for example, UNHCR 2007a: 2–5, 11; 2007g). It was a concept that easily caught on. While it had a hint of a technical term relating to political economy and demographics, it also effectively conveyed, through a striking image, the difficulties and contradictions presented by repatriation to an economically poor country that was once again submerged in conflict. It was deployed strategically, as part of the discursive framework that the UNHCR put in place to counter the pressure for return from the Iranian and Pakistani authorities. It was thus an effective weapon in the ongoing political struggle over how Afghan migrants should be governed.

The ACSU project offers a perfect illustration of the UNHCR engaging in a confrontation that took place primarily at the cognitive and discursive level. The aim of the project was precisely to alter the way in which the Iranian and Pakistani authorities viewed Afghan migration, so that they would consequently modify their way of governing it. Justifying its proposals in terms of the prolonged nature of the Afghan crisis, the UNHCR argued, through the project's strategy documents, that the question should now be posed in different terms: 'we should move our thinking' (AREU and MoRR 2007: 12) and therefore create 'new arrangements'. This approach went hand in hand with, and was conveyed through, a specific mode of expression, made up of key messages and a vocabulary that was continually promoted. In short, this was a conceptual, theoretical and terminological framework that shaped the UNHCR's discourse and made it proactive. Each time the organisation spoke, it was practising a cognitive lobbying.

This framework is evident in the strategy documents and studies commissioned under the aegis of the ACSU project. As soon as Saverio arrived in post to lead the Afghan Operation, it began to be integrated into the Operation's external communications through the communications strategy. Familiar with and indeed a keen supporter of this strategy, I was concerned to ensure the accounts I produced were consistent with its discursive register – for example, in my choice of vocabulary. As in the strategy papers produced by Eric and Saverio, I strove to use the term 'refugee' in a restricted and considered way in order to make clear that the Afghan population in Iran and Pakistan no longer consisted only of persons 'in need of protection', but was more complex. A plethora of other expressions was used and highlighted in place of 'refugee': 'population movements', 'second-generation Afghans' and 'cross-border movements'. The concept of the 'residual population', on the other hand, which is fairly frequently used within the UNHCR to describe populations in host countries who are yet to be repatriated, was eliminated from my vocabulary, because it gave the impression that return was the standard choice for all Afghans in Iran and Pakistan.

Extensive and systematic dissemination of these discourses was integral to the implementation of the ACSU strategy. In addition to ensuring that it pervaded external communications, Eric and Saverio concerned themselves with the publication and dissemination of studies. As they were published, these successive studies also formed the basis for organising targeted forums that offered opportunities and tools for lobbying (AREU and MoRR 2005, AREU and CSSR 2006, AREU and UNHCR 2007). These meetings – variously titled 'strategic consultations', 'high-level workshops' or 'conferences' – brought together government decision-makers and representatives of international organisations, but were particularly targeted at the Iranian and Pakistani authorities. Presented as initiatives aimed at 'raising the awareness' of Afghan migration among those present, these meetings in fact operated as the main channel through which the UNHCR tried to influence how the Pakistani and Iranian authorities perceived and governed migrations.

The Source of Authority of the UNHCR's Accounts

What makes the UNHCR's accounts persuasive, convincing and influential, or even 'final' in some cases? How do they become established and recognised by a broad range of actors as plausible, reliable and indeed truthful? What makes them so difficult to equal and to challenge? Here I note five factors, linked to the UNHCR's expert status, the characteristics of these narratives and the legitimacy they draw from the UNHCR's relationship with academic research.

The accounts that the UNHCR produces are authoritative first of all because they are issued by an institution widely considered to have unrivalled expertise on the subject of refugees. As the refugee regime became institutionalised and expanded over the second half of the twentieth century, the niche of this domain of government extended and became 'filled' with norms, technologies and contexts of intervention. As the regime expanded, a political-epistemological space emerged within which people fleeing conflict and violence and the phenomenon of their migration were constituted as objects of knowledge and government. The UNHCR, riding the tide of this expansion, acquired and then consolidated its position as the number-one expert. Hence, its expertise grew exponentially. As Barnett and Finnemore (2004) note, 'expert' authority was gradually added to and superimposed on the 'delegated authority' and 'moral authority' the UNHCR held when it was set up. Legal norms (treaties and directives) proliferated, and the UNHCR promoted, negotiated and even wrote them. Contexts of intervention became increasingly diverse, and the UNHCR established a presence in each case and extended its geographical range. It also designed and implemented all the technologies (camps, repatriation programmes, etc.), and thus became the source of all the refugee regime's areas of specialisation. The UNHCR therefore possesses an unrivalled capacity to position itself and control the international norms relating to refugees, and to align new norms and new initiatives with what has gone before. It also manages and controls the collection of most of the data on refugees, which it gathers through its own programmes. As such, the organisation has a unique authority to 'fill' this epistemic field and shape it through its accounts. This space could be seen as an 'epistemic jurisdiction' within which the UNHCR holds a pivotal role. The accounts, analyses and recommendations it issues are those of a specialist body. They form what amounts to a technical, competent knowledge – an expertise.

Three features of the UNHCR's accounts help to make them attractive and convincing. These are their internal consistency, their universal explanatory capacity and the fact that they are embedded in an already hegemonic episteme.

A large part of my work involved writing UNHCR reports on Afghan refugees. Over time, I realised that producing these texts was essentially an exercise in consistency. The UNHCR's accounts are usually consistent and 'armoured'. The strategic considerations and recommendations are backed up by empirical data. These accounts align with the organisation's previous policies and with the analysis and programmes of other international organisations. Initially, when I was drafting the reports, I thought I was *restoring* consistency: my aim was to seek consistency between the multiple elements from which I could compose my accounts, and make it evident. But I realised that it was more a question of *giving* them consistency at the point when I was putting them together.

The 'ingredients' I used to fulfil my task were, first, analytical frameworks: they consisted essentially of the refuge episteme and the Afghan Operation's strategic directives, which I internalised by reading strategy documents and listening to the senior managers talking. Second, there were all the data and accounts produced within the context of the Afghan Operation, which I absorbed and learned to source and handle. I followed the course of events by attending internal meetings, I looked at and analysed data on repatriation, reports from Sub-Offices, the material produced by my predecessor, and I could also go directly to colleagues in the Sub-Offices to obtain specific data. Then I would assemble and shape this 'raw material' in line with analytical frameworks and strategic directives. The consistency I succeeded in giving my texts was an internal consistency, derived from the self-referential and non-verifiable nature of the data and accounts I was working with. Producing these accounts required discernment, but not in terms of questioning the substance of the elements that made up my raw material. At that time, I was not a specialist on migration and I almost never left the office. My discernment related to the form: how to assemble the elements, which data to discard and which to highlight, how to link some to others depending on the type and function of the document I had to produce. Over time, I began to find this role frustrating: rather than gaining a better understanding of the context around me, it seemed on the contrary that I was completely losing contact with reality. I was floating in a world of discourse and could not relate the representations I was manipulating to the reality they claimed to describe. But it was precisely this self-referentiality and nonverifiability that allowed me to manipulate them with no regard to their relation to reality, and to produce credible, influential texts.

The capacity of the UNHCR's accounts to provide apparently universal explanatory models – in other words, models that effectively articulate the contextual and the global – also helps to make these accounts attractive. Each account finds its place in a global system of knowledges that offers keys to interpretation, explaining and comparing what is happening throughout the world. Two elements make this possible: first, the refugee episteme, a vision of the world that is universal in scope and structures the thinking of the organisation's employees; and, second, the globally deployed translocal structure of the UNHCR, which enables the organisation to produce accounts and data from a multitude of contexts. Created on the basis of internally developed standardised legibility tools (see Chapter 4), these elements make it possible to produce data and reports on transnational phenomena, which states and many other organisations that are less widely established than the UNHCR find more difficult to do. In addition, the translocal structure makes it possible to produce and disseminate tailor-made reports adjusted to the context, target readership and the language they speak.

It should also be noted that the refugee episteme is itself attached to an already hegemonic episteme. I noted above that this incorporates a vision centred on the state: all the fundamental categories through which the political and migrations are understood are framed by the state and the principle of state sovereignty. The state is the principal and final actor, and migration is classified first and foremost as internal or external, legal or illegal. The UNHCR's activity and knowledge are all the more attractive and convincing because they coincide with the conception shared by a large proportion of the world's population, including many researchers (Foucault 1979; Wimmer and Glick Schiller 2003), of the political and of migration.

The UNHCR's Relationship with the Academic World

One final factor contributes to making the UNHCR's accounts convincing: the organisation's proximity to the academic and research sectors. Academic knowledge is often deployed to substantiate its analyses and validate its recommendations, lending greater legitimacy to the UNHCR's expertise. This relationship is constructed through the creation of a zone of intersection, or 'grey' zone, where expert knowledge and academic knowledge interweave, allowing the UNHCR to appropriate scientific knowledge and integrate it into its own discourse. The UNHCR devotes substantial financial and human resources to creating and maintaining this grey zone in which expert knowledge is fabricated. This possibility rests both on funding provided by the organisation and on the desire of many researchers to see the impact of their work in the real world.

During the 1990s and 2000s, the UNHCR's Policy Development and Evaluation Service (PDES) was in permanent contact with academic researchers, always listening and ready to digest new approaches and critiques. Its primary academic partners were university research centres that have made refugees a specialist academic field. The Refugee Studies Centre in Oxford, set up in 1982, was followed by others, such as those at the Universities of York and Cairo. These centres receive funding from the UNHCR, providing a pool for recruiting consultants. Since the 1990s, the grey areas inhabited by both practitioners and academics have proliferated, ranging from the Association for the Study of Forced Migration, which brings together researchers working in this field, to the many journals such as the *Journal of Refugee Studies*, the *Forced Migration Review* and *Refugee Studies Quarterly*: UNHCR representatives sit on their editorial and/or review boards, and help to fund them. The former director of the PDES himself created the series *New Issues in Refugee Research* in 1992: the material it published includes the results of some consultancies, reflections from UNHCR officers, and articles by academics critiquing the refugee regime. Many UNHCR officers published in 'grey' journals or collections (see, for example, the articles by Crisp, Feller, Grandi, Lombardo, Macleod and Ogata cited in the bibliography). The texts produced by the former director of the PDES, an influential senior officer in the organisation, are emblematic of the 'grey' nature of this knowledge about refugees and the multiple forms it can take: while he was the principal (and anonymous) author of many UNHCR strategy documents, he also published in academic journals in a personal capacity. In these articles he might explain the UNHCR's point of view or its internal thinking in order to publicise them more widely, or express personal reflections where he revealed his own critique, putting forward points of view that contrasted with the organisation's official approach.

In this 'grey' zone, academic knowledge is often absorbed and manipulated to serve the UNHCR's ends. One example is consultancy reports, often written by academic researchers: these documents read more like the normative texts produced by the UNHCR than academic papers. There is always a prescriptive aspect; there are few academic references. It is these reports that are likely to be cited by experts rather than the academic articles upon which they may rely. But the refugee episteme is particularly greedy for analytical frameworks and concepts. The most striking example is the fact that the category 'refugee' has come to define an academic discipline, in which it is used as a descriptive sociological category. This is also true of a whole series of other concepts. In a book published in 2008, for example (Loescher et al. 2008), UNHCR officers and academic researchers write alongside one another, addressing 'protracted refugee situations'. The academics seek to conceptualise and theoretically refine this notion, but ultimately remain embedded in the refugee episteme. In addition to its role of validation and legitimisation, this proximity with the academic world often extends the influence of the UNHCR's expert knowledge because it fosters the production of an academic knowledge 'contaminated' by the refugee episteme.

The ACSU project offers an excellent illustration of the UNHCR engaging with academic research as a way of reinforcing the authority of its recommendations. The project made production of knowledge about Afghan migration a priority. Numerous studies were commissioned from research centres and consultancy companies such as the Afghanistan Research and Evaluation Unit and Altai Consulting, based in Kabul, the Sustainable Development Policy Institute and the Collective for Social Science Research, based in Pakistan, the University of Tehran and individual consultants. Between 2003 and 2009, no fewer than twenty-four case studies and research summaries were conducted and published.[4] All of this research supported and corroborated the recommendations contained in the ACSU strategy, demonstrating that they were 'grounded' (AREU and UNHCR 2007), and therefore relevant and appropriate. Both the form and the content of these studies reveal a strong influence from the UNHCR. All the central arguments put forward by the ACSU project as to the most appropriate way to understand, classify and manage Afghan migration are present here. The specific themes of the various series of studies conducted cover the central points in the arguments of the ACSU strategy: cross-border movements and transnational networks, Afghanistan's 'absorption capacity', the role of Afghans in the Iranian and Pakistani labour markets, and the propensity of second-generation Afghans living in Iran and Pakistan to return. The conclusions and recommendations often broadly reiterate (sometimes word for word!) the classifications and reasoning of UNHCR strategy papers,[5] and for good reason: Saverio and Eric monitored the conduct of these studies closely. They wrote terms of reference for the research teams, reviewed the texts and sometimes even edited them, particularly the summaries, conclusions and recommendations, where they checked to ensure that the UNHCR's key messages were clearly articulated.

The example of anthropologist Alessandro Monsutti's collaboration with AREU nevertheless shows that while collaboration with researchers often works to legitimise the organisation's recommendations, the relationship between researchers and the UNHCR is not always one of one-way epis-temic and political submission. As the academic author of the most detailed ethnographic study of Afghan migration, Monsutti was contacted by Eric and Saverio and agreed to act as advisor for the first pilot series of studies on transnational networks on behalf of the Afghanistan Research and Evaluation Unit (Monsutti 2006; Stigter and Monsutti 2005). Monsutti took on this consultancy because the approach of the ACSU project was fundamentally in agreement with his work, and in many respects was attempting to go beyond the limits he had identified in the refugee regime (see Chapter 2). He saw it as an 'illuminated' approach and respected Eric and Saverio, who, he said to me one day, 'had understood everything' even before they encountered his work (published in 2004). He saw this consultancy as 'a unique opportunity in the life of a researcher'. Participating in the research project gave him the opportunity to put forward a critical approach and to ensure that the results of his own research influenced the way in which Afghan migration was gov-erned by states. Moreover, it is worth noting that his papers, although they took the form of consultancy reports, were not 'swallowed up' by the refugee episteme; while they produced a knowledge that sat within this episteme and was understood through it, he retained control over the vocabulary and an-alytical categories. For example, he asserts that it is not possible to establish a clear distinction between refugees and migrants (Monsutti 2006; Stigter and Monsutti 2005), whereas it would be difficult to find a similar asser-tion in a UNHCR document.[6] Moreover, after participating in these studies, Monsutti published a critical reflection on the limitations of the three 'tra-ditional solutions' (Monsutti 2008), probably prompted by his proximity to the UNHCR during his consultancy.

The five factors considered above explain why the UNHCR's accounts are particularly authoritative. Despite an academic literature critical of the organisation's activity, despite many internal proposals for reform, among the media and many of those involved in the international refugee regime, the UNHCR's accounts are often accepted as truth. Their self-referentiality makes them unique and immune to all criticism of substance, and their inte-gration into the universal analytical framework of the refugee episteme rein-forces their consistency and their attraction; at the same time, the UNHCR's multilocalised presence gives them a solid, unrivalled empirical foundation, and their global dissemination reinforces their influence. Unless one is to contradict the appropriateness of the UNHCR's accounts on the basis of an even more localised and/or distributed presence, or question the refugee episteme as a whole (but by this token in a different register, alternative to rather than challenging that of the UNHCR), the UNHCR's accounts are difficult to equal or to challenge.

The Naturalisation of the National Order

The five factors identified above also operate as mechanisms of depoliticisation. By obscuring the fact that these accounts are interpretations, and the hypotheses and strategic goals that structure them, they help to produce narratives and recommendations that claim to be objective and not subject to any moral-political scrutiny. Yet, in fact, the UNHCR's accounts are highly 'political'. As I have pointed out, they are always the product of internal negotiations and, as I have shown above, they serve to promote specific objectives with regard to how migration is to be viewed and approached,[7] and are often used for strategic ends. In the remainder of this chapter I examine how these accounts are embedded in a hegemonic episteme and in international power relations. This episteme defines the field of what is thinkable within the UNHCR, and is at the same time naturalised and indeed reinforced by the performativity of the UNHCR's accounts.

A number of those who have researched international humanitarian and development institutions have noted the existence of powerful depoliticisation mechanisms that elide the power relations and dominance structures at work, presenting interventions as purely technical operations (Andrijasevic and Walters 2010; Chandler 2006; Ferguson 1994; Murray Li 2007; Monsutti 2012a).[8] In his pioneering study of a World Bank-funded development project in Lesotho, James Ferguson (1994) describes the bureaucratic structure put in place to run this project as an 'anti-politics machine', because it reduced poverty to a purely technical issue. The structural political and economic relations, particularly the unequal and asymmetric distribution of resources and power, were completely ignored in the construction of the problem and the solutions, concealing them while at the same time fostering the expansion of state bureaucratic power. Tania Murray Li, in her study of the World Bank in Indonesia, reveals the depoliticised and depoliticising approach taken by those working in development, who see the villages targeted by their projects as 'incarcerated localities' (2007: 275) and fail to take into account local, national and global power relations, eliding their own positioning in these relations entirely.

Following on from these studies, here I approach the UNHCR's narratives as historical and situated productions. Despite their normative tone, which presents the refugee 'problem' and the concomitant 'solutions' to it as self-evident, these texts are located in an epistemic space with a defined and specific validity and legitimacy that determines in advance what it is possible and acceptable to say. This space arises out of the UNHCR's positioning as an interstate institution, and has consequences at both the epistemic level (what can be seen within the UNHCR and how it is seen and spoken about) and the moral level (what is considered normal and abnormal, legitimate and illegitimate). Here I focus on two factors that shape the field of power-knowledge at issue: the national order, and the unequal power relations between the states of the Iran-Afghanistan-Pakistan region and European states.

As I noted in Chapter 2, the cognitive framework within which the UNHCR's accounts are set is structured by the national order, skewing them towards the nation- and state-centred, sedentary model. The background to migration is the set of mutually exclusive territorial state jurisdictions: the state holds the ultimate power, and nationality is the criterion for classification and distribution of human beings over the earth. Any discourse and any knowledge produced by the UNHCR are situated within this cognitive framework, but this is never explicitly stated. Accounts are formulated as if the world really worked this way. This is reinforced by the declarative and normative tone of the organisation's statements: its discourses are worded as if they were setting out observations that go without saying, as if they described universally valid facts, mechanisms and phenomena.

Take, for example, the selective way in which Afghan migration is represented in the range of UNHCR texts that I have analysed in this chapter, including those from the ACSU project. The spatiality of migration is rigidly anchored in the geopolitics of the interstate system, and the institutions of state sovereignty and citizenship. Migrants are first Afghans before they are human beings, Pashtuns or others. What counts, in their migration, is the fact that they have left the jurisdiction of the Afghan state and are non-nationals in another state jurisdiction. A series of other phenomena and realities derived from other sociopolitical orders than the nation and the state – for example, tribal solidarity or circular migration – remain largely elided and obscured in the organisation's narratives. When they are taken into account, they are read purely through the state-centred lens of the nation-state order, emphasising their 'irregularity', 'informality' or their 'social' nature.

By naturalising the national order, the UNHCR contributes not only to reproducing this order but also to strengthening its effects. Because the organisation's discourses and interventions are shaped by this cognitive framework, its activity works to reinforce it, making it operative and influential – in short, shaping the world to align with this view of the world. Through its discourse, the UNHCR roots this order in the minds of all those who hear it. Through its activity, it imposes it on the real world, imprinting it. The actors who in their turn situate their discourse and practices in relation to the UNHCR and within the refugee regime (NGOs and donors) do the same.

By reproducing the national order and rendering it operative, the UNHCR helps to naturalise the framework within which its activity and its existence are set and acquire meaning: it is within this framework that the 'refugee problem' is posed, and therefore that the UNHCR's mission and the 'solutions' it proposes are appropriate. What defines refugees is precisely that they are 'displaced' in relation to the national order; without this order, there would be no refugees – and no UNHCR. The UNHCR's accounts thus shape the world into one where the organisation's existence and activity are legitimate, relevant and indeed essential.

The Restricted Holism of the ACSU Project

The UNHCR's narratives naturalise not just the national order, but also power relations within the interstate arena. Here I focus particularly on the power relations between the countries of the Iran-Afghanistan-Pakistan region and European countries. The latter, which are wealthier and have greater influence in the international arena, are also affected by Afghan migration, though to a lesser degree than the former.[9] A comparison of the UNHCR's policies towards Afghans in the two regions pushes the analysis of the ACSU project's strategy documents further and reveals the regional impact of the innovations it introduced. This is why the 'comprehensive solutions' approach can appropriately be described as *restricted holism*.

A comparison of the ACSU strategy adopted in Asia and the UNHCR's policies in Europe in the mid-2000s[10] reveals a number of differences in the way in which the situation was analysed, migration flows were understood, and the problem and priorities were formulated in the two contexts. In Asia, the UNHCR proposed 'comprehensive solutions' to address Afghan 'population movements'. It thus adopted a holistic approach and took into consideration all kinds of movement, seeking appropriate solutions for each of them. In Europe, the focus was on identifying the 'refugees' amid 'mixed migration' and reducing 'secondary movements'. In other words, the aim was to pick out the refugees from among all the migrants in order to offer them access to European countries and to reduce the level of unauthorised migration to Europe.

There are three significant differences between the two approaches. First, the 'comprehensive solutions' strategy highlighted the need to look beyond the refugee paradigm and take the entire spectrum of migrants into consideration. However, in Europe, a 'refugee focus' prevailed, hand in hand with a selective approach: the UNHCR was concerned only to identify, among all migrants, those under its mandate, in order to ensure them the right of entry and residence. The aim was to carve out and preserve a space for asylum in European immigration policies. There was a strict binary logic, with a division between the two categories of migrants ('migrants' and 'refugees', who mix to produce 'mixed migration'), and the difference in treatment reserved for each was brutally apparent.

Second, the formulation of the problem faced at the gates of Europe was much less contextualised. The long-term strategy for Afghanistan was based on fine-grained analysis of the political, economic and social context and of migration patterns. The situation was understood in terms of 'population movements' that needed to be studied in all their complexity in order to arrive at 'comprehensive solutions'. In the policies developed for Europe, on the other hand, migration was approached in a more piecemeal way. Apart from a few generic references to 'globalisation', the phenomenon of migration was neither contextualised in relation to historical, economic, social and political processes nor related to the migrants' situation in their country of origin. The notions of 'development' and 'poverty' were never raised. No particular attention was paid to the situation in Afghanistan and its migration flows because the migrants who reached Europe were seen as an indistinct mass, regardless of their origin. No one asked if these migrations were an irreversible phenomenon or how they might evolve in the long term. The problem was formulated as one of access to asylum for the population that fell under the UNHCR's mandate; it was therefore an isolated question that could be resolved by isolated measures.

Finally, the way in which mobility was seen also differed. The ACSU strategy recognised the importance of migration, its history and its irreversibility. However, in the UNHCR's policies for Europe, movement was seen as a problem (even as *the* problem) to be solved. What states see as a problem automatically becomes the UNHCR's problem. These policies therefore aimed quite explicitly to put a brake on movement. This is clear in the information campaigns the organisation instigated in regions of origin, and the statement that priority would be given identifying migrants as close as possible to their country of origin. The documents I examined also recommended reducing undocumented 'secondary' migration in order to preserve the institution of asylum and ensure protection of (potential) migrants, reducing their risk of being trafficked.[11] The fact that 'secondary movements'[12] are unauthorised because there are no legal avenues for migration or that it is precisely the most vulnerable people who are at risk of exploitation in migrating seem to be relegated to the background. As noted earlier, the ACSU strategy also saw irregular movement as a problem. But it was precisely this observation that led it to seek ways to increase the legal possibilities for migration – not to eliminate movement altogether.

Moreover, in documents relating to the UNHCR's policies in Europe, the organisation readily recognises the right of states to control their borders and decide their immigration policies. It even asserts that granting asylum should not make controls more difficult, and that irregular immigration breaches states' rights to control the entry and stay of non-nationals in their territory.[13] This position is particularly ambiguous because these countries have systems of asylum, besides resettlement procedures, and the UNHCR seeks to improve them. The attitude of supporting reduction of 'irregular' and 'secondary' migration, while actively working in support of those who manage to reach countries not contiguous with their country of origin 'spontaneously' thus conceals a perverse logic whereby the possibility of legal settlement in Europe is only offered to those who manage to get there by clandestine routes.

Comparing the UNHCR's policy documents on Europe and the Iran-Afghanistan-Pakistan region starkly reveals the regional scale of the organisation's policies vis-à-vis Afghan refugees, including in the ACSU project. The 'problem of Afghan displacement' is presented in UNHCR documents as a pre-eminently regional issue. The contiguous states of Iran, Afghanistan and Pakistan (identified as 'South-West Asia') are the spaces pertinent to both understanding the phenomenon of Afghan displacement and formulating the problem and the solutions to it. The region is seen as a self-sufficient space, cut off from the rest of the world.

A number of anthropologists and geographers have shown that scales, as cognitive devices through which we understand and interact with reality, are social constructions (see, for example, Hill 2007; Marston 2000; Smith 1992). The point here is also to ask what 'will to knowledge' the policies formed in relation to Afghan refugees are expressing. What kind of division governs the discontinuity in the UNHCR's understanding of the phenomenon of Afghan migration, and its formulation of problems and solutions, in two regions of the world at a particular moment in history?:

> Certainly, as a proposition, the division between true and false is neither arbitrary, nor modifiable, nor institutional, nor violent. Putting the question in different terms, however – asking what has been, what still is ... the kind of division governing our will to knowledge – then we may well discern something like a system of exclusion (historical, modifiable, institutionally constraining) in the process of development. (Foucault 1971: 10)

Murray Li describes the operation whereby decision-makers omit certain elements in constructing the problems that determine their programmes – elements such as global political and economic relations, and macrolevel inequalities – as 'constitutive exclusion' (Murray Li 2007: 27).

Up to this point, I have presented the ACSU project as the fruit of an encompassing, holistic approach and 'in-depth' analysis of Afghan migration. But this depth is at the same time selective, in that it is structured on the regional scale: not only is the region the space delimiting the phenomenon to be analysed, but the influence of all external factors and actors also remains completely concealed. The general effect of this regional focus is to create a dissociation between the region and the rest of the world, which aligns with a split between regional and extraregional migration.

The centrality of the regional focus is evident in the way in which the problem is formulated. Everything that goes beyond the region remains out of consideration.[14] The source of the 'displacement' (and hence of the problem) is the situation in Afghanistan. The causes of this situation are not entered into in detail, and nor are the external factors that had contributed and continue to contribute to it (for example, the circumstances under which the Afghan state had been created, interstate power relations and the intervention of foreign powers). Chimni and Duffield make a similar observation: Chimni describes the 'internalist causes' that are emphasised in refugee policy (Chimni 1998), while Duffield remarks that in accounts furnished by humanitarian and development bodies intervening in a crisis, the only causes of conflict referred to are those that are internal to the country (Duffield 2001). Not only is migration beyond the region not taken into account, but the links with the outside are also passed over. Transnational networks and money transfers, for example, are only referred to in relation to migration within the region. While Iran and Pakistan's restrictive policies are highlighted, those of other countries are not mentioned.

The solutions are also sought within this regional space. The place that the UNHCR must create has to emerge within one of these three state jurisdictions. In order to solve the 'equation', the organisation strives to balance the two solutions of repatriation and integration in Iran or Pakistan: the possibility of resettlement further afield is never mentioned. The few hundred people who leave each year for Western countries under 'resettlement programmes' are not mentioned. Countries outside the region are only referred to as external agents, donors and actors who might put political pressure on governments in the region. Their role in history and in the conflicts in Afghanistan, past and present, is not mentioned at any point. As donors, and stakeholders in the post-2001 future of Afghanistan, they are instead the target readership of the UNHCR's strategy documents. An examination of the use of the word 'Europe' in these documents reveals that this set of countries appears not as a potential region of destination, but exclusively as a donor to the UNHCR.

As soon as Afghans leave 'South-West Asia', they are no longer seen in terms of their nationality and are therefore no longer the focus of policies targeted specifically at Afghans. Thus, UNHCR policies towards Afghans seeking to reach Europe treat them as members of an undifferentiated flow of migrants making their way to Europe. It is therefore no longer the relation to the situation in Afghanistan, or the fact of being reducible to the phenomenon of Afghan migration, that counts. The phenomenon to which Afghan migrants are reduced, and to which the UNHCR seeks solutions, is no longer 'Afghan displacement', but 'mixed migration' or 'secondary movements'. Chimni (1998) highlights the 'myth of difference' in the way in which migration flows that began to reach Western countries from African and Asian countries in the 1980s were constructed as qualitatively different from those within the migrants' region of origin, thus justifying different policies.

The emphasis on the regional scale in the understanding and management of 'Afghan displacement' is also reflected in the volume of knowledge produced on the subject of Afghan migration. The UNHCR produces a huge quantity of data on migration in 'South-West Asia', as all of the statistics, commissioned research, analyses and strategy documents cited in this book show. However, a search for data on Afghan migration outside the region, even taking into account documents produced to give a global overview of forced migration (UNHCR 2006a, 2008a) or in other regions of the world (UNHCR 2008b), turns up very fragmentary, much less complete information.[15]

The Internal Economy of UNHCR Policies

Thus, an internal economy of UNHCR policies emerges, revealing on the one hand the attempt to optimise solutions within the region (repatriation, integration and migration), by way of an innovative approach, and on the other hand the limited solutions offered to those who leave the region – despite the fact that the 'equation' within the region becomes more insoluble each year. Taken together, the two regional policies of restricted holism in the long-term regional strategy, and the system of selection and restriction on movement at the borders of Europe implicitly collude to discourage migration of Afghans outside the region.

This position is fundamentally consistent with European countries' openly declared aim of containing the flows. It also aligns with the structure of European countries' bureaucracies, splitting the perspective of the donor, for whom Afghan refugees are a foreign policy issue (victims who should be helped) from that of the host country, for whom they represent an internal political issue (illegal migrants from a Muslim country close to a source of terrorism and drug production, representing a danger to European societies). This structure defines two separate domains – 'humanitarianism' and 'immigration' – that are seen and managed as if they were fundamentally different questions.

The genesis and reach of the ACSU project can thus be contextualised in a web of power relations that go beyond internal relations in the UNHCR. The reason the strategy came about was also because the structural conditions were favourable to it. These conditions supported the emergence of an innovative project, but at the same time limited its reach. The holism of the 'comprehensive solutions' was thus the counterpoint to selection at European borders. European donors' willingness to countenance attempts to move beyond the impasse in the region, even by way of such an innovative project, was the obverse of the restrictive policies being adopted at Europe's borders. Indeed, the first funding from the European Commission, the project's main funder, came in 2003, the year in which European countries began to call more forcefully for the externalisation of international protection for refugees. Their proposals included the concept of 'region of origin', and the creation of partnerships with countries contiguous with the country of origin so as to increase their capacity to manage migration flows and create conditions where 'persons in need of international protection' could obtain it 'as rapidly and as close to their country as possible'. In this way, they would not need to seek this protection elsewhere (European Commission 2003, 2004, 2005).

Thus European countries' priorities helped to produce a configuration favourable to the introduction of the ACSU strategy. This helps to explain how, in the European Commission, such a project found a partner willing to fund it. It explains not only how the strategy became conceivable and fundable, but also why until 2008 it did not feature strongly in the UNHCR's external communications. It was seen more as a technical strategy, developed in response to a specific, particularly complex problem. Internally, it remained a unique and isolated project. Documents describing the strategy often asserted that it was the complexity and longevity of the Afghan crisis, and the nature of the population concerned, that justified such a specific approach. The singular strategy was thus justified by the exceptional nature of the Afghan refugee crisis.[16] In this way, its innovative, destabilising potential was 'contained'. As such, the organisation effectively produced a highly innovative, even revolutionary project for an interstate organisation. But this project could only be rolled out within precise limits. Its conception of migration as positive and irreversible related solely to the region. The state sovereignty that the UNHCR was directly, robustly challenging was that of Iran and Pakistan, while that of European countries continued to reign in Europe. Ultimately the project was caught up in the global power relations in which the organisation is enmeshed, which are immanent to it and in which the priorities of European countries carry particular weight.

For the UNHCR, this set of power relations constitutes a systemic and structural system of constraint. The organisation can neither ignore them nor radically transform them. Thus, they define the UNHCR's field of possibilities, including its cognitive repertoire. Before they determine the content of its policies, global power relations shape the way in which policy sectors are constituted, and the concepts and context within which the UNHCR understands the phenomenon of migration, conceptualises problems and formulates its recommendations.

It is widely acknowledged that refugee policy is shaped by the interests of the wealthiest industrialised countries, which fund the UNHCR's programmes while remaining concerned to limit immigration by some non-nationals (including Afghans). Many researchers have highlighted the UNHCR's dependence on donor states and have noted that this allows these countries to forward their interests at the level of the organisation's policies (Agier 2003, 2011; Chimni 1998; Duffield 2008; Valluy 2009). In this chapter I have shown that the influence of European donors on UNHCR policies is not mechanical and direct, a sort of blackmail in exchange for funding. On the one hand, I have shown that in some contexts, when UNHCR officers interact with European countries in their 'donor mode' rather than their 'host country mode', it has powerful authority, as they need its expertise in order to be 'good donors'. On the other hand, I have also shown that European countries' priorities are furthered through the UNHCR's policies, even before funding is provided, through bureaucratic and cognitive procedures that determine in advance the divisions between policy domains, the concepts that govern how phenomena are understood, how problems and solutions are constructed, and how the bureaucratic structure is organised.

The configuration of power relations within which the UNHCR's expansive bureaucracy is enmeshed thus shapes the field of possible policies. The UNHCR can neither ignore these power relations nor radically transform them: operating through bureaucratic and cognitive mechanisms, they shape the organisation's cognitive repertoire and its repertoire of possible actions. In their turn, the UNHCR's policies refresh, reassert and help to reproduce these same power relations.

Notes

1. Abbasi-Shavazi 2005a, 2005b, 2005c; Abbasi-Shavazi and Glazebrook 2006; Abbasi-Shavazi et al. 2008; AREU and CSSR 2006; AREU and MORR 2005; Aftab 2005; Altai Consulting 2006, 2009; CSSR 2005, 2006a, 2006b, 2006c; Gulbadan and Hunte 2006; MPI 2005; Monsutti 2006; Saito 2007; Saito and Hunte 2007; SDPI 2003, 2006; Stigter 2004, 2005a, 2005b; Stigter and Monsutti 2005; Wickramasekara et al. 2006.

2. The briefing notes presented twice a week at press conferences in Geneva, *Global Appeal* and *Global Report*, the magazine *Refugee* and the five-yearly publication *The State of the World's Refugees*, widely cited by researchers and institutions. There are also the strategy and discussion papers, the position papers presented at international forums, the directives on 'refugee status determination', etc.

3. For example, the NRC stated that the deportees included holders of the *Amayesh* card and that Iran had not signed the 1951 Convention. The UNHCR countered that the few *Amayesh* cardholders were immediately returned to Iran (unlike the NRC, the UNHCR was present at the border and had dealt with this issue directly). The UNHCR also pointed out that Iran had signed the 1951 Convention and recommended the NRC read certain documents, including UNHCR-commissioned research.

4. See the list of references in note 1.

5. In the review of the series of case studies conducted by the Collective for Social Science Research on Afghans in Quetta, Peshawar and Karachi (CSSR 2006), for example, the arguments put forward are entirely aligned with UNHCR strategy documents

(UNHCR 2003a, 2004a, 2007a). The final summary suggests the three questions decision-makers should consider as a priority: transnationalism and money transfers; cross-border movements; and changes in 'population movements' over the decades and why they need to be rethought. Finally, the 'way forward' urges readers to recognise that Afghans in Pakistan have diverse needs, particularly those of the second generation, migrant workers and Afghans 'in need of protection', and recommends setting realistic goals for repatriation, taking into consideration Afghanistan's limited 'absorption capacity'.

6. The ACSU strategy instead states that not all Afghan migrants can be seen indistinguishably as refugees – a different position.

7. In the same vein, Barnett and Finnemore (2004) remark that the International Monetary Fund presents its analyses as neutral and technical, whereas in fact their aim is to reconstitute the economies of certain countries so that they conform to the model of the Washington Consensus.

8. Similar mechanisms have been noted in the work of state bureaucracies (Arendt 2006; Herzfeld 1992; Spire 2007).

9. The migration pathways Afghans have established also extend to countries further away than Iran and Pakistan: first to the Middle East and the Gulf States, then to the Central Asian republics, India and Russia, and finally to Europe, North America, Australia and New Zealand. While during the 1980s and 1990s emigration to the West was almost exclusively the province of the educated, urbanised elite (Centlivres and Centlivres-Dumont 2000; Gehrig and Monsutti 2003), since the 2000s it has become more generalised (see, for example, Monsutti 2009).

10. The following outline of the UNHCR policies at European borders is based on these documents: UNHCR 2000a, 2003b, 2004f, 2005a, 2006a, 2006c, 2007c.

11. '[B]y virtue of its mandate for the protection of refugees, UNHCR has a broader interest in initiatives that are intended to reduce the number of migrants who move in an irregular manner and who submit unfounded applications for refugee status ... the people involved in such movements have to spend large amounts of money for the services of human smugglers, and are then obliged to undertake very hazardous journeys in which their lives and liberty are at constant risk. Even then they have no guarantee that they will reach their destination. It is for this reason that UNHCR gives such priority to building capacities in countries of asylum' (UNHCR 2006c: 3–58).

12. This concept emerged in the 1990s, as transcontinental migration expanded worldwide. It concerns asylum seekers who arrive in countries not contiguous with their country of origin by clandestine routes, like Afghans who arrive in a European country. They come 'spontaneously', a term often used to emphasise that their migration does not fit into any of the institutional frameworks designed for it. This is a phenomenon not provided for within the three 'traditional solutions'. From the point of view of noncontiguous countries, these people circumvent the institutional resettlement system, which by contrast ensures an ordered and quantitatively limited flow of non-nationals from unstable countries.

13. See, for example, the following passage: 'UNHCR is especially mindful of the need to ensure that the provision of protection and asylum to refugees and other people of concern to the Office does not compound the difficulties that states experience in controlling more generally the arrival and residence of foreign nationals and in combating international crime' (UNHCR 2007n: 2).

14. The only exception is the eligibility guidelines for the status determination of Afghan asylum seekers (UNHCR 2007c). In this document, reference is made to external causes, although they remain discreet: there is mention, for example, of 'open conflict' ongoing in the country (the informed reader knows that foreign troops are involved in such a conflict) and the list of at-risk categories includes 'Afghans associated with international organisations and the security forces'. Furthermore, the very existence of this document indirectly implies that there are Afghan asylum seekers outside of the region and that these countries are potential host countries. The singular nature of this document was counterbalanced by the fact that it was disseminated to a very limited number of people in the region and among UNHCR staff and partners dealing with 'South-West Asia'. Although largely written by the Protection Department at the Kabul Branch Office, it was then published by Headquarters and distributed to the authorities responsible for 'refugee status determination' in states that had established such procedures. The document was not designed for the general public, but for specialists and lawyers.

15. The only exception I found was a document published in 2005 that compared data on repatriation with the number of asylum applications made in Europe (UNHCR 2005b). Its aim was to establish a link between the situation in Afghanistan, the high rate of return from Iran and Pakistan under the repatriation programme, and the fall in asylum applications from Afghans in European countries since 2001. This is clearly a document written for European partners, aiming to show that donations were well used, in line with their interests.

16. '[U]nder normal circumstances a population movement of this dimension would signal an end to a refugee situation' (UNHCR 2003a: 2).

CHAPTER 11

Surveillance as Protection – or Protection as Surveillance?

Collection and processing of statistical data was an important part of the work of the Kabul Branch Office. An entire section (the Data Section) was dedicated to this work, and controlled a vast, region-wide IT system. The section was networked with all the Sub-Offices in Afghanistan, which were themselves linked to the Encashment Centres and the border crossing points, and with the Data Sections in Tehran and Islamabad, controlling their own nationally centralised systems. This structure produced an impressive amount of data that could be used to determine the location of the Afghan population in Iran and Pakistan as well as returnees in Afghanistan, and to classify them in terms of 'place of origin' and demographic characteristics, all updated daily. All of these data, presented in the form of maps or statistical tables, were assembled in a fifty-page folder that was my bible, kept at hand to help me to answer donors' questions and write my reports (UNHCR 2007d). The UNHCR's main source of legibility for Afghan migrants was the documents they possessed – the *Amayesh* cards discussed earlier, and the 'Proof of Registration' cards and repatriation certificates considered in this chapter. Establishing administrative surveillance mechanisms, in the form of procedures for census, identification, registration and issue of documents, forms an essential part of the UNHCR's activity. As an illustration, between 2001 and 2008, as the organisation committed substantial resources to the region, four million Afghans were counted in Pakistan and three million biometric cards were issued. In addition, all of the four million Afghans returned from Iran or Pakistan under the repatriation programme were registered and issued repatriation cards.

The UNHCR's administrative surveillance has been studied mainly in localised contexts, such as the camps, or at distribution points for individual aid packages. In such contexts, enumeration and census procedures are often seen as the expression of an ideology of control and the nonparticipatory nature of refugee aid programmes (Harrell-Bond 2002: 61–62; Harrell-Bond et al. 1992; Hyndman 2000: 130–31). But these authors seem to forget that administrative surveillance underpins the work of all kinds of bureaucratic institutions, including those of liberal states. As for the studies that examine the UNHCR's work at large, they mainly focus on the camps and on the selection of migrants, and the resulting effects of confinement and containment (Agier 2011; Scheel and Ratfisch 2014; Valluy 2009); less attention has been given to identity documents and administrative surveillance mechanisms. However, the latter have been extensively studied by researchers focusing on the policies of control and externalisation of migration adopted by Western states since the 1990s (Bigo and Guild 2005; Broeders 2007; Farraj 2011; Schuster 2011; Torpey 2000). Even so, in these studies it is usually the role of the IOM rather than that of the UNHCR that is highlighted (see, for example, Andrijasevic and Walters 2010).

In this chapter I examine the mechanisms of administrative oversight of Afghans that the UNHCR helped to establish in the Afghanistan-Pakistan region between 2001 and 2008. I first consider why the UNHCR needed to create these mechanisms. I then describe three key UNHCR programmes in the region and the forms of administrative surveillance that accompanied them: the census of Afghans in Pakistan, the monitoring of flows under the repatriation programme, and the monitoring of movement recommended in the ACSU strategy. Analysis of these surveillance mechanisms reveals the paradoxical nature of the UNHCR's policies: aiming to incorporate migrants administratively into states, they effectively integrate them into systems of state control that necessarily restrict their movement. For the millions of Afghans concerned, these programmes naturalised their link with the Afghan state, emplaced them definitively in Afghan territory and made any subsequent movement illegal. This paradox is particularly striking in a region where states had not developed surveillance mechanisms comparable to those of modern liberal states – it is precisely this absence of monitoring that has enabled Afghans to move relatively freely within the region in recent decades. I further show that the government of Afghan migration promoted by the UNHCR is not purely a matter of confinement, exclusion and selection; a rationale of *incorporation* is at work that, at the same time as it promotes a sedentary order in which the relationship between populations and territories is subjected to the national order, operates to exclude Afghan migrants by *emplacing* them and by *illegalising* their movement. It therefore becomes clear that even though it is presented as a strategy to support movement, the ACSU project ultimately does not escape this rationale, because state control of movement is considered the fundamental prior condition.

The UNHCR and Administrative Surveillance of Non-nationals

Mechanisms for enumeration and registration are established by bureaucratic institutions operating over vast territories, their aim being to govern a population. In order to create and then implement public policies, the institution needs to capture and get a grip on the population. It was in the seventeenth century that European states began to develop mechanisms of administrative surveillance enabling them to exert authority over the population from a distance. These mechanisms were based on a key moment of contact between the individual and the institution. The link thus created was sanctioned by the issue of a document unique to its bearer, thanks to elements the institution could verify (birth and marital status, signature, or indeed biometric data such as a photograph or fingerprints). For the individual, the administrative identity thus established determined their status vis-à-vis the institution concerned, including the entitlement to enjoy the treatment or rights of which the institution was guarantor. This procedure enabled the institution not only to identify individuals, but also, since the standardised information gathered could be processed statistically, to get a hold of the population as a whole.

Administrative surveillance mechanisms are therefore central to the 'governmentalization of the state' (Foucault 2009), particularly its capacity to exert regulatory authority over a population. James Scott introduces the concept of *legibility* to describe the state's effort to organise the population in way that facilitates the exercise of its administrative functions of taxation, conscription and suppression of revolt, and also of redistribution of resources and access to rights. Its aim was 'rationalizing and standardizing what was a social hieroglyph into a legible and administratively more convenient format' (Scott 1998: 3).

The state developed tools for capturing the population (censuses, the land register, registration of births, marriages and deaths), and standardised categories for structuring this knowledge (property, location and identity). The population thus became fixed on paper, containable in a single gaze; it was henceforth accessible and manageable (Scott 1998). Gérard Noiriel (2001) describes the process whereby the state developed the capacity to identify each citizen, to track them from birth to death, and to situate them in their proper location, as an 'identification revolution'.

This infrastructure of identification also underpins states' capacity to draw a distinction between members and nonmembers, and to assign different treatments to each (Noiriel 2001; Torpey 2000), including preventing or punishing unauthorised residence. The distinction between nationals and non-nationals can only be established by reference to documents that thus become the signifiers of nationality.[1] Foreigners who do not possess documents certifying their eligibility to enter the territory (passport, visa or residence permit) are not authorised to be there. And as the state is able to identify nationals, regulation of immigration also takes place passively, since the mere physical presence of foreigners in state territory does not confer access to rights. Documents thus establish a genuine border: if the geographical boundaries of a state mark the perimeter of its territory, identity documents mark the perimeter of its population.

The UNHCR's needs are similar in many respects to those of states. Whether in order to identify the population 'under its mandate', to formulate appropriate recommendations, to plan its programmes or to administer the distribution of aid, or indeed to seek funds from donors or negotiate with host states, the organisation needs to get a grip on the populations concerned. This requires quantitative data that capture the population in question and thus render it accessible to administration (Crisp 1999b): how big is it, what are its demographic characteristics and its location? The establishment of mechanisms of identification, enumeration, registration and issue of documents is therefore often a priority in UNHCR interventions. There is a 325-page manual entirely devoted to this process, which opens with the words: 'Registration of refugees and asylum-seekers is, first and foremost, a key protection tool' (UNHCR 2003c).

Conclusions 91 (LII) and 102 (LVI) of the Executive Committee encourage the UNHCR and states to introduce and improve mechanisms of identification and the issuing of documents to refugees and asylum seekers, and to enhance them through the use of new technologies. For the UNHCR, these procedures are first and foremost a way of making a population visible and accessible. To be gotten hold of and identified is to exist for the organisation; this is thus the only way to gain access to its assistance. Here, then, surveillance, in the UNHCR's understanding, returns to its etymological meaning of 'watching over'.

The mechanisms for surveillance of Afghan non-nationals established by the UNHCR were strongly linked to state machinery. While the UNHCR can easily set up registration procedures at a local level – in a camp, for example – it is more complex on a bigger scale. The organisation did not have a large enough infrastructure or a sufficiently extensive presence in the territory. Logistically data collection can only be carried out at a local level, going over entire regions with a fine-tooth comb or by intercepting people as they move. The UNHCR is therefore forced to fall back on, or at least to collaborate with, states, which are better equipped in terms of their presence in the territory, staff and infrastructure. This creates a screening effect: it is difficult or even impossible for the UNHCR to capture individuals and flows in places where the state has not established its own administrative hold.

The link with state machinery is not only a matter of operational requirements: one of the UNHCR's explicit objectives is that states should identify and regulate non-nationals. The state is seen as the ultimate frame within which people and things are governed. Absence of state action is the source of refugees' vulnerability, and it is by reinserting the refugee into a state framework that protection is re-established (see Chapter 2). A protection situation therefore implies that the non-nationals concerned be incorporated with a defined status into a state jurisdiction. Associating them with states, making them discernible and governable by the state, is consequently seen as a prerequisite for their protection.

The methods and issues involved in the concrete implementation of the administrative surveillance procedures promoted by the UNHCR thus depend strongly both on the control states have over their jurisdiction and on their attitude towards the population concerned. If this attitude is not compatible with the UNHCR's priorities, the establishment of such mechanisms becomes the focus of delicate negotiations.

Like European countries, Iran has developed a centralised, efficient system of identification and documentation. The 2001 census of Afghans was conducted at the initiative of the Iranian government, without the UNHCR having any say in the matter. Tellingly, it did not include any questions on 'protection needs', a criterion that was fundamental for the UNHCR, but inconvenient for the government. Furthermore, the Iranian authorities were always reluctant to share data from the census and from renewal of cards, and this was a continual point of contention with the UNHCR. The Afghan and Pakistani states, on the other hand, had much less administrative command of the territories and populations in their jurisdiction. Here the UNHCR had a much greater role and influence in establishing and running these mechanisms. But it still had to compromise with the Pakistani authorities' priorities.

An Illegible Population

Up to the early 2000s, the Afghan population in Pakistan was a submerged, illegible world for the UNHCR. Neither the UNHCR nor the Pakistani government had a precise idea of its size, its demographic characteristics or its location outside of the camps. The figure of two to three million put forward at the end of 2001 was merely an approximate estimate based on the population in the camps, and was impossible to verify, owing to the size of the population and the regions involved (millions of individuals, an entire country, a border over 2,000 km long), and also to the fact that Afghans' movements and their presence in Pakistan had not previously been subject to administrative surveillance by the Afghan and Pakistani states.

The Afghan state had not developed documentation mechanisms comparable to those of European states, and the decades of conflict had disrupted those that were in place. Since that time, the majority of people had not been registered at birth and had no identity document (*taskira*). The most recent census dated back to the 1970s. The UN plan to organise one did not come to fruition. Since 2002, electoral registers and voting cards had been the most widespread means of identification and documentation in the country. Passports, which were only available in Kabul, were not common and remained too expensive for the majority of the population.

Up to the 2000s Afghans had always entered Pakistani territory freely, without being subject to state monitoring. There is a strong history of cross-border movement and the border is porous. It was drawn in 1893 to suit British colonial policy and did not correspond to any ethnic or geographical reality. It bisected Pashtun territory, which extended from the Peshawar valley to Kabul, as well as the Kandahar valley and the Helmand valley as far as Quetta. The Pashtuns share a language (Pashto) and a customary law (*Pashtunwali*) (Barth 1998; Centlivres 1988; Edwards 1996). This border therefore never represented a real separation (Green 2008; Nichols 2008). It is in any case more visible on maps than on the often mountainous ground, where it is sometimes not even marked. Moreover, the two states themselves had not officially recognised it: Afghanistan had not renounced its claims to the Pashtun zones located on the Pakistani side, and Pakistan exploited this fact to exert its influence over Afghanistan (American Institute of Afghanistan Studies and Hollings Center for International Dialogue 2007). These interests combined with the two states' physical inability to truly control it. During the 1980s, this border was a key site of resistance, transfer of weapons and Mujahideen activities; in the 2000s, it was the nerve centre of drug trafficking and Taliban guerrilla activities in Afghanistan. People moved freely across it, including at Torkham, one of the two main border crossings, where the state authorities often did not ask to see any documents.[2]

The Pakistani government had never granted formal status to Afghans present in its territory or issued documents authorising their residence. The only exception was in the 1980s, when some of the families living in camps were issued cards (*shanakhti*) for the purposes of organising food distribution. Afghans had never been counted or identified: the 1998 census completely ignored this population.

Some Afghans settled in camps in the North-West Frontier Province (NWFP) and Balochistan, officially designated 'Afghan Refugee Villages'; others spread freely through the remainder of the territory, mainly in cities. The regions where the Afghan presence was densest were the Pashtun regions adjacent to the border, known as the Federally Administered Tribal Areas (FATA). Here the Pakistani state's hold was weak. Since the colonial era, this region, with a population of some three million people, had always enjoyed semi-autonomous status, and the state had never been able to establish direct control. Pashtun tribal custom was the inescapable frame within which security and individual access to resources were negotiated, where *Pashtunwali* was more powerful than the state's law and justice, and state infrastructures was reduced to the minimum (Abou Zahab 2010; Rashid 2008). Here the tribal order was an essential intermediary for the Afghan and Pakistani states. For individuals, the relationship to the state via the bond of nationality was not the only nor the most important criterion for gaining access to the resources essential to subsistence and to social and political participation. This is clear from the welcome offered to Afghans in the frontier regions of Pakistan during the 1980s: the dominant criteria for settling there were being Muslim and Pashtun, in a Muslim and Pashtun area, rather than being an Afghan in Pakistan (Centlivres 1988; Centlivres and Centlivres-Dumont 1999; Edwards 1986; Shahrani 1995). *Pashtunwali* advocates hospitality (*melmastia*) and asylum (*panah*) for all members of the ethnic group. Islam prescribes the duty to migrate from lands where its practice is repressed (*dar al-kufr*) to those where it is freely practised (*dar al-Islam*).

Finally, it should be noted that by the end of the 2000s, the Pakistani state still had not developed an identity documentation structure efficient enough to identify its own citizens, and thus distinguish them clearly from foreigners. Kamal Sadiq (2009) shows that in Pakistan, as in other postcolonial contexts, many immigrants had access to basic rights without having a formal status, and that some obtain formal citizenship by illegal means, paradoxically becoming more official than locally born people who still do not enjoy citizenship. During the 1980s, many Afghans found conditions sufficient for subsistence and settled in the long term. Some even acquired Pakistani identity cards.

The Census of Afghans in Pakistan

Prior to the 2000s, the UNHCR had never attempted to grasp the Afghan population in Pakistan in its entirety. This was initially because the attention of humanitarian agencies was focused on the camps. Then, during the 1980s, Afghans were well received, and the absence of regulation meant that they could enter and settle in Pakistan freely. Subsequently, lack of funding and the size of the task discouraged any urge to establish administrative surveillance mechanisms. However, after 2001, more accurate data became essential for the UNHCR, for two reasons: first, in order to better manage and coordinate repatriation and reintegration programmes (information on the population's places of origin, for example, would have enabled reintegration programmes to be adapted in advance to the potential locations for return); and, second, given the now overtly restrictive policies in Pakistan, the organisation needed to be better informed to argue its case. In this new situation, the UNHCR had more resources and authority. It therefore proposed that the Pakistani government conduct a census to count and establish a profile of the Afghan population in Pakistan.

The organisation of the census was the subject of lengthy negotiations between the UNHCR and the Pakistani government. The UNHCR secured the right to organise the process, but at the price of compromising with the Pakistani authorities, who were more interested in encouraging repatriation than in granting rights to Afghans. Negotiations focused on two central issues: the information to be gathered and the legal consequences of the census.

By common agreement, assessment of the 'protection needs' of Afghans in Pakistan was deferred. Pakistan would have risked having to manage an enormous population that it could not easily get rid of. The UNHCR preferred to wait until it was able to screen a smaller population. The 2003 Tripartite Agreement had in fact specified that at the end of the repatriation programme, there would be screening of 'residual caseloads' to identify Afghans 'in need of international protection' (Agreement 17/03/2003, Article 6.2). The UNHCR had succeeded in getting this clause included, under which Pakistan indirectly recognised that not all Afghans would have left the country and that some of those who remained might need long-term residence permits.

The UNHCR ultimately had substantial input into the design of the questionnaires. It was thus able to include questions seeking information it required for planning its programmes and arguing against the Pakistani authorities' restrictive policies. These included, for example, place of origin in Afghanistan, date of arrival in Pakistan, intention to return to Afghanistan and the motivation for this choice. These data subsequently served as evidence for the assertion that the Afghan population was made up of individuals who were durably settled, had little inclination to return, often originated from regions where conflict was ongoing and owned no property in Afghanistan. Moreover, the census enabled the UNHCR to identify hundreds of thousands of people raising 'special concerns' who were priority for aid.[3]

In terms of the status of Afghans in Pakistan, the interests of the Pakistani authorities prevailed. It was agreed that the count and data collection would be followed by the issuing of temporary residence permits lasting three years. Called a 'Proof of Registration' (abbreviated to 'PoR card'), these were biometric documents showing the photograph and fingerprints of the bearer (see Figure 11.1). Given the pressure for return that the Pakistani authorities had been exerting since 2003, it is clear that in their eyes, the census was primarily a way of legally getting rid of a substantial proportion of Afghans, since the repatriation programme involved cancelling the residence permit. This formalised residence permit can therefore be seen as the formalised end of residence. Moreover, these documents conferred only right of residence, and not the right of movement or to work. They also made it possible to take a harsher stance towards Afghans who had no residence permit. This mechanism was similar to that initiated by the 2001 census of Afghans in Iran (see Chapter 7) and to the strategy common in EU countries whereby some migrants are registered in order to better exclude or even deport them (Engbersen and Broeders 2009).

From the UNHCR's point of view, the situation was certainly not ideal, but the census was seen as an efficient way of saving time. UNHCR staff hoped that at the end of these three years, with concessions from the organisation, negotiations would result in the establishment of an adequate asylum system, procedures for controlling cross-border movements, and provisions for long-term residence. Moreover, since all those counted were officially protected from deportation until 2009, the UNHCR would have had a strong argument to counter the growing pressure for return. The organisation had also secured assurances that residence permits would be renewable (under procedures to be decided later). From this point of view, they offered a form of protection, even if it was basic and uncertain.

The census operation, sanctioned by two agreements (Memorandum 19/04/2004, Memorandum 19/04/2006), was jointly conducted, drawing on the parties' respective resources and priorities. The UNHCR provided much of the funding. These funds came primarily from the European Union, the United Kingdom and the United States, which were well disposed towards the census in view of their security concerns regarding the 'war on terror' and combating the Taliban. The Pakistani state made its infrastructure available:

Figure 11.1. 'Proof of Registration' (PoR) card. https://media.unhcr.org/
© UNHCR/Duniya Aslam Khan

the census was conducted by the Population Census Organization, which assigned 3,143 agents who went over the whole of the national territory with a fine-tooth comb. The registration process employed over 1,000 agents distributed through 100 registration centres, as well as mobile teams; here it was the National Database and Registration Authority, a department of the Interior Ministry responsible for issuing Pakistani identity cards, that made its infrastructure available. The UNHCR supervised the operations, organised training for the agents and monitored their work throughout the process.

The census took place early in 2005. A total of 3,049,268 Afghans were counted, a figure that far exceeded the UNHCR's predictions.[4] The data collected were statistically processed and compiled into a seventy-page publication (UNHCR, SAFRON, and PCO 2005). Subsequently, between October 2006 and February 2007, 2,153,088 residence permits were issued (SAFRON, NADRA and UNHCR 2008).

The census marked a turning point in the government of Afghans in Pakistan. From a situation of generalised informality, a large proportion of them had become visible, legible and quantifiable for the UNHCR and the Pakistani government. From this point onwards, only Afghans who held a PoR card existed in the eyes of these two institutions. They could either apply to the repatriation programme or be protected against deportation. For those who could not produce this magic key (those who had chosen not to present themselves for the census and all those who had arrived after it took place), the Pakistani state's decrees were final: from April 2007, they would be considered 'illegal migrants' and treated in accordance with national laws (in other words, deported or punished).[5]

Oversight of Returns

The programme for repatriation from Pakistan was introduced in the early 1990s, following the retreat of the Soviet Union from Afghanistan. But it was not until late 2001 that it was adapted to allow thousands of people to take advantage of it each year.[6] The programme rested on a transnational infrastructure. Here too, the UNHCR drew on state administrations at the same time as providing essential resources in the form of funding, its transnational presence, its expertise in repatriation programmes, and its data collection and processing technology. In late 2001, all the states concerned were in favour of the programme, its introduction did not involve difficult negotiations, and the UNHCR was free to organise and run it as it wished.

The programme infrastructure consisted of Repatriation Centres in Pakistan, run by teams from the Pakistani Commissionerate for Afghan Refugees (CAR) and the UNHCR. Those who wished to take advantage of the programme had to register and were issued a Voluntary Repatriation Form.[7] At the same time, Encashment Centres were set up in Afghanistan, on the main access routes, where teams from the UNHCR and the Afghan Ministry for Refugees distributed return aid. In 2007 there were still five active Repatriation Centres in Iran, as well as two in Pakistan and six Encashment Centres in Afghanistan. The journey was made independently. The repatriation card was the keystone of the programme: when they arrived at an Encashment Centre in Afghanistan, returnees had to present this document in order to receive aid (see Figure 11.3).[8] This showed details of the registration procedure that made the document unique and identifiable, followed by information on the bearer and their family, place of residence in the country of asylum and place of origin (or destination) in Afghanistan. This card certified the movement of the individual from one state jurisdiction to another. The person ceased to be considered a refugee by the UNHCR, but could receive return aid and would be oriented towards reintegration programmes for which only returnees were eligible. During field visits, I noted that UNHCR officers regularly asked to see the repatriation card in order to verify the eligibility of the person concerned (see Figure 11.4). People kept these documents carefully on their person, often in plastic bags to prevent them getting damaged, given that this was often the only document the individual, and indeed the entire family, possessed.

At the end of 2002, a further surveillance procedure was introduced in these centres in order to prevent return journeys aimed at obtaining the aid several times over. When the repatriation card was issued, the holder was subject to an iris scan. The resulting database could be used to verify that the person in question was indeed accessing the programme for the first time.

For the UNHCR, the repatriation card also represented a powerful tool of legibility. Not only did it make it possible to identify each returnee and their family – and hence, for example, to verify that he had indeed received the aid he was due, or to reunite families – but it also gave access to an overview of the whole of the repatriated population. In addition, computer processing of the data enabled the UNHCR to monitor the progress of return day by day, as noted in Chapter 8. The result was a synoptic view of returns over time (see Figure 11.5). In addition to making it possible to adjust reintegration programmes, these data were also presented as tangible proof of the 'success' of the programme, and helped to secure further funds for its continuation.

This infrastructure made it possible to control the returns of Afghans and to orchestrate it in such a way that they were 'processable' by the UNHCR and the Afghan state. Return migration took place in an orderly way that was transparent to the UNHCR, in a predictable timeframe and following an expected trajectory, since there were points that people had to pass through: if the person wanted to receive aid, they could only do so at point B, on condition that they had first passed through point A.

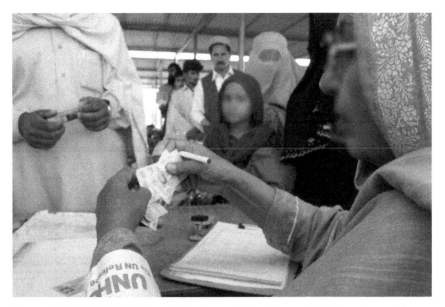

Figure 11.2. Checking PoR cards in a Repatriation Centre in Pakistan. https://media.unhcr.org © UNHCR/Vivian Tan

Figure 11.3. A returnee showing his repatriation card to a UNHCR officer. Photo by the author.

WEEKLY RETURN TRENDS 2007

Week	Week Period	Pakistan						Iran		Other Countries		Total	
		Non-PoR Holders[z]		PoR Holders[zz]		Total							
		Families	Individuals	Families	Individuals	Families	Individuals	Families	Individuals	Families	Individuals	Families	Individuals
01	01 Jan - 06 Jan	0	0	0	0	0	0	3	23	5	27	8	50
02	07 Jan -13 Jan	0	0	0	0	0	0	0	0	0	0	0	0
03	14 Jan - 20 Jan	0	0	0	0	0	0	0	0	0	0	0	1
04	21 Jan - 27 Jan	0	0	0	0	0	0	2	27	0	0	2	27
05	28 Jan - 03 Feb	0	0	0	0	0	0	0	0	6	83	6	63
06	4 Feb - 10 Feb	0	0	0	0	0	0	0	0	0	0	0	0
07	11 Feb - 17 Feb	0	0	0	0	0	0	0	0	1	0	1	0
08	18 Feb - 24 Feb	0	0	0	0	0	0	5	30	0	0	5	30
09	25 Feb - 03 Mar	4	25	0	0	4	25	0	0	4	71	8	96
10	04 Mar - 10 Mar	53	273	0	0	53	273	10	82	0	1	63	356
11	11 Mar - 17 Mar	274	1,658	0	0	274	1,658	0	0	0	2	274	1,660
12	18 Mar - 24 Mar	2,021	12,958	0	0	2,021	12,958	0	0	0	1	2,021	12,959
13	25 Mar - 31 Mar	3,566	23,124	0	0	3,566	23,124	0	0	0	0	3,566	23,124
14	01 Apr - 07 Apr	4,782	32,828	0	0	4,782	32,828	0	0	5	39	4,787	32,867
15	08 Apr - 14 Apr	7,022	47,926	0	0	7,022	47,926	0	0	0	0	7,022	47,926
16	15 Apr - 21 Apr	8,611	59,938	16	88	8,627	60,026	0	0	0	0	8,627	60,026
17	22 Apr - 28 Apr	3,740	27,159	514	2,785	4,254	29,944	9	38	1	7	4,264	29,989
18	29 Apr - 05 May	31	223	648	3,582	679	3,805	109	509	9	120	797	4,434
19	06 May - 12 May	2	13	881	3,675	883	3,688	66	324	3	750	4,015
20	13 May - 19 May	0	0	614	3,347	614	3,347	50	250	0	2	664	3,599
21	20 May - 26 May	0	0	696	3,909	896	3,909	70	352	0	0	766	4,261
22	27 May - 02 Jun	0	0	778	4,409	778	4,409	68	344	4	40	850	4,793
23	03 Jun - 09 Jun	0	0	1,127	6,304	1,127	6,304	9	50	0	0	1,136	6,354
24	10 Jun - 16 Jun	0	0	1,350	7,916	1,350	7,916	113	562	0	5	1,484	8,483
25	17 Jun - 23 Jun	0	0	1,614	9,441	1,614	9,441	69	334	1	9	1,884	9,784
26	24 Jun - 30 Jun	0	0	2,059	12,195	2,059	12,195	43	254	0	1	2,102	12,450
27	01 Jul - 07 Jul	0	0	1,838	10,856	1,838	10,856	76	404	2	28	1,916	11,288
28	08 Jul - 14 Jul	0	0	2,056	12,317	2,056	12,317	54	292	1	7	2,111	12,616
29	15 Jul - 21 Jul	0	0	1,283	7,653	1,283	7,653	31	147	0	1	1,314	7,701
30	22 Jul - 28 Jul	0	0	604	3,477	604	3,477	18	80	0	27	623	3,584
31	29 Jul - 04 Aug	0	0	759	4,491	759	4,491	28	133	2	37	789	4,661
32	05 Aug - 11 Aug	0	0	811	3,494	811	3,494	48	235	0	0	859	3,729
33	12 Aug - 18 Aug	0	0	861	3,890	861	3,890	39	191	0	0	700	4,081
34	19 Aug - 25 Aug	0	0	1,304	7,324	1,304	7,324	29	141	0	0	1,333	7,465
35	26 Aug - 01 Sep	0	0	2,339	12,977	2,339	12,977	37	164	5	54	2,381	13,195
36	02 Sep - 08 Sep	0	0	1,825	9,407	1,625	9,407	50	242	0	0	1,675	9,649
37	09 Sep - 15 Sep	0	0	863	4,951	863	4,951	45	230	0	0	908	5,182
38	16 Sep - 22 Sep	0	0	296	1,698	296	1,698	37	195	0	0	333	1,893
39	23 Sep - 29 Sep	0	0	224	1,352	224	1,352	29	156	2	11	255	1,519
40	30 Sep 06 Oct	0	0	255	1,577	255	1,577	21	125	7	61	283	1,763
41	07 Oct - 13 Oct	0	0	119	691	119	691	21	104	0	7	141	802
42	14 Oct - 20 Oct	0	0	21	122	21	122	11	62	0	0	32	184
43	21 Oct - 27 Oct	0	0	481	2,898	461	2,898	14	66	0	0	475	2,964
44	28 Oct - 03 Nov	0	0	858	5,008	5,008	5,008	36	170	7	68	900	5,246
45	04 Nov - 10 Nov	0	0	0	0	0	0	29	154	0	0	29	154
46	11 Nov - 17 Nov	0	0	0	0	0	0	26	113	0	0	26	113
47	18 Nov - 24 Nov	0	0	0	0	0	0	23	131	0	0	23	131
48	25 Nov - 01 Dec	0	0	0	0	0	0	10	56	3	24	13	80
49	02 Dec - 08 Dec	0	0	0	0	0	0	12	72	0	0	12	72
50	09 Dec - 15 Dec	0	0	0	0	0	0	25	156	0	2	25	158
51	16 Dec - 22 Dec	0	0	0	0	0	0	2	6	0	0	2	6
52	23 Dec - 29 Dec	0	0	0	0	0	0	12	57	0	0	12	57
53	30 Dec - 31 Dec	0	0	0	0	0	0	3	13	0	0	3	13
	Total	30,106	206,125	26,274	151,734	56,380	357,859	1,388	7,054	71	721	57,839	365,634

Weekly Return Trends -2007

DAILY & MONTHLY RETURN 2007

Month	Date	Pakistan						Iran		Other Countries		Total	
		Non-PoR Holders[z]		PoR Holders[zz]		Total							
		Families	Individuals	Families	Individuals	Families	Individuals	Families	Individuals	Families	Individuals	Families	Individuals
January		0	0	0	0	0	0	5	50	5	28	10	78
February		0	0	0	0	0	0	5	30	6	84	11	84
March		5,918	38,038	0	0	5,918	38,038	10	82	4	75	5,932	38,175
April		24,179	168,026	750	4,099	24,929	172,125	15	62	6	46	24,950	172,233
May		9	61	3,149	17,446	3,158	17,507	357	1,755	11	132	3,526	19,394
June		0	0	6,198	36,106	6,102	35,517	234	1,200	5	48	6,341	36,825
July		0	0	6,221	36,811	6,221	36,811	192	1,000	7	63	6,420	37,874
August		0	0	5,234	29,568	5,234	29,568	165	787	3	42	5,402	30,397
September		0	0	3,045	17,621	3,045	17,621	163	840	6	61	3,214	18,522
October		0	0	1,677	10,083	1,729	10,388	99	503	8	68	1,836	10,959
November		0	0	0	0	0	0	89	461	7	68	96	529
December		0	0	0	0	0	0	54	304	3	26	57	330
Total		30,106	206,125	26,274	151,734	56,336	357,635	1,388	7,054	71	721	57,795	365,410

CUMULATIVE RETURNS FROM 03 MAR 02 - 07 Dec 07

Year		Pakistan						Iran		Other Countries		Total	
		Non-PoR Holders[z]		PoR Holders[zz]		Total							
		Families	Individuals	Families	Individuals	Families	Individuals	Families	Individuals	Families	Individuals	Families	Individuals
2002	In 2007, we have two phases of return. Phase	281,402	1,585,066	37,231	259,792	2,273	9,679	320,906	1,834,537
2003	1 started on 1 March and ended on 15 April;	58,942	332,183	22,240	142,280	205	1,176	81,387	475,639
2004	during this phase, UNHCR assisted Afghans	66,554	333,321	68,262	377,151	115	650	134,931	781,122
2005	without PoR cards to return from Pakistan	79,234	449,391	11,532	63,559	65	1,140	90,831	514,090
2006	UNHCR assists Afghans with PoR cards to	24,046	133,338	913	5,204	103	1,202	25,062	139,804
2007		30,106	206,125	26,274	151,734	56,336	357,635	1,388	7,054	71	721	57,795	365,410
TOTAL		30,106	206,125	26,274	151,734	566,514	3,220,934	141,566	855,100	2,832	14,568	710,912	4,090,602

" "PoR card holders' refer to Afghans who possess PoR cards in Pakistan and return to Afghanistan with UNHCR's assistance.

Figure 11.4. Statistical data relating to the repatriation programme (2001–7) (UNHCR 2007d: 14) © UNHCR

The Management of Movement Recommended by the ACSU Project

The third administrative surveillance system promoted by the UNHCR was that recommended in the ACSU strategy. 'Management of population movements' of Afghans in the region is an expression that recurs frequently in the project's strategy documents (UNHCR 2003a, 2007a). It refers to one of the project's aims: to reach a situation where all international movements, and therefore all Afghan presence in any of the three countries, were known to and managed by the respective states. This strategy did not call either repatriation procedures or the census into question. The census in particular, in addition to being a tool for good 'management of population movements', was seen by the strategy's authors as a crucial source of information to be used in negotiating with the Pakistani authorities.

Through the ACSU strategy, the UNHCR encouraged the Afghan, Iranian and Pakistani states to establish bilateral systems to regulate the movement of migrant workers. The aim was to render the 'hieroglyph' of Afghan movements legible and therefore subject to management by states. To this end, the ACSU project recommended establishing a process similar to that of the repatriation programme, but to be run by the states themselves, initially with support from the IOM and the ILO. Training was organised to support more efficient management on both sides of the border: an improved infrastructure, an increased number of state agents (police and administrative staff), efficient border control procedures. The UNHCR also advocated establishing a more efficient and accessible system for the issue of visas by the Pakistani and Iranian embassies and consulates in Afghanistan. In order for this to become possible, Afghanistan had first to improve its own system for issuing passports – hence the need to support the Interior Ministry. This institutional infrastructure would enable states to manage movements in both time and space.

Although the UNHCR does not usually concern itself with the movement of nonrefugee migrants, the thinking behind the ACSU project here aligned with one of the institution's unwavering positions: migration that takes place in full view of institutions helps to reduce the vulnerability and precarity arising from recourse to people traffickers and undocumented residence (UNHCR 2000b, 2005d, 2006e, 2007a: 5, 9, 2009). In the UNHCR's view, having to resort to smugglers or people traffickers made migration financially expensive and personally dangerous. In the host country, the lack of official status exposed migrants to exploitation in the labour market and to punishment by the police (arrest or deportation).

The Establishment of the National Order

The administrative surveillance mechanisms introduced (or promoted) by the UNHCR were centred on strictly nation-based principles. The organisation's work is dedicated to associating 'displaced' people with a state and incorporating them effectively into a state jurisdiction, by defining and activating a link based on nationality. Within a few years, the people who had been counted in the census and/or participated in the repatriation programme were administratively identified as 'Afghans', and had thus become governable by the UNHCR and by the Afghan and Pakistani states, either as citizens in Afghanistan or as non-nationals in Pakistan.

Thus, the UNHCR's activities worked towards establishing the national order in this region of the world. The organisation strove to enact an order in which the relationship between individual and territory was subject to the logic of the nation-state – a logic that partitions the world and its population, by means of exclusive bonds between portions of the world's population and their states of nationality – and sought to incorporate 'displaced' people into that order. In this order, nationality is the principal characteristic of human beings, the criterion that determines their place in the world and how they should be governed (Hindess 2000, 2002).

A number of those who have studied the spread and establishment of the nation-state have argued that rather than pre-existing the state, the 'nation' derives from institutional activity, particularly the capacity of states to instil a sense of national belonging in the population (Anderson 2006; Balibar and Wallerstein 1991: 88; Hobsbawm and Ranger 1983; Noiriel 2001; Roy 1997). These studies focus on the institutional infrastructure essential to nation-building, a process often led by the elites who control the state. Anderson's definition (2006), in his description of the nation as an 'imagined community', emphasises precisely the material means (the press, censuses and museums) without which it is impossible to imagine the nation as a sociopolitical community. Hobsbawm and Ranger (1983) analyse the role of the state in the 'invention of tradition', the production of a common history. Noiriel and Roy focus on nation-building as a process of state expansion and manufacture of a habitus: the reality of state institutions is manifested in the everyday gestures of people, contributing to constituting them as a nation.

In the current case, the vectors of nation-building were the documents issued (PoR cards, repatriation certificates, passports and visas) and the systems of administrative surveillance dependent on them. The UNHCR was active at the level of both individuals and states, first connecting them and then shaping their relations in accordance with the nation-state model. The UNHCR's nation-building project was split into two parts: first, it had to establish the national distinction between Afghans and non-Afghans, and to demarcate the Afghan and Pakistani jurisdictions territorially; and, second, it had to ensure that the two state administrations were capable of making these differences operative, and used them for the purposes of governing.

The census and the repatriation programme thus worked to manufacture the Afghan nation. These mechanisms sanctioned individuals' identity as Afghan nationals subject to the Afghan state. By identifying its bearer as an 'Afghan citizen temporarily resident in Pakistan', the PoR card assigned an administrative identity based on nationality. The repatriation certificate was effectively an identity document for returnees, since possession of it ensured eligibility for reintegration programmes and facilitated the issue of an Afghan identity document. Individuals were thus marked as nationals: through the use of biometric data (iris scans, fingerprints and photographs), nationality was permanently bound to their bodies. Rooted in the physical, it thus became naturalised (Douglas 1986). The relationship was unique: no one can be bound by this same bond to two states at once. This was evident from the fact that the UNHCR and the Pakistani government, aware that some people had been able to procure Pakistan identity documents, forbade all those who possessed them from taking part in the census.[9] For an individual, being classified as an Afghan national had important consequences: their exclusive bond with the Afghan state was now certified. In the rest of the world, they would be merely a foreigner.

In addition to acting on individuals, the UNHCR also intervened with states, encouraging them to promote national difference and to use it as a basis for governing. Although the establishment and management of these mechanisms could often be a source of tension, the UNHCR worked to consolidate and extend the Afghan and Pakistani states' control over migrants. The model followed by the UNHCR is that of a state with a legal apparatus and an efficient identity infrastructure that enables it to monitor and regulate migration. States' power to control was strengthened through the training and supervision the UNHCR provided to Pakistani government staff employed on the census and to staff from the Afghan Ministry of Refugees assigned to the repatriation programme, as well as through training offered to Afghan and Pakistani border officials by the ILO and the IOM, which the UNHCR recommended. In the interim the UNHCR partially replaced the states; for the time being, it was the repatriation programme that made the international border operative, through the Repatriation and Encashment Centres.

In contrast to the nation-building processes studied by most researchers, this project is distinctive in that it was promoted not by a state, but by an international organisation: it was not the state elites who first imagined the nation and sought to make it tangible, but the officials of an international organisation.[10] The aim was not to establish the internal and interstate legitimacy of a particular state as a nation-state, but rather to consecrate a link between

individuals and territories, seen as the fundamental criterion for global government and modernity. Its other distinctive feature was that the first to be
defined as nationals were located in other countries. Rather than as nationals,
they had to be recognised as non-nationals so that they could be governed as
foreigners.

UNHCR officials pursued this nation-building process largely uncon-
sciously. In this interstate agency whose mission is rooted in the national order, that order is understood as the normal state of affairs. The nation-state
is seen as the only viable form of political organisation, *the* premier context
in which politics and social relations are conducted. Individuals are national
citizens before being, for example, Pashtun or Baloch. Thus, 'ethnicity' usually
does feature only as a demographic or socioeconomic characteristic. UNHCR
officers imagine that mutually exclusive national populations exist by nature.
'Afghans' in Pakistan are therefore theoretically immediately identifiable, as if
there was a direct natural link between them and the Afghan state that pre-ex-
ists identification procedures, and is merely formalised by these procedures.
The inability of the Afghan and Pakistani states to make national difference
effective was seen as a deviance to be rectified, since 'normal' states were able
to control their borders. The nation-building process was therefore seen and
presented as the remedy for a lack of competence, a normalisation. The fact
that the UNHCR Head of Mission in Kabul argued for the 'normality' of controlled borders clearly demonstrates this teleological focus towards an ideal
model of the regulatory nation-state with strong control:

> there are a very large number of Afghans moving in both directions every day. This is
> an entirely normal situation. However what is not normal about it ... is that the vast
> majority of these movements are not regulated ... I think you will agree that this is
> not a normal situation for any international border. (UNAMA 2009)

The UNHCR's nation- and state-centred vision incorporates a reductive and
false understanding of power and the reality of migration. The hypotheses that
structure it fail to grasp the complexity of exercising power in Afghanistan and
Pakistan. In this region, the logic of the nation-state only partially explains
the formation of states, political organisation and social belonging. The nation-state model appeared there in the nineteenth century, imposed by British
imperialism. Experts on the region agree that rather than this exogenous model
being 'imported', it was 'grafted' (Bayart 1996, 2006), in an implantation process specific to each historical context. Thus, although the model did result
in political reorganisation and shifts in identity (Pakistan, after all, emerged
from the division between Muslims and Hindus in India), it also had to be
articulated with other pre-existing political, social and moral institutions, such
as tribal or ethnic systems. This resulted in states that root their legitimacy

and assert their authority in ways different from those of modern Western nation-states, and a situation where several political, legal and social systems co-exist. It is precisely the complexity of the relationship between the state and the political institutions that pre-existed it that shapes the contemporary politics of the two countries (Barfield 2010; Edwards 1986; Roy 1985).

How, then, is the UNHCR's position to be explained? I have noted that the hypothesis of the national order underpins the paradigm of the 'refugee problem' and therefore the UNHCR's mission, making it difficult for the organisation to distance itself from that order. Moreover, the nation-building process promoted by the UNHCR can be seen to have the implicit goal of constructing a world in which the organisation's activity is both legitimate and facilitated. Implanting the nation-state order implies reinforcing the UN's legitimacy and raison d'être, which is based on the hypothesis of a world organised politically and socially around nation-states. Strengthening the Afghan and Pakistani states' control in line with the nation-state model was therefore an exercise in making the world conformable. This resulted in the creation of a more legible and negotiable field, thus facilitating the pursuit of the organisation's own project. The nation-state as a tool of legibility of the world is particularly important for an international body that acts at the planetary scale: it is through this vision that the world can be grasped as a homogeneous whole and thus becomes 'manageable'. Ultimately, nation-building contributes to shaping the world in accordance with the organisation's viewpoint, making its mission meaningful and viable, so that it can rightfully participate in the government of the world.

The establishment of the national order promoted by the UNHCR has two consequences. At the political level, the effect is as noted in Chapter 9: the organisation is indirectly involved in creating a hierarchy among models of political organisation, and thus in a hegemonic process. The UNHCR presents a specific form of political organisation – the nation-state as it developed in Western countries during the nineteenth and twentieth centuries, as a direct consequence of the assertion of democratic and liberal principles of political legitimacy – as a universal model. This immediately establishes a hierarchy between states – normal versus abnormal, those that 'already' operate as they should versus those that do not 'yet' do so.

In terms of the UNHCR's activity, I show below that this nation- and state-centred position also gives rise to a paradox and a serious shortcoming. The paradox lies in the effort to enact the nation-state order and to incorporate migrants into it with the aim of protecting them, when this sedentary order actually works to emplace them in Afghanistan and restricts their possibilities for movement. The shortcoming emerges in the failure to recognise processes that in fact have a much greater impact than state action on the dynamics of migration and migrants' decisions.

Exclusion through Emplacement and Illegalisation

There is no denying that the state framework can offer real resources. To the extent that states exist and are, to varying degrees, effective, being able to claim an official link with them can allow people to claim rights and to benefit from certain services. But state control of migration can also impose powerful restrictions on the movement of any individual. As holders of 'legitimate means of movement' (Torpey 2000), in the national order states are free to decide the conditions under which non-nationals may enter and stay in their territory. This power also extends to the legitimate use of force to expel foreigners not authorised to stay. There is therefore often a misalignment between the aspirations of people who wish to migrate and their possibilities for doing so legally.

This was the case for Afghans in the 2000s. Conflict and poverty were still raging in Afghanistan. In Pakistan the state's attitude was now openly hostile. The UNHCR advocated introducing more effective and forceful border control, and stricter application of the law on foreigners in Pakistan. This unconditional support for the state also risked enabling or amplifying the constraint the Pakistani state was able to exert over Afghans. What the UNHCR saw as benevolent oversight could easily tip over into disciplinary surveillance. Migrants were at risk of being stuck, held in a sedentary system in which they were more dependent on and more exposed to states that manifestly did not want to or were not capable of offering them anything, despite the fact that migration was for them an essential survival and subsistence strategy.

Many studies have shown that stronger state administrative surveillance of migrants goes hand in hand with an increase in the obstacles, costs and risks associated with movement. The restrictive immigration policies adopted by EU countries – nation-states where administrative control and the ability to instil national difference is an important element of their constitution and their current operation (Noiriel 2001; Scott 1998; Torpey 2000) – are a telling example. Since the 1990s, these countries have tried to increase their control over migrants in order to stem immigration, seal their borders and increase the costs of illegal residence for non-European citizens. The strategies adopted include interception (in Mediterranean waters, at the border and within their territories) and a plethora of increasingly sophisticated remote administrative surveillance techniques. The Eurodac system, a Europe-wide database of the fingerprints of asylum seekers designed to prevent migrants from making several applications within the Schengen zone, has received the most attention, but it is not the only one (Broeders 2007; Engbersen and Broeders 2009; Farraj 2011). Researchers increasingly recognise that being identified by a state does not necessarily mean inclusion; administrative surveillance can just as well form part of a deliberate strategy of exclusion of foreigners (and even some nationals) (Engbersen and Brodeers 2009; Muller 2004; Sprokkereef and de Hert 2007; Thomas 2005; Wilson 2006). In the Afghanistan-Pakistan region, it was precisely the lack of state regulation that enabled millions of Afghans facing war and poverty to leave Afghanistan and settle in Pakistan from the 1980s onwards. This situation changed radically after 2001, a time when state control was intensifying in parallel with a major UNHCR intervention in the region. The combination of the repatriation and census programmes formed part of a mechanism that worked towards emplacement in Afghanistan and illegalisation of any subsequent movement. To the extent that states were able to exert control over Afghans, they became fixed, 'held' in a sedentary order and a situation of relative distress, either in a country where life and subsistence were extremely difficult, but that was considered to be the portion of the planet where they naturally belonged, or in Pakistan or anywhere else in the world as undesirable non-nationals.

I now turn to consider in more detail the two principles of the mechanism established during the 2000s: emplacement and illegalisation. The repatriation programme can be seen as a mechanism of emplacement aimed at sedentarising and definitively implanting Afghan migrants in the only portion of the planet where their presence was considered legitimate. In his article on the introduction of the iris scan into the repatriation programme, Jacobsen (2010) clearly demonstrates that the programme was designed as a one-way process whose aim was to return Afghans to their country of nationality, so that they would remain there permanently. The iris scan was introduced precisely to discourage returnees from going back to Pakistan and receiving aid again on their return. The fact that international aid was overwhelmingly concentrated in Afghanistan clearly shows that it was in this country that Afghans were now supposed to live and find the means of subsistence. In the logic of the programme, returnees were supposed not to move again after their return. This was seen as normalisation of their position in the world. The idea was that a migration cycle was coming to an end, and any subsequent movement was to be seen as an indicator of the programme's failure. The possibilities of legitimate movement ended with return. It was no longer possible to leave Afghanistan legally. Passports, which could only be obtained in Kabul, were extremely expensive for most Afghans, and visas were rare.

Although UNHCR officers saw the census as a way of ensuring more secure status for Afghans settled in Pakistan, in fact it reinforced the mechanism of emplacement in Afghanistan. In a context where the Pakistani authorities were determined to 'close the chapter on refugees' as quickly as possible and the UNHCR was increasingly powerless, the census in fact gave the Pakistani state a way of funnelling the Afghans counted towards repatriation and legitimately getting rid of them. This phrase from the report on the census is telling, emphasising 'the importance and need to enumerate Afghans in Pakistan and to issue documentation to better manage this population and to *facilitate voluntary repatriation* as the most preferred solution' (SAFRON, NADRA and UNHCR 2008: 4, emphasis added).

Moreover, as noted above, for thousands of residents of the Jalozai and Kacha Gari camps, the PoR card did not guarantee that they could stay in Pakistan. For the other Afghans counted, little changed in terms of benefits or rights, but they had become legible to the Pakistani authorities, who now had detailed data on all those who had left under the repatriation programme (who could now be punished in the event they returned to Pakistan) and on all those recorded who remained (who could thus be more easily pressured to return to Afghanistan).

Emplacement in Afghanistan was the counterpoint to the illegalisation of their subsequent movement. By recognising the status of migrants in relation to the state, repatriation and the census made the boundary between legality and illegality more effective. States became more able to impose their own criteria for legitimate and illegitimate movement, through law and administrative surveillance. While those who had been brought under the sway of state law (returnees and holders of the PoR card) were caught up in the restrictive mechanism of emplacement in Afghanistan, the costs rose correspondingly for those who remained outside this sway (those who had chosen not to be counted in the census and those who moved between the two states out of sight of state surveillance).

These costs came first in the form of exclusion from the benefits that could be claimed by Afghans who had an official status (legitimate residence in Pakistan, international aid in Afghanistan). But, above all, they now found themselves in a situation seen not as part of a generalised 'informality', but rather as 'illegal' – in other words, an illegitimate situation that implied a breach of the state's authority and could therefore be legitimately repressed and punished. Afghans who were unable to produce a PoR card could theoretically now be deported – and the Pakistani state had the means to punish them. It was also possible for the Pakistani authorities to use the biometric data they held to refuse entry and residence. Moreover, in the new context, the Pakistani state had greater scope for applying the law selectively, in a precise strategic way, as did the Iranian authorities (see Chapter 7). In these circumstances, remaining invisible in order to avoid state control became more difficult, more costly and more dangerous.[11]

The UNHCR presented its initiatives as working to 'regularise' migrants, but following Nicholas de Genova's work (2002) on the 'production of illegality', they could be seen as helping to *illegalise* migrants, since they introduced a distinction between legality and illegality, and enabled states to enact that distinction.[12] As there was no possibility of legitimate residence other than as a returnee in Afghanistan or PoR cardholder in Pakistan, or any possibility of movement in conformity with state laws, any other movement or presence in Pakistan became by definition illegal and, as such, illegitimate and subject to sanction.

The bilateral migration regime for migrant workers proposed by the ACSU project appeared to have the aim of remedying this situation of immobilisation in Afghanistan and illegalisation of movement out of the country. But by 2008, when the census took place, no progress had been made towards establishing this regime. The Pakistani state showed no inclination to introduce it, and even if it had wished to, it may reasonably be doubted whether such a system would have permitted the thousands who might have wished to move to do so legally.

Agier (2008, 2011), studying the mechanism of encampment in Africa, which confines migrants to isolated camps, points out that the international government of refugees operates to exclude an undesirable population. In the Pakistan-Afghanistan region, a similar mechanism of exclusion is in operation. But here, the mechanism does not operate through confinement within small spaces. Many of the camps in Pakistan had become quasi-urban centres, and a large proportion of the Afghan population in Pakistan lived in the country's cities. The logic operating here was not so much one of confinement as one of incorporation into a sedentary order in a subaltern position; it operated not through the technology of the camp, but through administrative surveillance and the law. This order assigned 'displaced' Afghans a place-in-the-world, and both restricted and regulated their movements outside of this place. Movement was not completely eliminated. Some movement was even encouraged (particularly the movement of return), while others were not prevented, but were rather hampered and rendered reprehensible. In contrast to camps, the spaces of exclusion were the much larger ones of the Afghan state jurisdiction and the domain of illegality.

A fundamental paradox thus emerges in the UNHCR's work. In order to resolve the 'problem of Afghan displacement', which derived from the national order, the organisation's response was to make that order more operative. In other words, the order that produced these 'dis-placed' people as surplus was also the order into which the UNHCR sought to absorb them. While international refugee law and the UNHCR were created precisely in order to circumvent the restrictions that states could impose on non-nationals, the solutions brought in fact increased states' capacity to impose those restrictions. As surplus people, refugees threaten the national order: they show that it is not a viable order for the global population. Identifying this population and making it manageable, consecrating the unique relationship that binds it to a specific portion of the planet and re-placing it in the 'country of origin' thus becomes a 'repair' operation that restores rather than challenging the order that has produced it. In this way, the danger represented by refugees is neutralised, and the national order gains greater legitimacy and thus becomes more effective. But this comes at the cost of restricting the movement of populations for whom migration is an essential survival and subsistence strategy, and relegating them to a subaltern, excluded position.

The Nonstate Sphere as Refuge

In order to grasp the concrete restrictive effects of the UNHCR's activity, its intervention needs to be situated in the broader context of 'overlapping sovereignties' particular to this region of the world. The UNHCR's nation-building work in the Afghanistan-Pakistan region is part of a vast political and social engineering project. The operation and political legitimacy of states in modes other than the national order, and the coexistence of several political systems, remain powerful realities, the product of particular historical processes. We need only to imagine what achieving a situation of total state control of the Afghanistan-Pakistan border would mean, particularly to the many political interests and relations that are at play – between Pashtuns and the state, between the Afghan and Pakistani states, but also the interests of smuggling and drug networks, etc., over which the UNHCR has no direct control. This is why the organisation was unable, alone and within a few years, to fully impose its model of political organisation, and its projects were therefore destined to remain partially incomplete.

People's strategies develop in this more complex sociopolitical field, and generally involve engaging various different orders and playing on the diverse statuses they have within each in order to maximise resources and minimise risk (Monsutti 2012b). They may thus invoke nationality in situations where it entitles them to assistance, but at the same time draw on other systems that govern 'means of movement', such as Pashtun ethnic or tribal belonging (Centlivres 1988; Edwards 1986), the transnational trust networks established by the Hazaras (Monsutti 2005, 2009), smugglers and clandestine channels (Bathaïe 2008; Monsutti 2005, 2009). It is precisely because the state field is not the only operative one that the effects of state and international policies are mitigated, and some at least find the space of manoeuvre necessary to circumvent the constraints exerted by states and international bodies.

In his study of the spread of the state in South-East Asia, Scott (2009) shows that for many people, the spaces to which the state had not extended its control (often regions that were difficult to access, particularly mountainous areas) formed zones of refuge that enabled them to escape state violence and demands (taxation, conscription, etc.). If we apply this idea to a world where there is no longer any physical space not under state jurisdiction, orders that coexist with the state order could be seen as dimensions that offer a form of externality, or refuge – albeit no longer a physical space – where people can escape the exercise of state power (in this case emplacement in Afghanistan).

There were at least two ways in which Afghans articulated their migration strategies with the policies of the Pakistani state and the UNHCR in order to reduce their dependence on these institutions and circumvent the constraints they imposed. The first was strategies of invisibility: migrants sought to remain illegible and hence uncontrollable. Either they avoided all contact with surveillance mechanisms or, if that was not possible, they muddied the waters, confusing state and international bureaucracies by altering their administrative identity. Migrants might give false names, or a different name each time, or create several administrative identities, sabotaging bureaucratic administrative surveillance systems. The second strategy was to engage with institutions to benefit from the resources and opportunities they might offer while avoiding or minimising control and dependence. The widespread use of false documents in the region formed part of this strategy (Monsutti 2005).

For Afghans in Pakistan, the census was a highly unpredictable project that involved rendering themselves legible to the Pakistani and Afghan states and to the UNHCR, with no guarantee that this would bring more benefits than restrictions. Would registering entitle them to aid, or would it simply make them visible to the state and therefore more exposed to pressure to return? Strategies were employed to mitigate this uncertainty. The Social Development Policy Institute noted that a substantial number of people chose invisibility; they did not register for fear of being exposed to the Pakistani authorities (SDPI 2006). Many families adopted a strategy of family differentiation in order to spread the risk: some members registered, while others did not. Several individuals came purposely from Afghanistan to register so that they could enjoy the potential benefits associated with the status of Pakistani resident. Others chose to register for the census, but not to present themselves for it the following year. Hundreds of thousands of people participated in the census, but then did not register to obtain the residence permit or apply to the repatriation programme. This population, which the UNHCR and Pakistani state thought they had rendered legible, ultimately disappeared from the radar, briefly surfacing before being 'reabsorbed' into a world that remained impenetrable to the UNHCR.

Under the repatriation programme, in 2002 many people made several return journeys in order to receive UNHCR aid more than once. The needed only to give a different name and present themselves at an Encashment Centre. And as the amount of the payment depended on the number of family members, names were often added to the repatriation card, particularly children. Entire families could be found 'for hire' at border crossings, for the purpose of increasing the aid payment. It was these practices that led the UNHCR to introduce the iris scan, including for children over the age of five. Another strategy used from 2006 onwards consisted of returning to Afghanistan outside of the repatriation programme in order to keep the PoR card, thus retaining the possibility of returning to Pakistan if the situation in Afghanistan deteriorated.

The contrast between the return of the majority of residents of Kacha Gari and Jalozai (see Chapter 8) and that of a group of Kuchi Pashtuns who also went back to Afghanistan during the summer of 2007 shows that only those with substantial alternative resources were able to circumvent the constraints imposed by the emplacement process. Key resources that make it possible to reduce dependence on state and international bodies include the possibility of operating in alternative orders that can provide the means of subsistence and 'means of circulation' for members of the group, and an understanding of the reasoning behind state and international initiatives that allows for more strategic engagement with them. The Kuchi group was a close-knit and very well-organised tribe whose chief was a well-known wealthy warlord. Their return was based on a rational decision to settle and take over a vast area that the group claimed as its ancestral pasture lands – a claim that had been recognised by the Afghan state. Return was deliberately organised outside of the repatriation programme in order to retain the PoR cards and the possibility of moving between the two countries. Thus, by choosing to return after the PoR cards had been issued and making selective use of the services offered (yes to the census, no to repatriation), this group succeeded in engaging strategically with state and UNHCR policies, turning them to its advantage. It was able to secure legal rights in both countries (land ownership in Afghanistan and right of residence in Pakistan), even though the emplacement mechanism introduced by the Afghan and Pakistani states and the UNHCR worked towards sedentarisation in one country.

The UNHCR's nation- and state-centred position, and the need to make its recipients legible, often leads the organisation's officers to view any behaviour that does not comply with its programmes with distrust if not outright hostility. Such behaviour upsets the order essential to the organisation and demonstrates that statistics (the product of labour and money, and a source of authority for the UNHCR) do not in fact reflect reality as accurately as the organisation claims; they offer only an illusion of legibility and control of migrants. UNHCR staff tend to make a moral judgement, criticising those who receive aid without entitlement as 'cheats' who abuse aid, or as ungrateful (Bakewell 2000b: 104; Harrell-Bond 2002: 58; Malkki 1996: 383). The pejorative terms 'recyclers' (used to describe people who resorted to the repatriation programme several times over) or, in Europe, 'bogus asylum seekers' (for those who make an application for asylum when they are 'manifestly ineligible') offers further evidence of this.

Similarly, political authorities and projects other than those of the state – categorised indiscriminately as 'nonstate actors' – are seen only as potential vectors of persecution rather than orders or actors that could provide a form of protection (UNHR 2007c: 7). For example, Afghans' ethnicity is a factor that the UNHCR associates primarily with the risk of persecution arising from interethnic conflict and the existence of minorities. Clandestine migration channels are seen purely as potential sources of vulnerability or even persecution, and migration that does not conform with state laws as a phenomenon to be reduced and discouraged (UNHCR 2005d, 2006c).

This attitude reveals the UNHCR's incapacity either to value the strategies of its recipients or to recognise the constraints that may derive from its own activity. From this point of view, while it is true that the authors of the ACSU project saw mobility as a resource and sought to facilitate it, their approach remained strictly state- and nation-centred. The absence of state control was seen purely as a shortcoming. The presence of the state and controls became an end in itself, giving rise to paradoxical statements like the following, from a study commissioned by the UNHCR: 'The main obstacle at the border is currently the lack of a systematic implementation mechanism for counting and screening individuals crossing the border' (Altai Consulting 2009: 5).

Seeing protection as the exclusive domain of the state prevents the UNHCR from taking into account the nonstate actors and fields that structure migrants' strategies and the constraints states may impose on them. The result is ultimately a failure to reflect on the paradoxical effects of its activity: in order to resolve the 'refugee problem', the UNHCR strives to make operative the national order that is itself at the root of the 'problem'. This is a sedentary order that controls the relationship between individuals and territories according to the criterion of nationality. While this is the order on which the UNHCR's mission and existence rest, it also enables states to erect substantial obstacles to movement. The administrative surveillance mechanisms analysed here thus ultimately form part of a mechanism that operates to emplace Afghan migrants in Afghanistan (seen as their only legitimate place of existence in the world) and to illegalise their movement (the boundary between legality and illegality is introduced and rendered more effective in a situation where the possibilities of legal movement are minimal). Afghans are thus incorporated into the national order, but in a marginal position that heavily restricts migration strategies.

Notes

1. In this respect, Sadiq talks of 'documentary citizenship' (Sadiq 2009) and Bakewell of 'handheld nationality' (Bakewell 2007).
2. An unpublished 2005 study by the IOM cites more than 25,000 individuals passing through the Torkham crossing each day. The UNHCR, which recorded the number of crossings once a month in 2007, reported even higher numbers (UNHCR 2007p). Studies confirm the absence of checks, even at the main border crossings (Geda 2011: 25; Monsutti 2004: 197).
3. See, for example, the entry 'special needs', which included the categories 'woman at risk', 'child at risk', 'unaccompanied child', 'important medical condition' and 'special legal and physical protection' (SAFRON, NADRA and UNHCR 2007).
4. Indeed, if the number of those who had taken up the repatriation programme since March 2002 is added to those counted in the census, the figure is over five million – substantially more than the UNHCR's 2002 estimate suggested.
5. The situation thus came to resemble what I have already described in Iran: the Afghan population was now divided into a population that was correctly documented, visible to institutions, and enjoyed relatively preferential treatment, and a population in an irregular situation. This division was not based on assessment of 'protection needs'.
6. The discussion here concerns only Pakistan, but the repatriation programme from Iran was similar.
7. From 2007 onwards, the issue of the Voluntary Repatriation Form required the cancellation of the PoR card.
8. The aid provided included an amount to cover travel expenses and a sum to support resettlement.
9. See Article 1 of the 2005 Afghan census.
10. Kelly and Kaplan's work (2001) on the decolonisation of Fiji is a notable exception: they emphasise the role of the UN in promoting the nation-state as the model of modernity and highlight the logics of postcolonial domination at work.
11. A comparison with migration to Europe is illuminating. While within the Iran-Afghanistan-Pakistan region, border crossings were often made by van on secondary tracks, using Pashtun or Baloch smugglers and with few intermediaries (Geda 2011; Monsutti 2005), some Afghans then travelled to Europe hidden under lorries or in containers (Bathaïe 2008; Geda 2011). These journey conditions sometimes put migrants' life in danger, as indicated by the number of those who drowned at sea or suffocated in containers.
12. See also Dauvergne's work (2008) on the role of international law in the illegalisation of migrants.

Conclusion

On a trip to Greece in the summer of 2008, a few months after leaving my post in Kabul, I visited an unofficial camp that had arisen on the outskirts of the port of Patras. It was home to young Afghans waiting for the right moment to cross the Adriatic Sea by clinging to the underside of lorries driving onto the ferry, in the hope of reaching Western or Northern Europe. Having entered the European Union by way of a perilous crossing of the Aegean Sea, they were keen to leave Greece, where the economic crisis was deepening and xenophobia was rising, as soon as possible. It was here that there began the long process of distancing whereby I moved from my initial enthusiastic support of the ACSU project to resituating it in its context of production and implementation, and using it as a heuristic tool with which to analyse the UNHCR and its work.

In Patras I realised for the first time that the existence of a 'comprehensive' strategy in Asia was the counterpart to the system of selection at European borders. Not without surprise, I realised that throughout my posting in Geneva and the year spent in Kabul, I had never thought about the situation of Afghans in Europe and the relationship between the UNHCR's policies in Europe and Asia. I had remained enclosed in a cognitive framework that I had internalised and that induced me to see the migration of Afghans to Europe as 'secondary movements', to perceive 'South-West Asia' as the only true geographical context of the 'Afghan refugee problem', to view repatriation and reintegration in Afghanistan as legitimate key concerns, and the ACSU project as the only solution, unfortunately jeopardised by the attitude of the Iranian and Pakistani authorities.

Leaving the organisation and considering the issue of 'Afghan displacement' from the vantage point of Greece thus opened up the way for reflection that enabled me to recognise how Afghans' migrations are shaped by a highly restrictive mechanism, of which UNHCR programmes are a part. The deportations from Iran, the closure of the camps in Pakistan, and the land allocation programme analysed in this volume show that ultimately the UNHCR is unable to mitigate the arbitrariness and violence to which Afghan non-nationals are subjected by states. The organisation is therefore itself induced to regulate the relationship between people and territories in accordance with the nation-state logic, becoming part of a mechanism structured around emplacement in Afghanistan, illegalisation of international migration of Afghans, and the containment of that movement within the Iran-Afghanistan-Pakistan region.

The emplacement of returnees in Afghanistan was instituted under pressure from the Iranian and Pakistani states, and it was legitimised by the bureaucratic production of the 'voluntariness' of repatriation. The UNHCR's process was centred, financially and administratively, on Afghan territory – the only portion of the planet deemed the legitimate place of residence of Afghans. Here the organisation sought to implant returnees at any cost, in a project funded by donors and implemented in collaboration with dozens of NGOs. International migration was illegalised through the establishment of systems of surveillance and control of Afghan non-nationals (censuses, issue of residence permits and passports, border controls). Whilst they were presented as ways to 'regularise' Afghan presence in Iran and Pakistan, these measures were in fact introduced in a way that encouraged repatriation, discouraged subsequent migration, and increased the costs and risks of any movement undertaken outside this framework. Finally, the containment of Afghans in the region, sought by European countries and consistent with the objectives pursued by the UNHCR in 'South-West Asia' and at the gates of Europe, removed any legal way to reach Europe: an Afghan who wanted to go to a European country and obtain refugee status there had to take a new clandestine route, which was much more costly and dangerous than those within the region.

Assessing the ACSU Project

In this volume I have shown how the ACSU project encountered various obstacles, both internal and external, that prevented it from making any major change to the UNHCR's sedentary, state-centred worldview. Within the organisation, it was contested, and its implementation generated a great deal of tension. And even when Saverio and Eric arrived in Kabul in early 2007, despite the new impetus that this gave to the long-term strategy, it was relegated to the background amid the emergencies of camp closures, deportations and the rise of violence in Afghanistan. The longer-term promotion of the project remained on the 'back burner'; it continued to be partially detached from other programmes and occupied only a tiny part of its authors' time and energy. They themselves had to admit that the times were not conducive to the achievement of their vision.

Externally, the steps taken to advance the project were blocked by the wall of Iranian and Pakistani state sovereignty. The UNHCR's expert discourse came up against the arbitrary power to manage immigration that states enjoy in the interstate arena. The results of the UNHCR's negotiations with the Iranian and Pakistani authorities were modest. The latter refused to revise their official position that all Afghans should leave their territory. They thus made any discussion or agreement conditional on completion of the repatriation programme, at a time when their policies were becoming increasingly aggressive and restrictive.

While Afghan mobility was an idea that met with little acceptance, my study also reveals that the ACSU project was in fact less innovative than it appears at first sight. It claimed to promote a different conception of mobility, but without questioning the episteme of the national order, thus incorporating the nation- and state-centred bias at the heart of the organisation's thinking. Ultimately, the ACSU project did not challenge either the relationship between people and territories assumed by the nation-state order or the logic whereby finding a solution involves promoting the effective incorporation of 'displaced' people into a state's jurisdiction. Mobility is thinkable provided that it is regulated and controlled by states. Thus, the project ultimately recommended more regulation and more management – and hence more control – of migrants by states, despite the fact that these states were adopting an overtly repressive approach. Even though the project advocated recognising the agency of Afghan migrants, it continued to treat them as victims and failed citizens. Other sociopolitical orders, such as the tribal order, were not considered to be on an equal footing with the state order, despite the fact that they have a real impact on the lives of Afghans, sometimes greater than that of the state. Analysis of this project thus confirms that institutions influence, frame and very often hamper reforms by restricting the space of the thinkable and defining their repertoire of action (Bezes and Le Lidec 2010).

To this should be added the function of this relatively innovative EU-funded project, given the aim of European countries' to curb Afghan migration. By confining to the regional space the movement that it recommended accepting as inevitable and by limiting its applications to only the Iranian and Pakistani authorities, the project contributed to the containment and illegalisation of extraregional migration, in contradiction with its declared principles and objectives. The fact that the innovative solutions proposed applied only to the region distracted attention from extraregional migration and from the ultimately highly accommodating position the organisation took in relation to European states.

Subsequently, the project was very quickly discontinued. After 2008, the ACSU venture was gradually wound down, and with it the challenge it raised to the organisation's thinking. In mid-2008, Saverio, learning that he was soon to be a father, left Afghanistan for a senior post in a calmer capital. Eric would remain at the helm of the Afghan Operation for two further years. In 2010, under the rotation system, he returned to Geneva, where he took up a senior post, but was no longer involved in the Afghan crisis. The strategy developed by the new leadership in Kabul was presented at a conference two years later (UNHCR 2012). The theme of mobility had completely disappeared, and there was an even stronger emphasis on repatriation as the 'most preferred solution' and on reintegration. The geopolitical context of the 2010s, marked by the gradual disengagement of donor countries from Afghanistan, helped to discourage any urge to put these ideas into practice.

The initiative led by the director of the Policy Development and Evaluation Service between 2007 and 2010 might have enabled the ACSU project to continue. As noted in Chapter 2, this initiative sought to shift the position of the UNHCR, international organisations and states in regard to refugee mobility. In the autumn of 2007, donor states and others gathered at a forum in Geneva. Drawing on the work of researchers (Betts 2010b; Crisp 2008; Long 2009, 2010), the strategy documents presented by the UNHCR proposed approaching mobility as an 'inevitable human phenomenon', inviting those present to think of 'migration as a solution', and even referred to 'freedom of movement' and the need to ensure that the rights of undocumented migrants were respected (UNHCR 2007o, 2007r, 2007s, 2008c). It was in this context that the ACSU project was promoted as never before, that anthropologist Monsutti's articles were extensively cited, and that studies on Afghans in Europe were commissioned (Cipullo and Crisp 2010; Mougne 2010; UNHCR 2010). But the reluctance of state representatives, the competition among international organisations and the retirement a few years later of the director who had promoted the initiative resulted in an institutional impasse.

Should the decline of the ACSU project be seen as a failure? Those who hoped for a radical reform of the organisation's policy view it as one. But it can be assessed differently if we consider the functions that this project performed in the careers of its authors and for the organisation. While the project's career ended after eight years, those of Saverio and Eric continued, leading both of them to occupy the most senior positions at UNHCR headquarters a few years later. The ACSU project thus benefited them in the internal competition for jobs. Certainly, their main springboard was the leadership posts they had held in the regional operation, but the ACSU project played a decisive role in distinguishing them as competent, committed and proactive professionals. They certainly took a risk in addressing the issue of mobility head-on, but this was a calculated risk (particularly given that the ACSU project was presented as a pragmatic solution to a specific problem) and ultimately paid off. Moreover, in Kabul, while they did not disown their ideas, they proved themselves aware and respectful of the limits imposed by the institutional order. Bringing their ideas to completion would have prevented them from fulfilling the institution's expectations.

Furthermore, the ACSU project enabled the UNHCR to present itself as a dynamic organisation capable of innovating and welcoming reforming projects – an organisation that was reflective and in permanent contact with the world of research (see, for example, Long and Crisp 2010). This image is of great value for an intergovernmental organisation that aspires to remain influential on the world stage.

The ACSU project also played an important role in my own career. Being associated with an unorthodox project that valued academic research, and believing in its innovative impact, enabled me to obtain a post in the organisation where I could reconcile a critical approach with commitment, and they legitimised this decision in the eyes of a number of interlocutors (researchers, NGOs, activists, asylum seekers and refugees) who were highly critical of the organisation.

The Implantation of the National Order and the Paradoxes of the UNHCR

The uncertain future of sites for landless returnees, the violence exerted through camp closures in Pakistan and deportations from Iran, and the restrictions that force Afghans to travel at risk of their lives if they wish to reach Europe raise serious questions about the relationship among people, territories and states that forms the core of the national order. As surplus humanity produced by the national order, the figure of the refugee reveals the flaws in, and the inequitable nature of, that order. As Agamben and, before him, Hannah Arendt (1951) point out, because they breach the alignment between a person and a citizen, the refugee is 'a border concept that radically calls into question the principles of the nation-state and, at the same time, helps clear the field for a no-longer-delayable renewal of categories' (Agamben 1995: 117).

What is problematic about the figure of the refugee is not only their destitution, but the larger, highly symbolic danger that it represents for the national order by pointing out its limits.

Far from challenging the national order, the UNHCR's activity reinforces it and makes it more fully functional. This activity, which is structured by a state-centred, sedentary mentality and dedicated to creating a physical and legal place for refugees within states (conceived as nation-states), has the effect of implanting the national order. Acting on states, migrants and collective imaginaries, the UNHCR's interventions imprint the national order on the world, at both the material and symbolic levels.

I have examined this process of establishment of the national order at work from various angles, such as when I considered the type of state promoted by UNHCR programmes in Pakistan and Afghanistan: a liberal-democratic, law-based state with absolute power that works through the production and application of the law, a state endowed with administrative surveillance mechanisms that enable it to distinguish between nationals and non-nationals. I have also noted this process in the habitus of the UNHCR expatriate staff, whose points of reference and sociopolitical allegiances are defined in relation to a national order seen as the normal state of affairs, even when they oppose it. Thus, through their lifestyle and their professional practices, the international officers of the UNHCR reproduce and reinforce the principle of nationality, the myth of state sovereignty and the sacredness of national law. I have also pointed out the transformative power of the categories, modelled on the national order, through which the UNHCR grasps and defines phenomena and problems: by structuring knowledge and action, these categories actively transform the populations and political systems with which the UNHCR intervenes, and they also influence the imaginaries of thousands of officers and observers. Finally, and more fundamentally, we have seen that the production of a population of 'refugees' – through the mechanisms of selection, identification, enumeration, attribution of status and issue of documents – in order to render it tangible and govern it, makes the national order more effective. As a corollary of the distinction between nationals and non-nationals, the figure of the 'refugee' is an integral part of that order, and the exception that the UNHCR advocates for refugees validates, consolidates and reasserts it.

Thus, the organisation maintains the sedentary, statist order that lies at the heart of the 'refugee problem' it is supposed to resolve. The UNHCR's repertoire of action thus incorporates a structural limitation on how it approaches mobility. Incorporating 'displaced' Afghans into the national order means restricting their movement and their access to transnational resources, despite the fact that this movement and these resources continue to be crucial not only for the survival of these populations but also for the viability of the Afghan state. It is clear that the 'refugee problem' is defined *by states* as a problem *for states* caused by the presence of undesirable non-nationals. These people, who are often undesirable and mobile, are destined to remain surplus, to not 'fit' into the national order, making the 'problem' insoluble.

The national order is not only at the root of this major structural limitation on the UNHCR's activity; it is also the foundation of the organisation, which continues in existence and grows in authority. Without it, there would be neither refugees nor the UNHCR; with it, on the other hand, the UNHCR sees its work guaranteed and its existence legitimised. The insolubility of the 'refugee problem' ensures the need for the UNHCR. Through measures aimed at reinstating the national order, the state of exception of the 'refugee' is normalised. My analysis thus shows why, despite the jargon and practices that focus on emergency, exception and the temporary nature of programmes, the 'refugee' has become a standard feature of the contemporary international order. 'Refugee situations' have proliferated throughout the world. The Afghan case resonates with other 'insoluble' situations, from the longstanding case of the Palestinians to the more recent plight of the Syrians.

My analysis highlights the fundamental paradox underpinning the UNHCR's activity, but it also reveals the influence of the nation-based thinking that continues to shape the world and justify political action that is no longer under the sway of state elites, but operates through the work of the staff of international organisations, and no longer with the aim of establishing a particular state regime, but rather as an ideology and a technique to govern the world's population. In this regard, the promotion of the national order has two significant effects on the UNHCR's activity.

First, this study shows that the implantation of the national order promoted by the UNHCR makes it contribute to the hegemonic liberal project. The type of state put forward as the model for how the world should operate is that of the nation-state as developed in the liberal democracies of Europe and North America. This view makes it difficult to see not only nonstate forms of political organisation, but also other ways to manage a state as equally legitimate. Self-determination is conceived only in terms of nationality and democracy. This effectively turns a particularism, a vernacular political model (what the Comaroffs call 'Euromodernity' (2012)), into a universalism. It is in this way that the UNHCR supports the liberal model's claim to superiority and its use as a measure of civilisation. The equality among the states of the world that is in principle at the basis of the UN's work is in fact replaced by a hierarchy between those countries that can claim the authorship and exemplariness of the liberal-democratic political system, and those that are inadequate and in need of therapeutic and normalising interventions. I have shown, for example, that by aligning itself with the reconstruction project in Afghanistan, the UNHCR contributed to defining the Afghan state as inferior, marginal, incapable of governing and maintaining order, thereby justifying external intervention. Similarly, I have examined the different standards that the UNHCR applies in its relations with the Iranian and Pakistani states, which it asks to radically alter their policies, and European countries, which it considers as a whole to be champions of human rights capable of managing their immigration policies.

Second, the gap between the nation-state model and the particular political and social characteristics of the contexts in which the UNHCR intervenes –

a gap that is very rarely taken into account within the organisation – explains the profound changes and the risks of destabilisation resulting from the UNHCR's activity in those contexts. Although the nation-state model has spread far and wide and has proved to be adaptable (Anderson 2006), many states, including Iran, Afghanistan and Pakistan, operate in a partially different way. Thus, the implantation of the nation-state may in fact involve substantial engineering that can give rise to major sociopolitical reconfigurations. I have demonstrated this in the case of Afghanistan, whose state authorities are torn between internal and external criteria of legitimacy.

Moreover, the inability to recognise the legitimacy of forms of political organisation other than the nation-state is a second paradox in regard to the UNHCR. The increasing number of attacks on its staff, and the security rationale that now governs the organisation's presence not only in Afghanistan but also in many other regions of the world, suggest that the UNHCR's political and epistemic position, and its incapacity to recognise and take responsibility for it, may be detrimental to it and generate insoluble conflicts of legitimacy.

The Perilous Path of an Immanent Bureaucracy in the World

Following the trajectory of the ACSU project also enabled me to observe the operation of the UNHCR from within. I conceptualised it as a ramified, polymorphous apparatus, shaped by its contexts of intervention and embedded in power relations that extended beyond it and framed its repertoire of action, its room for manoeuvre and its range of options. This is far from the image of the organisation presented in normative approaches, and by the UNHCR itself, which primarily emphasise its coherence and verticality.

Rather than being a monolithic body, the UNHCR apparatus only exists by virtue of a multitude of offices and officials, among whom negotiations and tensions are omnipresent. Hence, its operation often requires achieving a compromise among different conceptions of problems and priorities. The organisation is enmeshed in diverse realities, systems of meaning, and power relations that shape its various offices. Each of these offices is engaged in a particular arena where it must establish its legitimacy and develop the global project of an organisation whose activity has to be viable everywhere – in Kabul, Islamabad, Brussels, Geneva, Peshawar and Jalalabad – and for all its interlocutors. I have described, for example, the severe tensions that arose between the Kabul and Islamabad offices, and how the concept of 'voluntary return' was stretched to the limits of contradiction in an attempt to reconcile the Pakistani authorities' pressure for return and Afghanistan's capacity for hosting. Rather than being an institutional reality, unity (of the UNHCR as a collective actor acting with a single purpose and speaking with one voice) is a representation and an objective sought by the institution.

The alleged verticality of the UNHCR (the conception of the organisation as acting from a position of transcendence, like a *deus ex machina*, from the elevated sphere of the international arena) is also a representation that bases its claims on neutrality and global encompassment. It derives from the organisation's links with the state system and its conception of power, in which the state is the fundamental actor and form of political organisation. Observing the UNHCR in action in fact reveals an organisation in a position of immanence in, rather than exteriority to, the world. It is embedded in it, not only from the spatial point of view, by the territorialised islets of its offices, but also because each office is an integral part of a particular arena. In its way, the UNHCR has an osmotic relationship with the world, in the sense that its deployment and its interventions are shaped, from the inside, by its contexts of intervention and its interlocutors.

I have shown, for example, the extent to which a set of power relations over which the organisation has no control, structured primarily by the United States' 'war on terror' and the marginal and subaltern position of Afghanistan in the interstate system, restricts and shapes the UNHCR's activity in Afghanistan. The organisation is caught up in an irresolvable conflict of legitimacy: by aligning itself with the international project of 'state-building', it forgoes the support of the Taliban and therefore access to half of the country. While in 2001 these power relations offered the organisation plenty of room for manoeuvre, this was reduced to a minimum after 2007. The UNHCR was then forced to make difficult compromises and resort to extreme measures – issuing a press release threatening to condemn violation of the 'voluntary nature' of return, the decision to embark on an audacious programme of land allocation to returnees, and resignation in the face of European countries' restrictive migration policies.

Several researchers who have studied the UNHCR point out, often using corporeal metaphors, that a number of aims coexist in tension. Verdirame and Harrell-Bond (2005) define the UNHCR's activity as 'Janus-faced' – one face turned towards states, the other towards refugees. Barnett speaks of the 'sovereign face' of the UNHCR, emphasising the difficulty the organisation has in freeing itself from the supervision of states, and suggests it has two 'hands' – one working on behalf of refugees and the other against them (Barnett 2001: 246). My work suggests pushing this polymorphism further: the organisation has as many facets as it has offices (or even officials) who think and express themselves in their own context.

The diffuse, multiscalar nature of the UNHCR provides opportunities to act, but also imposes constraints. In his book on the history of the UNHCR, Gil Loescher (2001a) uses the term 'perilous path' to evoke this choice between seeking room for manoeuvre and dependence on power relations between states. This is an appropriate image with which to describe the subtle balance that the institution has to maintain in order to stay on the scene and establish its authority in the contemporary world. But my study offers a more nuanced account of the shifting waters the UNHCR must navigate. Interstate relations are in fact just one of the many elements in the constant pull of contradictory priorities that the UNHCR as institution has to balance and manage.

First, the organisation has to show that its activity is appropriate, necessary and successful, despite the fundamental paradox that underpins its mission and makes any resolution of the 'refugee problem' illusory. But it must also ensure that its activity is viable in multiple arenas, engaging with a vast number of actors, while at the same time establishing its own legitimacy and its reputation on multiple levels. Another discrepancy arises in the UNHCR's quest for institutional consistency and unity (both internally and in the way in which it represents itself and its work), which is countered by inconsistencies and disconnections in its practice, and by the multiple faces and voices that it adopts in different contexts. I have also shown that as a global bureaucracy, the UNHCR has to deal with the disparity between an order in which reality must be represented as manageable (a 'disorder that can be put in order') and the complexity of a reality that evades standardised categorisations owing to the incommensurable specificities of diverse contexts of intervention.

My study has focused particularly on a central tension underlying the UNHCR's activity, a tension that derives from the organisation's interstate character. Although it is designed to transcend this system, the latter inevitably shape its repertoire of action. Thus, the organisation stands in opposition to the system from which it originates, within which its mandate has meaning, and which circumscribes and shapes its authority and its actions. The UNHCR's repertoire is inextricably entangled with the interstate system: states are not only its primary interlocutors, but also the basis on which it defines itself, understands the world and grounds its claims to universalism, encompassment, neutrality and moral superiority. This explains the deep and complex interweaving of the state and interstate dimensions. Because the UNHCR strives to influence state policy on non-nationals, relations between the organisation and its state interlocutors are often confrontational. But the state is ultimately reasserted and reinforced by the state-centred activity of the UNHCR, which is the first to recognise its ultimate power. States remain the organisation's primary interlocutors, the only actors it believes capable of providing protection for populations – to the extent that the UNHCR reinforces the myth of state sovereignty and reproduces, extends and implants the state regime on both the material and symbolic levels.

In order to prosper and to maintain its authority, the UNHCR must somehow manage these dilemmas and discrepancies, either by attempting at any cost to reconcile contradictory priorities, imperatives and constraints or by concealing their irreconcilability. The organisation has to demonstrate that its mission is relevant and its interventions are successful. It must give the illusion of managing reality, of being able to deal with difference. It must show that it has the capacity to influence states' policies while respecting the principle of state sovereignty. It must give an impression of consistency and unity. In short, it must constantly re-establish itself and continually recreate its myth.

The procedures through which the UNHCR apparatus is organised (including the combination of local and expatriate staff, the production of standards) are conceived precisely in order to manage complexity and ensure internal consistency. The distributed nature of this apparatus is such that its activity takes place in multiple arenas on multiple scales: no single instance encompasses it or can give a sense of the global scope of its work. Consequently, the UNHCR has, if not the monopoly, at least an 'oligopoly' over discourse about its activities and their effects, whence derive the mechanisms of depoliticisation that cloak the organisation's initiatives in technicality, but conceal or absorb frictions and paradoxes while legitimising its activity. Moreover, the UNHCR has powerful frames of reference that are already hegemonic in the contemporary world. The ACSU project also evidences the organisation's ongoing capacity to adapt and adjust, as demonstrated by its constant search for new conceptual and operational tools, and particularly its capacity to channel its policies in directions that are both feasible and innovative.

In the early 2020s, the UNHCR remains a key international organisation, still expanding, constantly sought-out and cited, and that young graduates dream of joining. Its 'success' thus needs to be reconsidered in these terms: it is not so much the resolution of the 'refugee problem' by way of a suitable strategy, but the fact that the UNHCR manages to travel the 'perilous path' that enables it to continue to exist, to reproduce the system in which it can exist, and thus to continue to exert authority in the contemporary world. The impossibility for the organisation to achieve its stated mission, which is kept in the background and reformulated in positive terms, justifies its tenacity in achieving all that 'remains to be done' and addressing the 'challenges ahead'.

Glossary

Absorption capacity: an expression used by UNHCR employees with regard to Afghanistan to describe the number of returnees that the country can accommodate.

Advocacy: raising awareness and advocating (or refugees).

Branch Office: a UNHCR office that heads a 'Country Operation'.

Briefing kit: a folder containing documents of various types (statistics, reports, maps, budgets, etc.) that aims to provide concise but exhaustive key information on a given case or context, offering an overview.

Bureau: an administrative unit of the UNHCR within the Department of Operations, combining several Desks.

Capacity building: work to support an institution perceived to be operating poorly.

Country Operation: the basic unit of UNHCR deployment in the world.

Desk: an administrative unit of the UNHCR within the Department of Operations, serving as a link between sections at Headquarters and offices in the field.

Discussion paper: a paper (often internal) written to launch a strategy discussion on a given theme.

Displacement: an expression often used in formulating the 'problem' that the UNHCR's mission is to resolve. It conveys the idea of a place of origin from which a person has been separated against their will.

Durable solutions: the three traditional solutions to the refugee problem: repatriation, integration (in the first host country) and resettlement (in a third country).

Encashment Centres: centres that formed part of the repatriation programme in Afghanistan. Located on entry routes to the country, returnees received reintegration aid here.

Expats: the term used by expatriates on mission to describe themselves.

Failed asylum seeker: individuals who under procedures for determining refugee status have been designated ineligible for protection under the terms of the 1951 Convention.

Family duty station/nonfamily duty station: a classification that determines whether or not expatriates may be accompanied by their spouses.

Field: the zone of direct intervention with aid recipients.

Hardship allowance: added to the salaries of expatriate staff posted to missions in difficult contexts.

Hardship duty station: classification of a posting based on security conditions, isolation, etc.

Host country: in the UNHCR, a country in whose territory the organisation establishes an office.

International protection: the protection that should be granted to refugees under the 1951 Convention in order to mitigate the shortcomings of the state of nationality.

Mixed migration: migration combining migrants 'in need of protection' and those who do not need it.

Needs assessment: the process of analysing a situation in order to determine the intervention to be made.

People of concern: persons who come under the UNHCR's mandate.

Policy paper: strategy document.

Protection needs: what defines the refugee who has lost the protection of their state of nationality.

Protracted refugee situation: a specific context of displacement that has not been resolved after five years.

R&R (rest and recuperation leave): compulsory leave added to annual leave in order to take into account working conditions that are considered particularly stressful.

Refugee status determination: legal-administrative procedures designed to assess 'protection needs' and grant refugee status to those considered eligible.

Refugee studies: a field of academic research that emerged in the 1980s.

Returnee: a refugee who has returned to their country of origin through a repatriation programme.

Rotation: the process that underlies the UNHCR's operations, whereby expatriate staff circulate around the organisation's offices, in missions that last on average two years.

Secondary movements: an expression referring to people who arrive clandestinely in countries not contiguous with their country of origin, whose situation is such that they may be considered refugees.

Situational approach: in the context of the decentralisation process under way in the UNHCR in 2007, an approach that aims to create regional platforms so that decisions are taken closer to the field and to foster cohesion between operations involved in the same 'situation'.

Sub-Office: a UNHCR office accountable to a Branch Office.

Technical assistance: assistance provided by a specialist organisation to reinforce the institutional capacities of another organisation in a given domain.

References

Abbasi-Shavazi, Mohammad. 2005a. *Return to Afghanistan? A Study of Afghans Living in Tehran, Islamic Republic of Iran*. Kabul: Afghanistan Research and Evaluation Unit.
———. 2005b. *Return to Afghanistan? A Study of Afghans Living in Zahedan, Islamic Republic of Iran*. Kabul: Afghanistan Research and Evaluation Unit.
———. 2005c. *Return to Afghanistan? A Study of Afghans Living in Mashad, Islamic Republic of Iran*. Kabul: Afghanistan Research and Evaluation Unit.
Abbasi-Shavazi, Mohammad, and Diane Glazebrook. 2006. *Continued Protection, Reintegration: Afghan Refugees and Migrants in Iran*. Kabul: Afghanistan Research and Evaluation Unit.
Abbasi-Shavazi, Mohammad et al. 2008. *Second-Generation Afghans in Iran: Integration and Return*. Kabul: Afghanistan Research and Evaluation Unit.
Abélès, Marc. 1992. *La Vie Quotidienne au Parlement européen*. Paris: Hachette.
———. 1995. 'Pour une Anthropologie des Institutions', *L'Homme* 135: 65–85.
———. 2008. 'Michel Foucault, l'Anthropologie et la Question du Pouvoir', *L'Homme* 187–88: 105–22.
———. (ed.). 2011. *Des Anthropologues à l'OMC : Scènes de la Gouvernance Mondiale*. Paris: CNRS Editions.
Abou Zahab, Mariam. 2010. 'Frontières dans la Tourmente : La Talibanisation des Zones Tribales', *Outreterre* 24(1): 237–57.
Adelkhah, Fariba. 2007. 'Le Réveil de Khorassan : La Recomposition d'un Espace de Circulation', in Fariba Adelkah and Jean-François Bayart (eds), *Voyages du Développement : Émigration, Commerce, Exil*. Paris: Karthala, pp. 116–82.
———. 2013. 'Guerre et Terre en Afghanistan', *Revues des mondes musulmans et de la Méditerranée* 133: 19–41.
———. and Jean-François Bayart (eds). 2007. *Voyages du Développement : Émigration, Commerce, Exil*. Paris: Karthala.
Adelkhah, Fariba, and Zuzanna Olszewska. 2006. *Les Afghans Iraniens*. Paris: Sciences Po/ CERI, Les Études de CERI 125.
Adepoju, Aderanti, Alistair Boulton and Mariah Levin. 2007. 'Promoting Integration through Mobility: Free Movement and the ECOWAS Protocol', *New Issues in Refugee Research* 150. Retrieved 16 January 2023 from https://digitallibrary.un.org/record/627747?ln=fr.

Afghanistan Research and Evaluation Unit (AREU), and Collective for Social Science Research (CSSR). 2006. *Conference on Afghan Population Movements*. Islamabad.

Afghanistan Research and Evaluation Unit (AREU), and Ministry for Refugees. 2005. *Conference on Afghan Population Movements*. Kabul.

Afghanistan Research and Evaluation Unit (AREU), and UNHCR. 2007. 'Second-Generation Afghans in Neighbouring Countries: From Mohajer to Hamtawan?' Workshop, Kabul.

Aftab, Opel. 2005. *Bound for the City: A Study of Rural to Urban Labour Migration in Afghanistan*. Kabul: Afghanistan Research and Evaluation Unit.

Agamben, Giorgio. 1995. 'We Refugees', *Symposium* 49(2): 114–19.

———. 1998. *Homo Sacer: Sovereign Power and Bare Life*, trans. Daniel Heller-Roazen. Stanford: Stanford University Press.

———. 2005. *State of Exception*, trans. Kevin Attell. Chicago: University of Chicago Press.

———. 2009. *'What Is an Apparatus?' and Other Essays*, trans. David Kishik and Stefan Padatella. Stanford: Stanford University Press.

Agier, Michel. 2003. 'La Main Gauche de l'Empire : Ordre et Désordres de l'Humanitaire', *Multitudes* 11: 67–77.

———. 2008. *On the Margins of the World: The Refugee Experience Today*, trans. David Fernbach. Cambridge: Polity.

———. 2011. *Managing the Undesirables: Refugee Camps and Humanitarian Government*, trans. David Fernbach. Cambridge: Polity.

Altai Consulting. 2006. 'Integration of Returnees in the Afghan Labor Market'. Kabul.

———. 2009. 'Study on Cross-Border Population Movements between Afghanistan and Pakistan'. Kabul

Akoka, Karen. 2020. *L'Asile et l'Exil : Une Histoire de la Distinction Réfugiés/Migrants*. Paris: La Découverte.

Al-Ali, Nadje, and Khalid Koser (eds). 2002. *New Approaches to Migration? Transnational Communities and the Transformation of Home*. London: Routledge.

Ambrosetti, David, and Yves Buchet de Neuilly (eds). 2009. 'Organisations internationales et crises'. *Cultures et Conflits* 75: 7–14.

American Institute of Afghanistan Studies, and Hollings Center for International Dialogue. 2007. 'The Durand Line: History, Consequences, and Future'. Conference Report.

Anderson, Benedict. 2006. *Imagined Communities: Reflections on the Origin and Spread of Nationalism*, 2nd edn. London: Verso

Andrijasevic, Rutvica, and William Walters. 2010. 'The International Organization for Migration and the International Government of Borders', *Environment and Planning* 28: 977–99.

Arce, Alberto, and Norman Long. 1993. 'Bridging Two Worlds: An Ethnography of Bureaucrat-Peasant Relations in Western Mexico', in Mark Hobart (ed.), *An Anthropological Critique of Development: The Growth of Ignorance*. London: Routledge, pp. 179–210.

Arendt, Hannah. 2006. *Eichmann in Jerusalem: A Report on the Banality of Evil*. London: Penguin.

———. 2017. *The Origins of Totalitarianism*. London: Penguin

Atlani-Duhault, Laëtitia. 2005. *Au Bonheur des Autres : Anthropologie de l'Aide Humanitaire*. Paris: Éditions Société d'Ethnologie, Université Paris X.

Aymes, Marc. 2008. 'Affaires Courantes pour Marcheurs d'Empire : Le Métier d'Administrateur dans les Provinces Ottomanes au XIXe Siècle', *Genèses* 72: 4–25.

Bakewell, Oliver. 2000a. 'Repatriation and Self-Settled Refugees in Zambia: Bringing Solutions to the Wrong Problems', *Journal of Refugee Studies* 13(4): 356–73.

———. 2000b. 'Uncovering Local Perspectives on Humanitarian Assistance and its Outcomes', *Disasters* 24(2): 103–16.

———. 2007. *The Meaning and Use of Identity Papers: Handheld and Heartfelt Nationality in the Borderlands of North-West Zambia*. Oxford: International Migration Unit Working Paper.

———. 2010. 'Some Reflections on Structure and Agency in Migration Theory', *Ethnic and Migration Studies* 36(10): 1689–708.

Balibar, Étienne, and Immanuel Wallerstein. 1991. *Race, Nation, Class: Ambiguous Identities*. London: Verso.

Barfield, Thomas. 2010. *Afghanistan: A Cultural and Political History*. Princeton: Princeton University Press.

Barnett, Michael. 1997. 'The UN Security Council, Indifference and Genocide in Rwanda', *Cultural Anthropology* 12(4): 551–78

———. 2001. 'Humanitarianism with a Sovereign Face: UNHCR in the Global Undertow', *International Migration Review* 35(1): 244–77.

———. 2004. 'Defining Refugees and Voluntary Repatriation at UNHCR', in Michael Barnett and Martha Finnemore (eds), *Rules for the World: International Organizations in Global Politics*. New York: Cornell University Press, pp. 73–120.

Barnett, Michael, and Martha Finnemore. 2004. *Rules for the World: International Organizations in Global Politics*. New York: Cornell University Press

Barth, Fredrik. 1998. *Ethnic Groups and Boundaries: The Social Organization of Cultural Difference*. New York: Little Brown

Bathaïe, Azita. 2008. 'Casser les Frontières : Circulation et Mobilité des Jeunes Migrants Afghans depuis l'Iran jusqu'en France'. *Vivre et Tracer les Frontières dans les Mondes Contemporains*, Conference paper, Centre Jacques Berque, Tangiers, 31 January to 2 February 2008.

———. 2009. 'La Grèce, une Étape Cruciale dans le Parcours Migratoire des Afghans Depuis la Frontière Iranienne Jusqu'en Europe', *Méditerranée* 113: 71–77.

Bauman, Zygmunt. 1998. *Globalization: The Human Consequences*. Cambridge: Polity.

———. 2004. *Wasted Lives: Modernity and its Outcasts*. Cambridge: Polity.

Bayart, Jean-François. 1996. *L'Historicité de l'État Importé*. Paris: Les Cahiers du CERI 15.

———. 2004. *Le Gouvernement du Monde: Une Critique Politique de la Globalisation*. Paris: Fayard.

———. 2006. *L'État en Afrique: La Politique du Ventre*, 2nd edn. Paris: Fayard.

Beauguitte, Laurent. 2011. 'La Surprenante A-Spatialité des Bâtiments Onusiens'. Mensuelles. Retrieved 16 January 2023 from https://www.espacestemps.net/articles/la-surprenante-a-spatialite-des-batiments-onusiens/.

Beck, Ulrich. 2006. *The Cosmopolitan Vision*, trans. Ciaran Cronin. Cambridge: Polity

Becker, Howard. 1963. *Outsiders: Studies in the Sociology of Deviance*. New York: Free Press.

Bendix, Regina. 2012. 'Une Salle, Plusieurs Sites : Les Négotiations Internationales Comme Terrain de Recherche Anthropologique' *Critique Internationale* 1(54): 19–38.

Betts, Alexander. 2009a. *Forced Migration and Global Politics*. Hoboken: Wiley-Blackwell

———. 2009b. *Protection by Persuasion: International Cooperation in the Refugee Regime*. New York: Cornell University Press.

———. 2010a. 'Survival Migration: A New Protection Framework', *Global Governance: A Review of Multilateralism and International Organizations* 16(3): 361–82.

———. 2010b. 'The Refugee Regime Complex', *Refugee Survey Quarterly* 29(1): 12–37.

Bezes, Philippe, and Patrick Le Lidec. 2010. 'Ordre institutionnel et genèse des reformes', in Jacques Lagroye and Michel Offerlé (eds), *Sociologie de l'Institution*. Paris: Belin, pp. 55–74.

Bhabha, Jacqueline. 1998. 'Enforcing the Human Rights of Citizens and Non-citizens in the Era of Maastricht: Some Reflections on the Importance of States', *Development and Change* 29: 697–724.

Bhagwati, Jagdish. 2003. 'Borders beyond Control' *Foreign Affairs* 82(1): 98–104.

Bialczyk, Agata. 2008. *'Voluntary Repatriation' and the Case of Afghanistan: A Critical Examination*. Oxford: RSC Working Paper 46.

Bierschenk Thomas, Jean-Pierre Chauveau and Jean-Pierre Olivier de Sardan. 2000. 'Les Courtiers Entre Développement et État', in Thomas Bierschenk, Jean-Pierre Chauveau and Jean-Pierre Olivier de Sardan (eds), *Courtiers en Développement: Les Villages Africains en Quête de Projets*. Paris: Karthala, pp. 5–42.

Bigo, Didier, and Elspeth Guild. 2005. *Controlling Frontiers: Free Movement into and within Europe*. Aldershot: Ashgate.

Black, Richard. 2001. 'Fifty Years of Refugee Studies: From Theory to Policy', *International Migration Review* 35(1): 57–78.

Black, Richard, and Khalid Koser (eds). 1999. *The End of the Refugee Cycle? Refugee Repatriation and Reconstruction*. Oxford: Berghahn Books.

Blitz, Brad K., Rosemary Sales and Lisa Marzano. 2005. 'Non-voluntary Return? The Politics of Return to Afghanistan', *Political Studies* 53(1): 182–200.

Blundo, Giorgio. 1995. 'Les Courtiers du Développement en Milieu Rural Sénégalais', *Cahiers d'Études Africaines* 137: 73–99.

Boome, André, and Leonard Seabrooke. 2012. 'Seeing Like an International Organisation', *New Political Economy* 17(1): 1–16.

Bourdieu, Pierre. 1977. *Outline of a Theory of Practice*, trans. Richard Nice. Cambridge: Cambridge University Press.

———. 2003. 'Participant Observation', *Journal of the Royal Anthropological Institute* 9(2): 281–94.

Broeders, Dennis. 2007. 'The New Digital Borders of Europe: EU Databases and the Surveillance of Irregular Migrants'. *International Sociology* 22(1): 71–92.

Burawoy, Michael. 2000. 'Introduction: Reaching for the Global', in Michael Burawoy et al. (eds), *Global Ethnography: Forces, Connections, and Imaginations in a Postmodern World*. Berkeley: University of California Press, pp. 1–40.

———. 2001. 'Manufacturing the Global'. *Ethnography* 2(2): 147–59.

Carens, Joseph H. 1987. 'Aliens and Citizens: The Case for Open Borders', *Review of Politics* 49: 251–73

Cassarino, Jean-Pierre. 2004. 'Theorising Return Migration: The Conceptual Approach to Return Migrants Revisited', *International Journal on Multicultural Societies*, 6(2): 253–79.

Centlivres, Pierre. 1988. 'Les Trois Pôles de l'Identité Afghane au Pakistan', *L'Homme* 28(4): 134–46.

Centlivres, Pierre, and Micheline Centlivres-Demont. 1999. 'État, Islam et Tribus Face aux Organisations Internationales : Le Cas de l'Afghanistan 1978–1998', *Annales* 4: 945–65.

———. 2000. 'Exil et diaspora afghane en Suisse et en Europe', *Cahiers d'Études sur la Méditerranée Orientale et le Monde Turco-Iranien* 30: 151–71.

Chandler, David. 2006. *Empire in Denial: The Politics of State-Building*. London: Pluto Press.

Chimni, Bhupinder. 1998. 'The Geopolitics of Refugee Studies: A View from the South', *Journal of Refugee Studies* 11(4): 350–74.

———. 2004. 'From Resettlement to Involuntary Repatriation: Towards a Critical History of Durable Solutions to Refugee Problems', *Refugee Survey Quarterly* 23(3): 55–73.

Cipullo, Lucia, and Jeff Crisp. 2010. 'The Road from Kabul', *Forced Migration Review* 36: 65–66.

Cleton, Laura, and Sébastien Chauvin. 2019. 'Performing Freedom in the Dutch Deportation Regime: Bureaucratic Persuasion and the Enforcement of "Voluntary Return"', *Journal of Ethnic and Migration Studies* 46(1): 297–313.

Cling, Jean-Pierre, Mireille Razafindrakoto and François Roubaud. 2011. 'La Banque Mondiale, Entre Transformations et Résilience', *Critique internationale* 4(53): 43–65.

Coburn, Noah. 2016. *Losing Afghanistan: An Obituary for the Intervention*. Stanford: Stanford University Press.

Cole, Georgia. 2018. 'How Friends Become Foes: Exploring the Role of Documents in Shaping UNHCR's Behaviour', *Third World Quarterly* 39(8): 1491–507.

Collective for Social Science Research. 2005. *Afghans in Karachi: Migration, Settlement and Social Networks*. Kabul: Afghanistan Research and Evaluation Unit.

———. 2006a. *Afghans in Pakistan: Broadening the Focus*. Kabul: Afghanistan Research and Evaluation Unit.

———. 2006b. *Afghans in Quetta: Settlements, Livelihoods, Support Networks and Cross-Border Linkages*. Kabul: Afghanistan Research and Evaluation Unit

———. 2006c. *Afghans in Peshawar: Migration, Settlement and Social Networks*. Kabul: Afghanistan Research and Evaluation Unit

Coll, Steve. 2004. *Ghost Wars: The Secret History of the CIA, Afghanistan and Bin Laden, from the Soviet Invasion to September 10, 2001*. London: Penguin.

Comaroff, John, and Jean Comaroff J. 2012. *Theory from the South: Or, How Euro-America Is Evolving toward Africa*. London: Paradigm.

Crisp, Jeff. 1984. 'Voluntary Repatriation Programmes for African Refugees: A Critical Examination', *British Refugee Council Working Papers on Refugees* 1(2). Refugees Studies Programme, Queen Elizabeth House.

———. 1999a. 'Policy Challenges of the New Diasporas: Migrant Networks and Their Impact on Asylum Flows and Regimes', *New Issues in Refugee Research* 7. Policy Research Unit, UNHCR, Geneva.

———. 1999b. '"Who Has Counted the Refugees?" UNHCR and the Politics of Numbers', *New Issues in Refugee Research* 12. Policy Research Unit, UNHCR, Geneva.

———. 2003. 'A New Asylum Paradigm? Globalization, Migration and the Uncertain Future of the International Refugee Regime', *New Issues in Refugee Research* 100. Evaluation and Policy Analysis Unit, UNHCR, Geneva.

———. 2004. 'The Local Integration and Local Settlement of Refugees: A Conceptual and Historical Analysis', *New Issues in Refugee Research* 102. Evaluation and Policy Analysis Unit, UNHCR, Geneva.

———. 2008. 'Beyond the Nexus: UNHCR's Evolving Perspective on Refugee Protection and International Migration', *New Issues in Refugee Research* 155. Policy Development and Evaluation Service, UHNCR, Geneva.

———. 2017. 'Finding Space for Protection: An Inside Account of the Evolution of UN-HCR's Urban Refugee Policy', *Refuge* 33(1): 87–96.

Crisp, Jeff, and Damtew Dessalegne. 2002. 'Refugee Protection and Migration Management: The Challenge for UNHCR', *New Issues in Refugee Research* 64. Evaluation and Policy Analysis Unit, UNHCR, Geneva.

Daulatzai, Anila. 2006. 'Acknowledging Afghanistan: Notes and Queries on an Occupation', *Cultural Dynamics* 18(3): 293–311.

Dauvergne, Catherine. 2008. *Making People Illegal: What Globalization Means for Migration and Law.* New York: Cambridge University Press.

Dauvin, Pascal, and Johanna Siméant (eds). 2002. *Le Travail Humanitaire: Les Acteurs des ONG, du Siège au Terrain.* Paris: Presse de Sciences Po.

De Genova, Nicholas P. 2002. 'Migrant "Illegality" and Deportability in Everyday Life', *Annual Review of Anthropology* 31: 419–47.

De Guchteneire, Paul, and Antoine Pécoud (eds). 2008. 'La Convention des Nations Unies sur les Droits des Travailleurs Migrants. Enjeux et Perspectives', *Hommes & Migrations* 1271: 1–129.

Decorzant, Yann. 2011. 'La Société des Nations et l'Apparition d'un Nouveau Réseau d'Expertise Économique et Financière (1914–1923)', *Critique Internationale* 52: 35–50.

Dezalay, Yves. 2004. 'Les Courtiers de l'International : Héritiers Cosmopolites, Mercenaires de l'Impérialisme et Missionnaires de l'Universel', *Actes de la Recherche en Sciences Sociales* 1(151–52): 4–35.

Donini, Antonio. 2006. *Humanitarian Agenda 2015. Afghanistan Country Study.* Boston: Feinstein International Center Briefing Paper.

———. 2010a. 'The Far Side: The Meta Functions of Humanitarianism in a Globalised World', *Disasters* 43: 220–37.

———. 2010b. 'Between a Rock and a Hard Place: Integration or Independence of Humanitarian Action?', *International Review of the Red Cross* 93: 141–57.

Donini, Antonio, Alessandro Monsutti and Giulia Scalettaris. 2016. 'Seeking Protection and Refuge in Europe: Afghans on the Move in Europe'. Geneva: Graduate Institute of International and Development Studies, Global Migration Research Paper Series 17.

Douglas, Mary. 1986. *How Institutions Think.* Syracuse: Syracuse University Press.

Dubois, Vincent. 2012. 'Ethnographier l'Action Publique : Les transformations de l'État Social au Prisme de l'Enquête de Terrain', *Gouvernement et Action Publique* 1: 83–101.

Duffield, Mark. 2001. *Global Governance and the New Wars: The Merging of Development and Security.* New York: Zed Press.

———. 2008. 'Global Civil War: The Non-insured, International Containment and Post-interventionary Society', *Journal of Refugee Studies* 21(2): 145–65.

———. 2010. 'Risk-Management and the Fortified Aid Compound: Everyday Life in Post-interventionary Society', *Journal of Intervention and Statebuilding* 4(4): 453–74.

Dulong, Delphine. 2010. 'Au Dedans et en Dehors : La Subversion en Pratiques', in Jacques Lagroye and Michel Offerlé (eds), *Sociologie de l'Institution*. Paris: Belin, pp. 249–66.

Dupree, Louis. 1975. 'Settlement and Migration Patterns in Afghanistan: A Tentative Statement', *Modern Asian Studies* 9(3): 397–413.

Edwards, David B. 1986. 'Marginality and Migration: Cultural Dimensions of the Afghan Refugee Problem', *International Migration Review* 20(2): 313–25.

———. 1996. *Heroes of the Age: Moral Fault Lines on the Afghan Frontier*. Berkeley: University of California Press.

Engbersen, Godfried, and Dennis Broeders 2009. 'The State versus the Alien: Immigration Control and Strategies of Irregular Immigrants', *West European Politics* 32(5): 867–85.

European Commission. 2003. 'Toward More Accessible, Equitable and Managed Asylum Systems'. Communication from the Commission to the Council and the European Parliament, 3 June.

———. 2004. 'On the Managed Entry into the EU of Persons in Need of International Protection and the Enhancement of the Protection Capacity of the Regions of Origin: Improving Access to Durable Solutions'. Communication from the Commission to the Council and the European Parliament, 4 June.

———. 2005. 'On Regional Protection Programmes'. Communication from the Commission to the Council and the European Parliament, 1 September

Eyben, Rosalind. 2011. 'The Sociality of International Aid and Policy Convergence', in David Mosse (ed.), *Adventures in Aidland: The Anthropology of Professionals of International Development*. New York: Berghahn Books, pp. 139–60.

Farraj, Achraf. 2011. 'Refugees and the Biometric Future: The Impact of Biometrics on Refugees and Asylum Seekers', *Columbia Human Rights Law Review* 42(3): 891–941.

Fassin, Didier. 2018. *Life: A Critical User's Manual*. Cambridge: Polity

Feller, Erika. 2006. 'Asylum, Migration and Refugee Protection: Realities, Myths and the Promise of Things to Come'. *International Journal of Refugee Law* 18: 509–36.

Ferguson, James. 1994. *The Anti-politics Machine: 'Development', Depoliticization, and Bureaucratic Power in Lesotho*. Minneapolis: University of Minnesota Press.

———. 2006. *Global Shadows: Africa in the Neoliberal World Order*. Durham, NC: Duke University Press.

———, and Akhil Gupta. 2002. 'Spatializing States: Toward an Ethnography of Neoliberal Governmentality', *American Ethnologist* 29(4): 981–1002.

Fielden, Matthew B. 1998. 'The Geopolitics of Aid: The Provision and Termination of Aid to Afghan Refugees in the North West Frontier Province, Pakistan', *Political Geography* 17(4): 459–87.

Foucault, Michel. 1971. 'Orders of Discourse: Inaugural Lecture Delivered at the Collège de France', *Social Science Information* 10(2): 7–30.

———. 1979. *The History of Sexuality, Vol. 1: The Will to Knowledge*, trans. Robert Hurley. London: Allen Lane.

———. 1994. 'Le jeu de Michel Foucault', in *Dits et Écrits II*. Paris: Gallimard, pp. 298–329.

———. 1995. *Discipline and Punish: The Birth of the Prison*, trans. Alan Sheridan. London: Penguin.

———. 2009. *Sovereignty, Territory, Population: Lectures at the Collège de France, 1977–78*, trans. Graham Burchell. London: Palgrave Macmillan.

Fouilleux, Ève. 2009. 'À Propos de Crises Mondiales... Quel Rôle de la FAO Dans les Débats Internationaux sur les Politiques Agricoles?', *Revue Française de Science Politique* 4(59): 757–82.

Fresia, Marion. 2006. 'Des "Réfugiés-Migrants" : Les Parcours d'Exil des Réfugiés Mauritaniens au Sénégal'. *Esquisses 7*, TERRA-Editions. Retrieved 24 April 2023 from http://reseau-terra.eu/article540.html.

———. 2009a. *Les Mauritaniens Réfugiés au Sénégal : Une anthropologie Critique de l'Asile et de l'Aide Humanitaire*. Paris: L'Harmattan.

———. 2009b. 'L'Action du Haut Commissariat aux Réfugiés au Sénégal', *Tsantsa* 14: 17–26.

———. 2010. 'Une Élite Transnationale : La Fabrique d'une Identité Professionnelle Chez les Fonctionnaires du Haut Commissaire des Nations Unies aux Réfugiés', *Revue Européenne des Migrations Internationales* 25(3): 167–90.

———. 2012. 'La Fabrique des Normes Internationales sur la Protection des Réfugiés au Sein du Comité Exécutif du HCR', *Critique internationale* 54(1): 39–60.

———. 2018. 'Pourquoi les Institutions de l'Aide se Laissent-Elles Prendre pour Objet d'Étude?', in Philippe Lavigne Delville and Marion Fresia (eds), *Au Cœur des Mondes de l'Aide: Regards et Postures Ethnographiques*. Paris: Karthala, pp. 41–74.

Fund for Peace. 2011. *The Failed States Index 2011*. Washington, DC: Fund for Peace.

Garnier, Adele. 2014. 'Migration Management and Humanitarian Protection: The UN-HCR's "Resettlement Expansionism" and Its Impact on Policy-Making in the EU and Australia', *Journal of Ethnic and Migration Studies* 40(6): 942–59.

Geda, Fabio. 2011. *In the Sea There Are Crocodiles: The Story of Enaiatollah Akbari*, trans. Howard Curtis. London: Harvill Secker.

Gehrig, Tina, and Alessandro Monsutti. 2003. 'Territoires, Flux et Représentations de l'Exil Afghan : Le cas des Hazaras et des Kaboulis', *A Contrario* 1(1): 61–78.

Ghani, Ashraf, and Clare Lockhart. 2008. *Fixing Failed States: A Framework for Rebuilding a Fractured World*. Oxford: Oxford University Press.

Ghosh, Bimal. 1995. 'Movements of People: The Search for a New International Regime', in *Issues in Global Governance: Papers Written for the Commission on Global Governance*. The Hague: Kluwer Law International, pp. 405–24.

Ghufran, Nasreen. 2011. 'The Role of UNHCR and Afghan Refugees in Pakistan', *Strategic Analysis* 35(6): 945–54.

Gibney, Matthew J., and Randall Hansen. 2003. 'Deportation and the Liberal State', *New Issues in Refugee Research* 77. Evaluation and Policy Analysis Unit, UNHCR, Geneva.

Gilbert, Geoff. 1998. 'Rights, Legitimate Expectations, Needs and Responsibilities: UN-HCR and the New World Order', *Journal of Refugee Law* 10(3): 349–88.

Giustozzi, Antonio. 2007. *Koran, Kalashnikov and Laptop: The Neo-Taliban Insurgency in Afghanistan*. London: Hurst & Company.

Glasman, Joël. 2017. 'Seeing Like a Refugee Agency: A Short History of UNHCR Classifications in Central Africa (1961–2015)', *Journal of Refugee Studies* 30(2): 337–62.

Glazebrook, Diana, and Mohammad Abbasi Shavazi. 2007. 'Being Neighbours to Imam Reza: Pilgrimage Practices and Return Intentions of Hazara Afghans Living in Mashhad, Iran', *Iranian Studies* 40(2): 187–201.

Global Commission on International Migration. 2005. *Migration in an Interconnected World: New Directions for Action*. Report of the Global Commission on International Migration.

Grandi, Filippo. 2002. 'Hope on the Brink', *Forced Migration Review* 13: 11–13.

Grare Frédéric. 2003. 'The Geopolitics of Afghan Refugees in Pakistan', in Steven John Stedman and Fred Tanner (eds), *Refugee Manipulation: War, Politics, and the Abuse of Human Suffering*. Washington DC: Brookings Institution Press, pp. 57–94.

Green, Nile. 2008. 'Tribe, Diaspora, and Sainthood in Afghan History', *Journal of Asian Studies* 67(1): 171–211.

Greslier, Florence. 2007. 'La Commission des Recours des Réfugiés ou "l'Intime Conviction" Face au Recul du Droit d'Asile en France', *Revue Européenne des Migrations Internationales* 23(2): 107–33.

Guilhot, Nicholas. 2005. *The Democracy Makers: Human Rights and the Politics of Global Order*. New York: Columbia University Press

Gulbadan, Habibi, and Pamela Hunte. 2006. *Afghan Returnees from NWFP, Pakistan, to Nangarhar Province*. Kabul: Afghanistan Research and Evaluation Unit.

Gupta, Akhil, and James Ferguson. 1997a. 'Beyond "Culture": Space, Identity and the Politics of Difference', in Akhil Gupta and James Ferguson (eds), *Culture, Power, Place: Explorations in Critical Anthropology*. Durham, NC: Duke University Press: 6–23.

———. 1997b. *Anthropological Locations: Boundaries and Grounds of a Field Science*. Berkeley: University of California Press.

Gusfield, Joseph R. 1981. *The Culture of Public Problems: Drinking-Driving and the Symbolic Order*. Chicago: University of Chicago Press.

Habermas, Jürgen. 1998. 'The European Nation-State: On the Past and Future of Sovereignty and Citizenship', *Public Culture* 10(2): 397–416.

Haddad, Emma. 2008. *The Refugee in International Society:*

Hall, Nina. 2013. 'Moving beyond Its Mandate? UNHCR and Climate Change Displacement', *Journal of International Organizations Studies* 4(1): 91–108.

Hammerstad, Anne. 2014. *The Rise and Decline of a Global Security Actor: UNHCR, Refugee Protection and Security*. Oxford: Oxford University Press.

Hammond, Laura. 2004. *This Place Will Become Home: Refugee Repatriation to Ethiopia*. Ithaca: Cornell University Press.

Hanifi, Shah Mahmoud. 2008. *Connecting Histories in Afghanistan*. New York: Columbia University Press.

Hannerz, Ulf. 2004. 'Cosmopolitanism', in David Nugent and Joan Vincent (eds), *A Companion to the Anthropology of Politics*. Malden, MA: Blackwell, pp. 69–85.

Hansen, Thomas Blom, and Finn Stepputat. 2005. 'Introduction', in Thomas Blom Hansen and Finn Stepputat (eds), *Sovereign Bodies: Citizens, Migrants and the State in the Postcolonial World*. Princeton: Princeton University Press, pp. 1–38.

Harper, Ian. 2011. 'World Health and Nepal: Producing Internationals, Healthy Citizenship and the Cosmopolitan', in David Mosse (ed.), *Adventures in Aidland: The Anthropology of Professionals of International Development*. New York: Berghahn Books, pp. 123–38.

Harrell-Bond, Barbara. 1986. *Imposing Aid: Emergency Assistance to Refugees*. Oxford: Oxford University Press.

———. 1989. 'Repatriation: Under What Conditions Is It the Most Desirable Solution for Refugees? An Agenda for Research', *African Studies Review* 32(1): 41–69.

———. 2002. 'Can Humanitarian Work with Refugees be Human?', *Human Rights Quarterly* 24(1): 51–85.

Harrell-Bond, Barbara, Eftihia Voutira and Mark Leopold. 1992. 'Counting the Refugees: Gifts, Givers, Patrons and Clients', *Journal of Refugee Studies* 5: 205–25.

Helton, Arthur C. 2003. 'People Movement: The Need for a World Migration Organisation', *openDemocracy*. Retrieved 20 April 2023 from https://www.opendemocracy.net/en/people-movement-need-for-world-migration-organisation.

Herzfeld, Michael. 1992. *The Social Production of Indifference*. Chicago: University of Chicago Press.

Heyman, Josiah. 2001. 'Class and Classification at the U.S.-Mexico Border', *Human Organization* 60(1): 128–40.

Hibou, Béatrice. 1998. 'Retrait ou Redéploiement de l'État?', *Critique Internationale* 1: 151–68.

———. 2015. *The Bureaucratization of the World in the Neoliberal Era: An International and Comparative Perspective*, trans. Andrew Brown. Basingstoke: Palgrave Macmillan.

Hill, Matthew J. 2007. 'Reimagining Old Havana: World Heritage and the Production of Scale in Late Socialist Cuba', in Saskia Sassen (ed.), *Deciphering the Global: Its Scales, Spaces and Subjects*. New York: Routledge, pp. 59–78.

Hindess, Barry. 2000. 'Citizenship in the International Management of Populations', *American Behavioural Scientist*, 43(9): 1486–97.

———. 2002. 'Neoliberal Citizenship', *Citizenship Studies* 6(2): 127–43.

Hindman, Heather. 2007. 'Outsourcing Difference: Expatriate Training and the Disciplining of Culture', in Saskia Sassen (ed.), *Deciphering the Global: Its Scales, Spaces and Subjects*. New York: Routledge, pp. 155–78.

Hobbes, Thomas. 1996 [1651]. *Leviathan*. Cambridge: Cambridge University Press.

Hobsbawm, Eric. 1992. 'Ethnicity and Nationalism in Europe Today', *Anthropology Today* 8(1): 3–8.

Hobsbawm, Eric, and Terence Ranger. 1983. *The Invention of Tradition*. Cambridge: Cambridge University Press.

Holmes, Douglas R. 2009. 'Economy of Words', *Cultural Anthropology* 24(3): 381–419.

Horst, Cindy. 2006. *Transnational Nomads: How Somalis Cope with Refugee Life in the Dadaab Camps of Kenya*. Oxford: Berghahn Books.

Hull, Matthew H. 2012. *Government of Paper: The Materiality of Bureaucracy in Urban Pakistan*. Berkeley: University of California Press.

Human Rights Watch. 2007. 'Iran: Halt Mass Deportation of Afghans', 19 June. Retrieved 19 April 2023 from https://www.hrw.org/news/2007/06/19/iran-halt-mass-deportation-afghans.

Huttunen, Laura. 2010. 'Sedentary Policies and Transnational Relations: A "Non-sustainable" Case of Return to Bosnia', *Journal of Refugee Studies* 23(1): 41–61.

Hyndman, Jennifer. 2000. *Managing Displacement: Refugees and the Politics of Humanitarianism*. Minneapolis: University of Minnesota Press.

Islamic Republic of Afghanistan. 2008. 'Afghan National Development Strategy 2008–2013', Kabul.

Jacobsen, Katja Lindskov. 2010. 'Making Design Safe for Citizens: A Hidden History of Humanitarian Experimentation', *Citizenship Studies* 14(1): 89–103.

Jacobsen, Katja Lindskov, and Kristin Bergtora Sandvik. 2018. 'UNHCR and the Pursuit of International Protection: Accountability through Technology?' *Third World Quarterly* 39(8): 1508–24.

Joppke, Christian. 1998. 'Why Liberal States Accept Unwanted Immigration', *World Politics* 50(2): 266–93.

Karatani, Rieko. 2005. 'How History Separated Refugee and Migrant Regimes: In Search of Their Institutional Origins', *International Journal of Refugee Law* 17(3): 517–41.

Kelly, John D., and Martha Kaplan. 2001. *Represented Communities: Fiji and World Decolonization*. Chicago: University of Chicago Press.

Koepke, Bruce. 2011. 'The Situation of Afghans in the Islamic Republic of Iran Nine Years after the Overthrow of the Taliban Regime in Afghanistan'. Middle East Institute, Fondation pour la Recherche Stratégique.

Kott, Sandrine. 2011. 'Les Organisations Internationales, Terrains d'Étude de la Globalisation: Jalons pour une Approche Socio-Historique', *Critique Internationale* 3(52): 9–16.

Kronenfeld, Daniel A. 2008. 'Afghan Refugees in Pakistan: Not All Refugees, Not Always in Pakistan, Not Necessarily Afghan?', *Journal of Refugee Studies* 21(1): 43–63.

Lagroye, Jacques, and Michel Offerlé (eds). 2010. *Sociologie de l'Institution*. Paris: Belin.

Latour, Bruno. 2010. *The Making of Law: An Ethnography of the Conseil d'État*, trans. Marina Brilman and Alain Pottage. Cambridge: Polity.

Lavenex, Sandra. 2016. 'Multilevelling EU External Governance: The Role of International Organizations in the Diffusion of EU Migration Policies', *Journal of Ethnic and Migration Studies* 42(4): 554–70.

Lazard, Gilbert. 2000. *Dictionnaire Persan-Français*. Paris: Beladi.

Lewis, David, and David Mosse (eds). 2006. *Development Brokers and Translators: The Ethnography of Aid and Agencies*. Bloomfield: Kumarian Press.

Lipsky, Michael. 1980. *Street-Level Bureaucracy: Dilemmas of the Individual in Public Services*. New York: Russell Sage Foundation.

Lister, Sarah. 2006. *Moving Forward? Assessing Public Administration Reform in Afghanistan*. Kabul: Afghanistan Research and Evaluation Unit.

Littoz-Monnet, Annabelle (ed.). 2017. *The Politics of Expertise in International Organizations: How International Bureaucracies Produce and Mobilize Knowledge*. Oxford: Routledge.

Lochak, Danièle. 2002. *Les Droits de l'Homme*. Paris: La Découverte.

Loescher, Gil. 1993. *Beyond Charity: International Cooperation and the Global Refugee Crisis*. Oxford: Oxford University Press,

———. 2001a. *The UNHCR and World Politics: A Perilous Path*. Oxford: Oxford University Press.

———. 2001b. 'The UNHCR and World Politics: State Interests vs. Institutional Autonomy', *International Migration Review* 35(1): 33–56.

Loescher, Gil, Alexander Betts and James Milner (eds). 2008. *The United Nations High Commissioner for Refugees (UNHCR): The Politics and Practice of Refugee Protection into the Twenty-First Century*. Abingdon: Routledge.

Loescher, Gil, James Milner, Edward Newman and Gary Troeller (eds). 2008. *Protracted Refugee Situations: Political, Human Rights and Security Implications*. Tokyo: United Nations University Press.

Lombardo, Salvatore. 2004. 'The Military's Role in Major Humanitarian Crises: The Case of Afghanistan from a Refugee Point of View', *Refugee Survey Quarterly* 23(4): 116–20.

Long, Katy. 2009. 'Extending Protection? Labour Migration and Durable Solutions for Refugees. *New Issues in Refugee Research* 176. Policy Development and Evaluation Service, UNHCR, Geneva.

———. 2010. 'Home Alone? A Review of the Relationship between Repatriation, Mobility and Solutions for Refugees'. UNHCR Policy Development and Evaluation Service. Retrieved 23 January 2023 from https://reliefweb.int/report/world/home-alone-review-relationship-between-repatriation-mobility-and-durable-solutions.

———. 2013. *The Point of No Return: Refugees, Rights and Repatriation*. Oxford: Oxford University Press.

Long, Katy, and Jeff Crisp. 2010. 'Migration, Mobility and Solutions: An Evolving Perspective', *Forced Migration Review* 35: 56–57.

Long, Norman (ed.). 1989. *Encounters at the Interface: A Perspective on Social Discontinuities in Rural Development*. Wageningen: Pudoc Scientific Publishing.

Lucassen, Jan, and Leo Lucassen (eds). 1999. *Migration, Migration History, History: Old Paradigms and New Perspectives*. Bern: Lang.

Macdonald, Ingrid. 2011. 'Landlessness and Insecurity: Obstacles to Reintegration in Afghanistan'. Middle East Institute, Fondation pour la Recherche Stratégique.

Macleod, Ewen. 2008. 'Afghan Refugees in Iran and Pakistan', in Gil Loescher, James Milner, Edward Newman and Gary Troeller (eds), *Protracted Refugee Situations: Political, Human Rights and Security Implications*. Tokyo: United Nations University Press, pp. 333–50.

Majidi, Nassim. 2013. 'Home Sweet Home! Repatriation, Reintegration and Land Allocation in Afghanistan', *Revue des Mondes Musulmans et de la Méditerranée* 133: 207–25.

Majidyar, Ahmad K., and Ali Alfoneh. 2010. 'Iranian Influence in Afghanistan: Refugees as Political Instruments'. American Enterprise Institute for Public Policy Research, Middle Eastern Outlook. Retrieved 23 January 2023 from https://www.criticalthreats.org/analysis/iranian-influence-in-afghanistan-recent-developments.

Maley, William. 2001. 'Security, People-Smuggling and Australia's New Afghan Refugees', *Australian Journal of International Affairs* 55(3): 351–70.

Malkki, Liisa. 1992. 'National Geographic: The Rooting of People and the Territorialization of National Identity among Scholars and Refugees', *Cultural Anthropology* 7(1): 24–44.

———. 1995a. 'Refugee and Exile: From "Refugee Studies" to the National Order of Things', *Annual Review of Anthropology* 24: 495–523.

———. 1995b. *Purity and Exile: Violence, Memory, and National Cosmology among Hutu Refugees in Tanzania*. Chicago: University of Chicago Press.

———. 1996. 'Speechless Emissaries: Refugees, Humanitarism, and Dehistoricization', *Cultural Anthropology* 11(3): 377–404.

———. 1998. 'Things to Come: Internationalism and Global Solidarities in the Late 1990s', *Public Culture* 10(2): 431–42.

Marcus, George. 1995. 'Ethnography in/of the World System: The Emergence of Multi-sited Ethnography', *Annual Review of Anthropology* 24: 95–117.

Marsden, Peter. 1992. 'Afghans in Pakistan: Why Rations Decline', *Journal of Refugee Studies* 5(4): 289–99.

Marston, Sallie A. 2000. 'The Social Construction of Scale', *Progress in Human Geography* 24(2): 219–42.

Martin, Susan. 2004. 'Making the UN Work: Forced Migration and Institutional Reform', *Journal of Refugee Studies* 17(3): 301–18.

———. 2001. 'Global Migration Trends and Asylum', *New Issues in Refugee Research* 41.

Masud, Muhammad Khalid. 1990. 'The Obligation to Migrate: The Doctrine of *Hijra* in Islamic Law', in Dale F. Eickelman and James Piscatori (eds), *Muslim Travellers: Pilgrimage, Migration, and the Religious Imagination*. Berkeley: University of California Press, pp. 29–49.

McKittrick, Ann. 2008. 'UNHCR as an Autonomous Organisation: Complex Operations and the case of Kosovo.' Working Paper Series, 50, Refugee Studies Centre, Oxford.

Médecins Sans Frontières. 2006. *Annual Report 2005*.

Merlingen, Michael. 2003. 'Governmentality: Towards a Foucauldian Framework for the Study of IGOs', *Cooperation and Conflict* 38(4): 361–84.

Merry, Sally Engle. 2006. *Human Rights and Gender Violence: Translating International Law into Local Justice*. Chicago: University of Chicago Press

Migration Policy Institute. 2005. 'Afghanistan and Regional Population Movements: A Time of Change'. Retrieved 23 September 2005 from https://www.migrationpolicy.org/.

Ministry of States and Frontier Regions, Government of Pakistan, National Database and Registration Authority, and United Nations High Commissioner for Refugees, Pakistan. 2008. *Registration of Afghans in Pakistan 2007*. Islamabad: Government of Pakistan/UNHCR.

Monsutti, Alessandro. 2004. *Guerres et migrations. Réseaux sociaux et stratégies économiques des Hazaras d'Afghanistan*. Neuchatel: Editions de l'Institut d'ethnologie.

———. 2005. *War and Migration: Social Networks and Economic Strategies of the Hazaras of Afghanistan*, trans. Patrick Camiller. London: Routledge, 2005.

———. 2006. *Afghan Transnational Networks: Looking beyond Repatriation*. Kabul: Afghanistan Research and Evaluation Unit.

———. 2008. 'Afghan Migratory Strategies and the Three Solutions to the Refugee Problem', *Refugee Survey Quarterly* 27(1): 58–73.

———. 2009. 'Itinérances Transnationales : Un Éclairage sur les Réseaux Migratoires Afghans', *Critique Internationale* 44: 83–104.

———. 2012a. 'Fuzzy Sovereignty: Rural Reconstruction in Afghanistan between Democracy Promotion and Power Games', *Comparative Studies in Society and History* 54(3): 563–91.

———. 2012b. 'States, Sovereignties and Refugees: A View from the Margins?' Elizabeth Colson Lecture, Refugee Studies Centre, University of Oxford, 6 June.

Morris, Julia. 2017. 'Power, Capital, and Immigration Detention Rights: Making Networked Markets in Global Detention Governance at UNHCR', *Global Networks* 17(3): 400–22.

Mosse, David. 2005. *Cultivating Development: An Ethnography of Aid Policy and Practice*. London: Pluto Press.

———. 2006. 'Anti-social Anthropology? Objectivity, Objection, and the Ethnography of Public Policy and Professional Communities', *Journal of the Royal Anthropological Institute* 12(4): 935–56.

Mougne, Christine. 2010. *Trees Only Move in the Wind: A Study of Unaccompanied Afghan Children in Europe*. Geneva: UNHCR.

Moulin, Carolina, and Peter Nyers. 2007. '"We Live in a Country of UNHCR": Refugee Protests and Global Political Society', *International Political Sociology* 1: 356–72.

Müller, Birgit (ed.). 2013. *The Gloss of Harmony: The Politics of Policy-Making in Multilateral Organisations*. London: Pluto Press.

Murray Li, Tania. 2007. *The Will to Improve: Governmentality, Development, and the Practice of Politics*. Durham, NC: Duke University Press.

Nader, Laura. 1972. 'Up the Anthropologist: Perspectives Gained from Studying up', in Dell Hymes (ed.), *Reinventing Anthropology*. New York: Vintage, pp. 284–331.

Nay, Oliver. 2012. 'How do Policy Ideas Spread among International Administrations? Policy Entrepreneurs and Bureaucratic Influence in the UN Response to AIDS', *Journal of Public Policy* 32: 53–76.

———. 2014. 'International Organisations and the Production of Hegemonic Knowledge: How the World Bank and the OECD Helped Invent the Fragile State Concept', *Third World Quarterly* 35(2): 210–31.

Nay, Oliver, and Franck Petiteville. 2011. 'Éléments pour une Sociologie du Changement dans les Organisations Internationales', *Critique Internationale* 4(53): 9–20.

Nichols, Robert. 2008. *A History of Pashtun Migration, 1775–2006*. Oxford: Oxford University Press.

Nixon, Hamish. 2007. *Aiding the State? International Assistance and the Statebuilding Paradox in Afghanistan*. Kabul: Afghanistan Research and Evaluation Unit.

Noiriel, Gérard. 1991. 'Représentation Nationale et Catégories Sociales, l'Exemple des Réfugiés Politiques', *Genèses* 26: 25–54.

———. 1997. *La Tyrannie du National: Le Droit d'Asile en Europe 1793–1993*. Paris: Calmann-Lévy.

———. 2001. *Etat, Nation et Immigration: Vers une Histoire du Pouvoir*. Paris: Gallimard.

Norwegian Refugee Council (NRC). 2007. 'Refugee and Population Movements along the Iranian and Pakistani Borders'. Briefing document, 21 May.

Novak, Paolo. 2007. 'Place and Afghan Refugees: A Contribution to Turton', *Journal of Refugee Studies* 20(4): 551–77.

Nyers, Peter. 2006. *Rethinking Refugees: Beyond States of Emergency*. New York: Routledge.

Ogata, Sadako. 2005. *The Turbulent Decade: Confronting the Refugee Crises of the 1990s*. New York: W.W. Norton

Ong, Aihwa. 1999. *Flexible Citizenship: The Cultural Logics of Transnationality*. Durham, NC: Duke University Press.

Ong, Jonathan Corpus, and Pamela Combinido. 2018. 'Local Aid Workers in the Digital Humanitarian Project: Between "Second Class Citizens" and "Entrepreneurial Survivors"', *Critical Asian Studies* 50(1): 86–102.

Paris, Roland. 2002. 'International Peacebuilding and the Mission Civilisatrice"', *Review of International Studies* 28: 637–56.

Pécoud, Antoine. 2015. *Depoliticising Migration: Global Governance and International Migration Narratives*. London: Palgrave Macmillan.

———. 2018. 'What Do We Know about the International Organization for Migration?', *Journal of Ethnic and Migration Studies* 44(10): 1621–38.

Peters, Rebecca Warne. 2016. 'Local in Practice: Professional Distinctions in Angolan Development Work', *American Anthropologist* 118(3): 495–507.

Petric, Boris-Mathieu. 2005. 'Post-Soviet Kyrgyzstan or the Birth of a Globalized Protectorate"', *Central Asian Survey* 24(3): 319–32.

Pinéu, Daniel. 2009. 'The Pedagogy of Security: Police Assistance and Liberal Governmentality in American Foreign Policy', PhD thesis. Aberystwyth: University of Aberystwyth.

Pouligny, Béatrice. 2004. *Ils Nous Avaient Promis la Paix*. Paris: Presses de la Fondation Nationale de Sciences Politiques.

Pouliot, Vincent. 2006. *International Pecking Orders: The Politics and Practice of Multilateral Diplomacy*. Cambridge: Cambridge University Press.

Pupavac, Vanessa. 2006. 'Refugees in the "Sick Role": Stereotyping Refugees and Eroding Refugee Rights', *New Issues in Refugee Research* 128. Policy Development and Evaluation Service, UNHCR, Geneva.

Pyasiri, Wickramasekara et al. 2006. *Afghan Households in Iran: Profile and Impact*. Geneva: ILO/UNHCR.

Rajak, Dinah, and Jock Stirrat. 2011. 'Parochial Cosmopolitanism and the Power of Nostalgia', in David Mosse (ed.), *Adventures in Aidland: The Anthropology of Professionals of International Development*. New York: Berghahn Books, pp. 161–76.

Rajee, Bahram M. 2000. 'The Politics of Refugee Policy in Post-revolutionary Iran', *Middle East Journal* 54(1): 44–63.

Ramji-Nogales, Jaya, Andrew I. Schoenholtz and Philip G. Schrag. 2007. 'Refugee Roulette: Disparities in Asylum Adjudication', *Stanford Law Review* 60(2): 295–411.

Randeria, Shalini. 2007. 'The State of Globalization: Legal Plurality, Overlapping Sovereignties and Ambiguous Alliances between Civil Society and the Cunning State in India', *Theory, Culture & Society* 24(1): 1–33.

Rashid, Ahmed. 2000. *Taliban: Islam, Oil and the Great New Game in Central Asia*. London: I.B. Tauris.

———. 2008. *Descent into Chaos: The United States and the Failure of Nation Building in Pakistan, Afghanistan, and Central Asia*. London: Penguin.

Ray, Kakoli. 2000. 'Repatriation and De-territorialization: Maskhetian Turks' Conception of Home', *Journal of Refugee Studies* 13(4): 391–414.

Redfield, Peter. 2012. 'The Unbearable Lightness of Ex-pats: Double Binds of Humanitarian Mobility', *Cultural Anthropology* 27(2): 358–82.

Revet, Sandrine. 2009. 'Vivre dans un monde plus sûr', *Cultures & Conflits* 75: 33–51.

Richmond, Anthony H. 1988. 'Sociological Theories of International Migration: The Case of Refugees', *Current Sociology* 36(7): 7–25.

Richmond, Oliver P., and Jason Franks. 2009. *Liberal Peace Transitions: Between Statebuilding and Peacebuilding*. Edinburgh: Edinburgh University Press.

Rizvi, Gowhan. 1990. 'The Afghan Refugees: Hostages in the Struggle for Power', *Journal of Refugee Studies* 3(3): 244–61.

Roberts, Adam. 1998. 'More Refugees, Less Asylum: A Regime in Transformation', *Journal of Refugee Studies* 11(4): 375–95.

Roth, Silke. 2012. 'Professionalisation Trends and Inequality: Experiences and Practices in Aid Relationships', *Third World Quarterly* 33(8): 1459–74.

Rousseau, Cécile, François Crépeau, Patricia Foxen and France Houle. 2002. 'The Complexity of Determining Refugeehood: A Multidisciplinary Analysis of the Decision-Making Process of the Canadian Immigration and Refugee Board', *Journal of Refugee Studies* 15(1): 43–70.

Roy, Olivier. 1985. *Afghanistan, Islam et Modernité Politique*. Paris: Seuil.

———. 1988. 'Iran, Schiisme et Frontière', *Revue de l'Occident Musulman et de la Méditerranée* 48–49: 266–80.

———. 1997. *La Nouvelle Asie Centrale, ou la Fabrication des Nations*. Paris: Seuil.

———. 2004. *Afghanistan : La Difficile Reconstruction d'un État*. Paris: Institut d'Etudes de Sécurité.

———. 2007. *Le Croissant et le Chaos*. Paris: Hachette Littératures.

Rubin, Barnett R. 1995. *The Fragmentation of Afghanistan*. New Haven: Yale University Press.

———. 2006. 'Peace Building and State-Building in Afghanistan: Constructing Sovereignty for Whose Security?', *Third World Quarterly* 27(1): 175–85.

Sadiq, Kamal. 2009. *Paper Citizens: How Illegal Immigrants Acquire Citizenship in Developing Countries*. Oxford: Oxford University Press.

Safri, Maliha. 2011. 'The Transformation of the Afghan Refugee: 1979–2009', *Middle East Journal* 65(4): 587–601.

Saïd, Edward. 2003 [1978]. *Orientalism*. London: Penguin.

Saito, Mamiko. 2007. *Second-Generation Afghans in Neighbouring Countries: From Mohajer to Hamwatan: Afghans Return Home*. Kabul: Afghanistan Research and Evaluation Unit.

Saito, Mamiko, and Pam Hunte. 2007. *To Return or to Remain: The Dilemma of Second-Generation Afghans in Pakistan*. Kabul: Afghanistan Research and Evaluation Unit.

Sandvik, Kristin Bergtora. 2011. 'Blurring Boundaries: Refugee Resettlement in Kampala – Between the Formal, the Informal, and the Illegal', *PoLAR: Political and Legal Anthropology Review* 34(1): 11–32.

Sassen, Saskia. 1996. *Losing Control? Sovereignty in an Age of Globalization*. New York: Columbia University Press.

Scalettaris, Giulia. 2007. 'Refugee Studies and the International Refugee Regime: A Reflection on a Desirable Separation', *Refugee Survey Quarterly* 26(3): 36–50.

———. 2019. 'L'Ethnographe Embarqué et la Pensée Institutionnelle du HCR: Sortir du Terrain, Entrer dans la Critique Anthropologique', in Philippe Lavigne Delville and Marion Fresia (eds), *Au Cœur des Mondes de l'Aide Internationale*. Paris: Karthala, pp. 75–92.

Scheel, Stephan, and Philipp Ratfisch. 2014. 'Refugee Protection Meets Migration Management: UNHCR as a Global Police of Populations', *Journal of Ethnic and Migration Studies* 40(6): 924–41.

Schöch, Rüdiger. 2008. 'UNHCR and the Afghan Refugees in the Early 1980s: Between Humanitarian Action and Cold War Politics', *Refugee Survey Quarterly* 27(1): 45–57.

Schuster, Liza. 2011. 'Dublin II and Eurodac: Examining the (Un)intended(?) Consequences', *Gender, Place and Culture* 18(3): 401–16.

Scott, James C. 1998. *Seeing Like a State: How Certain Schemes to Improve the Human Condition Have Failed*. New Haven: Yale University Press.

———. 2009. *The Art of Not Being Governed: An Anarchist History of Upland Southeast Asia*. New Haven: Yale University Press.

Sending, Ole Jacob, and Iver B. Neumann. 2006. 'Governance to Governmentality: Analyzing NGOs, States, and Power', *International Studies Quarterly* 50: 651–72.

Shahrani, M. Nazif. 1995. 'Afghanistan's Muhajirin (Muslim "Refugee-Warriors"): Politics of Mistrust and Distrust of Politics', in E. Valentine Daniel and John C. Knudsen (eds), *Mistrusting Refugees*. Berkeley: University of California Press, pp. 187–206.

Sharma, Aradhana, and Anil Gupta. 2006. 'Rethinking Theories of the State in an Age of Globalization', in Aradhana Sharma and Anil Gupta (eds), *The Anthropology of the State: A Reader*. Malden, MA: Blackwell, pp. 1–42

Shevchenko, Olga, and Renée C. Fox. 2008. '"Nationals" and "Expatriates": Challenges of Fulfilling "Sans Frontières" ("Without Borders") Ideals in International Humanitarian Action', *Health and Human Rights* 10(1): 109–22.

Shore, Cris, and Susan Wright. 1997. 'Policy: A New Field of Anthropology', in Cris Shore and Susan Wright (eds), *Anthropology of Policy: Critical Perspectives on Governance and Power*. London: Routledge, pp. 3–33.

Siméant-Germanos, Johanna. 2012. 'Localiser le Terrain de l'International', *Politix* 100: 129–47.

Slaughter, Amy, and Jeff Crisp. 2008. 'A Surrogate State? The Role of UNHCR in Protracted Refugee Situations', in Gil Loescher, James Milner, Edward Newman and Gary Troeller (eds), *Protracted Refugee Situations: Political, Human Rights and Security Implications*. Tokyo: United Nations University Press, pp. 123–40.

Smirl, Lisa. 2008. 'Building the Other, Constructing Ourselves: Spatial Dimensions of International Humanitarian Response', *International Political Sociology* 2(3): 236–53.

Smith, Neil. 1992. 'Contours of a Spatialized Politics: Homeless Vehicles and the Production of Geographical Scale', *Social Text* 33: 54–81.

Spire, Alexis. 2007. 'L'Asile au Guichet: La Dépolitisation du Droit des Étrangers par le Travail Bureaucratique', *Actes de la Recherche en Sciences Sociales* 4(169): 4–21.

Sprokkereef, Annemarie, and Paul de Hert. 2007. 'Ethical Practice in the Use of Biometric Identifiers Within the EU', *Law, Science and Policy*, 3: 177–201.

Standing, Guy. 2008. 'The ILO: An Agency for Globalization?', *Development and Change* 39(3): 355–84.

Stepputat, Finn. 2004. 'Dynamics of Return and Sustainable Reintegration in a "Mobile Livelihoods" Perspective'. Working Paper 2004/10, Danish Institute for International Studies, Copenhagen.

Stigter, Elca. 2004. *The Kandahar Bus Stand in Kabul: An Assessment of Travel and Labour Migration to Iran and Pakistan*. Kabul: Afghanistan Research and Evaluation Unit.

———. 2005a. *Transnational Networks and Migration from Faryab to Iran*. Kabul: Afghanistan Research and Evaluation Unit.

———. 2005b. *Transnational Networks and Migration from Herat to Iran*. Kabul: Afghanistan Research and Evaluation Unit.

Stigter, Elca, and Alessandro Monsutti. 2005. *Transnational Networks: Recognising a Regional Reality*. Kabul: Afghanistan Research and Evaluation Unit.

Strand, Arne et al. 2008. *Return in Dignity, Return to What? Review of the Voluntary Return Programme to Afghanistan*. Bergen: Chr. Michelsen Institute.

Suhrke, Astri. 2011. *When More Is Less: The International Project in Afghanistan*, New York: Hurst & Co.

Sustainable Development Policy Institute. 2003. 'Assessment and Recommendations for the Rehabilitation of Refugee Hosting Areas in Balochistan and the North-West Frontier Province'. Islamabad: SDPI.

———. 2006. 'Report on Stakeholder Consultations on the Future of Afghan Refugees in Pakistan'. Islamabad: SDPI.

Takahashi, Saul. 1997. 'The UNHCR Handbook on Voluntary Repatriation: The Emphasis of Return over Protection', *International Journal of Refugee Law* 9(4): 593–612.

Tarrius, Alain. 2002. *La Mondialisation par le Bas: Les Nouveaux Nomades des Économies Souterraines*. Paris: Balland.

Teitelbaum, Michael S. 1980. 'Right versus Right: Immigration and Refugee Policy in the United States', *Foreign Affairs* 59(1): 21–59.

Thomas, Rebekah. 2005. *Biometrics, International Migrants and Human Rights*. Geneva: Global Commission on International Migration.

Torpey, John. 2000. *The Invention of the Passport: Surveillance, Citizenship and the State*. Cambridge: Cambridge University Press.

Tsing, Anna. 2000. 'The Global Situation', *Cultural Anthropology* 15(3): 327–60.

Turner, Simon. 2005. 'Suspended Spaces: Contesting Sovereignties in a Refugee Camp', in Thomas Blom Hansen and Finn Stepputat (eds), *Sovereign Bodies: Citizens, Migrants and the State in the Postcolonial World*. Princeton: Princeton University Press, pp. 312–32.

———. 2006. 'Negotiating Authority between UNHCR and "the People"', *Development and Change* 37(4): 759–78.

———. 2010. *Politics of Innocence: Hutu Identity, Conflict and Camp Life*. New York: Berghahn Books.

Turton, David. 2003. 'Refugees, Forced Resettlers and "Other Forced Migrants": Towards a Unitary Study of Forced Migration', *New Issues in Refugee Research* 94, Evaluation and Policy Analysis Unit, UNHCR, Geneva.

———. 2005. 'The Meaning of Place in a World of Movement: Lesson from Long-Term Field Research in Southern Ethiopia', *Journal of Refugee Studies* 18(3): 258–80.

Turton, David, and Peter Marsden. 2002. *Taking Refugees for a Ride? The Politics of Refugees Return in Afghanistan*. Kabul: Afghanistan Research and Evaluation Unit.

United Nations. 1992. 'An Agenda for Peace: Preventive Diplomacy, Peacemaking and Peace-Keeping'. Report of the Secretary-General.

———. 2002. 'Strengthening of the United Nations: An Agenda for Further Change'. Report of the Secretary-General.

United Nations Assistance Mission in Afghanistan (UNAMA). 2007. 'United Nations Concerned Over Deportation of Afghans from Iran'. Press release, Kabul, 7 May.

———. 2009. 'Afghanistan', Press conference by Ewen MacLeod, UNHCR Country Representative; Nassim Majidi, Project Director, Altai Consulting; Nazifullah Salarzai, UNAMA Strategic Communication and Spokespersons Unit. Kabul, 15 June.

United Nations General Assembly. 2008. 'Safety and Security of Humanitarian Personnel and Protection of United Nations Personnel'. Report of the Secretary-General, 18 August.

United Nations High Commissioner for Refugees (UNHCR). n.d. 'Model UNHCR Co-operation Agreement'. Retrieved 1 June 2023 from https://www.refworld.org/docid/3ae6b31b27.html.

———. 1992 [1979]. *Handbook on Procedures and Criteria for Determining Refugee Status under the 1951 Convention and the 1967 Protocol Relating to the Status of Refugees*. Geneva: UNHCR.

———. 2000a. 'Reconciling Migration Control and Refugee Protection in the European Union: A UNHCR Perspective'. Discussion Paper.

———. 2000b. 'UNHCR Summary Position on the Protocol Against the Smuggling of Migrants by Land, Sea and Air and the Protocol to Prevent, Suppress and Punish Trafficking in Persons, Especially Women and Children, Supplementing the UN Convention Against Transnational Organized Crime'. Retrieved 18 January 2023 from https://www.unhcr.org/publications/unhcr-summary-position-protocol-against-smuggling-migrants-land-sea-and-air-and.

———. 2002. 'Guidelines on International Protection No. 2: "Membership of a Particular Social Group" Within the Context of Article 1A(2) of the 1951 Convention and/ or Its 1967 Protocol Relating to the Status of Refugees'. Retrieved 18 January 2023 from https://www.unhcr.org/media/guidelines-international-protection-no-2-membership-particular-social-group-within-context.

———. 2003a. 'Towards a Comprehensive Solution for Displacement from Afghanistan'. Discussion Paper. Geneva: UNHCR.

———. 2003b. *Agenda for Protection*. Geneva: UNHCR.

———. 2003c. *Handbook for Registration: Procedures and Standards for Registration, Population Data Management and Documentation. Provisional Release (September 2003)*. Geneva: UNHCR.

———. 2004a. *Afghanistan: Challenges to Return*. Geneva: UNHCR.

———. 2004b. 'Making Comprehensive Approaches to Resolving Refugee Problems More Systematic'. Paper for the High Commissioner's Forum, Geneva.

———. 2004c. *The UNHCR Code of Conduct and Explanatory Notes*. Geneva: UNHCR.

———. 2004d. *Protracted Refugee Situations*. Executive Committee of the High Commissioner's Programme.

———. 2004e. 'Refugees and Migrants: Defining the Difference'. Ruud Lubbers, BBC.

———. 2004f. 'Addressing Irregular Secondary Movements of Refugees and Asylum Seekers'. Convention Plus Issues Paper.

———. 2005a. 'Refugees Are not Migrants'. Presentation to the 10th Annual Humanitarian Conference by Erika Feller, Geneva.

———. 2005b. *Afghan Refugee Statistics*. Geneva: UNHCR.

———. 2005c. *Framework Document for the Comprehensive Plan of Action (CPA) for Somali Refugees*. Geneva: UNHCR.

———. 2005d. 'Joint Statement of the Convention Plus Core Group on Addressing Irregular Secondary Movements of Refugees and Asylum-Seekers'. High Commissioner's Forum, 8 November 2005.

———. 2006a. *The State of the World's Refugees 2006: Human Displacement in the New Millennium*. Oxford: Oxford University Press.

———. 2006b. *UNHCR and International Protection: A Protection Induction Programme*. Geneva: UNHCR.

———. 2006c. 'UNHCR, Refugee Protection and International Migration'. Discussion Paper.

———. 2006d. 'Humanitarian Considerations with Regard to Return to Afghanistan'. UNHCR, May 2006. https://www.refworld.org/pdfid/4561c4094.pdf.

———. 2006e. *Guidelines on International Protection No. 7: The Application of Article 1A(2) of the 1951 Convention and/or 1967 Protocol Relating to the Status of Refugees to Victims of Trafficking and Persons at Risk of Being Trafficked*. Geneva: UNHCR.

———. 2007a. 'Finding Durable Solutions for Refugees and Displacement'. Paper for the Afghanistan Development Forum.

———. 2007b. 'Afghanistan Situation. Operational Update'.

———. 2007c. *UNHCR's Eligibility Guidelines for Assessing the International Protection Needs of Afghan Asylum-Seekers*. Kabul: UNHCR.

———. 2007d. *Operational Information: Monthly Summary Report, December 07*. Kabul: Operational Information Unit.

———. 2007e. *Questions and Answers: Deportations from Iran*. Kabul: UNHCR.

———. 2007f. *Handbook for Emergencies*, 3rd edn. Geneva: UNHCR.

———. 2007g. 'UNHCR Appeals for Temporary Suspension of Jalozai Camp Closure'. Press release, 22 August.

———. 2007h. 'Afghan Township Struggles to Make Magic out of Mud and Mines'. News Stories, June.

———. 2007i. 'Opening as Many Doors as Possible for Long-Term Refugees'. New Stories, 5 July.

———. 2007j. 'Kacha Ghari Refugee Camp Closes in Pakistan after 27 Years'. News Stories, 27 July.

———. 2007k. 'Weekly Update, 2 August 2007'. Kabul: UNHCR Afghanistan.

———. 2007l. *UNHCR Global Report 2006*. Geneva: UNHCR.

———. 2007m. *UNHCR Global Appeal 2008–2009*. Geneva: UNHCR.

———. 2007n. *Refugee Protection and Mixed Migration: A 10-Point Plan of Action*. Geneva: UNHCR.

———. 2007o. 'Refugee Protection and Durable Solutions in the Context of International Migration'. Discussion Paper, High Commissioner's Dialogue on Protection Challenges, 19 November.

———. 2007p. 'Weekly Update, 6 December 2007'. Kabul: UNHCR Afghanistan.

———. 2007q. 'Voluntary Repatriation'. Kabul: UNHCR Afghanistan.

———. 2007r. 'Opening Statement by Mr. António Guterres, United Nations High Commissioner for Refugees, at the Fifty-Eighth Session of the Executive Committee of the High Commissioner's Programme'. Retrieved 18 January 2023 from https://www.unhcr.org/publications/opening-statement-mr-antonio-guterres-united-nations-high-commissioner-refugees-1.

———. 2007s. 'Opening Statement by Mr. António Guterres, United Nations High Commissioner for Refugees, Geneva, 11 December 2007, High Commissioner's Dialogue on Protection Challenges'. Retrieved 18 January 2023 from https://www.unhcr.org/publications/opening-statement-mr-antonio-guterres-united-nations-high-commissioner-refugees-high.

———. 2007t. 'Over 350,000 Afghans Repatriate from Pakistan before Winter'. News Stories, 2 November.

———. 2007u. 'Help Us Revive Our Traditional Lands, Ask Afghan Kuchi Returnees'. News Stories, 24 December.

———. 2008a. *Statistical Yearbook 2007: Trends in Displacement, Protection and Solutions*. Geneva: UNHCR.

———. 2008b. *Asylum Levels and Trends in Industrialized Countries, 2007*. Geneva: UNHCR.

———. 2008c. 'Refugee Protection and Durable Solutions in the Context of International Migration: Report on the High Commissioner's Dialogue on Protection Challenges, December 2007'. Retrieved 18 January 2023 from https://www.unhcr.org/media/refugee-protection-and-durable-solutions-context-international-migration-report-high.

———. 2008d. 'UNHCR Position on the Return of Asylum-Seekers to Greece under the "Dublin Regulation"', 15 April. Retrieved 18 January 2023 from https://www.unhcr.org/media/unhcr-position-return-asylum-seekers-greece-under-dublin-regulation.

———. 2009. 'Human Trafficking and Refugee Protection: UNHCR's Perspective'. Conference paper, Brussels.

———. 2010. *Voices of Afghan Children: A Study on Asylum-Seeking Children in Sweden*. Stockholm: UNHCR Regional Office for the Baltic and Nordic Countries.

———. 2012. International Conference on the Solutions Strategy for Afghan Refugees, to Support Voluntary Repatriation, Sustainable Reintegration and Assistance to Host Countries. 2–3 May, Geneva.

———. 2019. *UNHCR Global Report 2018*. Geneva: UNHCR.

———. 2022. *UNHCR Global Report 2021*. Geneva: UNHCR.

United Nations High Commissioner for Refugees, and Pakistan Ministry of States and Frontier Regions, Population Census Organization and Statistics Division. 2005. *Census of Afghans in Pakistan*. Islamabad: UNHCR.

Valluy, Jérôme. 2009. *Rejet des Exilés. Le Grand Retournement du Droit de l'Asile*. Paris: Editions du Croquant.

Van Aken, Mauro. 2003. *Facing Home: Palestinian Belonging in a Valley of Doubt*. Maastricht: Shaker Publishing.

Van Hear, Nicholas. 2012. 'Forcing the Issue: Migration Crises and the Uneasy Dialogue between Refugee Research and Policy', *Journal of Refugee Studies* 25(1): 2–24.

———. 2002. 'From "Durable Solutions" to "Transnational Relations": Home and Exile among Refugee Diasporas'. CDR Working Paper 02.9, Centre for Development Research, Copenhagen.

Verdirame, Guglielmo, and Barbara Harrell-Bond. 2005. *Rights in Exile: Janus-Faced Humanitarianism*. New York: Berghahn Books.

Vrasti, Wanda. 2008. 'The Strange Case of Ethnography and International Relations', *Millennium* 37(2): 279–301.

Wagner, Anne-Catherine. 2007. *Les Classes Sociales dans la Mondialisation*. Paris: La Découverte.

Warner, Daniel. 1994. 'Voluntary Repatriation and the Meaning of Home: A Critique of Liberal Mathematics', *Journal of Refugee Studies* 7(2–3): 160–72.

Weber, Max. 1968. *Economy and Society: An Outline of Interpretive Sociology*. Berkeley: University of California Press.

———. 2004. *The Vocation Lectures*, trans. Rodney Livingstone. Indianapolis: Hacker Publishing Company.

Wedel, Janine R. 2009. *Shadow Elite: How the World's New Power Brokers Undermine Democracy, Government, and the Free Market*. New York: Basic Books.

Weller, Jean-Marc. 2018. *Fabriquer des Actes d'État. Une Ethnographie du Travail Bureaucratique*. Paris: Economica.

Wickramasekara, Piyasiri, Jag Sehgal, Farhard Mehran, Ladan Noroozi and Saied Elisazedah. 2006. *Afghan Households in Iran: Profile and Impact*. Geneva: ILO/UNHCR.

Wigley, Barb. 2005. *The State of UNHCR's Organization Culture*. Geneva: UNHCR.

Wilson, Dean. 2006. 'Biometrics, Borders and the Ideal Suspect', in Sharon Pickering and Leanne Weber (eds), *Borders, Mobility and Technologies of Control*. Dordrecht: Springer, pp. 87–109.

Wimmer, Andreas, and Nina Glick Schiller. 2003. 'Methodological Nationalism, the Social Sciences, and the Study of Migration: An Essay in Historical Epistemology', *International Migration Review* 37(3): 570–610.

Zetter, Roger. 1988. 'Refugees and Refugee Studies: A Label and an Agenda', *Journal of
Refugee Studies* 1(1): 1–6.

———. 1991. 'Labelling Refugees: Forming and Transforming a Bureaucratic Identity',
Journal of Refugee Studies 4(1): 39–62.

———. 2007. 'More Labels, Fewer Refugees: Making and Remaking the Refugee Label
in an Era of Globalisation', *Journal of Refugee Studies* 20(2): 172–92.

Zieck, Marjoleine. 2008. 'The Legal Status of Afghan Refugees in Pakistan, a Story of
Eight Agreements and Two Suppressed Premises', *International Journal of Refugee
Law* 20(2): 253–72.

Zimmermann, Susan. 2009. 'A Safe Return? The Deportation of Afghan Asylum Seekers',
RSC Newsletter Winter/Spring: 4–5.

International Agreements and Treaties and Other Multilateral Legal Texts

United Nations Charter, 26 June 1945.

Convention on the Privileges and Immunities of the United Nations, 13 February 1946.

Universal Declaration of Human Rights, 10 December 1948.

Statute of the Office of the United Nations High Commissioner for Refugees, 14 December 1950.

Convention Relating to the Status of Refugees, 28 July 1951.

International Covenant on Civil and Political Rights, 16 December 1966.

Protocol Relating to the Status of Refugees, 30 January 1967.

Convention Governing the Specific Aspects of Refugee Problems in Africa, 10 October
1969.

Protocol Relating to Free Movement of Persons, Residence and Establishment. ECOWAS,
1 May 1979.

International Convention on the Protection of the Rights of All Migrant Workers and
Members of Their Families, 18 December 1990.

Conclusion on International Protection No 91 (LII). The Registration of Refugees and
Asylum-Seekers, 2001.

Agreement on Provisional Arrangements in Afghanistan Pending the Re-establishment of
Permanent Government Institutions, 5 December 2001.

Joint Programme between the Government of the Islamic Republic of Iran, the Interim
Authority of Afghanistan, and UNHCR for Voluntary Repatriation of Afghan Refugees and Displaced Persons, 2002.

Agreement between the Government of the Islamic Republic of Pakistan, the Transitional Islamic State of Afghanistan and the United Nations High Commissioner for Refugees Governing the Repatriation of Afghan Citizens Living in Pakistan, 17 March 2003.

Conclusion on International Protection No. 96 (LIV). Return of Persons Found Not to Be in Need of International Protection, 10 October 2003.

Mexico Declaration and Plan of Action to Strengthen the International Protection of Refugees in Latin America. 16 November 2004.

Memorandum of Understanding between the Government of the Islamic Republic of Pakistan and the Office of the United Nations High Commissioner for Refugees (UNHCR) on the Census and Registration of Afghan Citizens Living in Pakistan, 17 December 2004.

Conclusion on International Protection No. 102 (LVI), 2005.

Conclusions of the 12ᵗʰ Tripartite Commission Meeting, Geneva, 17 January 2006.

The Afghanistan Compact, 31 January 2006.

Memorandum of Understanding between the Government of the Islamic Republic of Pakistan (GOP) and the Office of the United Nations High Commissioner for Refugees (UNHCR) on the Registration of Afghan Citizens Living in Pakistan, 19 April 2006.

Conclusions of the 13ᵗʰ Tripartite Commission Meeting, Dubai, 8 June 2007.

Agreement between the Government of the Islamic Republic of Pakistan, the Government of the Islamic Republic of Afghanistan, and the United Nations High Commissioner for Refugees Governing the Repatriation of Afghan Citizens Living in Pakistan, 2 August 2007.

Joint Programme between the Government of the Islamic Republic of Iran, the Islamic Republic of Afghanistan, and the United Nations High Commissioner for Refugees for Voluntary Repatriation of Afghan Refugees and Displaced Persons, 2 August 2007.

Index

Milton Keynes UK
Ingram Content Group UK Ltd.
UKHW022253151123
432643UK00006B/101

9 781805 391685